INIUM
FABIOM
(ONFAB
AIOG
IONTAM

The Interpretation
of Psychological Tests

The Interpretation
of Psychological Tests

JOEL ALLISON
Yale University

SIDNEY J. BLATT
Yale University

CARL N. ZIMET
University of Colorado

Taylor & Francis
Publishers since 1798

Acknowledgements

Material from the Babcock Test presented in Chapters 2 and 6 by permission. Copyright (renewed) 1940 by C. H. Stoelting Company.

Plates from the Rorschach Psychodiagnostics presented in Chapter 4 by permission. Copyright 1921 (renewed 1948) by Hans Huber, Medical Publisher.

Material from the Wechsler Adult Intelligence Scale presented in Chapters 2 and 6 by permission. Copyright 1947, © 1955 by The Psychological Corporation.

Dedicated to:

Millicent and Benjamin

J. A.

Ethel, Susan, Judith, and David

S. J. B.

Sue, Andrew, and Gregory

C. N. Z.

This book represents a truly collaborative effort in which each author shared equal responsibility for formulating and presenting the material and therefore the authors are listed in alphabetical order.

THE INTERPRETATION OF PSYCHOLOGICAL TESTS

3 4 5 6 7 8 9 0   B C B C   9 8 7 6 5

Library of Congress Cataloging-in-Publication Data

Allison, Joel.
    The interpretation of psychological tests.

    Reprint. Originally published: New York : Harper & Row, [1968].
    Includes bibliographies and index.
    1. Psychological tests.   I. Blatt, Sidney J. (Sidney Jules)   II. Zimet, Carl N.   III. Title.   [DNLM:
1. Psychological Tests.   BF 431 A438i 1968a]
BF176.A497   1988   150'.28'7   87-23632
ISBN 0-89116-326-3

Contents

Preface

This book sets forth basic assumptions and principles of test administration and interpretation according to a psychoanalytic ego-psychological point of view. As such it is in a direct line with the work of Rapaport and of Schafer and in large part serves to restate and extend their views about psychological testing. What it also attempts to add to earlier presentations of the ego psychological approach is a fuller demonstration of how the test rationales can be applied to the understanding of any particular individual. Whereas in previous writings various aspects of patients' test batteries have been selected to illustrate a specific test principle or the operation of a specific defense mechanism, we have attempted here—through the intensive discussion of a single patient's tests—to demonstrate in detail the complete process of test interpretation and communication of test results via the test report. Instead of presenting many cases briefly, as is usually done in order to cover the broad range of diagnostic conditions, personality disorders, or defense mechanisms, our goal is to show how a psychologist working in an ego-psychological framework goes about the process of analyzing a patient's test battery from start to finish and how he synthesizes a rich array of inferences into a meaningful description of personality functioning.

In this approach to personality assessment major consideration is given to diverse test data—to scores, response content, style, and process of response and interpersonal interaction—with the aim of integrating these data into a comprehensive picture of an individual's thinking, feeling, and acting including in an important way subjective experiential dimensions. This approach is neither score centered, content centered, nor interaction centered but instead encompasses all three. Often action, thought, and feeling will be synchronous and similar hypotheses from these different sources will supply an internal consistency or cross validation of the clinician's inferences. But one may also encounter seemingly discrepant hypotheses from each of several sources of data. For example, a person may experience a sense of failure even though his orientation to a task may be ultimately successful. On the other hand he may protest depressively his lack of energy while exhibiting an active fantasy life (e.g. in an abundance of movement responses on the Rorschach) the content of which is relatively lively and gay. It is in these cases that a multifaceted orientation particularly demonstrates its full potential. For such an approach may then point toward ways of integrating seeming discrepancy. Many instances both of congruity of functioning throughout the test battery and of seeming contradiction will be discussed within this book.

Consistent with an ego-psychological approach, the guides to test administration presented here have been derived from Rapaport's theoretical analyses of how psychological functioning is expressed in tests. Although in this approach some details of test administration and of scoring and interpretation deviate to some extent from more common and popular practice, our experience nonetheless has been that the most crucial tenets of interpretation—the reliance on a variegated concern with scores, content, style, and interpersonal interaction and their integration—are equally applicable to other systems of test administration and scoring as long as the test data have been obtained in a systematic way. In psychological testing, as in scientific pursuits more generally, a basic orientation to gathering data which is well grounded in theory not only offers maximum possibility of obtaining systematic observations, but it also permits fuller integration of test data. It is for this reason that we have included an intensive discussion of test administration and rationales in each chapter before proceeding with a more extensive discussion of actual test data. The selection of the WAIS, TAT, and Rorschach also resulted from considerations based on ego-psychological theory, in that these tests permit a systematic sampling of behavior along a continuum of separate but interdependent facets of psychological functioning. This continuum ranges from functioning in situations which put a premium on highly logical, reality-oriented, secondary process modes of thought (WAIS) to those which allow for more personal, less conventionally constrained thinking (TAT) and finally those which allow for considerably novel, personalized, and regressive modes of thinking (Rorschach). On occasion, however, when there is marked constriction in the tests or when there is a specific question of organic brain damage or malfunction we may include other tests as well.

The importance of a systematic approach to test selection, administration, and interpretation is especially highlighted if we consider that testing is fundamentally a research endeavor which involves the study of perception, cognition, affect, action, and interpersonal relationships. Personality theory can illuminate each of these areas and show how they are interrelated. Thus the tester needs to be grounded in psychological theory and needs to be aware of the potential of psychological testing for expanding and revising our present conceptions of personality. A relevant example is the recent use of the Rorschach test by Holt and his colleagues (e.g. *Nebraska Symposium on Motivation,* 1966) to systematically explore the concepts of primary and secondary thought processes and of regression in the service of the ego. The common pessimism surrounding the frequent failures in validation studies of clinical tests does not seem to be consistent with the reality in clinical settings when tests are skillfully used. Much of the research on the Rorschach has focused on general and gross scoring categories and has neglected the additional differentiations and elaborations of the basic scoring system routinely made by a clinician. A research approach to the Rorschach like that of Holt, however, pays full attention to the diversity and complexity of test data. Despite thousands of research reports on the Rorschach and other clinical tests only a few studies have used tests as they are capable of being used. Merely counting numbers of studies pro and con gives a false view of the quality of the research. It is for these reasons that we decided not to attempt in this book to review the massive research literature on tests but instead to concentrate on a presentation of an ego-psychological approach to testing.[1] For it is our strong conviction that a view toward tests based on psychoanalytic ego-psychology can yet provide the basis for rigorous and meaningful research endeavors into testing and psychological functioning more generally. Even further, one of the major purposes of this book is to present, as clearly as possible, the assumptions made in the interpretation of psychological tests. It is our hope that clarification of these assumptions will lead to more

[1] A critical review of recent research with the WAIS by two of the authors (Blatt and Allison) is included in a chapter: "The Intelligence Test in Personality Assessment" in the forthcoming *Projective Methods in Personality Assessment* (A. Rabin, Ed.).

meaningful systematic research in the area of diagnostic testing, directed toward examining the underlying assumptions of tests rather than solely concentrating on test scores or on the comparison of imprecisely defined diagnostic groups.

The patient whose test battery comprises a large section of this book is a highly intelligent, verbal woman who was tested in a hospital setting in which intensive psychoanalytically-oriented psychotherapy and milieu treatment are important components of the therapeutic program. Nevertheless, when one tests less verbally articulate people or tests for purposes other than for psychotherapy, the same battery of tests (WAIS, TAT, Rorschach) can usually supply important information. These tests in skillful hands supply rich information regarding flexibility of approach, persistence, frustration tolerance, and reaction to novelty beyond indicating overall achievement. Even if test content is sparse, productivity constricted, or the interaction similarly constrained, nonetheless, stylistic factors of response—how tasks are approached, and the process of attempted solution—can lead to inferences about psychological functioning more generally. It is in fact in such instances that an orientation derived from ego-psychology is particularly valuable for it puts in the forefront an emphasis on ego assets and functions, not just in terms of defense mechanisms but in terms of more general cognitive styles and modes of perceiving, thinking, and acting.

A further issue is the move of clinical psychologists (along with other mental health professions) into an increased variety of settings and toward supplying rapid treatment for large segments of society with procedures which require a minimum of time, effort, or training. It is the feeling among many clinicians that complex or time consuming forms of treatment and assessment are a cumbersome and unnecessary luxury. This view however often does not fully recognize that any justification for brief forms of therapy will have to be based on complex, careful, and detailed evaluation of their effects and on a discrimination of the people and conditions for which they can be most effectively utilized. Similarly, training to employ brief assessment procedures may require greater rather than less skill because the clinician using such procedures has to function with only minimal cues and data. It is our belief therefore that training in intensive and systematic assessment must continue to be a major vehicle for teaching a wide range of clinical skills which are vital in practice and research. In this way the intellectual obligation of the scientist-practitioner to contribute to the knowledge and understanding of psychological processes will also be best served.

This book is intended to be an introduction to clinical testing and it is addressed primarily to graduate students, advanced undergraduates, and psychiatric residents all of whom we have had experience teaching, using the bulk of the material presented here. However, it also may be of interest to clinicians who wish to familiarize themselves with a psychoanalytic ego-psychological approach to testing and to those with a research orientation toward the inference process in clinical endeavors.

The organization of the book is intended to facilitate its use for teaching. Each test is covered in a separate chapter. Moreover, each chapter presents the student at the outset with principles of test administration and with rationales of test interpretation before proceeding to the full presentation of the test material of a single patient. The format also permits the student to analyze this patient's test responses sequentially and then check his hypotheses against the authors'.

The authors are listed in alphabetical order and each of us came to this task better equipped because of contact with Roy Schafer as colleague or teacher. At various points in writing we have also received good suggestions from Miriam A. Kohn, Frances Kaplan, and Leonard Suchotliff and from a myriad of unnamed students who were introduced to clinical testing by means of portions of this book.

We are also grateful to Lydia Holquist and Ruth Hartman for editorial assistance and to Andrea Adams and Edith Venti for a conscientious and careful job of typing the manuscript.

Finally we wish to express our gratitude to Mrs. T., her therapist, and the hospital director for their permission to present her clinical material with the hope of contributing to clinical theory, research and practice.

Joel Allison
Sidney J. Blatt
Carl N. Zimet

September, 1967

1

Introduction

Psychological testing provides the skilled clinician with a wide range of behavioral observations and a variety of responses to relatively standard stimuli. These observations and responses include cognitive and affective, adaptive and pathological dimensions that can lead to a finely modulated understanding of aspects of personality. To achieve such an understanding it is essential to elicit idiosyncratic responses which range from reality oriented, goal directed functioning to more fantasy derived and possibly primitive and regressive modes of experience and expression. These various levels of psychological functioning can be observed and evaluated through a basic test battery comprised of the Wechsler Adult Intelligence Scale (WAIS), Thematic Apperception Test (TAT), and Rorschach Test.

Though it is possible to view each of these tests in the clinical battery as assessing particular psychological functions, any specific segment of behavior contains, in varying degrees, all levels of psychological functioning. For example, the WAIS is frequently considered solely as a test of intelligence, the TAT as a method of assessing interpersonal transactions, and the Rorschach as an instrument which elicits primitive drives or archaic fantasies. However, responses on any of these tests may contain representations of drive, conflict, defense, and adaptive endeavors. In studying a Wechsler protocol, for example, one gains more than an estimate of intelligence or even a global appraisal of adaptive functions. For one can specify the situations in which adaptive efforts are effective and also the specific characteristics of any disruptions that are present. In this approach, psychological processes are viewed as an interweaving of ego functions, instinctual forces, defensive maneuvers, and reality demands; in an analysis of a WAIS protocol, therefore, the relative balance of these various factors can be specified. Likewise, on the Rorschach and TAT one can identify when and how representations of drives are successfully integrated in an adaptive way and when synthesizing ego functions are overwhelmed or fail to operate effectively.

Psychological test evaluations which concentrate on categorizing people according to current nosological fashion make little contribution to the understanding of and planning for a particular individual. Diagnostic labels are summary statements which are frequently derived from symptom formation alone, only intimating the presence of certain processes within the individual. Rather, a psychological evaluation should attempt to fully specify the processes and organizing principles which are typical of an individual and which serve to tie together a variety of complex psychological characteristics. In this regard we believe that the major role of psychological testing should not be prediction, but, instead, the development of hypotheses which best describe the given individual and which constitute a "best fit" for the data and the observations which are available. The broader purpose of these hypotheses is to enrich and extend the understanding of the patient or client and to make available dimensions of the individual which may have been unavailable or not considered previously.

The types of questions that psychological tests are capable of answering may involve such issues as: adequacy of reality testing, adaptive strengths, degree of impulse control, the major array of defenses and their degree of rigidity, and prominent areas of conflict. A therapist might be interested in whether the constellation of pedantic intellectual sensitivity to details, concerns about autonomy, and argumentativeness which have adaptive value really mask a hyperalertness, suspiciousness, and guardedness and indicate a highly defended person. Or interest might be in whether a bland, hypersocial, conventional individual is attempting to ward off intense feelings of estrangement, alienation, and depersonalization. It is not sufficient, however, to simply cite the presence and the layering of these factors; a formulation should strive to specify how these processes interact. For example, when ego integration is brittle, it may, in certain situations, give way to increased disorganization. The tester's attention, therefore, also needs to be focused on such questions as the patient's motivation or capacity for psychotherapy, possibly as related to issues of how chronic and settled or ego-syntonic the patient's problems are and the amount of subjective distress. Testing also offers a major contribution in assessing organic brain damage which is not evident in a mental status examination or in the routine neurological evaluation, by extending, clarifying, and detailing the extent and nature of cognitive deficit.

To attempt to answer these questions, psychological testing seeks varied types of observations and information. These include:

1 Test scores
2 Content or themes of responses
3 Style of verbalization, i.e., the subject's attitude toward his responses and his affective reactions that accompany them
4 Interpersonal relationship between the tester and the subject

Fundamental to our approach to clinical testing is the assumption that an understanding of the complexities of individual personality organization can be best achieved through an integration of the above four sources of data and that each is relatively limited by itself.

A comprehensive clinical test evaluation should be a synthesis of test scores, content analysis, attitudes and affect toward responses, and transactional dimensions. These, in conjunction with the tester's empathic and introspective cues to the patient's communication and some general biographical information about the patient such as his educational and cultural background, offer a sample of behavior which is representative of many facets of the subject's personality organization and which frequently serve as microcosmic examples of his reactions and experiences in a variety of situations. Nonetheless, one finds current indications of the more limited view that "the way" of analyzing tests is either by means only of test scores, or the interpretation of content or the interpersonal transaction. Each of these sources of data will be taken up in turn and both their potential contribution to personality assessment as well as their limitations when considered in isolation will be touched on briefly. In later chapters, when each test is discussed and case examples given, these points will be amplified further.

Test Scores

When clinical psychological testing consists of procedures such as the administration of a questionnaire by a clerk or a psychometrician who may or may not be present and whose interest is limited to seeing that the test form is correctly completed, test scores are the sole source of data. In such an approach, there is no cognizance of the individual's style of responding and his behavioral reactions to specific test items or the test situation generally. It is not the usual practice to note on which items he blocks, blushes, becomes uncomfortable, smiles, grimaces, laughs out loud, takes a rest, or erases and changes his responses. Moreover, the processes that enter into the decision to respond one way or another or the effects of a previous question upon a subsequent one are ignored. The clinician here is relegated to a task which is primarily that of evaluating a profile, which, in fact, may be more efficiently accomplished by a computer (Meehl, 1954; Holt, 1958). Frequently levels of integration and patterns of defenses may be inferred from these types of personality tests through an analysis of interscale variation, i.e., through the pattern of the individual's scores. Even in the most sophisticated analyses of this kind, however, the more intricate dimensions of personality organization are unavailable because the subject is not given the opportunity for a wide range of expression or the clinician the possibility of observing the individual's functioning. An exclusive emphasis on such seemingly "objective" test measures loses sight of the valuable information which can be obtained from the observation of the response process, from the interpersonal transaction, and the clinician's empathic and introspective observations.

A mechanical approach to psychological testing through a concentration on test scores is not limited to diagnostic instruments of the self-report, objective type. Even with a Rorschach protocol, for example, one can formulate hypotheses solely from the scoring summary and never see the person. Although hypotheses about dimensions of personality organization derived in this manner can often be found to be valuable, they are short-sighted in that they are based on only one of many facets of the Rorschach.

Content of Themes of Responses

Probably the most common partial approach to projective techniques is in the speculative association to content without consideration of the structural dynamics. These structural dynamics are inextricably intertwined with the content of the responses and are reflected in the scores and in the style of responding. While content analysis can also offer leads, in its own right, about major preoccupations and areas of conflict, it offers only limited information about how these conflicts are handled and where they fit into the overall organization of the individual's personality.

For example, when confronted with a preponderance of passively toned oral content in a Rorschach, we may infer issues around passivity, dependency, and neediness, but these issues would take on different meanings depending on other features of the test responses or behavior. In a woman who is acting in a flirtatious way with the tester we may be led to infer that her seductive behavior primarily serves an underlying need for interpersonal warmth and closeness of an oral, infantile nature. In another person similar test content might be more congruent with interpersonal behavior, e.g., in a person who more directly leans on the tester for support by often requesting feedback about his performance and help in the solution of any felt difficulties. As a further example, prominent oral aggressive content in a timid person whose scores show a schizophrenic degree of reality distortion may reflect his fear that interpersonal contact is essentially devouring and destructive; whereas in a hyperactive salesman similar oral aggressive content may be consonant with overt behavior that is aggressive and controlling. In general, test reports based primarily on an analysis of content often do no more than enumerate a variety of infantile wishes, expressions of hostility and anxiety, and areas of personal concern without clarifying the broader personality configuration into which the content fits.

Style of Verbalization

In addition to a scoring summary and the areas of preoccupation and conflict which emerge in the content, the attitude toward the response and the affect which may accompany the response is another important dimension of the response process. Valuable leads are frequently communicated by the individual's affective reaction to his responses and by his asides, comments, gestures, and posture. Often crucial test information stems from how a subject feels about his response, whether he enjoys it or is critical of it and devaluates it; whether he feels he is using his imagination in a playful way or is terrified by its productions; whether he tries to hold onto his responses and is guarded about them, letting them go grudgingly or suddenly; whether he feels bereft and depleted from giving his numerous responses to the tester or acts nurturant and overflowing; and whether, in a variety of other ways, he reveals special attitudes toward his responses (Schafer, 1954). Noting these aspects of the response process and the patient's reaction to a given test or to the test situation more generally adds extensive dimensionality to the test battery.

Interpersonal Relationship

Another partial approach to testing practice is the utilization of tests primarily as a vehicle for interpersonal interaction. Here, subjects' reactions during testing constitute the bulk of the clinical evaluation. Although a full battery of tests is given, the interpretation is concentrated on only one aspect of the test situation, namely, the interaction, and little attention is paid to other facets of the test material. Psychological tests in this approach are sometimes used as the springboard for a clinical interview, and the tests themselves are essentially ignored.

Also pertinent in viewing the test transaction is the tester's understanding of his own role in the clinical situation. Sarason (1954), for example, has stressed the vital role of the clinical interaction and how certain personal characteristics of the tester may influence the material he obtains. Schafer (1954) has also treated at length the interpersonal aspects of testing, and he has explored the ways in which the relationship of the tester to himself, to his professional colleagues, and to patients may influence his observations and conclusions. These personal attributes of the tester, be they controlling, seductive, demanding, or paternalistic, may affect patients' productions. As expressed by Schafer (1954, p. 6), the clinician, "being human and having to make a living—facts often ignored—the tester too brings hopes, fears, assumptions, demands, and expectations into the test situation. He too responds personally and often intensely to what goes on—in reality and in fantasy—in that situation, however well he may conceal his personal response from the patient, from himself and from his colleagues."

The same personal attributes and characterological features that influence a tester's relationship with a patient may also affect the relationship between the tester and the referring therapist. The characterological features of the tester may affect the degree to which he is able to establish an effective relationship with the therapist and thereby the degree to which his test findings will be used to contribute to understanding the patient. As with the relationship between the tester and the patient, the relationship between members of the professional staff can be influenced by feelings of competition, anger, inadequacy, professional rivalry, or unrealistic positive evaluation. And the quality of the relationship existing between tester and therapist may not only be expressed between them directly, but indirectly it may also influence the patient's approach to testing and his views about therapy following testing. While patients can manipulate and set members of the professional staff against each other on occasion, the reverse may also occur; the patient can become the vehicle through which the tester's and the therapist's feelings are expressed or acted out. Therefore, discordant feelings between tester and therapist cannot only interfere with the contribution of testing, but can have detrimental effects upon the patient as well. On the other hand, if feelings and goals are congruent, if the therapist and the tester work in a truly collaborative effort, the therapeutic process of the patient can be markedly facilitated.

Feelings of mutual trust and respect are essential for establishing a collaborative effort. The tester's concerns over his self-esteem, his perception of testing as an ancillary function, or his belief that his formulations will contribute little to the therapeutic process are some of the frequent hinderances to establishing such a relationship. The therapist, on the other hand, may feel that a request for psychological testing reveals his inability to formulate the case accurately and that testing, rather than being a collaborative effort, is instead an implicit plea for help and evidence of his inadequacy. When tester and therapist are working together with only a minimal and superficial degree of collaboration, the psychological test report frequently is the sole source of communication between them, supplemented on occasion by a passing remark in the hall or a casual query over coffee. When diagnostic testing is a fuller collaborative effort, however, the test report serves as a springboard for a joint discussion about the patient, not only immediately after testing, but also subsequent to testing to evaluate change or progress.

WHEN TO TEST: ASPECTS OF THE CONTRIBUTION OF TESTS

Psychological testing is most frequently used in the initial stages of the clinical process and often aids in deciding which patients to accept for treatment, which forms of treatment may be indicated, and even which type of therapist might be most effective with a particular patient. Testing is also frequently used in the early stages of psychotherapy in order to obtain a fuller perspective of the patient and his psychological processes which is not ordinarily available until much later in the treatment process. Another contribution of testing, utilized all too infrequently, comes from its use in later stages of the therapeutic process. Testing can be of value when a particular problem arises in the treatment process and the therapist feels a need for extensive consultation. A therapist may want to evaluate the progress and current status of a patient or may feel a need for assistance in integrating his various observations of the patient. Though many of the same observations made from psychological tests may be available to the therapist after intensive psychotherapeutic work with a patient, psychological testing can offer a hierarchical integration of the juxtaposition of drives, impulses, and defenses which is often difficult to achieve and place in perspective through clinical interviews.

Testing, therefore, does not have to be, and should not be, a routine procedure prescribed for all patients; it is best utilized when it may make a unique contribution. Thus, when case history and interviews supply sufficient and consistent information on the basis of which clinical decisions or therapeutic plans can be made, there is little need for psychological testing. It is when there is inconsistency in the material, when the observations currently available are inadequate for the decisions that must be made, or when the clinical problem is unusually complex, that psychological testing is best utilized. But even when the results of clinical testing simply confirm the picture or the formulations available from other sources, testing makes some contribution. In this case it may serve to reassure the staff by offering confirmation of their impressions and allow decisions to be made with more certainty and confidence. It is often the situation, however, especially with complex cases, that psychological test findings may be discrepant with some important formulations derived from interviews or the case history. It is in these situations that the unrealistic attitudes of the tester and the therapist can most interfere with the effective utilization of testing. Certainly both interview data and inferences made from psychological test procedures are observations of the patient which are subject to disagreement stemming from a variety of sources, one source being a limitation in skill and experience on the part of the tester or therapist. Assuming a high level of professional competence in therapist and tester in their interviewing and testing skills, one is still often confronted with the need to resolve disparities in formulations. Since interview observations and test data may tap different levels of personality organization and functioning, the most reasonable alternative is to view these differences as existing within the patient. It is then incumbent upon the tester and therapist to attempt to integrate their observations. The occurrence of disparities in formulation is not surprising if we view personality as a hierarchial organization of functions. Thus, if one can specify the level at which the observations are pertinent, disparities may often turn out to be the result of the difference in the level of observation, and there may be greater consistency between seeming differences than was initially suspected. For instance, certain borderline schizophrenics may appear relatively intact in a fairly structured interview, show few classical signs of psychosis, and strike the interviewer as a severe neurotic. With these patients the tests will often reveal clearly schizophrenic looking projective test findings, but the ego assets observed in the interview will be seen in efficient, undisrupted WAIS functioning.

In this instance the data from the interview and WAIS are consistent, and apparently the projective tests have dipped to deeper levels of personality functioning. All too frequently, however, dissonances among formulations from clinical interviews, case history, and psychological tests are reduced by ignoring one or another source of information. In some clinical facilities, test formulations are accepted as valid only if they are in agreement with interview data. In other settings there is an uncritical acceptance of the "super-scientific" or "magical" test findings, and, against these, interviews or case history are considered inferior. It is not surprising that when the latter attitude exists the psychologist may be tempted to foster the myth of the scientific precision and objectivity of test data as against "interview impressions." Highlighting the numerical and scientific dimensions of testing, then, serves the function of establishing and maintaining the status, security and power of the tester, bolstered by his academic and scientific halo in a clinical world.

An essential point about testing is that there is relatively little difference between the therapist and the tester in the process of arriving at their formulations. The difference lies in the tools and methods, not in the interpretative processes. From somewhat different vantage points, testing and the clinical interview try to encompass the total organization of the individual. A truly full understanding of a patient can only be achieved through the integration of observations and formulations of the various members of the clinical team who have observed and worked with the patient from differing vantage points.

HISTORICAL DEVELOPMENT OF CLINICAL TESTING

Clinical psychological testing is a rather recent historical development. Psychology, as a discipline separate and distinct from philosophy on the one hand and physiology on the other, came into being in the latter part of the nineteenth century. The year Wundt founded his laboratory in Leipzig (1879), is often cited as the official beginning of psychology. Interest at that time was focused on sense organs and on reaction time, and the importance of making observations on subjects under standardized conditions was demonstrated. However, the approach was somewhat rigid, since variations found in the responses of subjects to experimentally induced changes were considered to be measurement errors, a result of observer negligence, or poor control of conditions. The "personal equation" which was of considerable interest to astronomers after finding that two observers may not fully coincide on the observed time of stellar transits, did not modify research thinking in the psychology laboratories. The tradition of quantitative measurement was established, however, and this provided an important foundation for the development of psychometrics. The biologist Francis Galton (1883) laid the groundwork for psychological testing by studying individual differences. This was at first limited to the study of physical traits and sensory discrimination, but later he became interested in the use of rating scales for evaluating psychological functions as well as the free association technique. One other important contribution by Galton was his development of statistical techniques for the analysis of data on individual differences.

The term "mental tests" was introduced by Cattell (1890) in an article where he described the annual administration of a series of tests to college students in order to evaluate intellectual functioning. The test battery was quite different from what today would be considered an adequate procedure for establishing intellectual level; it consisted of tasks that measured reaction time and sensory discrimination on the assumption that intelligence is reducible to sensations and motor speed. At that time the decision to use such tasks rather than more complex ones was that they could be precisely measured, while more complex and abstract functions could not be evaluated as accurately and objectively.

Cattell's approach to mental testing was strongly criticized by Binet and Henri (1895) on the basis that these tests were too simple and concentrated too exclusively on sensory tasks. Taking issue with Cattell's avoidance of complex tasks, they stated that there was much greater individual variability in the complex functions and therefore great precision was unnecessary. Making use of a variety of functions such as attention, memory, suggestibility, and comprehension, to name a few, Binet and his associates worked toward developing ways of measuring intelligence. This resulted in the first educational application of psychological testing in the Paris schools in 1905 when children suspected of being of low intellectual capacity were evaluated by the Binet-Simon Scale

(1905). Two subsequent revisions of the test appeared in 1908 and 1911, and with them the term "mental age" was introduced. It was Binet who was first to step out of the psychological laboratory, and he was followed in the United States by Lewis Terman, whose revision of the Binet Scale gave clinical psychology its start. This revision was called the Stanford-Binet, and it became the major instrument used by applied psychologists until the 1940s. Terman's work in this area proceeded through the 1916 and 1937 revisions, his interest unshaken by the generally hostile attitude of many psychologists toward his endeavors.

During that same period, performance tests came into use as a result of the need for evaluating foreign speaking or linguistically handicapped individuals. Another major step at that time was the development of group tests. The impetus for this development came from the pressing practical need to rapidly evaluate the general intelligence level of recruits in World War I and led to construction of the Army Alpha and Beta scales. The former was a verbal test, the latter, a nonlanguage scale designed for illiterates and the foreign born. After the war these tests and others like them were brought into general use; unfortunately, however, they were often misused by being applied indiscriminately.

In the late 1920s and in the following decade the primary preoccupation of psychological testers was measurement and the methodological considerations involved in obtaining a unitary score which could represent a diverse series of psychological functions (e.g., IQ for intelligence). In contrast to the psychologists' interests in limited types of intelligence testing and in the evaluation of motor skills, psychiatrists and psychoanalysts at the same time were attempting to assess individual psychological functioning through a variety of other methods which over time have worked their way into psychology. Through clinical interviews, observations were made about patients' ways of expressing their thoughts and feelings, about their style of speech and behavior, and these observations led to a multitude of diagnostic conceptions and prognostic formulations. These clinicians, beginning with Freud, explored the complexity, and intricate organization of human personality and the subtle and powerful forces operating within it. By means of psychodynamic insights and structural concepts, Freud studied nonconscious aspects of personality and made it clear that they could only be understood by a very sensitive, flexible, and detailed inquiry.

If we turn back to the development of clinical testing as we now know it, we find that psychoanalytic theory and practice paved the way for the development of techniques which complemented and extended inquiry into conscious and rational thoughts and feelings as well as into areas which were outside of the individual's full awareness. One of the first clinical techniques was the Free Association Test used by Jung (1910) and earlier described by Galton (1879). Jung chose a series of words having general emotional impact and examined the content of the associations, reaction time, and expressive behavior, such as blushing and laughing. In administering the test, Jung also introduced a memory dimension by asking the subject to attempt to recall his original responses. Memory impairment, such as changes in association and blocking, served as additional diagnostic observations. About the same time Kent and Rosonoff were also preparing a free association test that utilized more objective scoring and statistical norms. The more unstructured form of the Free Association Test is the one more generally used today (Rapaport, Gill, & Schafer, 1945).

Undoubtedly the technique that was to have the greatest impact on psychology and, in particular, the future development of clinical psychology, was the highly original contribution of Hermann Rorschach. He began his investigations into the use of inkblots for personality diagnosis in 1911, experimenting with large numbers of inkblots which he administered to various groups of psychiatric patients. Differentiating the response characteristics on the basis of various psychopathological syndromes, he developed a scoring system which was then further refined by testing nonpsychiatric groups, such as artists, laborers, scholars, mental defectives, and others. Ten years after the beginning of his research he published a monograph (1921) on the inkblot technique and its relationship to psychoanalysis. Tragically, Rorschach died soon after the completion of this book at the age of 37. Oberholzer, his pupil, carried on the work started by Rorschach. His was the first publication in the United States to describe the method (Rorschach & Oberholzer, 1924). Oberholzer also trained American psychologists and psychiatrists who introduced the Rorschach Test in this country. The first of these was David Levy. Later, Samuel Beck went to Switzerland to study with Oberholzer and subsequently wrote the first Ph.D.

dissertation on the Rorschach Test. Beck was also the first to write a complete manual in English on the application of the Rorschach (1937). It was the same year that *Rorschach Research Exchange,* which later became the *Journal of Projective Techniques,* made its appearance.

While the Rorschach came into prominence with clinical psychologists and psychiatrists in the midthirties in the United States, it was stubbornly resisted both by the academic psychologists and the psychometricians, much as it had been earlier resisted in Europe. Both groups objected to the experimentally uncontrolled procedures of the Rorschach, a situation which persists in some degree even today. In the following years a number of psychologists (e.g., Beck, Hertz, Klopfer, Piotrowski, Rapaport, Schachtel, and Schafer) contributed greatly to the Rorschach literature. What is noteworthy is that the ten blots and the major scoring categories devised by Rorschach have remained in use during the evolution and maturation of clinical psychology, and only recently has there been a serious attempt to develop other series (Holtzman et al., 1961).

One early effort to reconcile the divergent clinical and academic viewpoints in the late 1920s, when clinical psychology was only beginning to get started, was seen in the founding of the Harvard Psychological Clinic by Morton Prince. Though one of the major purposes of the Harvard Psychological Clinic was to bring together clinical and academic psychology, and though the clinic represented such an integration for some years, it is clear from the present sharp division within psychology at large that this integration is far from being achieved. After Prince, Henry Murray took over the leadership of the Clinic and further extended the frontiers of clinical and academic psychology; these efforts are still best expressed in Murray's classic, *Explorations in Personality* (1938). In this book, the results of the Thematic Apperception Test, published three years earlier, were integrated with a general theory of personality which was developed by Murray and a large group of collaborators including Nevitt Sanford and Robert White. The first report on the Thematic Apperception Test was published in 1935 by Morgan and Murray and was based on the observation, already demonstrated by the Rorschach Test in a somewhat different way, that when a person interprets an ambiguous situation he reveals many facets of his personality organization. A number of variations and adaptations of the TAT for special populations have appeared (Campbell, 1950; Thompson, 1949), but aside from special research applications, the original TAT stands largely unchanged.

About the same time that the TAT came upon the psychological scene, the Wechsler-Bellevue, a new test for the evaluation of adult intelligence, became available. Until its appearance at that time, the Stanford-Binet, which had been revised in 1937, had an undisputed monopoly as the individually administered intelligence test for both children and adults. But there had been dissatisfaction with the Binet, because it had been originally designed for children; only later was it extended to adult levels, and consequently it had retained a kind of child-like orientation. In addition to the fact that many of the tasks were of little interest to an adult population,[1] the use of a mental age concept with adults is based on a number of questionable methodological assumptions (Freeman, 1962). The Wechsler-Bellevue, which incorporated a point scale rather than a mental age scale, was especially designed for adults and produced a Total IQ score and separate Verbal and Performance IQ scores. Another major distinction between the Binet and Wechsler scales was that the former was developed primarily on an empirical basis, while Wechsler chose subtests which tapped a specific series of psychological functions. Items were selected for the Binet because they discriminated effectively on various age levels; the subtests of the Wechsler-Bellevue, on the other hand, were conceptualized as being major facets of intellectual ability. It is, in fact, the systematic measurement of different cognitive functions which has enabled the Wechsler to provide an evaluation of personality organization. The Wechsler-Bellevue was rapidly accepted, and subsequently a children's scale (The Wechsler Intelligence Scale for Children) was developed. In 1955 the Wechsler Adult Intelligence Scale (WAIS) was published, and, while it included the same subtests, it improved on a number of technical deficiencies, such as standardization and age range, and it introduced a system of age-grading in the computation of the IQ.

[1] Wechsler (1944, p. 17) points out, "asking a housewife to furnish you a rhyme to the words, 'day, cat, and mill,' or an ex-army sergeant to give you a sentence with the words, 'boy, river, ball,' is not particularly apt to evoke interest or respect."

The Wechsler-Bellevue, TAT, and Rorschach, the three major diagnostic tools of clinical psychology, were already on the scene at the start of World War II. But the utilization of these tests lagged for a number of years for various reasons. Clinical psychology programs had not yet been established and, therefore, only a handful of people had adequate training for the administration and interpretation of these tests. Another difficulty stemmed from the lack of a systematic and well articulated theory of personality which would enable the clinician to integrate and understand the observations which were available from these clinical procedures. Nevertheless, during World War II most of the 1500 psychologists in the Armed Services were confronted with the demand to perform clinical functions for which they had had little training. A vast majority of these psychologists had received their academic training in experimental, physiological, or social psychology or in psychometrics. The desire to cope with the need for clinical services and still maintain theoretical and scientific interests resulted in the development of test rationales and theoretical formulations for the diagnosis and treatment of psychological disorders. In addition, an equal number of psychologists were asked to participate in the selection of men for special functions within the Armed Forces. Assessment procedures ranged from selecting personnel for simple jobs such as clerk-typists to highly complex and responsible positions in the Office of Strategic Services (OSS). It was in the OSS project, under the direction of Henry Murray, that major strides were made in the understanding and utilization of assessment methodology, particularly involving projective techniques.

The need for psychologists to participate in clinical services did not diminish with the end of World War II. Quite to the contrary, with the rapid growth of Veterans Administration hospitals and clinics, the role of the clinical psychologist was now firmly established. Recognizing the value of psychologists in clinical settings, the United States Public Health Service began to support graduate training programs in clinical psychology; in addition, the Veterans Administration started a program of clinical internships which was integrated with the newly established graduate training programs.

Though some progress had been made during the early 1940s in evolving theoretical bases for clinical practice and projective techniques, a major statement about the utilization of a test battery in psychodiagnostic procedures was made by Rapaport, Gill and Schafer in 1945. In their *Diagnostic Psychological Testing* (1945) they discussed a number of psychological procedures and attempted to specify the psychological functions tapped by each test. These test rationales evolved from the viewpoint of psychoanalytic ego psychology, and for the first time a major systematic attempt was made to bring together diverse psychological tests on the basis of a unified personality theory. On the basis of psychoanalytic theory and extensive clinical experience, Rapaport and his colleagues specified the particular psychological functions tapped by the clinical instruments and how these functions related differentially to various psychopathological states. One of the major points made in *Diagnostic Psychological Testing* was that the diagnosis and description of patients through the use of a single test falls short of a full understanding of complex processes within the individual. In order to fully evaluate an individual, emphasis was placed on the importance of administering a battery of different tests. The value of a test battery for an integrated interpretation was given further impetus by Schafer (1948) who also used a relatively standard battery consisting of the Rorschach, Wechsler Intelligence Scale, Thematic Apperception Test, Word Association Test, Memory Efficiency Test, and Object Sorting Test. He discussed test protocols of patients from a variety of diagnostic categories in terms of the adaptive and pathological mechanisms which seem characteristic of the disorders. Placing his earlier work in a more explicit theoretical cast Schafer (1954) presented, in great detail, the psychoanalytic interpretation of drives, defenses, and adaptive styles as expressed in Rorschach protocols. Like Schachtel earlier, Schafer also presented an extensive discussion of the interpersonal, situational dynamics of testing which he integrated with Rapaport's focus on formal thought processes.

In our historical survey, the work of Rapaport and Schafer brings us up to the present. Their work has supplied much of the foundation of our own clinical approach and supplies the psychoanalytic ego psychological model which serves as the specific theoretical framework of this book.

REFERENCES

BECK, S. J. *Introduction to the rorschach method*. New York: American Ortho-psychiatric Assoc., 1937, No. 1.

BINET, A., & HENRI, V. La psychologie individuelle. *Annee psychol.*, 1895, **2**, 411–465.

CAMPBELL, D. T. The indirect assessment of social attitudes. *Psychol. Bull.*, 1950, **47**, 15–38.

CATTELL, J. MC K. Mental tests and measurements. *Mind*, 1890, **15**, 373–380.

FREEMAN, F. S. *Theory and practice of psychological testing*. (3rd ed.) New York: Holt, Rinehart and Winston, 1962.

GALTON, F. Psychometric experiments. *Brain*, 1879, **2**, 149–162.

GALTON, F. *Inquiries into human faculty and its development*. London: Macmillan, 1883.

HOLT, R. R. Clinical and statistical prediction: a reformulation and some new data. *J. abnorm. soc. Psychol.*, 1958, **56**, 1–13.

HOLTZMAN, W. H., THORPE, J. S., SWARTZ, J. D., & HERRON, W. E. *Inkblot perception and personality*. Austin: Univer. of Texas Press, 1961.

JUNG, C. G. The association method. *Amer. J. Psychol.*, 1910, **21**, 219–269.

MEEHL, P. E. *Clinical vs. statistical prediction*. Minneapolis: Univer. of Minnesota Press, 1954.

MORGAN, C. D., & MURRAY, H. A. A method for investigating fantasies: the thematic apperception test. *Arch. neurol. Psychiat.*, 1935, **34**, 289–306.

MURRAY, H. A., ET AL. *Explorations in personality*. New York: Oxford Univer. Press, 1938.

RAPAPORT, D., GILL, M., & SCHAFER, R. *Diagnostic psychological testing*. Chicago: Year Book Medical Publishers, 1945.

RORSCHACH, H. *Psychodiagnostik: Methodik und ergebnisse eines wahrnemungs-diagnostischen experiment. deutenlassen von zufallsformen*. Bern: Ernst Bircher, 1921. In English, Lemkau, P., & Kronenberg, B. (Trans.) *Psychodiagnostics*. Bern: Huber, 1942. New York: Grune & Stratton, 1942.

RORSCHACH, H., & OBERHOLZER, E. The application of the interpretation of form to psychoanalysis. *J. nerv. ment. Dis.*, 1924, **60**, 225–248, 359–379.

SARASON, S. B. *The clinical interaction: with special reference to the rorschach*. New York: Harper & Row, 1954.

SCHAFER, R. *The clinical application of psychological tests*. New York: International Universities Press, 1948.

SCHAFER, R. *Psychoanalytic interpretation in rorschach testing.* New York: Grune & Stratton, 1954.

THOMPSON, C. E. *Thematic apperception test: thompson modification.* Cambridge, Mass.: Harvard Univer. Press, 1949.

WECHSLER, D. *The measurement of adult intelligence.* Baltimore: Williams & Wilkins, 1944.

2

The Wechsler Adult Intelligence Scale

Although the WAIS was originally developed as a measure of intelligence, in the last fifteen years the potential of the Wechsler scales for more extensive clinical assessment has begun to be realized. This new use of the test came with the expanded conceptualization of intelligence as an expression of ego functioning and with the view that each of the components of the intellectual process represent general cognitive modes of interacting, functioning, and meeting reality demands. The rationale for including the Wechsler in a diagnostic test battery, therefore, is based on more than an attempt to assess a general intellectual level but, rather, in order to look beyond the gross IQ measure and tap the various cognitive abilities or ego functions that make up "intelligence." For if one is interested in the intellectual quotient alone, there are at present more rapid and less cumbersome methods available for its estimation than administering an entire intelligence test. For example, the Vocabulary scale of the WAIS correlates 0.86 with full scale IQ and therefore the time and energy required in giving the remaining ten scales add, for the usual case, little to the assessment of the IQ. There have also been numerous abbreviations of the Verbal and Performance sections, and the experienced clinician can usually estimate the intellectual level fairly accurately even in a brief interview.

In the Introduction, we have already discussed the importance of making extensive observations and integrating them into a multidimensional conceptualization of adaptive as well as pathological trends rather than making fragmentary observations from limited data to support discrete diagnostic formulations. In this way we hope to clarify the hierarchy and organization of defenses, the unique pattern of ego functions or cognitive styles, the role of affects and impulses, and of the primitive processes of thought. The primary function in the test battery of the WAIS is to assess certain adaptive potentials of the individual, namely, his ability to function effectively in relatively impersonal situations which involve past achievements and current problem solving efforts. The WAIS plays the unique role in the test battery of presenting the subject with a number of types of situations with the request that he respond in as organized and realistic a way as possible and remain relatively unaffected by trends coming from unconscious fantasy life. In contrast to the TAT and Rorschach test which encourage less logical ideation and more preconscious and even unconscious derivatives to embellish and enrich one's responses, the intelligence test requires no such elaborative enrichment (Rapaport et al., 1945; Waite, 1961). In fact, a correct response to the WAIS requires the subject to avoid this type of functioning. Adequate functioning on the WAIS, regardless of the intellectual level, demands the maintenance of ego boundaries, so that primitive fantasies and wishes do not invade reality oriented thought. Intact responses to an intelligence test should be relatively free of these trends which, if they are present, are important aids in clarifying the extent to which psychological functioning in routine, neutral situations is undermined by personal preoccupations and autistic elaborations. Excursions into fantasy on the WAIS, therefore, represent at least a momentary loss of reality focus and orientation and suggest that to some degree secondary process thinking can be infused by more archaic modes of thought. This does not mean that there is a single correct response for each item on the WAIS, for one can cope successfully with the many tasks presented by the WAIS in a variety of ways which show little infiltration by primitive, archaic and possibly pathological trends. Generally, however, since the WAIS places such a high premium on habituated, logical thinking it is important for personality assessment to use a battery of tests which include a diversity of types of thinking, some of which permit relatively little variation in cognitive approach and discourage the embellishment of responses by drives (like the WAIS) and others (like the TAT and Rorschach) which encourage more variation in style of approach and enrichment by drives.

A major role of the WAIS is to assess for the individual the characteristic and unique patterns of ego processes which he uses to integrate and adapt to reality demands. It is hypothesized that these ego processes or styles evolve from inborn predispositions (Hartmann, 1958) and from the interaction of these predispositions with ongoing maturational processes combined with the vicissitudes of drive development and with areas of conflict. The cognitive styles represent generalized modes of behavior which are characteristic of adaptive functioning as well as of defensive maneuvers. In Kroeber's (1964) terms, "the mechanisms of the ego (can) be thought of as general mechanisms which may take on either defensive or coping functions." That is, defenses are viewed, in part, as cognitive processes, and the preferred cognitive styles of an individual represent relatively stable processes used in adaptive as well as defensive endeavors. Observing operations in one sphere, adaptive or defensive, permits one to infer the presence of these modes in the other sphere. This view of the congruence of cognitive styles and defensive processes has also been well supported by the research of Gardner et al. (1959, 1960) who show that defense mechanisms relate differentially to capacities on a number of cognitive-perceptual tasks.

THE SCATTER OF SUBTEST SCORES

By using the WAIS to study organization of cognitive processes and the relative balance of primary and secondary process thinking, intellectual processes are considered as a more integral part of personality. A great deal of understanding about the organization of ego functions can be achieved through an analysis of the patterns of subtest scores. Inasmuch as the scaled scores reflect an individual's standing on a number of specific abilities and psychological functions, variations between and within the different functions do occur as a result of the individual's uniqueness. The wide variations in adaptive capacity result from either strengths or weaknesses due to pathological impairment of certain processes. Each of these sources can contribute to variations in the subtest scatter and in each case they reflect the organization of psychological functions we call personality. The weighted subtest score, however, becomes meaningful only in the context of the total score pattern; for it is in the variation among scores that the particular organization of psychological processes is expressed and not in the absolute level of the scores. Thus, two people may have identical scores on a subtest, but for one it may be his highest subtest score, and for the other it may be his lowest subtest score. In interpreting a WAIS profile, then, a baseline must be established from which the variation in subtest scores can be viewed. This baseline assesses the general intellectual level of the individual and variations in subtest scores are considered in relation to it.

There are several baseline measures. The one most widely used is the Vocabulary subtest, since it is usually the single best estimate of intelligence and is relatively impervious to the effect of functional and organic conditions and to the overall decline in functioning which accompanies age. The subtests may be viewed as having positive or negative deviation from the Vocabulary score.

In order to fully utilize the concept of scatter, one must understand the particular psychological processes tapped by each of the subtests. In the section to follow, the psychological functions assessed by the subtests will be discussed. These interpretive rationales have been greatly influenced by the theoretical ego-psychological formulations of David Rapaport and his colleagues (1945, Mayman et al., 1951).

INTERPRETATIVE RATIONALE FOR WAIS SUBTESTS

Verbal Subtests

VOCABULARY. As indicated previously, this scale correlates most highly with the Total IQ. This is so primarily because it represents the breadth of concepts, ideas and experience gained during one's lifetime. The acquisition of these concepts and their availability to memory is contingent both on innate ability and on an enriched early life experience. Although emotional conflicts as well as characterological features may affect the acquisition of an adequate vocabulary, it is in general still the single best estimate of intellectual capacity, being stable over time and relatively resistant to neurological deficit and psychological disturbance. Because of its relative invulnerability, its reliability, and predictive capacity, the Vocabulary subtest offers an excellent baseline to which other tests can be compared.[1] It is in relation to the Vocabulary score that one may consider positive or negative scatter, the elevation and heightened investment in certain ego functions, or the disruption of ego functions due either to temporary inefficiencies or to more marked and permanent organic or psychogenic problems.

INFORMATION. This subtest is seen as measuring the wealth of available information which, like Vocabulary, is acquired largely as a result of native ability and early cultural experiences, but which, unlike Vocabulary, is more alterable by defensive processes or by schooling or persistent efforts at academic achievement. Self-made men, for example, often show a level of Information that exceeds their Vocabulary scores. Rapaport et al. (1945) indicated that the effort to acquire a general fund of information is frequently an indicator of "intellectual ambitiousness." Inasmuch as repression is geared toward blocking out memories from awareness, the acquisition of general knowledge is especially hindered by repression when it is a primary mode of defense. Repression may interfere with the fund of information either in the initial learning process in which the material is acquired or in later attempts to recall the material. This concept of memory further implies that experiences are delivered into consciousness when a situation again appeals to the same needs, strivings, interests, or affects with which the experience is linked in the subject's frame of reference (Rapaport et al., 1945). Repressive people, with their marked degree of memory blockage, therefore, are likely to show disruptions, inefficiency, and

---

[1] An exception to this general rule occurs when early life experiences have been intellectually impoverished in some way, where intellectual stimulation has been minimal, as in many economically and socially deprived families, and where very early school experience has been irregular and disrupted. With such people one must look to scores other than Vocabulary such as the mean of all the subtests, to establish a baseline for comparison.

variability on a task like Information which concerns long range memory, relates to active intellectual strivings, and deals with piecemeal, sharply defined bits of experience. The obsessive compulsive, on the other hand, with his characteristic pedantic emphasis on detail and his intellectual strivings, will tend to obtain a relatively high score.

COMPREHENSION. This subtest presents a subject with a series of more or less conventional social situations and asks about appropriate behavior and its rationale. Comprehension, therefore, measures a subject's grasp of social conventionality and social judgment (Rapaport et al., 1945). This subtest is frequently a very sensitive indicator of maladaptation; low scores may represent a need to defy or ignore social conventionality, or they may indicate an impairment of judgment or a diminished interest in social interaction, as in schizophrenic conditions. Frequently the Comprehension subtest, because it deals with social situations and judgments appropriate to these situations, may yield material related to issues of morality and superego organization. Antisocial trends are frequently expressed in the content of the subtest via such comments as "check to see whether there's any money in it," in response to the envelope item. There are some psychopaths, however, who tend to score very high on this subtest; these are the more glib and socially facile individuals. However, high Comprehension may also represent a push toward hyperconventionality or conformity and reflect the naivete, conventional thinking and moral strivings of individuals with hysterical features. High Comprehension, especially coupled with lower Information, therefore, is characteristic for hysterics. The reverse pattern, high Information and lower Comprehension, is generally seen in the obsessive-compulsive largely because of the obsessive's uncertainty and excessive qualification but excellent fund of information. It is important to note that three items on the WAIS Comprehension subtest require the interpretation of proverbs. These items assess primarily the capacity for abstract thought rather than social judgment. In drawing inferences from this subtest one must consider the extent to which the score was affected by these three items.

SIMILARITIES. This subtest is essentially a measure of verbal concept formation (Rapaport et al., 1945; Wechsler, 1958). Conceptual abstraction can be carried out on one of three general levels of cognitive development (Rapaport et al., 1945). The concrete similarity between two objects, a specific common feature of the objects (e.g., a table and a chair both have legs or a dog and a lion both have fur) represents the lowest level of cognitive development. This type of concept formation, which is correct in a limited sense, acknowledges a most direct and obvious feature of the objects without attempting to reach for broader and more abstract generalizations. The thinking is unusually specific, direct, limited in focus, and generally constitutes a rather poorly articulated concept which at best receives only a partial score. A second type of concept formation is the functional category which defines a utilitarian purpose as the basis for the conceptual category (e.g., piano and violin, play them both). Though this type of abstraction or concept formation is more sophisticated than a concrete conceptualization, it still falls short of a high level abstraction. In terms of personality functioning, the extensive use of functional categories may indicate an inability on the part of the ideational processes to serve as a buffer against impulsive action. Rather than ideation serving as a form of delay and planning, a general move toward activity and acting out may be indicated. The third type of concept formation is the abstract level, which captures the essential common characteristic of the objects. This is the highest level of thought and stands in marked contrast to the prior two forms of more concrete thought processes (Rapaport et al., 1945). From the general level of abstraction on the Similarities subtest, and also from its relationship to the Vocabulary baseline, and the qualitative features of the derived concepts, valuable clues can be derived concerning the level, flexibility, and appropriateness of conceptual thinking and the role of abstract ideational processes in the subject's total psychological organization.[2] When Similarities fall exceptionally low within the scatter, one may suspect central nervous system impairment. In acute schizophrenic states impaired thought processes would not be limited to Similarities, but, as will be discussed shortly, would also affect such other scales as Comprehension (judgment) and possibly Arithmetic (concentration). Similarities be-

---

[2] Concrete and functional responses may also be a function of impoverished educational experiences rather than reflecting psychopathology or intellectual limitations.

cause of its demand for abstraction tends to be elevated in patients such as the obsessive and the paranoid who emphasize abstract and symbolic modes of thought.

DIGIT SPAN. In presenting a subject with increasing lengths of rote material for immediate memory and recall, this subtest generally taps passive reception of stimuli and the automatic effortless process called attention (Rapaport et al., 1945). Attention functions best when it is not disrupted by preoccupations, anxiety or the intrusion of drive derivatives. A Digit Span score which is markedly below the Vocabulary level tends to indicate the presence of anxiety; whereas, a Digit Span score which is high in relation to Vocabulary indicates blandness of affect and is frequently found in detached, schizoid people. In schizoid records the blandness usually represents a lack of conscious anxiety, chronicity, and an acceptance of pathology. High Digit Span, which indicates a lack of anxiety, may also be seen in psychopathic protocols and in hysterics characterized by "belle indifference." Conversely, a low Digit Span may suggest a more positive prognosis, since it reflects an acute state of subjective distress in which the disorder has not become ego-syntonic or the person is comfortable with it and unmotivated to change. A one to three point difference may be expected in favor of digits forward over digits backward. If this pattern is reversed, one should also be alerted to blandness or negativism.

In other contexts, low Digit Span may have yet another meaning. One of the primary features of central nervous system damage is a severe distractability which accompanies diminished cortical control. The capacity to attend is adversely affected by distractability, and, therefore, an impoverished Digit Span with added indications of concrete concept formation and unusual motor impairments frequently is seen in brain damaged patients.

ARITHMETIC. Complex arithmetical reasoning requires extensive concentration and attention (Rapaport et al., 1945). Concentration is foremost in this task, since the subject has to actively focus his attention in order to acquire the information within the problem and to manipulate its complex dimensions. The subject must attend to the specific numbers of the problem, maintain an overview so that various elements are seen in their relative position in the problem matrix and the interrelationship between the various elements must be manipulated in order to arrive at a solution. The tasks on the Arithmetic subtest require the subject to utilize skills that have been attained comparatively early in development and during the educational process. In this sense the subject has to turn back to prior skills and apply them to a particular task. The test also introduces time pressures for the first time, and the subject is forced to apply himself actively to the problem while reducing various distracting elements from within or from the total environment. Arithmetic is like Vocabulary and Information in that it depends upon memory and prior learning, but it differs markedly in the fact that it requires concentration and active application of select skills to cope with a new and unique situation.

By comparing functioning on the Digit Span and Arithmetic subtests, the relative balance between attention and concentration can be ascertained. Attention is the relatively passive and automatic reception of stimuli without effortful attempts to organize the material or to establish mnemonic devices. It is usually a one step assimilation of a stimulus field which can be disrupted by internal preoccupations. Concentration is a more active, effortful process, and, though it depends on attention to some degree, it goes beyond it in organizing and manipulating a complex series of events. The relative balance and interweaving of these two psychological functions have important implications for understanding psychological organization (Rapaport et al., 1945). Attempts to compensate for disruptions in attention, for example, often involve extensive efforts at concentration to bolster processes which should occur in a relatively automatic way. Lapses in attention usually occur as a function of anxiety, whereas difficulties in concentration indicate more serious thought disorder. This interpretation of possible thought disorder, however, may be made only when Arithmetic and Digit Span are widely disparate. A low score solely on Arithmetic, relative to Vocabulary, for example, is typically found in hysterical and narcissistic individuals who avoid active, effortful ideation and the elaboration of internal experience. The diagnostic implication of an Arithmetic score lower than Digit Span becomes all the more critical when Digit Span is higher than Vocabulary, for then it indicates a lack of anxiety and a blandness when there are difficulties in concentration (Rapaport et al., 1945). Should both Arithmetic and Digit Span be low, as frequently occurs in anxious, unreflective hysterics (or in brain damage), impairments both in active concentration and attention are present. The differential relationship between Arithmetic and Digit Span and their relationship to the Vocabulary baseline, therefore, are most important diagnostic considerations.

Performance Subtests

PICTURE ARRANGEMENT. In arranging a series of sketches into a sequence which creates a meaningful story, the subject is required to understand the inner relationships of a series of events and to grasp the essential message of a social interaction. The skill necessary for seeing the inner connections between sequences of enduring, continuing, and causally related events, is really a capacity to recognize what effects one event has on the next. Meaningful continuity in everyday experiences is largely dependent on the capacity to anticipate, to judge, and to understand the possible antecedents and consequences of any event. Poor performance on this subtest frequently reflects an impaired capacity to anticipate events and their consequences and to plan effective courses of action (Rapaport et al., 1945). On the other hand, subjects with cautious, guarded, hyperalert paranoid features are frequently extremely sensitive to social events and consequent behavior and are highly involved in an attempt to anticipate the future. Their psychological orientation may be reflected in an elevation of the Picture Arrangement subtest score.

The Picture Arrangement subtest also reflects, as does the Comprehension subtest, the response to stimuli that are concerned with social interactions. These two subtests allow comparison of well learned social conventionalities (Comprehension) with the capacity to anticipate and plan in a social context (Picture Arrangement). A profile containing high Picture Arrangement but low Comprehension scores may be seen in a character disorder where there is sensitivity to interpersonal nuances, but a disregard for social conventionality. The glib psychopath with a social facade may receive high scores on both the Comprehension and Picture Arrangement subtests. It should also be noted that Picture Arrangement is the only subtest that contains an element of humor. Frequently the inability to see the humorous aspects of life interferes with an optimum capacity to function on this subtest.

PICTURE COMPLETION. This subtest requires visual organization and the capacity to attend to and observe the inconsistencies and incongruities within a picture. One must focus attention on the details of the picture and actively examine and check the drawing, either in terms of its symmetry or in terms of an internalized image of the object. In this sense the major function seems to be again concentration, but in contradistinction to Arithmetic, the concentration is directed towards an externalized form and there is only minimal demand for the more internalized processes required in the Arithmetic subtest (Rapaport et al., 1945). As in Arithmetic, the time limit is of considerable importance in placing additional demands upon the subject. The instructions of this subtest ask the subject to appraise critically and to look for defects within the stimuli. Occasionally this subtest may be affected by a subject's reluctance to criticize, to assert himself, to attack actively, or to find fault with an aspect of his environment. The Picture Completion score will be high and frequently have positive Vocabulary scatter in paranoid subjects for whom hyperalertness and hypervigilance are the prime modes of functioning. Obsessive compulsives may also have inflated scores because of their pedantic, meticulous examination of every aspect of the picture. Since the objects or people are shown in an incomplete state, a low score may reflect concerns over bodily intactness with a possible emphasis on castration concerns; a low score may also be seen as a function of passivity. Specific conflictual issues may be reflected in long delays, failures on relatively easy items, or failures involving particular content. This latter type of failure often takes the form of an emphasis on "supports" missing, e.g., someone holding a pitcher, or the flagpole or in an emphasis on people missing, e.g., no one in the rowboat. Depending on the context, missing supports may reflect feelings of helplessness and passivity and missing people may reflect feelings of estrangement from people and a need for contact.

OBJECT ASSEMBLY. In dealing with jigsaw puzzles, subjects are required to grasp a whole pattern by anticipating the inner relationship of the individual sections. On some items and for some subjects, anticipation of the final pattern is immediate and the task is one of simple visual-motor coordination (Wechsler, 1958). On more difficult items within the subtest, some subjects may not have immediate insight into the final pattern, in which case the subject frequently resorts to trial and error behavior. Bringing subparts together often furthers the progressive emergence of the total pattern, and in this press toward solution one can observe the subject's capacities for trying new leads, for shifting set, and for functioning on minimal cues. Equally important is observing the smoothness, accuracy, and rapidity of a subject's visual-motor coordination which may express habituated and stereotyped motor actions. Also, in presenting an object which has been broken apart, we implicitly confront the subject with something dismembered. Performance on this test, therefore, is adversely and particularly affected by concerns over bodily integration and intactness (Blatt, Allison, and Baker, 1965). It should be noted that on occasion blocking occurs on specific items which may also be related to conflictual issues (e.g., on the hand in subjects with concerns over aggression or masturbation).

BLOCK DESIGNS. In this test of visual-motor organization (Wechsler, 1958), the subject is presented with a pattern which he is asked to reconstruct out of blocks that are identical to each other in size and design. Block Design differs markedly from Object Assembly: in Object Assembly the end product must be anticipated from the part objects; in Block Design the final pattern is presented and must be broken down and then reconstructed in block size units (Rapaport et al., 1945; Wechsler, 1958). The differentiation of a part of a design and the specification of its interrelationships with other parts is essentially a concept formation task involving both analysis and synthesis. The visual organization demanded to differentiate partially a total design and the motor action needed to integrate the blocks is frequently interfered with by central nervous system damage. Since anxiety interferes with attention to small details, performance is facilitated by the blandness and lack of anxiety frequently seen in schizoid personalities. It is important to note the procedure which the subject uses to duplicate the pattern, i.e., whether it is orderly and follows along the outline of the blocks or is haphazard and goes from one section of the design to the other in a random pursuit to find the "magical" clue.

DIGIT SYMBOL. In comparison to the other performance tests, Digit Symbol is generally a measure of the capacity for imitative behavior. It requires relatively little learning, concept formation, anticipation, planning, or analytic-synthetic functioning. Rather, it involves the simple use of energy for a smooth and unhesitating duplication of simple patterns (Wechsler, 1958). In the past the Digit Symbol subtest was thought to be a measure of learning ability. Recent research (e.g., Murstein and Leipold, 1961), however, has indicated that a minimal degree of learning takes place during this task and also that few subjects rely on memory; therefore, we see the test primarily as a measure of the capacity to utilize energy in a simple task. Inasmuch as the subject is required to muster up energy and to apply it, this task reflects the amount of energy output a subject can generally bring to his work and his activities. Thus, a low Digit Symbol, markedly below Vocabulary, is frequently a sign of a depressive lack of energy output, whereas Digit Symbol above Vocabulary may be evidence of an overcompliant striving and a desire for achievement going beyond one's intellectual capacities. It is also noteworthy that this is the first subtest in which subjects are asked to write, to use a pencil. Particularly for school-age subjects this test may arouse feelings about classroom demands. Digit Symbol, when it is elevated above other Performance tests, indicates that reduced functioning in the other Performance tests may not be due to a lack of speed and low energy output, but rather to specific problems related to the unique functions tapped by these other subtests.

The relationship of Digit Symbol to Digit Span is often of particular diagnostic import. We have observed a frequent pattern in which Digit Span is relatively low and suggests considerable anxiety and Digit Symbol is relatively high and reflects a marked energy output. In these cases, the individual seems to be controlling strong and pressing anxiety by excessive activity. The activity may represent an attempt to conform and win approval and acceptance. Such passivity, conformity and even ingratiation could be in the service of reducing the level of anxiety by minimizing the possibility of attack and criticism.

When we find the reverse pattern, a high Digit Span and a low Digit Symbol, we are usually confronted with an essentially depressed person who is attempting to ward off recognition of depressive affect perhaps in a hypomanic way, usually via denial, but not necessarily through activity and acting out behavior.

Digit Symbol, also, like Digit Span and Block Design, deals with essentially neutral, content-less material and it may be for this reason that some people, e.g., schizophrenics, at times do especially well on these subtests despite the fact that these patients clinically may show highly anxious behavior and despite the finding that performance on these subtests is particularly vulnerable to the effects of anxiety. With such schizophrenics it is their basic blandness, their isolation from, and lack of relatedness to their seemingly intense affects and also their heightened powers of attention and passive receptivity in contrast to their impaired concentration that is revealed through their high scores on these subtests.

INTRA-SUBTEST SCATTER

Since each subtest of the WAIS presents items of increasing difficulty, there should be a gradual tapering off of efficiency and accuracy. In cognitive functioning, which is relatively unimpaired by pathological processes, there should be a gradual tapering off in the adequacy of the response. Initially the responses should be intact and well articulated, giving way to responses which indicate that the level of the question is beyond the subject's capacities. This tapering off of efficiency should be gradual and relatively regular on each of the subtests. However some test records, particularly of patients, show a certain degree of variability of passes and failures within some subtests. Occasionally this takes the form of missing easy items initially but at other times the pattern is more one of intermittent fluctuation. In general, marked intra-subtest variability indicates a considerable degree of psychological disruption due to temporary inefficiencies or to a permanent loss of capacities such as in organic brain damage. On occasion, variability also can occur in a person with consistently disturbed school experiences where information and ways of coping with the various tasks of an intelligence test will have been acquired in a sporadic and uneven way. In hysterical patients it is usual to find variability primarily on the Information subtest since in these patients repression often serves as a general defensive orientation and serves to block out access to information even distantly associated with particular areas of conflict. Variability and disruption on Blocks and Similarities likely reflects an organically based problem as does recurrent variability throughout the tests. Epileptics, for instance, have a typical pattern of alternations of passes and fails with a waxing and waning quality usually regardless of the subtest or of the specific content of the items. An important rule of thumb in assessing the degree to which organicity is suggested by intra-subtest variability is whether the test disruptions seem unrelated to specific preoccupations of the individual. Disruptions which are unrelated to specific concerns but are more associated with general cognitive functioning, occur in organically based interference with ego functioning. In schizophrenics the fluctuation is likely to be due more to areas of preoccupation although in more chronic, longstanding patients, ego efficiency may be affected in a more global way and result in poorer efficiency with some easier items. In such instances other test data may be crucial for ruling out organic brain damage.

Differences in Verbal and Performance IQ

In addition to hypotheses about specific subtests, inferences can be obtained from the comparison of the Verbal and Performance IQs. In the Bright Normal and Superior ranges, the Verbal IQ usually tends to be a little higher than the Performance IQ, and the difference increases as the Full Scale IQ rises because marked abilities and accomplishments in one area may lead to a relative de-emphasis on the development of other functions. Thus, for the highly ideational person, efficiency in motor activities will often lag behind verbal efficiency. An eight to ten point difference between Verbal and Performance IQs where there is, for instance, a Total IQ of 135 (e.g., Verbal IQ, 138, Performance IQ, 127, Full Scale IQ, 135) is of limited diagnostic significance and indicates only a highly verbal subject with possible obsessive-compulsive tendencies. When the Verbal IQ begins to have a marked imbalance over the Performance IQ (by greater than 15 points), more serious pathological trends may be considered. A markedly obsessive preoccupation with words and thoughts or an extreme variability in functioning such as might result from a psychotic condition may be apparent. Usually, however, and depending on the subtest scores, two additional possible inferences are suggested by a marked elevation of the Verbal over the Performance IQ: depression and/or central nervous system pathology. Depression often involves psychomotor retardation and tasks with time limits and those subtests which require active manipulation tend to reflect this retardation. On the Performance scale, Digit Symbol in particular but also Object Assembly and Block Design are generally lowered. The Performance IQ is also lowered in brain damaged patients, but rather than solely affecting subtests on which speed is an issue, brain damage involving visual-motor deficits is reflected on those Performance subtests which require planning, organization, concept formation, concentration, and attention. Block Design in particular is a difficult task for these patients, and the score on this test is usually lower than any of the other Performance subtests. Several Verbal subtests, Vocabulary and Information, are often unaffected in brain damaged patients, since much of the material is explicitly contingent upon prior experience and has been overlearned. Thus, while there may be some decrements in the Verbal IQ of organic patients because of low scores on Digit Span, Arithmetic, and Similarities, the Verbal IQ is maintained at a level closer to the premorbid intellectual level than is the Performance IQ.

In the lower intelligence ranges, the Performance IQ tends to be a little higher than its Verbal counterpart, largely because the emphasis on motor functioning tends to be associated with a reduced investment in ideational modes. But a Performance IQ greater than a Verbal IQ in individuals of at least average intelligence is atypical. Three major diagnostic trends, all of which have acting out as a primary feature, are suggested by such a pattern: hysteric, narcissistic, and psychopathic character disorders. In the hysteric, the repression of impulses and impulse derivatives usually results in restriction of intellectual and cultural interests and pursuits. Functioning on the Verbal scales of the WAIS is often strikingly influenced by repression, naivete, and inability to remember, and although hysterical women from rich cultural backgrounds may acquire a superficial cultural and intellectual veneer that can lead to an elevated Verbal IQ, this "modern" hysterical pattern still maintains much of the subtest scatter seen in the more classical hysterical states (especially Comprehension above Information). Performance IQ is also often higher in narcissistic character disorders and in individuals with psychopathic trends (Wechsler, 1958), since these are generally "action oriented" people who are unable to establish the delay necessary for dealing with questions requiring thought and concentration and internal elaboration. They are much more comfortable with tasks which require external manipulation and action, and thus function better on the

Performance subtests. The comparison of the Verbal IQ and Performance IQ and the examination of the pattern of the subtests of the WAIS is an important step in the diagnostic process. It allows the clinician to describe the individual's unique organization of psychological functions and from this to infer the defenses, the nature and quality of the drives and impulses, the degree and type of pathology, as well as assets and capacities for adaptation and coping.

CASE EXAMPLES

To illustrate further the development of hypotheses from WAIS scatter, six WAIS score patterns which cover a variety of diagnostic categories will be presented and discussed. Also, a detailed analysis of the full WAIS protocol of a patient, Mrs. T., will be presented and discussed. Cases are presented here, and in subsequent chapters, for specific diagnostic groups to illustrate broad and general personality types. As stressed earlier, these are only global categories in which there are extensive and subtle variations. Also, though one does not base conclusions on subtest scatter alone, the analysis of WAIS subtest scatter is presented here because it is often a relatively neglected but valuable source of data.

Neurotic Depression

33-year-old hospitalized married woman

Verbal Subtest Scaled Scores		Performance Subtest Scaled Scores	
Comprehension	11	Picture Arrangement	12
Information	12	Picture Completion	8
Digit Span	14	Block Design	8
Arithmetic	13	Object Assembly	12
Similarities	12	Digit Symbol	9
Vocabulary	11		

Verbal IQ 112   *Performance IQ* 99   *Full Scale IQ* 107

This is a woman of average intelligence with a Performance IQ 13 points below her Verbal IQ. The Verbal IQ with its relative lack of scatter is probably an adequate reflection of this woman's intellectual capabilities. The imbalance between her Performance and Verbal IQs is suggestive of depressive or organic trends. The latter diagnostic possibility is unlikely since Similarities, Arithmetic, and Digit Span are so high. Rather, the probability of depressive features is supported by the fact that Digit Symbol, a test of psychomotor speed and energy, is one of her lowest subtests and also because the lower Performance IQ is a function of a decrement of most of the Performance subtests rather than one or two. Noteworthy, in addition to the depressive features, is the suggestion of blandness and lack of anxiety indicated in the high Digit Span and Arithmetic, which have positive Vocabulary scatter. A record which has a depressive pattern yet has indications that many functions are relatively free of interference by anxiety, especially one in which Digit Symbol is low but Digit Span high, suggests that the depression is being defended against, probably through denial. It is important to note in this record that Vocabulary is the lowest of the Verbal subtests. This may reflect some degree of impoverishment of early intellectual stimulation which was then compensated for. Adaptive strengths are clearly present in her capacity to plan, anticipate and organize her experience (indicated by the intact Picture Arrangement and Object Assembly subtests). This capacity for anticipation and planning indicates a broad temporal orientation and concern with the future which counteracts the possibility of a depressive sense of life being over, and a preoccupation with the past or present. In a depressive record these assets indicate good ego strength, and the future orientation as well as signs of a lack of conscious anxiety show that she is not incapacitated by depression, at least not in the well structured WAIS. If anything, in fact, her ego assets may even complicate her involvement in therapy for efforts to defend against recognition of depression and anxiety may make it difficult for her to face these issues in therapy. If we consider the hypothesis of depression, then we might think that the lowered Picture Completion score stems from her defensive inability to acknowledge defect and fault. The lowered Block Design was possibly due to an inability to obtain time bonus scores.

Qualitative features in this woman's WAIS show that poor scores occur largely because of slow performance, and many of her responses are accompanied by expressions of inability.

Hysteria

26-year-old single female outpatient			
Verbal Subtest Scaled Scores		*Performance Subtest Scaled Scores*	
Comprehension	17	Picture Arrangement	15
Information	13	Picture Completion	11
Digit Span	12	Block Design	9
Arithmetic	11	Object Assembly	10
Similarities	13	Digit Symbol	15
Vocabulary	15		

Verbal IQ 120   *Performance IQ* 114   *Full Scale IQ* 118

While one would expect the Performance IQ to be greater than the Verbal IQ in hysterical records, in all other respects this pattern of subtests is classically hysterical. Comprehension is most notably the highest subtest and is the only one with positive Vocabulary scatter. Comprehension is also four points above Information which reflects the hysteric's conventionality, morality, naivete, and a corresponding lower fund of information. Digit Span and Block Design are often low in hysterical profiles when there is a high degree of subjective anxiety; the low Arithmetic is likely to result from difficulties in concentration, and also from a relatively passive orientation which is reflected in a lack of diligent application in active pursuits. Her ability for abstract thinking also falls short of her overall intellectual capacities and may also indicate her lack of success with active, complex thinking. The avoidance or shying away from active ideation in this woman is especially noteworthy in contrast to her high intellectual level. In fact, if we take her Vocabulary score as the baseline and estimate her potential from it, we arrive at an IQ close to 130. Despite her relative intellectual brightness, she appears from the WAIS scatter to be far from utilizing her full resources in a particularly ambitious or creative way. The higher Picture Arrangement is consistent with the high Comprehension and here reflects the marked externalizing and social orientation of a repressive individual.

There is extensive scatter from a scaled score high of 17 to a low of 9 on Block Design. This indicates that there is a fair degree of interference with functioning and that defenses are not operating effectively. But despite the strong anxiety that seems present, efforts to defend against it, perhaps through externally directed and compliant behavior, are indicated by the high Digit Symbol. Object Assembly is relatively low and along with Picture Completion seems indicative of strong preoccupations and concerns about body intactness.

The nature and extent of interpersonal difficulties and the preoccupation with body concerns are clearly reflected in a number of qualitative features in the record, typical of which is the definition of the word "sanctuary" in the Vocabulary subtest. She defines "sanctuary" as follows: "Home [laughs]. I guess I automatically think of my home as a sanctuary. It is a place of finding peace. I was trying to think of the Hunchback of Notre Dame and finding somebody in the church, in the bell tower. It is a place in which you are safe." In this response one sees her body concerns reflected in her reference to the hunchback. Strikingly evident is the fearfulness and danger she associates with places of safety (home and church), the failure of repressive defenses to contain these associations and her subsequent defensive efforts to combat these fears. Of further interest is her self-referential and egocentric way of relating the question to herself, her initially loosely associative quality which leads in the end to a clear definition. The theme of the hunchback and Esmeralda the Gypsy dancer also reflects her fear of sexuality, a depreciatory view of males as ugly, deformed, and aggressive, women being their passive victims.

Organic Brain Damage

21-year-old unmarried male outpatient

Verbal Subtest Scaled Scores		Performance Subtest Scaled Scores	
Comprehension	5	Picture Arrangement	4
Information	8	Picture Completion	8
Digit Span	6	Block Design	1
Arithmetic	5	Object Assembly	2
Similarities	0	Digit Symbol	0
Vocabulary	3		

Verbal IQ 68   *Performance IQ* 53   *Full Scale IQ* 59

This is a characteristic picture of organic brain damage of longstanding, with Performance markedly below Verbal in the mental defective IQ range. The 15 point difference between Performance and Verbal scales is particularly impressive, since one ordinarily expects the Performance IQ to be above the Verbal IQ in this range of intelligence. This pattern is suggestive of central nervous system pathology. While depression might also be considered as a possible feature of this record because of the lowered Performance score and the special lowering of Block Design, Object Assembly, and Digit Symbol, the marked difference between Performance and Verbal IQs and the zero scores calls for the primary interpretation of brain damage. The very low scores on Similarities and Block Design are classically organic in that they point to extreme concreteness of thinking, both in the verbal and visual-motor spheres. It is important to note that the Performance subtests that are impaired all require motor activity. On Picture Arrangement and Picture Completion, which require little or no motor coordination, his functioning is more intact. In fact, Picture Completion is one of his two highest subtest scores, the other being Information, both with a scaled score of eight. These two scores may offer us some indication that his premorbid intellectual level was around 90 to 100, and, therefore, in comparison to his baseline, the organic damage is quite severe. The fact that the patient's scores on Information, Picture Completion, and Digit Span are his highest shows that his ability to deal with specific concrete bits of experience has been retained. It is in the areas of motor efficiency, abstraction, and integration that he is most impaired. Since Digit Span is not lowered, it may also be that the patient has in some degree adjusted to his defects which would, therefore, suggest that the central nervous system damage is probably not of recent onset.

The Comprehension and Picture Arrangement scores are 5 and 4 respectively, and, though these are somewhat below Information and indicate some possible withdrawal from social interaction, these two subtests are not as badly impaired as others. Thus, in terms of social interaction he may appear more intact than he really is. Also, the relatively good social judgment indicated by the scores on Comprehension and Picture Arrangement contra-indicate the presence of psychosis. Somewhat atypical in this record is the fact that Vocabulary is quite low, for it is expected that his vocabulary will remain relatively unaffected by organic pathology. However, the qualitative features of the test show that memory is extensively impaired and that Information (like Digit Span and Arithmetic) is relatively high because the patient knew almost all the items dealing with numbers. Some special ability seemed retained as regards the memory of numbers, but in other respects, memory efficiency is so much affected that even the Vocabulary score has been lowered.

The primitive quality of this man's thinking is well illustrated in the zero score on Similarities. After the "orange and banana" item was explained to him in great detail, he gave the following response to the subsequent "coat and dress" item: "I don't even know how that is." [Asked to try and go ahead, he continues in the following way.] "Dress underneath a coat is very skinner than the outside of the coat." [In what way are they alike?] "I don't know. Put dress on first then put coat over the dress." This response not only indicates a severe primitivization of his thinking but also the complete loss of the abstract attitude.

Severe Obsessive-Compulsive Neurosis

30-year-old married male outpatient

Verbal Subtest Scaled Scores		Performance Subtest Scaled Scores	
Comprehension	13	Picture Arrangement	15
Information	18	Picture Completion	11
Digit Span	10	Block Design	9
Arithmetic	17	Object Assembly	14
Similarities	13	Digit Symbol	11
Vocabulary	16		

Verbal IQ 126   *Performance IQ* 114   *Full Scale IQ* 122

With a Full Scale IQ of 122 this is a man of superior intellectual ability, especially when we consider that if not for the lowered Digit Span his Verbal IQ would be above 130. The 12 point elevation of the Verbal over the Performance IQ is not unusual at this level of intelligence, but the fact that most Performance subtests fall below Vocabulary, especially the drop of Digit Symbol, suggests depressive features.

In examining the pattern of scores further, the difference between

Information (scaled score of 18) and Comprehension (scaled score of 13) could indicate either obsessive-compulsive or psychotic trends. Since Comprehension is also three points below Vocabulary, the possibility of psychotic trends might be considered. But when we see that Picture Arrangement is not simultaneously low, we can conclude that the drop in Comprehension most probably is the consequence of obsessive-compulsive qualification and the acquisition and retention of information in excess of the capacity to understand and critically appraise social situations. Judging by the fact that Information is also two points above Vocabulary, his acquisition of knowledge may be accomplished through an overstriving attitude, possibly with a pedantic quality. The somewhat lowered score on Similarities, however, suggests that the emphasis on detail is accompanied by some inefficiency in abstraction.

The Digit Span and Block Design scores point toward a serious intrusion of attention and visual-motor coordination by anxiety; this suggests that obsessive-compulsive defense mechanisms are not functioning effectively, with the result that the patient is vulnerable to intense feelings of anxiety. Another possibility is the presence of minimal brain damage. The extreme variation in scaled scores (from 9 to 18), furthermore, indicates a rather marked disruption in present functioning and could suggest a possible decompensation of defenses. On inspection, therefore, the low Comprehension and Similarities may turn out to reveal psychotic trends. Since the high Picture Arrangement may be, in part, a function of a hyperalert, paranoid orientation, we would be confronted with an individual whose obsessive-compulsive defenses were decompensating and who was moving toward a more psychotic and paranoid position. Further evaluation of this possibility would, of course, depend on data and observations from other aspects of the diagnostic battery.

Of immediate note is the highly significant elevation of the Verbal IQ over the Performance IQ which leads to the consideration of the following major alternatives: brain damage or depression. It becomes immediately clear that organicity is not present from the scatter of the Performance subtests, particularly the fact that Block Design (and, therefore, abstract thinking) is unimpaired and also from the high Digit Span and Similarities on the Verbal subtests. And, while depressive features might be suggested by the lowered Digit Symbol and Object Assembly scores, we see that

Schizophrenia, Acute

21-year-old single male inpatient

Verbal Subtest Scaled Scores		Performance Subtest Scaled Scores	
Comprehension	13	Picture Arrangement	8
Information	13	Picture Completion	9
Digit Span	16	Block Design	14
Arithmetic	11	Object Assembly	11
Similarities	13	Digit Symbol	10
Vocabulary	14		

Verbal IQ 120 *Performance IQ* 102 *Full Scale IQ* 113

it is primarily the drop in Picture Arrangement and Picture Completion which accounts for the discrepancy between Performance and Verbal IQs. This low a Picture Arrangement score shows that the adherence to social conventions and realistic ways of looking at things, as suggested by Comprehension, is not backed up by good planning and anticipation. Rather, there is at best a superficial grasp of conventionality which may mask a socially alienated position and an interference with planned, carefully thought out action. Other psychotic features of the scatter are the very high Digit Span and Block Design which reflect considerable blandness; the low Arithmetic which indicates difficulty in concentration; and the fact that Digit Span is above Arithmetic which suggests that the passive attentive process, the simple registering of stimuli, is intact but that experience cannot be dealt with actively and with sustained concentration. The Picture Completion score may be further evidence of this difficulty in concentration. Another consideration in this record is the possibility that some depressive features may be present but defended against by denial (low Digit Symbol with a high Digit Span).

On the adaptive side, the fairly high Comprehension reflects a capacity for some reality testing, and the high scores on Vocabulary, Information, and Similarities along with a Verbal IQ of 120 indicate that there are many ego assets which have been minimally affected, if at all. The intactness of these ego processes is an important aspect of this record, for this profile differs markedly from the records of more chronic schizophrenics in which one sees fewer retained ego assets. As a qualitative example of primitive thinking in this schizophrenic record is his response to item 14 ("swallow") of Comprehension: "Well, ordinarily summer is the time of plenty, when growing things grow and bloom, when crops can be raised and in a time of famine just because there is some means of, er, some small means of satisfying one's self would not really be an indication it was not a famine."

Schizophrenia, Chronic

27-year-old single female inpatient

Verbal Subtest Scaled Scores		Performance Subtest Scaled Scores	
Comprehension	0	Picture Arrangement	0
Information	10	Picture Completion	0
Digit Span	7	Block Design	10
Arithmetic	0	Object Assembly	9
Similarities	0	Digit Symbol	10
Vocabulary	4		

Verbal IQ 61 *Performance IQ* 73 *Full Scale IQ* 64

The Verbal, Performance, and Full Scale IQs all fall in the mentally defective range. When evaluating the scatter of subtest scores, however, there can be little doubt that this is not a mentally retarded individual, because some subtest scores fall in the average range. Organicity is counterindicated by the high Block Design and Digit Span scores. The wide range of scores on both the Performance and Verbal subtests, therefore, suggests a psychotic picture. Her complete failure on Arithmetic, Picture Completion, and Similarities represents a severe impairment in concentration and abstract conceptualization. The zero scores on Picture Arrangement and Comprehension are likely to be a function of social withdrawal and a failure to be able to establish reality ties in social situations. Such a subtest profile represents a marked disruption of ego controls of a chronic condition. Schizophrenia is also suggested in the extreme blandness without other indications of a struggle to preserve reality contact. Only when presented with inanimate objects or questions not related to social interaction can she venture forth and respond. The following example taken from Comprehension is not the result of a total lack of responsivity but, rather, represents an unsuccessful struggle to deal with the question. On item 5 ("movies") she responds as follows: "Where? What do you mean? Just what I said on the screen might be the end of the portration. If it is to the left, let the person know, if it is to the center, same thing. If it is to the other side, same thing. If it is touching you, put it out."

We have attempted to show in these preceding six cases how the profile of the scaled scores enables us to specify the general level of development and the efficiency of a number of psychological functions. We have also seen how comparisons between these functions allow us to describe each individual in terms of the specific array and pattern of his ego processes, adaptive endeavors, and organization of psychological defenses.

GENERAL RECOMMENDATIONS FOR ADMINISTRATION

A major source of data about cognitive processes is *how* the subject arrives at his response, i.e., his "style" of responding. Sheerer (1946), among others, has stressed the importance of understanding of underlying thought processes. And though many inferences about thought processes can be drawn from the pattern of scores, the inferences may be somewhat limited if not integrated with sensitive observations of the process through which the subject came to the correct or incorrect response. The clinician must continually ask himself how the subject arrived at his response. Even correct responses may have been arrived at by quite idiosyncratic methods, and certainly incorrect responses can range from an inexact but essentially correct approach to a mode of functioning which is completely irrelevant for the item. It is in the processes underlying the responses that the essential dynamics of the person's thinking can be observed. The clinician, therefore, must continually attempt to observe these processes by carefully noting the subject's behavior and by asking questions which will elicit information about the sequences of thought. This purpose is best served by a verbatim recording of the individual's responses which permits future study of the material that may have gone unnoticed during testing. In order to obtain a verbatim recording and at the same time make careful observations and view the complex transaction that occurs during any testing process, the clinician should memorize the entire test so that the test can be administered without the manual. This is especially important since all patients to a greater or lesser extent need face-to-face contact during testing. It is also useful for the purpose of recording observations to employ a revised expanded WAIS form which has more room for the tester's verbatim recording and for observations of the style of responding.

While the administration of the WAIS must adhere to the standardized instructions established by Wechsler, the following recommendations for each of the subtests offer the opportunity for further observation of the underlying thought processes. These procedures make available new levels of observations and inferences. In the section below, each of the subtests is discussed, and recommendations are presented for administrative procedures and observational techniques that go beyond those found in the WAIS manual.[3]

The WAIS is indirectly introduced to subjects along with the other tests with a comment that one of the tests will be an intelligence test but that it is used largely to evaluate personality. The WAIS is given in a matter-of-fact fashion, without any involvement in the "right" or "wrong" nature of the answers. An exception to this may be made with very anxious or severely depressed patients who cannot respond without external encouragement. Generally, however, the tester should avoid being too supportive even with upset patients. There is no need to comment "good" or "fine" after a correct answer, since this would imply that it is an achievement test and might make the test situation more tense and later failure more troubling. On the other hand, no attempt should be made to obscure the fact that this is an intelligence test or that parts of it are timed. It may be added, if necessary, that, since it is constructed as an intelligence test, it will contain some very easy items and some very difficult ones and that no one is expected to be able to do all the things he is asked.

The WAIS, as well as other tests, should be administered in a

[3] The authors are grateful to Dr. Roy Schafer for permission to use material from his mimeographed, *Supplementary Manual on the Administration of the WAIS to Psychiatric Patients.*

normal, informal, conversational tone. The tester should not sound like an authoritarian teacher drilling a student. If some WAIS instructions sound unnatural to the tester, he may have to depart a little from the exact wording so as to be able to say it naturally and with ease. The subject's statements are recorded verbatim. If a subject becomes upset, however, it may be necessary to sacrifice exact and immediate recording in the interest of maintaining good rapport until the disturbance has subsided. When the subject has again resumed the task or after the test appointment, notes should be made on what went on during the upset period. The tester should feel free to interrupt the subject if the latter speaks too fast asking him to slow down or to wait until he has caught up with writing down the answer. The tester can explain that this procedure is necessary in order to make a full analysis of the results. In principle, exact recording should never be given priority over maintaining contact with the subject. Some visual contact is especially important with depressed and anxious people in order for them to maintain sufficient motivation for testing but it is indispensable with any kind of patient; the tester should not appear to be a "recording machine."

If, during the test, the subject is obviously fatigued, very ill at ease, or resistant, it is advisable to comment upon this and try to discuss the impeding factors. If the subject admits that he feels very tired, the tester, if possible, should not volunteer to discontinue the testing session. On the other hand, it makes no sense to continue testing if the hostility and resistance of the subject cannot be overcome and if it seriously interferes with the procedure.

When the subject gives unusual, idiosyncratic, peculiar, or bizarre verbalizations, they must be explored by additional questioning as close in time to the original verbalization as possible. This inquiry permits the subject to make explicit the ambiguities in his atypical response. For example, neologisms should be defined, unusual phrasing clarified, and non sequiturs explained. Inquiry should be adapted to the apparent intellectual level of the subject. If it is obvious that he is at the upper limits of his knowledge, failing one question after another, a more casual attitude may be taken toward outlandish features. Inquiry should be gentle and simply reflect the tester's genuine curiosity about the subject's thinking and responses. Under no conditions should the words, tone of voice, or expressive movements of the tester convey a feeling of pressure to the subject. Although subjects probably feel pressured to some degree they generally tend to accept this type of inquiry if it is presented as a matter of standard procedure. If one suspects that the subject may not have heard correctly or may have over-looked part of the question, the tester should ask, "What was my question?" If the subject repeats the question and spontaneously corrects himself, he should receive credit.

We found it helpful to extend the scoring with scores which re-flect a subject's potential level not fully expressed in his formal subtest scores. As specified by Wechsler (1958), a score of 2 is given whenever an answer contains both a 1- and 2-point quality response. When an answer combines a 0 with 1- or 2-score value, the subject must be asked to make a choice. Usually subjects select the higher level response, but occasionally the 1- or 2-level response is rejected in favor of an incorrect answer. Formally, the response must be scored zero, but giving an additional score (1 or 2) reflects the fact that the subject has this material available even if he is unable to utilize it effectively. Additional scores are also helpful indicators when the subject gives a correct response but exceeds the time limit to a minimal degree. Here again the formal score reflects a failure within the prescribed time limit and the additional score indicates that the subject was eventually able to cope with the item. These additional scores, therefore, permit the tester to note the subject's potential level of functioning and they should be given when the tester believes that the subject has a good grasp of the item but cannot effectively communicate it. In circumstances when the tester has good reason to believe that a 1 response is not representative of the subject's level of functioning, an open-ended question may elicit further elaboration, giving it the quality of a 2 response. In such cases (e.g., on Vocabulary, "winter is a season") the answer will often be quickly extended on questioning to in-clude cold weather. The observation that the subject is willing to settle for a mediocre response when he is capable of a higher level of performance is an important piece of information, for it may call attention to the subject's inability to be self-critical. When the tester assumes this critical function for the subject by asking for further elaboration, the higher level response may be forthcoming. The evaluative function is an important part of the response process, and when the subject cannot maintain it on his own, it can represent an ego inefficiency. This type of impairment in ego functioning is also seen when a subject gives a high level response (1 or 2) along with an incorrect response (0) and is unable to differentiate between the levels unless the tester confronts him with the discrepancy and forces him to make a choice. Additional scores may not only designate higher potential but may also be used to reflect spoiled aspects of a response even though according to the manual it should receive a full score. Thus, a response could also be scored 2/1 or 2/0 or 1/0.

Although additional scores are very useful in providing an elaboration of the basic subtest scores for clinical purposes, it must be stressed that the extended scores are not used in the computation of the IQs.

Administration of Specific Subtests

Information

The procedures for administering this subtest are generally straight-forward. Occasionally the Information questions are viewed as demanding exact answers, and some subjects may need to be encouraged to guess on the quantitative items. If there is repeated refusal to guess, encouragement to do so should be discontinued. Individuals who have specialized backgrounds should be asked the Information items related to their particular background even when these items may occur beyond the point of five consecutive failures. Such items, answered correctly, receive an additional score. Thus, for instance, a nurse should be asked item 25 ("blood vessels").

A few items tend to present specific problems in administration. Item 6 ("Presidents") may be responded to incorrectly because the subject has overlooked the phrase "since 1900." In this case it is advisable to ask the subject to repeat the question, and the error is usually corrected spontaneously. If, however, the time dimension is still ignored, the question should be repeated in full. If the subject correctly answers the item, either through spontaneous correction or through the tester's repetition of the question, he should receive full credit. On item 18 ("Egypt") the subject must indicate the continent, and, if it is omitted, specific inquiry should be directed to this point. Because some time has elapsed since Alaska and Hawaii have been added to the 48 states, it is not unreasonable to regard any answer other than "100" to the "Senators" item as incorrect. On item 23, "water boil," the scale must be specified for the subject to receive full credit.

Comprehension

On occasion, subjects will refuse to give a conventional answer to some of the items on this scale. For instance, they may object to the concept of "bad company" and claim there is no such thing. In this case the subject may be asked what the conventional answer would be. Refusal to answer then indicates strong rebellion, possibly disillusionment with conventional reality, or both. If in answering questions 3 (what is the thing to do) and 5 (what should you do) the subject implies that he would personally do something which would be incorrect or have unfortunate consequences, he should be asked what one *should* do in such a situation. When a subject refers briefly to moss or to sun on question 9 ("forest"), he should be asked to elaborate his response. The same holds true for item 10 if the response is, "Because they cannot hear."

Arithmetic

Wrong answers should be inquired into and the subject asked, "How did you arrive at your answer?" Such a procedure gives the tester the possibility of viewing the response process. In this way flaws in logic or difficulties in arithmetic are exposed, or the fact that responses were guessed at will be revealed. The subject's attitude toward the error or guess is frequently very informative. The tester's query about the process through which the answer was obtained enables the subject spontaneously to discover his error and correct it. In this case additional scores may be given.

If the subject fails to solve a problem, particularly near his upper limits, graded help should be given. For example, upon failure on question 13, the subject might be asked, "What is 15 percent of 60?" If he is unable to do that, the problem can be broken down into simpler elements by asking the subject for 10 percent and/or 5 percent of 60 and observing if this facilitates solution of the problem. If the subject correctly answers the question with assistance he receives an additional score. Graded help should not be continued when the subject has repeatedly failed problems, unless they were failed by a common error or by miscalculation, and it is clear that graded help can aid the subject in arriving at an answer. If it seems that the subject has reached the upper limits of his ability, however, there is no need to have him struggle through the problem by giving graded help on each of the questions. Graded help plays a prominent role in test assessment in that it enables the subject to reveal more of the thought processes which enter into his responses and thereby permits increased understanding of his thinking. It can also determine a subject's degree of flexibility in being able to alter his approach to a problem. Moreover, in that the tester is helping him to reach a higher level of functioning it may also offer clues into the subject's perception of and reaction to a helping (therapeutic) person.

When the tester is asked by a subject to repeat a question, it is frequently better to ask him to state the question as he remembers it rather than to repeat it for him automatically. Knowledge of the degree to which he has distorted the question and the degree to which the receptive or memory function is impaired may be very important for arriving at one's final formulations about the subject. If the subject is unable to restate the question, then it may be repeated for him. In any case, the subject is timed from the end of the tester's initial question, and no extra time is given if the question is repeated by the tester. If time runs out before the subject answers correctly he does not receive formal credit for the item, although he may receive an extended score.

Similarities

The same general rules stated for Information and Comprehension apply to this subtest. Bizarre or atypical responses should receive further inquiry, and incomplete answers require further elaboration.

Vocabulary

Even though the subject has the card with the complete list of Vocabulary words in front of him, he should not be allowed to rush ahead of the tester. In order to establish this control, the following phrase should be added to the instructions: "Wait until I read the word before you define it." When the subject seems to be guessing or giving associations, it is appropriate to ask him, "What made you think this is what it means?" When he is obviously at his upper limits and failing difficult words, however, further inquiry should be avoided. Inquiry should always be made where responses are not sufficiently clear for the tester to make a judgment about the adequacy of the response. For instance, the word "obstruct" defined as, "close off," should be further inquired into by asking the subject to elaborate his response.

The same basic principles discussed for Information, Comprehension, and Similarities are also applicable to the Vocabulary subtest. The extended scoring procedure through the use of "additionals" is particularly important. Scoring should reflect the subject's understanding of the fundamental concept or definition of the word even though he may not be able to articulate it precisely enough to receive formal credit. This "additional" Vocabulary score, within a setting of severe disturbance of thought processes and verbal communication, allows for the establishment of a premorbid intellectual baseline to which one can compare the extent of deterioration as well as the negative and positive Vocabulary scatter.

Digit Span

In the administration of this subtest, one should be cautious not to vary one's voice, inflection, or timing across the series of digits. If the subject fails to get five or six digits forwards and four or five digits backwards, he should be given a third try after the usual two failures. (This does not apply to dull subjects.) For this, the appropriate number of digits may be selected from the last of the nine digit set. That is, the first five digits, for example, may be taken from the last series and presented to the subject as a third try for five digits. If the subject passes any subsequent stages after being successful on this third trial, no credit is given him for it. Any credit that is accumulated after double failure may only be scored as an additional credit and is not included in the basic score. This procedure is intended to appraise temporary inefficiencies, and allows the clinician thereby to discriminate to some degree the extent of the inefficiency in attention.

Digit Symbol

It is important that the subject does not start the test or the trial items until after the instructions have been completed. The tester must also see to it that no squares are omitted either in the sample or the test proper. If squares are omitted, the subject should be interrupted and told to do one after the other. Also added to Wechsler's instructions are the following words, "Keep going until I tell you to stop."

Picture Completion

The standard instructions should be supplemented with, "and I will turn the pages." Do not allow the subject to keep any picture more than 30 to 35 seconds unless he appears very anxious. Simply say, "time is up," or just turn the page. If the subject responds correctly past the time limit but under 30 or 35 seconds, the response is scored 0/1, indicating that the response itself was a 0 but that it had the potentiality of a score of 1. On the first misidentification of a missing part, the tester should ask, "What is intended to be missing?", a statement that frequently helps to clarify the test demands. Full credit is also given if the subject points to the correct missing part without being able to verbalize his answer. Since the subtest is designed to increase in difficulty, here, too, the subject should taper off in the correctness of his responses in a fairly progressive pattern. There should be a corresponding increase in the response time, and for this reason it is valuable to keep a record of the response times for each item. Occasional blocks in response time may indicate some involvement and investment in a particular card (e.g., one patient who had difficulty on the automobile door handles was severely depressed about losing his automobile sales agency franchise).

Block Design

In administering this subtest a record should be kept of the order in which the subject moves the blocks into position by assigning numbers to each position in the design as indicated in the pattern below. In this way, a sequential record block of the subject's attempts to duplicate the pattern may be kept by marking which position he attempts to fill in. The number is underlined only if the block is put in correctly; if a solid block (red or white) is inappropriately used the letter "R" or "W" is placed next to the number without underlining the number and if a block that is half-red and half-white is incorrectly used then the symbol "R/W" is placed next to the number without underlining it; a 0 is entered if a block is rotated or if it is rejected. In this manner, a running account is kept of the blocks which the subject handles and his procedure and method of attempting to duplicate the pattern. The diagnostic importance of this is obvious when we compare the more systematic, orderly way of normals with the chaotic, disorganized, and unplanned approach of the schizophrenic.

Record the order in which the subject moves the blocks into position, by assigning a number (1, 2, 3, . . . etc.) to each position in the pattern to be duplicated. Assuming the design to be facing the subject, the sequence of numbers should be as follows:

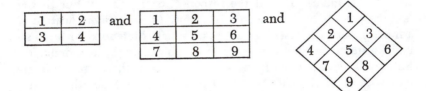

Only when the time allotted for the design has elapsed or when it is certain that the subject has completely given up trying, should graded help be introduced. This may be done by setting up two adjacent blocks in one corner which begin to form a section of the pattern of the failed design to see whether the idea is grasped by the subject. If the subject continues to fail, one may want to proceed further by setting up additional blocks, e.g., one row. The tester should not rush ahead to later items on this subtest if the subject begins failing items early. Rather, graded help should be given by having subjects check their designs or by doing a small section or row of the design for them. Also, detailed observation should be made, as it usually proves to be very valuable here. One must be careful, however, for if too much help is given, the subject may feel left out or may gain an added advantage on subsequent items. If the person is slowly approaching solution, but time has run out, it is advisable to let him continue without interruption and give him an additional score. Generally, graded help should be given when subjects fail items at a lower level than one might expect and if their approach seems especially haphazard or overly rigid and inflexible.

Picture Arrangement

In addition to noting the time and the pattern of the card placement in the subtest, it is helpful to have the subject tell the story to those series which he placed incorrectly. In addition, we ask subjects to tell the story on the last two series whether they are correct or incorrect. Before asking for the story, the pictures are removed and the subject is then asked, "What was the story?" If the subject is evasive, one might ask, "What did you have in mind?" or, "What did it seem to be about?" This material is very valuable in revealing distortions in thinking which may underlie an incorrect sequence or which may indicate specific idiosyncratic meaning that the pattern may have had for the subject. Frequently a correct sequence, and thus technically a correct response, occurs, but the subject does not know why he arranged the cards the way he did; this reflects a seeming capacity for planning with little essential understanding. It also indicates adherence to the external form of reality but a fuzzy conception of it. In such a case the additional score may be used to indicate the discrepancy between the sequence and the absence of an adequate story for it (4/0). It also sometimes happens that the sequence is incorrect but the general gist of the story is accurate (e.g., in people who see a broad but gross overview of a situation but are not able to manipulate its internal aspects). In such a case, an additional score can also be given (0/4).

Object Assembly

Generally no graded help is given during this subtest, because it is largely "a test of insight," and help will probably facilitate performance in subsequent retesting. If the subject's pattern is incorrect, he should be asked what he thinks it is or might be, and if he tends to give up before the allotted time, he should be encouraged to use all the time available. If, however, the subject seems to be very disoriented and is unable to grasp the instructions, the tester may give him help on items 1 and 2 by putting together a small section of the puzzle for him.

Also in Object Assembly a brief notation system should be used by which the tester can keep track of the parts which the subject selects, the order in which he selects them, and those which he uses correctly, incorrectly, or rejects. Such notation may reveal focal points of conflict or concerns about particular body parts as well as the orderliness or haphazardness of the subject's approach.

Story Recall Test

On the WAIS, long range memory efficiency is indicated by the Vocabulary and Information subtests. Immediate recall is assessed only by Digit Span, but these series of numbers are without content and meaning. There is no measure of immediate memory for more meaningful material which reflects memory organization as it is most frequently applied in everyday life. It has been helpful, therefore, to include as part of the WAIS administration the Story Recall procedure of the Babcock Test (1930) (Rapaport et al., 1945). This procedure requires memory organization rather than just immediate recall, and it also indicates how well material is retained for a longer time interval (10–15 minutes) following interpolated activity. In disturbed individuals the test at times elicits painful and/or disturbing associations which may be of diagnostic importance. Normal subjects have the capacity for receptive attention and full concentration which leads to reproductions in which some details may be missing or in which slight distortions may occur, but the story retains a high level of integration and accuracy and communicates the basic theme.

After Similarities, the subject is told that the tester is going to read a short passage and that the subject will be asked to repeat as much of it as he can remember. The following story is read (reading time about one half minute). "December 6 / last week / a river / overflowed / in a small town / 10 miles / from Albany./ Water covered the streets / and entered the houses./ Fourteen persons / were drowned / and 600 persons / caught cold / because of the dampness / and cold weather./ In saving / a boy / who was caught / under a bridge / a man / cut his hands./" Immediately after the story is read, the subject is told: "Begin at the beginning and tell me all that you remember of it." If the story is not recalled in sequence, the subject is not stopped; but the verbatim record of the tester should reflect the sequence in which it is recalled. There is no time limit for the recall, and when the subject is finished, the following instructions are given: "I will now read it to you again, because later on I will want to see how much of it you still remember." The story is then reread, and is followed by the administration of the Digit Span, Digit Symbol, and Picture Completion subtests. The second recall is then asked for.

There are 21 units in the paragraph, and each unit receives one point for being correctly recalled regardless of the sequence in which it is recalled; in addition, four extra points are added to the immediate recall score in order to minimize the advantage of the second reading and delayed recall. This makes the maximum score on immediate recall 25 and on delayed recall 21. Marked distortions receive minus scores, e.g., "April 6," "600 horses died," "in cutting the boy's hands," "600 miles from Albany." The minus scores are not subtracted from the total number of credits but are noted as such (e.g., on the first recall if 6 correct units are recalled and 2 minus scores are indicated the total score is 10 (6 + 4) —2). Introducing new material or recombining the elements of the story in this way reflects a marked disruption of memory and is likely to be pathognomonic of a borderline, a fully psychotic, or an organic condition. On delayed recall, normal subjects will improve their scores, whereas severely disturbed patients often become less efficient: psychotic patients because of the subjective experience of disaster stimulated by the content of the story, and organic patients because of an impoverished memory efficiency. Because disorganized memory functioning is sometimes an early sole indicator of severe psychic or organic disruption, this test, which takes so little time to administer and adds a dimension ignored in the WAIS, can be an important diagnostic tool. The Vocabulary test of the WAIS can be used as a rough baseline for the Story Recall test; a Vocabulary scaled score of 10 corresponds to an average recall score of 14, and both scales correspondingly increase and decrease in one point intervals.

In obsessive compulsive individuals, Story Recall is on a high level, and often intellectually impressive words are substituted for the original ones (e.g., "a town was inundated").[4] In hysterics,

- Such minor deviations in verbalization receive full credit.

where anxiety plays an important role, the story may be poorly integrated and contain many vague references, often accompanied by emotional elaboration, e.g., "terrible things happened." Emotional elaboration of the content may also occur revealing the hysteric's typically easy arousal by affective stimulation (e.g., people may be described as being left homeless, and more people as dead or ill). Usually the psychotic patient's recall is severely fragmented and contains non sequiturs and odd statements; acute or borderline psychotics, however, may often present a relatively intact story. Thus, one may find instances in which psychological disturbance is not reflected on Story Recall, but it is less likely that a disrupted Story Recall will not be accompanied by other test indications of pathology.

A 51-year-old male hypomanic patient with psychotic trends and a Full Scale IQ of 131 told the following story to the first recall, on which he received a score of 11 (7+ 4) —3. "A small town 10 miles from Albany suffered a severe flood, sometime, 10 days, [—1] I believe, before 6th of December. It was a severe catastrophe [—1] with many deaths and many people left stranded, homeless [—1] instead of stranded . . . and a man cut his hands." Another psychotic patient, with depressive and paranoid features, told the following stories. On the first recall he received a score of 15 (11 + 4) —2, and on the delayed recall his score was 9. Unlike the first patient's story which primarily introduced new elements, this patient's story, particularly the delayed recall, also shows increasing fragmentation and reveals increased confusion and impoverishment of his memory efficiency. "Last week, December 6, 10 miles from Albany a river overflowed. Fourteen people drowned and six people [—1] caught cold. In saving a boy, I remember a boy drowned. [—1] I don't remember any more now. Let's see if I can put the facts back together. Are you going to write down what I say? [Yes.] Then I'll stop here." The delayed recall story was as follows: "I know that fourteen people died and 600 people got sick. I thought you said 6 before but you said 600 got sick or had colds—that's it. You know, you remind me of—no, don't write it. It was 10 miles from Albany; now, that is not in the same sequence, and somebody cut their hand in trying to save a boy, and there was something about a flood—water flowed. The story is getting all balled up, but the facts are in there."

THE PATIENT: MRS. T.

At this point we shall turn to a more detailed discussion of the WAIS findings of Mrs. T., a randomly selected patient, whose WAIS, TAT, and Rorschach will be analyzed in full in the following chapters, thus illustrating how we approach the interpretation of a full battery of tests of a single individual.

At the outset, the referral for testing will be presented, including some sketchy biographical information. No effort will be made to present a full account of Mrs. T.'s background or of her clinical course; only the questions of the therapist and relevant but brief biographical material will be included. This method of presentation reflects the procedure we routinely follow in our clinical work. The initial emphasis is on gleaning as much independent information as possible from the tests themselves which is then presented along with other information (from the therapist, social worker, nurses, occupational therapist, activities director) and jointly integrated.

Before the patient was tested the following consultation request was received:

This is a 22-year-old, white Protestant woman admitted to the hospital because of long history of promiscuity, excessive use of alcohol, obesity, and depression. There is no clinical evidence of thought disorder. However, five months ago she took an overdose of unknown medication and this was followed by an episode involving outbursts of violence, depersonalization and derealization, and some question of hallucinations (auditory). There is, thus, some question of a schizo-affective disorder, and psychologicals should be helpful in evaluating this.

PRECAUTIONS OR OTHER COMMENTS: She is at present on suicidal precautions, although this does not seem a serious danger at present.

Additional biographical information elicited during the interview preceding formal testing revealed that Mrs. T. was brought up in a small Southwestern town where her father, a graduate of a major university, ran a rather successful family business. Six years prior to hospitalization, while Mrs. T. was away at boarding school, her mother, who was then separated from Mrs. T.'s father and in psychotherapy at the time, committed suicide. Mrs. T. states that only after her mother's death did she learn of her parents' separation. Shortly after her mother's death, her father remarried. In addition to Mrs. T.'s two siblings (a brother and a sister) from the first marriage, the father's remarriage added several step-siblings.

Four years prior to hospitalization, Mrs. T. began college, drifting among a series of colleges of high academic caliber, gradually choosing less well known schools closer to home. During the past two years she had been married her husband had changed his major repeatedly and at the time of Mrs. T.'s arrival in the hospital he was considering a business career.

Mrs. T.'s WAIS

Verbal Subtest Scaled Scores		Performance Subtest Scaled Scores	
Comprehension	17/15	Picture Arrangement	17
Information	12	Picture Completion	11
Digit Span	12	Block Design	13
Arithmetic	11	Object Assembly	10/13
Similarities	12	Digit Symbol	12
Vocabulary	16		

Story Recall: Immediate 19 (-1 tendency), Delayed 18
Verbal IQ 120/118   Performance IQ 116/120   Full Scale IQ 120

INTERPRETATION. A Total IQ of 120 and a Verbal IQ of 120 indicates that this is a person of superior intellectual ability. A four point difference in favor of verbal abilities is expected in an individual of high intellectual functioning and this small difference drops out entirely when we consider the additional scores; therefore, the difference between Verbal and Performance IQs is not of interpretive significance. Vocabulary, however, has a scaled score of 16, and when we consider that this subtest is the best single estimate of intellectual functioning, we can estimate the patient's intellectual capacity to be in the Very Superior range with an IQ around 135. Her present functioning is considerably below this, and in view of the marked scatter and the tendency for most subtest scores to fall consistently below Vocabulary, it is likely that she has not achieved this optimum level of functioning or that there has been a considerable regression from this level. Nonetheless, it represents an ideal level which she could conceivably attain. One might wonder whether, with this much variability in the subtest scatter, there has been a noteworthy interference with intellectual efficiency by a psychotic process. But the elevation of Comprehension (even with its slight spoiling to an extended scaled score of 15) and Picture Arrangement indicates an adherence to social conventionality, good judgment, and good planning which would rule out the likelihood of a psychosis, particularly schizophrenia. With Comprehension higher than Information, a predominantly hysterical organization or character structure would be indicated. This interpretation follows from the notion that her relatively reduced fund of information stems from the use of repression as a major defense mechanism and that the counterbalancing by high Comprehension indicates an outwardly directed orientation towards social conventionality and conformity. The high Picture Arrangement also reflects a high level of adaptive social sensitivity, but it may also imply a heightened, hyperalert investment in social interactions, in anticipating interpersonal cues and point towards possible paranoid features. The low Digit Span, the low Arithmetic, and the low Picture Completion all indicate difficulties in her capacity for attention and concentration. Interference with these ego processes show that the patient is experiencing a great deal of anxiety and discomfort. The low Arithmetic could also suggest the possibility of a thought disorder because of the typical psychotic difficulties in concentration, but the lowered Arithmetic is consistent with an hysterical and narcissistic picture in that it could reflect a shying away from an active and effortful use of thinking. The low Object Assembly points to some concerns over the intactness and integration of her body which may be reacted to in a depressive manner. At the same time, the fact that she receives an additional score on Object Assembly suggests some resiliency in counteracting the influence of these concerns. An additional suggestion of depressive features is the low Digit Symbol.

On the basis of lowered Similarities, Block Design, Picture Completion, Arithmetic, and Digit Span scores, one might also wonder whether organic features are also present. Her high memory efficiency, as measured by Story Recall, is congruent with her intellectual potential however, which contra-indicates any serious organic impairment. Nonetheless, it may be that some of the interference with attention, concentration, and abstract conceptual thinking may be organically based. This can be clarified through the study of the qualitative aspects of the WAIS.

In a totally blind interpretation of the scatter, therefore, one would make the judgment that this is a severely neurotic woman with probably predominant hysterical features, along with depressive and possibly paranoid trends and some mild organic signs. It is clear, too, that she is experiencing a fair degree of anxiety at the present time. Noteworthy adaptive features are indicated in the high Comprehension and Picture Arrangement subtest scores which indicate a good understanding of social interaction and social events. Although the extreme scatter on the WAIS suggests severe psychopathology, the investment in and reality contact with social events and social situations tends to contradict the diagnosis of schizophrenia. The degree of anxiety represented by the low Digit Span and to some extent, Block Design, and the depressive features indicated in the Digit Symbol would also tend to contraindicate the presence of a schizophrenic process because they suggest a lack of blandness and interpersonal withdrawal. These factors point to considerable current turmoil and suggest that she is still in an acute phase of her illness. This scatter also suggests that she may be able to form a therapeutic alliance, for she appears to be highly verbal and is not a bland, hysterical person or a rigid and hyperalert person whose paranoid features are comfortably ingrained in her basic character structure. Rather, the indications of anxiety and depression reflect a conscious sense of dysphoria and discomfort and suggest that this patient would be highly motivated to become involved in psychotherapy.

Thus far, the interpretations have been derived from an analysis of the overall IQ and the scatter of the subtest scores, excluding all of the qualitative and content information in the test material. In the next section this initial analysis of the test scores will be extended to include the quality, the style, and the content of the responses.[5]

---

[5] The reader will find in this book an emphasis on careful verbatim recording of test responses including all asides and gestures. Although this may seem an arduous task at the outset, it is made more possible by mastery of the test material—for example memorization of the WAIS instructions. But a close

Information

Raw Score: 20
Weighted Score: 12

Score	Item	Response
1	5. Rubber	From South America. [What does it come from?] A plant, tree.
1	6. Presidents	Roosevelt, Truman, Hoover, and Eisenhower.
1	7. Longfellow	Writer.
1	8. Weeks	[Patient repeats question] 52.
1	9. Panama	Chicago to Panama, South.
1	10. Brazil	South America.
1	11. Height	5' 6".
1	12. Italy	Oh, God, er . . . er . . . oh, hell. Venice? No, Rome, Rome.
1	13. Clothes	Absorbs heat.
1	14. Washington	February 22.
1	15. Hamlet	Shakespeare.
1	16. Vatican	In Rome, church where the Pope lives, holy place where the Pope is.
0	17. Paris	Oh, God, can I estimate? [Yes] 6000 miles? Actually, I have no idea.
1	18. Egypt	Egypt? In the . . . I can see it on a map off the Mediterranean, far right hand lower corner. [Continent?] Africa?
0	19. Yeast	[Patient repeats question.] Oh, God, some sort of chemical reaction. [More specific idea?] Studied it, can't remember.
0	20. Population	I have no idea. [Guess.] Let's see, 60 million.
0	21. Senators	Oh, Lord . . . er, 50, no, yes, one for each state.
1	22. Genesis	Beginning of humanity, the world.
0	23. Temperature	100. [Scale?] F.
1	24. Iliad	Homer.
1	25. Blood vessels	Three types of blood vessels? [Laughs.] No, I can't . . . Artery, that sort of thing? Capillary and veins.
0	26. Koran	Does it have something to do with Jewish religion?
0	27. Faust	Faust? I have no idea. I think Faust was a writer.
0	28. Ethnology	I don't know.
0	29. Apocrypha	I don't know.

INTERPRETATIONS. In discussing the responses, we will comment on them in order but only on those which are of particular import or suggestive of diagnostic inferences. Her misinterpretation of item 5 and her need to repeat items 8 and 9 raises the issue of her ability to attend to and concentrate on the task in front of her. On item 12 (capital of Italy) it is noteworthy that she juxtaposes God and hell and that her first association is the more romantic Venice. This represents a temporary inefficiency, for the item is relatively easy considering her intellectual level. This inefficiency may indicate conflict around religious morality, especially around themes of romance and sinfulness versus moral righteousness. Her relatively high score on Comprehension suggests an emphasis on conventionality and morality and the conflict suggested in the verbalization indicates the possibility of antisocial behavior and subsequent guilt. On item 17 the phrase, "Oh, God," appears again and may also be an expression of dependency needs, for she then turns to the tester and asks permission to estimate the answer. It is interesting to note that the disruptions thus far have occurred on Italy and Paris, both of which are geographical questions, and one wonders at this point about her sense of orientation in space. This impression receives additional support on item 18 where her response to Egypt's location is quite concrete; unable to conceptualize her answer, she has to resort to a visual image in order to come up with an adequate response. Her use of visualization raises several hypotheses here. It seems to serve her efforts at providing a stable spatial referent and, it may also reflect voyeuristic tendencies. Again, on item 19 there is a reference to, "Oh, God," when she feels unable to function, overwhelmed by the task at hand.

---

approximation to a verbatim recording is always an ideal to be striven for especially since a major advantage of testing is that it supplies verbalizations and responses whose meaning may only be evident in careful study following the testing session. For the sake of completeness and in order to indicate the potential of information which can be obtained, we tape recorded the testing of Mrs. T. whose test battery is presented in full. However, we do not use tape recording as a routine clinical procedure; inasmuch as the usual verbatim record kept by the clinician depends on a process of mutual regulation between patient and tester in the speed and clarity of communicating and recording, it offers an important inroad into the nature of the patient's interpersonal relationship, his use and conception of time, and the like. This information may be obscured by tape recordings.

Repressive trends appear on the "Yeast" item, where she states that she once knew but no longer remembers the answer. This interpretation is consistent with the pattern of Information being lower than both the Vocabulary and Comprehension. On items 20 and 21 we see further indication of repressive mechanisms, for she seems to have the general notion of the population of the United States and the number of senators, but her answers are inexact; her response is 60 million instead of 160 million on the "Population" item, and she has the basic concept of state representation but her answer is incorrect. Repressive forces are reflected in her partial remembering and partial recognition of a correct response with the inability to recapture the total memory.

One should note the repetition of reference to "God" on item 21. On the "Genesis" question, item 22, there is a tendency toward a personalized idiosyncratic response in the use of the word "humanity." Although a clear-cut interpretation of this word is difficult, it shows a focus on people which seems to have a charged quality to it. An inaccurate response is given to item 23 in which she confused the Fahrenheit and Centigrade scales. It is important to note that signs of repression occur on all three items related to numbers: population, the number of senators, and the boiling point of water. At the very least, one can infer at this point that these signs are consistent with the prior inference from the scatter about her hysterical character structure. The response to blood vessels has a histrionic quality in her immediate response of, "No, I can't," but after reflection she is able to give the correct answer, though with considerable laughter. This laughter may reflect her embarrassment about blood, but this inference is only tentative and will depend on subsequent material for further specification. In her response to "Koran" she has the idea of religion, but substitutes Jewish for Mohammedan. At the end of the subtest she commented that her interest in testing was, "going down the drain," an unusual phrasing which indicates her dissatisfaction with her performance on this subtest.

To summarize, the predominant features which emerge in the Information subtest are the indications of a hysterical character structure. She shows an unevenness in her performance on this subtest; there are frequent lapses, and a series of correct responses are interspersed with failures. These failures occur primarily on items concerned with numerical facts, a common finding in more passive or narcissistic hysterical persons who see numbers as active (and possibly as masculine) and thus avoid them. There is also a histrionic quality to her response on the "Blood Vessel" item, and grossness and inexactness is evident in her memory functioning on a number of items. In addition, there are suggestions of a passive helpless orientation in her frequent exclamation of, "Oh, God," and in her willingness often not to exert herself on difficult questions. All these factors taken together are indicative of a hysterical organization. Other noteworthy themes on the Information subtest are the juxtaposition of heaven and hell and concerns around moral issues, and her concreteness and difficulty in dealing with questions involving geographical location. From the latter we may infer feelings of being dislocated and disoriented.

Comprehension

   Raw Score: 25/23
   Weighted Score: 17/15

Score	Item	Response
2	3. Envelope	Has a used stamp? [Question repeated.] Probably stick it in the mail.
2	4. Bad company	Because we ourselves could become involved with them.
2	5. Movies	What should I do? . . . report it to the manager, I wouldn't jump up and start screaming.
2	6. Taxes	[Laughs.] [Patient repeats question.] That is a good question. Have to support the government.
1	7. Iron	You got your ideas and you are all fired up with ambition, you should go and do what you are planning to do.
2	8. Child labor	To prevent child being taken advantage of, cheap labor, etcetera.
2/0	9. Forest	Oh, God! [Patient repeats question.] Well, I'd figure out which direction the sun would go down; if I were going east, north, south, west, I would relate it to the sun as it was setting. If I were going north and sun setting west, it would help me. I'd probably be lost anyway; actually would sit til somebody found me.

Comprehension Subtest (*Continued*)

Score	Item	Response
2	10. Deaf	Because they have no idea how words sound. They learn to speak through imitation, I believe.
2	11. City land	Business opportunity, area, space involved, whole lot of reasons you know. [Be more specific.] More people per acre, less room, price of real estate goes up.
1	12. Marriage	First for blood test, age or blood test, whether a physical thing would prevent you, advisability to having children, age.
2	13. Brooks	People who have very little depth of thought yap on without real understanding of what they are talking about.
1	14. Swallow	One swallow, a physical swallowing of something? [Up to you.] [Patient repeats question.] Just the skimming the surface of something doesn't mean you have the whole thing, complete [coughs].

INTERPRETATIONS. Her questioning about whether the envelope has "a used stamp?" suggests a memory lapse and a mild distortion of the original stimulus. Moreover, her misperception of "new" as "used" suggests the presence of depressive feelings of being used up and no longer vital, effective, and purposeful. The other portion of her response to this item, "probably stick it in the mail," however, has a phallic intrusive quality which reflects an important shift from a depressive, inert position (the "used" stamp) to a more active position. On Information we saw many signs of strong passive trends and feelings of helplessness and her shift here after an initially depressive and passive start to increased activity indicates particular issues around activity and passivity and may thereby reveal sexual identity struggles. On item 4 ("Bad company") her use of the double pronoun "we ourselves" indicates a tendency to personalize her reactions, and this becomes further emphasized in the next item ("Movies") where, despite her understanding of the situation, she strongly involves herself personally by her comment, "What should *I* do?" Some difficulty in contain-

ing impulses is also expressed in her need to assert that she would
not jump up and start screaming. On the adaptive side it should be
noted that despite the tendency toward an impulsive reaction she
has the capacity to give an appropriate answer. Her initial laughter
and repetition of item 6 ("Taxes") and her asides also demonstrate
her need to delay an initial reaction. While the usual response to
item 7 ("Iron") generally includes a statement about external reality offering the opportunity for action, Mrs. T.'s concerns, however,
center primarily around her own capacities for constructive action.
There is an emphasis on spontaneous, immediate action, perhaps
of an impulsive nature. She also seems to imply that she questions
her ability to function actively, to have ideas, and to respond appropriately. Her repeated use of personal pronouns suggests an
egocentric orientation such that events seem to have an immediate
and personal implication for her. On the "Child labor" item her emphasis is on exploitation rather than on health, welfare, or education of the child, suggesting feelings of having been exploited and
a more general concern with being mistreated and abused by
others. The "Forest" item, number 9, is a very important one in
this record. She responds to a problem concerning the theme of isolation with a flood of ideational activity. Although she understands
the essentials of using the sun to indicate direction, she is unable to
put this knowledge to effective use. She gives up in despair, and at
the end spoils the quality of her response by accepting the role of the
helpless, lost little girl who sits passively, waiting for someone to res-
cue her. The degree of confusion evoked by this item is consistent
with what was observed on the Information subtest, where, on the
numerical items and those related to geographical locations, she
displayed impaired functioning in the nature of concreteness, and
some spatial disorientation. In addition, her repeated reference to the
setting sun confirms the initial depressive tone of the "used" stamp
and in this instance it may be particular to the theme of isolation
present in the question. Considering the obviously painful associations and affect stimulated by the "Forest" item, she is able to
integrate rapidly and respond effectively to the subsequent question. Her response to item 11 ("City land") is a fully adequate
one, and although some emphasis on the issue of confinement,
"less room," is indicated, its interpretive significance is unclear.
The response to item 12 ("Marriage") is colored by her concern
about physical well-being, venereal disease, and her role as a

parent. Apparently marriage has many painful and negative implications for her. On Item 14 ("Swallow") she is quite literal and concrete; she becomes preoccupied with the oral theme, and, although she approaches the correct concept, an oral theme still intrudes subtly in the phrase "skimming the surface." Considering her high overall IQ, her idiosyncratic response to this item seems to be determined more by the oral needs of a depressed person rather than by any general concreteness in her thinking. The conflict, discomfort, and difficulty with this item are indicated by blocking, coughing, and by the poorly articulated phrases.

In summary, her responses in this subtest are relatively intact as reflected by the scores she receives. At the same time the quality of her answers points to the fact that her high level of functioning is achieved with considerable effort and is punctuated with inefficiency, personalization, and concreteness. Noteworthy is an underlying sense of depression, helplessness, oral neediness, feelings of being isolated, abused, and unable to take constructive, spontaneous action. Also apparent are her efforts to defend against such feelings via a move toward intrusive behavior which seems masculine in quality, and is only a partially effective control over her impulsivity. Other themes of note are concerns over intimacy as it refers to marriage and problems in spatial orientation which were already seen in the Information subtest. Thematically this could be linked with feelings of helplessness generally.

Arithmetic

Raw Score: 12
Weighted Score: 11

Score	Item	Time	Solution
1	3. $4 + $5	6″	How much is . . . 9.
1	4. 10¢ − 6¢	7″	[Repeats question.] Oh, and gives clerk a dime has 4¢ left.
1	5. 25¢ from 6	2″	$1.50.
1	6. inches: 2½ ft.	4″	Er, 30.
1	7. 6¢/oranges: 36	2″	6.
1	8. 24 miles at 3/hr.	6–23″	24 miles, 3 miles an hours, 8. Wait a minute, 3 miles an hour, oh, takes him 8 hours, sure enough [laughs].
1	9. 7 2¢ stamps	8″	36.

Arithmetic Subtest (*Continued*)

Score	Item	Time	Solution
1	10. 18 — $7.50	7″	11, oh, no, $10.50 back.
1	11. 2/31¢: doz.	22″	Er, $1.21 . . . no, $1.26, $1.86. [Which is the correct one?] Last one.
1	12. $400 = ⅔	17″	Oh, golly, er . . . [points with finger] $600.
0	13. $60 less 15%	32″	Wait a minute, [writes in air] $50 not right, $40. [How did you get that?] Trying to divide 15 into 60, didn't do it right. [How?] Divide 15 into 60 . . . can't do a thing mathematical. I get 4. [What is 10% of 60?] 1/10 × 60, that's how you do it, he'd receive $55 . . . I am lousy at math. [What is 10% of 60?] . . . 4.
0	14. 8 men — 6 days	40″	[Sigh] . . . Oh, God, don't even know how to begin that . . . 16 in 3 days, 32 in 1 day, no. [If 16 men can do the job in 3 days, how many can do it in 1?] 32.

INTERPRETATION. On the first two items the patient has to repeat the question, and since this occurs so early in the subtest, it may indicate a difficulty in her initial adjustment to a new task. The patient's repetition of the question also serves as a delaying maneuver and may aid in focusing her attention and concentration. Once the initial adjustment seems to be made to the subtest, items 5, 6, and 7 proceed rapidly and correctly. On item 8 she does very well, getting the answer in 6 seconds, but feels quite uncertain about her solution and continues to work and finally (in 23 seconds) she supports her earlier response with a laughing statement about it. Items 9 and 10 go well except for an error at the outset of 10 which she quickly corrects and which indicates the capacity to be self critical. On item 11 she gives three answers in quick succession, only the last of which is correct and the first two seeming to be working stages in her effort to evolve the correct answer. It is impressive that this way she is able to get the correct answer in 22 seconds even though her impulsive, premature responses indicate some confusion and interference. Item 12 is done rapidly, but only by externalizing her thought processes through imagery notations. This reflects a similar emphasis on visual imagery that was evident in Information. She is overwhelmed by item 13 and again resorts to writing in the air. Two attempts at answering this question are far off, and even with graded help she cannot solve the problem. She encounters considerable difficulty on item 14, sighs, and mentions that she does not know how to begin. The first step of doubling the number of men and halving the number of days is correct, and her explanation of her procedure is logical and indicates her understanding of the arithmetical processes necessary for this item. Her confusion with the numbers, however, indicates a difficulty in concentration and her ability to focus her thinking is below what one would expect for her intellectual capacity.

In summary, we see on this subtest an extensive amount of temporary inefficiency and anxious uncertainty. Her efforts to delay responding are not successful. And it appears that her concentration is relatively easily disrupted. In order to counteract her difficulty, she resorts to visualizing the problem. In a situation which demands active internal manipulation, she tries to supply some external support and assistance. In this light, her functioning on Arithmetic would be consistent with problems noted earlier about activity in general. Another possibility is that a certain degree of her inefficiency in Arithmetic is due not only to anxiety and avoidance of active thinking, but to some organic dysfunction. Organic features were suggested in the discussion about her subtest scatter, and from the point of view of subjective experience her troubled sense of spatial orientation (evident in Information and Comprehension) could be one concomitant of it and her fluid, inefficient thinking in Arithmetic, another aspect. Clarification of this hypothesis will be sought in following subtests.

Similarities

Raw Score: 18
Weighted Score: 12

Score	Item	Response
2	1. Orange	Fruit.
2	2. Coat	Clothing.
1	3. Axe	Used to cut.

Similarities (*Continued*)

Score	Item	Response
2	4. Dog	Animals.
2	5. North	Directions.
2	6. Eye	They are . . . Oh, God. Sensory organs of the body.
2	7. Air	Air and water, two elements of life, basic chemistry. [What do you mean, elements of life?] Two necessary elements to have in life.
0	8. Table	They're both [laughs] to sit things on.
1	9. Egg	Egg and seed are basic forms of reproduction, for reproduction. [Explain further.] From egg form of human life, from seed, plant, or human life too, not human life.
2	10. Poem	Poem and Statue. Products of creative art.
0	11. Wood	Wood and alcohol, wood and alcohol . . . [laughs]. I don't know. [Guess.] Is wood something from which alcohol can be derived?
2	12. Praise	Er . . . both used as way of regulating human behavior.
0	13. Fly	Fly and tree . . . [laughs.] [Looks at examiner.] . . . I don't know. [Guess.] Fly and tree? I couldn't guess . . . I don't think.

INTERPRETATION. Two aspects of this subtest stand out: the weighted score is 12, which is 4 points below her Vocabulary score; and there is considerable variability in the intratest scatter. Instead of diminishing gradually from 2 to 0, a series of high level responses are interrupted by 1 or 0 scores. Such waxing and waning indicates a disruption in the efficiency of abstract cognitive functioning which may, as we shall see, be related to specific content concerns and may also support the suggestion of some organic features of a minor degree.

In examining the qualitative features of the responses, the first two are intact, concise, and to the point. It is on item 3 that the first lapse in efficiency occurs; here the response is on a more concrete cognitive level, describing the functional characteristics of the two objects rather than their abstract conceptual similarity. It is noteworthy that the loss of the abstract attitude occurs on an item which has potential aggressive implications. The quick return to an abstract level on items 4 and 5 indicates resiliency.

On item 6 there is a well articulated response after some delay, and the expression, "Oh, God," seen earlier on Information reoccurs. There are a number of alternative speculations about the meaning of this automatic phrase. There is no common content when this phrase is used, but, rather, it appears to occur when she is having difficulty, probably feeling helpless and overwhelmed, and therefore seems to appeal for support from a strong paternal authority and superior being. Item 7 is answered well, though some questioning is needed to help her clarify her response. She fails the eighth question ("table and chair") and seems to be somewhat embarrassed, as indicated by her laughter, which might have been inquired into by the tester. This failure may have occurred because the item evoked disturbed feelings about home, warmth, nurturance, and interpersonal relationships. The table and chair are described as impersonal objects for storage rather than being interrelated meaningfully. On item 9 ("egg and seed"), though her efficiency drops, she gets the essential idea. But in response to the request for further elaboration she becomes involved in the need to differentiate among reproduction in humans, in plants, and in animals, and does not seem to accept reproduction as a general process. Her difficulty here may reflect concerns on her part about her female reproductive role. Her answer to item 10 again indicates resiliency, for she gives an appropriately abstract response which is clearly phrased and to the point. The incorrect response to item 11 is of little consequence since it occurs too often in the general population to be of particular diagnostic significance. Again, her response to item 12 is extremely well phrased, direct, and appropriately abstract. She is unable to cope with the "fly and tree" item, and she looks toward the tester, possibly for support. Throughout the Similarities subtest, it should be noted, there seemed to be a change in the quality of her affect; her voice dropped, she seemed considerably less animated and much more subdued.

In summary, the findings on Similarities indicate some disruptions in thinking, particularly when she is dealing with concepts of home, aggression, and reproduction. These disruptions represent temporary inefficiencies, for there is little infusion of drive or archaic material, and she is quickly able to reestablish a high level of conceptualization. The possibility of some organic features is not ruled out, but since the inefficiencies are mostly at the higher levels and do not affect the overall score in a more major way, any organic difficulties are likely to be minor ones.

Story Recall

Story Recall [5] was given after the Similarities subtest, the delayed recall was asked for after Digit Span, Digit Symbol, and Picture Completion were administered.

Recall I Score: $15 + 4 = 19$ (—1 tendency). The response was: December 6 . . . last week . . . a river . . . overflowed into (—1) Albany, streets and houses . . . were flooded . . . 14 drowned . . . and 600 caught cold . . . er, a man rescuing a boy from under a bridge cut his hand.

Delayed Recall Score: 18. The response was: Oh, God, December 6 . . . last week . . . a river overflowed . . . into . . . small town 10 miles from Albany. Streets and houses flooded . . . 6 people drowned and 600 caught colds because of cold and damp-ness. Er, a man . . . saving a boy from bridge . . . bridge cut his hands.

Her recall for both the immediate and delayed presentation is excellent and at the level expected for her Vocabulary, except for the one weak distortion indicated by the single minus score. This distortion is quite minor and does not reach psychotic proportions, as it centers the flood directly in Albany, rather than 10 miles away. The larger and distant city, therefore, becomes directly involved in the flood and suggests some expansion of the amount of damage. Also suggested in this response is the difficulty in spatial orientation and a loss of distance.

On the second recall she minimizes the number of dead and perseverates to a mild extent around the number "6" (a number which also appeared in some of her failures on Information but the meaning of which is ambiguous). This latter distortion is close to the basic theme of the story and does not receive a minus score. Story Recall shows that her memory efficiency is not disrupted, at

[5] Dec. 6 / last week / a river / overflowed / in a small town / 10 miles / from Albany./ Water covered the streets / and entered the houses./ Fourteen persons / were drowned / and 600 persons / caught cold / because of the dampness / and cold weather./ In saving / a boy / who was caught / under a bridge / a man / cut his hands./

least not in a task involving relatively fresh material. Thus, her poorer functioning on Information, in contrast, could indicate that her repressive defenses affect the process of long range recall more than relatively new acquisition. It also indicates that her earlier need to have questions repeated and the fluidities and temporary inefficiencies do not point toward a significant memory difficulty. This consideration does not completely eliminate the possibility of organic trends in her thinking, but it does ascribe to them a minor role in Mrs. T.'s psychological functioning. In fact, since she is aware of her inefficiencies, and can often work her way back from them, they are more likely, if organic, to be recent and probably of toxic origin rather than reflecting any permanent loss.

Digit Span Subtest

Raw Score: (7 + 6) 13
Weighted Score: 12

Forward	Backward
(3) correct	(2)
(3)	(2)
(4) correct	(3) correct
(4)	(3)
(5) correct	(4) correct
(5)	(4)
(6) correct	1 5 2 8 6: 6 8 2 9 2
	I can't remember what you said.
(6)	(5) correct
5 9 1 7 4 2 8: 5 1 9 7 4 2 8	(6) correct
(7) correct	(6)
5 8 1 9 2 6 4 7: 5 1 8 9 6 2 7	8 1 2 9 3 6 5: 5 3 6 9 2 1 8
3 8 2 9 5 1 7 4: 3 8 7 5 1 9 2 3 4	4 7 3 9 1 2 8: 8 2 1 9 4 7 3
(9)	(8)
(9)	(8)

INTERPRETATION. The weighted score of 12 on Digit Span is one of her lowest subtest scores; she gets seven digits forwards and six backwards. Her performance on digits forwards tapers off gradually after six digits, beginning with a reversal of two numbers. On the eight digit series her responses have little resemblance to the original numbers, and she fails both trials. Also on digits backwards there is a gradual tapering off in her recall; she gets the series correct on the first trial up to the five digit series and is successful only on the second trial thereafter. She fails the first trial of the seven digit item by a simple reversal of two numbers, and on the second trial she reverses the first three numbers. Thus, there appears to be a relatively minor inefficiency which interferes with digits backwards on the level of seven digits. Though her method of recall was not inquired into, it seemed that she visualized the numbers and then read them off in reverse order, indicating that visual imagery plays an important role in her memory organization as well as in her thought organization more generally. Her low score on this subtest points to a difficulty in attention which is consistent with memory lapses involving the attentional processes noted on other subtests.

Picture Completion

Raw Score: 15/16
Weighted Score: 11

Score	Item	Time	Response
1	1. Door		
1	2. Pig		
1	3. Girl		
1	4. Car		
0	5. Card		Er, numbers in the corner. [What was intended to be missing?] Numbers in the corners.
0/1	6. Pitcher	3″	Water and the hand holding, [Which is the most important?] To me the water. Both are important. [Decide.] Hand.
1	7. Glasses	5″	
1	8. Violin	3″	Don't know what you call 'em.
1	9. Boat	4″	
0	10. Bulb	25″	I don't know about this one, something for it to be in.
0	11. Flag	3″	Staff.
1	12. Man, dog	4″	
1	13. Map	2″	
1	14. Ship	16″	Looks like it has sails instead of funnel. Missing big doflectches. [?] Where the steam comes out.

Picture Completion (*Continued*)

Score	Item	Time	Response
0	15. Crab	3″	Tail.
1	16. Vanity	3″	Reflection in mirror.
1	17. Man	9″	Finger.
1	18. Sun	2″	Shadow.
1	19. Horse	5″	Stirrup.
0	20. Woodpile	17″	Fence?
1	21. Girl	3″	Eyebrow.

INTERPRETATION. Picture Completion with a weighted score of 11 is one of the lowest subtests in this record, and it is marked by a fair amount of variability in efficiency. Mrs. T.'s errors generally tend to be those in which she does not accept the stimulus as a single unit looking for incompleteness within it. Instead she tries to enlarge the stimulus field by insisting that there should be other parts to it. The pitcher, for example, should be held by a hand, the bulb should have a socket, and the flag should have a staff. What seems to be suggested in these incorrect responses is a concern for contact and/or support which reflects her neediness and desire for external strength and security.

Several lapses in memory are evident, i.e., on "violin" (item 8) and "ship" (item 14), and her statement that the bulb goes into "something" rather than into a socket is also vague. As on Information, these vague responses show a spotty fund of specific bits of knowledge that is repressive in quality. Her perception that the crab is missing a tail shows the intrusion of a specifically anal and/or possibly phallic, sexual concern.

Block Design

  Raw Score: 43
  Weighted Score: 13

Score	Item	Time	Accur.	Solution
4	1ₐ	6″	ok	
	b			
4	2ₐ	12″	ok	
	b			

Block Design (*Continued*)

Score	Item	Time	Accur.	Solution
4	3	6″	ok	Finishes and immediately breaks up blocks.
4	4	7″	ok	*1 2 3 4*
4	5	6″	ok	*2 3 1 4*
4	6	60″	ok	W R R R R repeats *1 2 4 3*
4	7	43″		*3 6 9 2 5 8 1 4 7*
4	8	80″		*3 6 9 8 5 2 4 1 7*
5	9	62″		Well . . . several starts *3 6 9 8 5 2 1 4 7* (unbuttons sweater)
6	10	47″		*1 3 5 2 4 7 6 8 9*

Bonus Scores
(Basic Score 4)

Item	5	6
7	31″–40″	1″–30″
8	46″–70″	1″–45″
9	61″–80″	1″–60″
10	61″–80″	1″–60″

INTERPRETATION. Block Design (weighted score 13) is quite intact. Each design was reproduced in an orderly, accurate, and rapid fashion with relative ease and freedom from distraction. A temporary inefficiency appears on item 6, but it is quickly overcome, and if anything, her efficiency picks up momentum as she proceeds, since her time bonuses increase toward the end. It is of interest, in view of the fact that she often tries to contain impulsive trends in other subtests, that she is so orderly in her approach here. In items 7, 8, and 9, for example, she begins by putting the same three blocks in place first.

In general, her qualitative functioning on Block Design is discrepant with the possibility of an organic interference with her psychological functioning. As with Story Recall, Block Design suggests that any organic trends are quite minor.

Picture Arrangement

Raw Score: 35
Weighted Score: 17

Score	Item	Time	Seq	Solution
4	1.	a. 3″ b.	WXY	
4	2.	a. 4″ b.	PAT	
4	3.	5″	ABCD	
4	4.	14″	ATOMIC	
4	5.	18″	OPENS	Finished. I'm sorry. (Mrs. T. delayed slightly)
4	6.	33″	JANET	[Mrs. T. delays before saying finished.]
6	7.	20″	EFGHIJ	King was being supplied his fish by an underwater person. [Anything else?] Told him when he was leaving.
5	8.	25″	SAMUEL	Man walking with bust, got into car, looked behind him, thought that people were watching him, so he stuck her on the other side of the street, seat. [Mrs. T. blushes.]

Bonus and Partial Scores
(Basic Score 4)

6. JNAET—2
   AJNET—2
7. EGFHIJ—2
   EFGHIJ—5: 26″—40″
   EJFGHI—6: 1″—25″
8. SALMUE—2
   SAMUEL—5: 16″—25″
   AMUELS—6: 1″—15″

INTERPRETATION. As discussed in the analysis of scatter, Picture Arrangement (weighted score 17) together with Comprehension are Mrs. T.'s two highest subtests and point to a socially facile person who knows the correct or socially acceptable answers and is acutely alert to interpersonal nuances. Since her raw score on Picture Arrangement is only 1 point short of the possible maximum, her performance certainly seems impressive. As a part of the procedure Mrs. T. was asked to tell the stories for the last two series, and it is in this qualitative material that her performance seems less impressive because of the occurrence of several odd, idiosyncratic verbalizations. For instance, the story of item 7 is basically accurate, but the term "underwater person" has a strange quality. There is also a slight tendency to emphasize the issue of separation in the comment, "told him when he was leaving," for it is most frequent for the Little King to be described as merely indicating to the diver that he has caught enough without specifying the time of his departure. The next story, to item 8, represents personalization and suspicious trends in the statement that people were actually watching. The more usual story emphasizes the realization on the part of the man as to what it *might* look like and how it *could* be misunderstood. Impulsivity and the theme of rejection are expressed in the aggressively toned wording "stuck her," and the slip, "other side of the street . . . seat," also connotes rejection and simultaneously suggests a need for Mrs. T. to distance herself from the sexual implications. Her blushing further corroborates her discomfort with the sexual theme. An additional aspect of this response is the problem in locating the manikin as either close by (other side of the seat) or further away (other side of the street). This trend was noted previously, on one occasion during story recall when she located the flood "in" rather than "near" Albany. Since this trend appears in the context of the present response, it suggests that one factor in her concerns revolves around the degree of closeness and intimacy or distance between people.

Her excellent score on Picture Arrangement, especially the time bonuses, also reveals that her depressive concerns have not resulted in a significantly diminished output of energy nor a retardation of visual-motor coordination.

Object Assembly

Raw Score: 32/38
Weighted Score: 10/13

Score	Item	Time	Solution
7	1. (2′)	15″	Legs, head, arms.
13	2. (2′)	24″	Ear, eye, nose, mouth, hair, without hesitation.
1/7	3. (3′)	4′/40″	Looks at thumb, "Gads, what is it?", thumb, finger

Object Assembly (*Continued*)

Score	Item	Time	Solution
			to thumb, "Pete's sake," random, wrist wrong, start, "Oh for Pete's sake, darn it," takes wrist away. "It seems that I can't put it together." 1' 30". Looks. Wrist okay, "It does go together, right?" [Yes.] "That's nice"; has finger from wrist. 3' Thumb and wrist, "I'm not supposed to give up, am I?" Drums on table. "Oh, for Pete's sake. God." About 4' 25". "I hate to be dumb." OK at 4' 40". "I'm not so perceptive these days."
11	4. (3')	22"	Head, trunk, ok.

Scores for Perfect Performance with Bonus Scores

Bonus Scores	Item			
	1	2	3	4
6	16"–20"			
7	11"–15"			
8	1"–10"			
9			41"–50"	
10			31"–40"	31"–50"
11		36"–45"	1"–30"	21"–30"
12		26"–35"		1"–20"
13		1"–25"		

INTERPRETATION. The failure on the "hand" item of the Object Assembly stands in marked contrast to the high level performance on the other parts of this test where she receives maximum or near maximum credit. It is this failure which lowers her overall score rather than a general and depressive slowing down of her visual-motor functioning. Her difficulty with the hand may stem from conflictual association of hand and fingers with aggressive, masturbatory and/or more general issues around interpersonal closeness and contact. Despite her difficulties with this item and its possible painful associations, she did persist, and in 4 minutes and 40 seconds solved the puzzle and obtained an additional score. During this effort she commented in a mildly self-deprecatory way about her functioning.

Digit Symbol

Raw Score: 65
Weighted Score: 12

INTERPRETATION. Digit Symbol (weighted score 12) was carried out efficiently, and the symbols were written clearly and neatly with the exception of three "U" symbols which were reproduced as script "U's." From a qualitative point of view, therefore, there is little to add to the earlier hypotheses about the meaning of the Digit Symbol score.

Vocabulary

Raw Score: 71
Weighted Score: 16

Score	Response
2	Bed [laughs]. Piece of furniture upon which one lies down on to rest, sleep.
2	Seagoing vessel for transportation.
2	Form of American currency.

Vocabulary (*Continued*)

Score	Response
2	Er . . . the coldest month, season of year when sun is farthest away from earth.
2	To mend something that's been broken or torn apart.
2	Earliest meal of day.
1	Er . . . from . . . some sort of material. [Tell me more.] Material used to cover something.
1	Cut.
2	Congregate.
2	Hide.
2	Very large.
2	To do something fast.
2	Group of words expressing a complete thought.
2	Control.
2	Begin.
2	Think about, think upon.
2	Cave.
2	Point out.
1	Er . . . household . . . domestic is something . . . oh hell, everyday life sort of thing. [Be more explicit.] Oh, God, something that is a form of a . . . oh hell . . . house, no . . . can't be more specific, I know what it means.
1	Take in.
2	End.
1	Prevent.
2	Regret.
1	Hiding place.
2	Incomparable.
2	Hesitant.
2	Catastrophe.
2	Strength.
2	Quiet.
2	Building.
2	Sympathy.
2	Something material. [Tell me more.] You can see, feel, or touch, has substance.
1	Surrounding. [Tell me more.] Encompassing some sort of thing. [Be explicit.] Something that takes in a given area.
2	Brazen.
1	Evil.
2	Lecture. [Tell me more.] [Laughs.] Angry flow of language.

Vocabulary (*Continued*)

Score	Response
2	Hinder.
1	Copy. [Tell me more.] To use someone else's thought as your own.
2	Penetrate. [Tell me more.] Er . . . oh golly . . . let's see, no, I don't know how to express it, to hang up, to stick somebody. [Which?] To penetrate someone with an object. [Tell me more.] Someone is impaled upon a stick, something rammed into their body.
2	Mockery.

Vocabulary items can be found in the WAIS manual or the Record Form.

INTERPRETATION. The scaled score for Vocabulary is 16, which, if accepted as an estimate of her potential intellectual level, gives her an IQ of approximately 135. Using the scaled score of 16 as a baseline, we can then see the marked impairment of functioning indicated by the negative scatter below Vocabulary of most of the other subtests with the exception of Comprehension and Picture Arrangement. In terms of intratest scatter, Vocabulary proceeds fairly smoothly, except for items 7 and 8, up to item 19, "domestic." Starting at this point "1" scores become more frequent. In general, her responses are fairly intact and show only a few mild lapses.

A qualitative analysis of the responses reveals a number of important features. On the first word, "bed," she looked away from the tester, turned her face toward the wall, and ran her fingers through her hair. Sexual fantasies were apparently evoked by the connotation of "bed" and by the relationship with the male tester. In defining "bed," her statement was introduced by laughter, but the response itself was quite adequate. On the fourth item, "winter," she began with an incorrect answer indicating that she was restricting winter to one month, then quickly corrected herself and gave an appropriate response. By curtailing the duration of winter, she may be limiting an experience of coldness and discomfort and revealing her need for warmth and contact. The need for contact is further suggested by her elaboration of the response to include that it is during winter when the sun is furthest from the earth.

The next item, "repair," is again elaborated beyond what is required, and in this elaboration she conveys her own depressive self-concept and/or angry, aggressive feelings in a portion of her response, ". . . or torn apart." On "fabric" she has some difficulty in getting started and when asked to clarify her response, she resorts to a lower level conceptualization and a more functional definition. Her emphasis on material as a cover may relate to feelings of shame or a need for deception. Items from 8 through 18 are precise, very much to the point, and in fact, some of them have an almost dictionary-like clarity.

Probably the single most rich and informative response on the whole Vocabulary subtest is the response to item 19, "domestic." It is on this item that her thinking is disrupted by highly charged personal material. Her response is fragmented, the sequence is lost, and there are long delays between words and phrases. Her verbalizations are vague and uncertain, and the juxtaposition of "hell" and the appeals to "God" reappear in her side comments. She is finally able only to refer to household and to house, but the obvious difficulties around the issue of home are reflected most strikingly in her response. This is quite consistent with the observation made on the furniture item of the Similarities subtest and "fabric," as well as "slice." These difficulties clearly indicate a perception of home life as troubled, chaotic, and hellish, lacking in strong authoritative protection and control. Her inability to adequately define "domestic" may also reflect her own sense of inadequacy as regards a feminine role and her implied rejection of this role for herself.

The response to "consume" could have received further inquiry because of its uniqueness, but was overlooked because of the tester's continued preoccupation with the highly informative previous response. The tester's preoccupation with the "domestic" item may possibly reflect his own concerns about domestic issues and/or his need at that point in the testing to avoid issues around "consume." From item 21 through item 37 her responses are intact, though at times they drop to a 1-level. She gives an idiosyncratic definition to "plagiarize," when she elaborates the notion of copying by adding "to use someone else's thoughts as your own." The emphasis here on access to the direct thoughts of others rather than to the more external manifestation of these thoughts in written productions or words gives this response a somewhat over-ideational paranoid flavor, as if one could see beneath reality into the hidden reaches of others' minds. The next disruption occurs on item 39 with the definition to the word, "impale," which is infused with aggressive content. She starts out with the word "penetrate" as her definition, and when asked for further elaboration, she makes a rather infantile and disarming response of "oh, golly," and follows this with the statement "let's see," which relates to her frequent emphasis on visualizing and may suggest voyeuristic trends. In her definition she states that "impale" means "to hang up" or "stick somebody" or "to penetrate someone with an object," and here the reader should be reminded of her response, "stick it in the mail," on item 3 on Comprehension. Again, it may suggest trends toward a masculine identification; and her degree of disturbance indicates that she may have in mind a sexual penetration and a conception of intercourse as a directly aggressive and primitive activity. It is as though she were able to contain a great deal of this content in her initial response, but in being pressed further, the drive components entered into the ideational process and overwhelmed her defenses. It is important to note that on the next item, "travesty," she recovers and gives a one word, concise and perfectly appropriate response.

Overall, her functioning on the Vocabulary subtest was intact. What is particularly noteworthy is her resiliency after serious lapses on such items as "domestic" and "impale." This resiliency is an important adaptive function, and it constitutes a major factor in appraising her present difficulties and her potentiality for psychotherapy.

WAIS Summary

The data obtained on the WAIS indicates that Mrs. T. is a severely neurotic woman of very superior intellectual ability who appears to be functioning significantly below her intellectual potential. The extensive indications of the use of repression, her hypersocial facility, and the nature of her impairments in concentration, attention, and memory, as well as the frequent shifts in the quality of her responses, all suggest a predominantly hysterical organization. Her general high level of functioning is occasionally disrupted by personalizations and concreteness, but despite occasional lapses there is relatively little infusion of primitive and drive-laden material in her thinking. It must be stressed, however, that when disruptions occur, there is an impressive resiliency in her ability to return to her prior high level of functioning.

A certain degree of temporary inefficiencies and lapses in attention may be due to mild organic and probably toxic dysfunction associated with her alcohol intake, but it seems more generally due to Mrs. T.'s high level of anxiety. She seems acutely aware of her anxiety and discomfort, but at the same time appears to be attempting to cover over and ward off from conscious recognition pressing dysphoric feelings of passivity, helplessness, and neediness (for contact and support) by means of an aggressive, phallic, intrusive identification, and a rejection of female roles. She is not able successfully to sustain her efforts in this direction, and indications of giving up to feelings of depression and helplessness are apparent, as well as a typically hysterical avoidance of active ideation. Thus, while efforts at a more masculine identification seem evident, it does not appear to be an ingrained identification which has pervasive personality effects. She is not generally and significantly slowed up in her visual-motor coordination and does not show the typical retardation of a severely depressed person.

Despite her essentially conventional, moralistic strivings (reflected in the high Comprehension), problems concerning containment of impulsive activity and about moral and sexual issues appear to be central. Projective, paranoid trends are also suggested.

Mrs. T.'s high level of anxiety and the underlying depressive aspects suggest that she has the motivation to form a therapeutic alliance. Her superior intellectual ability and her resiliency in handling eruptions of primitive ideation and drive material indicate that she should be able to benefit extensively from psychotherapy.

The primary task of the other tests will be to provide cross-validation for the numerous hypotheses we have derived from the WAIS; to specify our impressions with more certainty and precision; to provide further clarification of Mrs. T.'s concerns; and to see whether her functioning in this impersonal, neutral, cognitive task is an adequate reflection of her functioning in diverse types of situations or whether alterations in the organization and effectiveness of defensive and adaptive efforts occur as we move into situations that present increased novelty and ambiguity and that put greater strain on ego processes.

REFERENCES

BABCOCK, H. An experiment in the measurement of mental deterioration. *Arch. Psychol.*, N.Y., 1930, No. 117.

BLATT, S. J., ALLISON, J., & BAKER, B. L. The Wechsler object assembly subtest and bodily concerns. *J. consult. Psychol.*, 1965, 29, 223–230.

GARDNER, R., HOLZMAN, P., KLEIN, G. S., LINTON, H., & SPENCE, D. P. Cognitive control: a study of individual consistencies in cognitive behavior. *Psychol. Issues*, 1959, 1(4).

GARDNER, R. W., JACKSON, D. N., & MESSICK, S. J. Personality organization in cognitive controls and intellectual abilities. *Psychol. Issues*, 1960, 2(4).

HARTMANN, H. *Ego psychology and the problem of adaptation.* New York: International Universities Press, (1939) 1958.

KROEBER, T. C. The coping mechanisms of ego functions. In R. W. White (Ed.), *The study of lives.* New York: Atherton Press, 1964. Pp. 178–200.

MAYMAN, M., SCHAFER, R., & RAPAPORT, D. Interpretation of the Wechsler-Bellevue intelligence test and personality appraisal. In H. H. Anderson and G. L. Anderson (Eds.), *An introduction to projective techniques.* New York: Prentice-Hall, 1951.

MURSTEIN, B. I., & LEIPOLD, W. D. The role of learning and motor abilities in the Wechsler-Bellevue digit symbol test. *Educ. psychol. Measmt.*, 1961, 21, 103–112.

RAPAPORT, D., GILL, M., & SCHAFER, R. *Diagnostic psychological testing.* Vol. 1. Chicago: Year Book Medical Publishers, 1945.

SCHEERER, M. Problems of performance analysis in the study of personality. *Ann. N. Y. Acad. Sci.*, 1946, 46, 655–678.

WAITE, R. R. The intelligence test as a psychodiagnostic instrument. *J. proj. Tech.*, 1961, 25, 90–102.

WECHSLER, D. *The measurement and appraisal of adult intelligence.* (4th ed.) Baltimore: Williams & Wilkins, 1958.

3

Thematic Apperception Test

Whereas the WAIS emphasizes the more realistic, secondary process modes of thinking and taps functioning in impersonal, routine situations, the TAT proceeds to less realistic, more personal levels. It permits more latitude of response variability, more elaboration by preconscious derivatives, and more representation of personal concerns and conflicts. But the TAT does not allow a freewheeling disregard of reality considerations. Our instructions, asking subjects to tell a story and to tell what the characters are thinking and feeling, stimulate imaginative elaboration. The story, however, is supposed to follow a specific temporal sequence (what led up, what is happening, and what the outcome will be), and the subject is supposed to adhere to the apparent reality of the picture (what is *happening in the* picture). Thus, an impetus to fantasy is provided but relative boundaries to it are set at the beginning. Since we do not tell subjects to let loose their full imaginativeness or to be as dramatic as possible but simply tell them to make up a story, the subjects have a certain degree of definition of the task, and we can observe their preferred modes of orientation.

The TAT, then, is more personal than the

varied tasks of the WAIS; it is also more interpersonal, since it presents, for the most part, people in scenes of everyday life activity. But it stops far short of the novel and unique situation of the Rorschach in which the subject must depend on internal processes to a large extent to mold and structure reality. In terms of a battery of tests, therefore, the TAT extends the variety of types of situations in which samples of behavior are obtained to partially-structured situations.

Some forerunners of the TAT made their appearance around 1907 at the time that psychology was beginning to reach beyond the physiological orientation of Wundt's laboratory to an interest in the psychology of thought (Binet & Henri, 1895; Ebbinghaus, 1897). In 1907, for example, Brittain presented a series of nine pictures to a group of boys and girls, aged 13 to 20 years, and asked them to write a story for each. He found consistent differences between the stories told by boys and those told by girls. The girls' stories revealed a considerably greater emphasis on social, religious, and moral themes and on clothes and food preparation. The girls also seemed to reflect more sadness and fear of being alone or abandoned. A year later, in 1908, Libby reported the use of pictures to evaluate the relationship between imagination and feelings in school children and showed that the imagination of high school students was no poorer than that of grade school pupils. After a fallow period of research with pictures, a psychiatrist (Schwartz, 1932) rediscovered the picture story technique for use as a clinical tool for personality assessment. His Social Situation Picture Test consisted of eight pictures representing scenes frequently encountered in the histories of delinquents. But it was not until the publication of *Explorations in Personality* (Murray et al., 1938) when TAT results were integrated with a general theory of personality that the test began to be widely used clinically by psychologists and became the vehicle for many research endeavors.

The earliest approach to TAT interpretation was based solely on the content of the stories. Although to this day there is still considerable emphasis on the TAT as a vehicle primarily for exploring the content of personality there is also increased recognition of the structural aspects of the TAT. These structural aspects include both "test-centered" formal aspects (the organizational characteristics of the stories) and the "person-centered" formal aspects (the manner in which the stories are told) (Holt, 1958). From an ego-psychological point of view, the conception that the TAT reveals the content of personality whereas the Rorschach test reveals the structure and organization of personality (Freeman, 1962) does not take sufficient cognizance of the degree to which the TAT also shows the imprint of personality structure. In our discussion therefore we shall emphasize equally content and structural aspects of the TAT. First we shall discuss the content, then the test-centered structural aspects of the stories, administration of the test, clinical case examples which illustrate the person-centered formal features and their interrelationship with content. Finally we shall present Mrs. T.'s TAT to show how all the dimensions of TAT analysis are brought together in its clinical use.

CONTENT

Murray's system of interpretation (1938) listed five elements of TAT content which can be examined in each story: the hero, the needs of the hero, the environmental forces, the theme, and the outcome. Other approaches to TAT content have also stressed similar elements of the story. Rapaport et al. (1945) for example recommends that one attend to the emotional tone of the narrative and also to the figures (or heros), their strivings, and the obstacles (internal and external) that confront them. Any listing of the possible needs or strivings of the TAT figures or of the environmental presses and obstacles would be extremely extensive and the possible combinations of these limitless. The reader is referred instead to Murray's list for basic orientation in this area.

Our focus in this section will be on some general principles involved in interpreting TAT content.

A basic rule in the interpretation of TAT content is that the interpersonal scenes described by the subject cannot be taken at face value to indicate his actual relationships, past or present. This bears emphasis because it is a common error in TAT analysis and leads to many incorrect inferences. While it is possible that the content may reflect one's actual relationships (e.g., for a male subject with his mother on 6 BM or his father on 7 BM) or permit genetic reconstructions of conflicts, other possibilities are equally likely. Clinical experience shows that TAT stories can reveal, in addition, relationships that are wished for, feared, defensively presented to cover significant issues even to the point of something representing its polar opposite, or are based on an accurate perception of the unconscious attitudes and feelings of the other person. TAT stories can also be composites of these possibilities and reflect several or more at the same time.

An example of a story in which a simple wished for relationship is expressed was told by a subject whose father had frequently been separated from the mother because of his infidelity, and with whom the subject felt unable to talk about a number of his important life goals because of the father's openly critical attitude. In this subject's story to 7 BM a son is described as going to a sympathetic and wise father for advice.

A more complex series of stories in which elements of a wished for and also a feared relationship with a paternal figure were evident was told by an adolescent boy who saw father figures as consistently destructive, punitive, and ferocious. No kindly, warmly responsive, interested, or even neutral adult male was seen. In a test report it was noted that the father seemed to have an uncontrollable rage which the boy found frightening to such an extreme degree that he was unable to cope with his fearful feelings. As a result of the test report, the therapist decided to interview the parents together. During the interview the mother did all the talking, and when the father started to respond to a question directed at him, the mother turned towards the father telling him to shut up. The father made no further attempt to speak again for the remainder of the hour.

In this boy's TAT, therefore, the strong aggressive and destructive father figures clearly did not represent the father as he might generally appear to others (at least in the presence of his wife). It may have represented an unconscious perception and fear of the father's pent-up rage and of his own (the father's) conception of his aggression as violent and destructive, or a description of possible sporadic, uncontrollable rage on the father's part which was hence more frightening than a more predictable anger. At the same time, the TAT representations of the father might show a wish for a strong male figure who could offer the boy an identity model and a source of protection against the mother. The tester in this case, instead of leaping to the conclusion that the boy's father was no different from the father in the TAT stories, should have limited himself to a description of the boy's representations of paternal figures and left open the derivation of the boy's perception. Sometimes considering other possibilities can alert one to details in the tests that might go unnoticed and might help clarify the derivation of a particular perception. As often as not, however, such further clarification may not be forthcoming, and it is best at such times not to go out on a limb and speculate too recklessly. Rather, one should discuss the subject's perceptions of particular relationships with general figures, e.g., maternal figures, paternal figures, etc., without specifying whether the subject's own mother or father is intended.

An example of the type of TAT stories in which a theme is presented defensively to cover other underlying issues is often seen in TAT stories in which potency and sexual prowess are stressed in a relentless way. An emphasis of this type is likely to be covering strong homosexual issues or feelings of weakness and inadequacy as a male via a masculine bravado. A story illustrating this point was given to 13 MF (man standing with arm over his eyes; woman on bed) by a 17-year-old boy with prominent homosexual problems disguised by hypermasculinity:

Looks like he's just gotten out of bed after a rough night, got dressed, and he's hiding his eyes from the light—I still think the light is hurting his eyes, and I don't know what else [pushes card away]. [What led up?] From the looks of it they're not married—he probably just picked her up or something the night before and brought her home. [What are his thoughts and feelings?] I don't know; he had a good time that night—looks like he's sorry the night's over. Probably has to go to work or something. [What will be the outcome?] What—I don't know—he'll see her again, I guess—still see her until he gets tired of her—if he doesn't get tired of her, he'll marry her.

Evaluating whether a particular theme is highlighted for defensive reasons follows the usual clinical guidepost that when we see only one aspect of a relationship, when it is presented as entirely one way (e.g., as all good and perfect), one should be alerted to diametrically opposed feelings—those which are conspicuous by their absence. On the other hand, when stories are monothematic in quality, e.g., when in almost every story someone dies or experiences an important loss, often a breakthrough of prominent preoccupations is represented. The fact that these concerns appear so persistently would then reflect their dominance in the subject's thinking and experience.

STRUCTURAL FEATURES

Structural Aspects of the Content

A basic assessment of TAT stories can establish the vividness and wealth of the subject's fantasy life. TAT stories can range from original and creative endeavors to banal and trite productions, and the degree of elaboration and originality of the stories is indicative of the range of fantasy activity and the subject's willingness to realize this capacity in the testing situation. The amount of energy invested in fantasy activity can also be assessed in the length of the stories, with longer stories often reflecting greater energy except when they are characterized by "detail-happy rumination" (Rapaport et al., 1945, p. 417), by an effortless accumulation of unessential, unintegrated details. Important information is also available from the degree to which the subject stays exclusively with the dimensions and stimulus properties of the cards or his relative willingness to introduce new content in the way of new figures and new situations. Such introduced content can also range from highly original to largely banal material, but it does indicate the capacity and willingness to go beyond the constraints of the immediate stimulus. This can also reach the other extreme, where there is an overinvestment in fantasy activity and where the picture merely serves as the springboard for an extensive and highly invested excursion into personalized and autistic material to the relative exclusion of the original stimulus, the picture.

One type of banal story consists of stereotyped, cliché elements derived from books or movies. Masserman & Balken (1939) express the view that since such material is selected from a wide range of possibilities, it is psychologically determined and may be considered to represent latent tendencies of the individual. It is important, however, that the tester be cognizant which of the material is a stereotype and which is more directly ideational and personal in nature. A more frequent type of banal story may merely indicate the most obvious aspects of each picture or may present a quite common theme with little or no personal touch added to it. Unlike the WAIS, where the most efficient functioning is based on perceiving and performing in primarily usual, conventional ways, TAT stories which adhere to the usual, conventional themes reflect a certain degree of stereotypy and lack of richness of imaginativeness, lack of creativity, and lack of access to free, spontaneous modes of experience. Subjects who perform in this manner fall short of adaptive functioning on the TAT because they are limited in their capacity to "make up" a story and have to rely on what they have derived from other sources or what is relatively easily apparent from the picture and requires no great ideational effort on their part. For instance, a frequently given story to Card 1 may proceed as follows:

> This is a boy who was told to practice his violin, he doesn't want to, would like to be out playing baseball with his friends. His mother will insist that he practice for a half hour. He decides that the only way to get out to play is to do as his mother says. He practices and then goes out to join his friends playing baseball.

A more personally relevant story to the same picture is:

> I'd say this boy had been practicing on his violin for a long time and his mother came into the room and told him he had no talent at all, and told him to stop practicing, consequently shattering his dream of becoming a Menuhin. And he is now staring at his violin remorsefully for the last time.

While the first story is not without interpretive potential, and while both are revealing as regards relationships with mother figures, attitudes toward self, intellectual tasks, and achievement, the latter story has much greater personal substance, and one can feel on safer ground in the interpretation of the subject's fantasy life.

Compliance with the Instructions

From TAT stories, one gleans representations of thinking, feeling, and acting. At times, however, one of these is emphasized to the exclusion of the others; in the stories of psychopaths, for example, one often sees action that proceeds without thought or deliberation and without much feeling. Or subjects may elaborate the thoughts of the characters but ignore or deemphasize feelings; in some stories characters get lost in thinking and fantasy and never act. The possibilities are, of course, unlimited in how thoughts, feelings, and actions are portrayed and balanced, the types of each that appear, and their degree of variety, complexity, wealth or narrowness, simplicity, and impoverishment.

From the point of view of ego processes, another important aspect of the structure of TAT stories is the light they shed on how subjects experience time, and plan and organize their experience over time. Since stories are requested with a temporal span (past, present, and future), the subject's relative investment in each of the three temporal dimensions may have important implications. For example, one expects depressed patients to have their primary investment in the past with relatively minor emphasis on the present and virtually no interest in the future. We may expect psychopathic and narcissistic individuals to be primarily present-oriented, without a more introspective focus on the past and future. Though hysterics may have an orientation toward the future, they are characterized often by childlike faith and the Pollyanna notion that without effort, somehow everything will be fine. Schizophrenics are likely to be confused in their time perspective and reflect this by mixing up time sequences, shifting fluidly among past, present, and future in an undifferentiated way. Obsessive compulsive individuals in a very orderly and meticulous way are likely to cover the full range of time but measure it out carefully, precisely, and affectlessly, as they measure out their own lives.

Another aspect of compliance with the test instructions is the degree to which the story mirrors correctly the details of the picture and is perceptually accurate. Although in some pictures the sex of the figures is ambiguous, on occasion one also finds misrecognition of the sex and age of TAT characters whose sex and age are clearly defined. Going against the reality of the picture in this way indicates a capacity to have a distorted perception of external reality and often indicates marked psychotic (usually paranoid) trends. If one sticks instead with a content oriented approach, trying to relate the content to the patient's fantasy and ignoring the properties of the stimulus, valuable data are ignored. An instance in which content was overemphasized appeared in the analysis of the tests of an 18-year-old girl who was hospitalized for promiscuous sexual behavior and who told the following story to #20 (A dim figure leaning against a lamp post):

> Looks like a man's face with a big nose. Modern art. Someone like Picasso. The paint or ink keeps eating him up until there's nothing left any more. [?] Just flows over the white. Man with a big nose. Eventually the white flows over it too. [Note—nose is located in the usual elbow area.]

The tester who diagnosed this girl as an hysterical character with psychopathic features referred to this TAT story in his report and discussed it in terms of the patient's hostile wish that her artist father's sexual prowess would be destroyed via oral incorporation. Although the inference as to the significance of the content may be in part accurate, by failing to emphasize the fact that these concerns in this girl could result in her seriously distorting her recognition of reality, the tester failed to spot this girl's psychotic potential. Not too long after the testing and during her hospitalization, the patient had several frankly psychotic episodes.

Organizational Structure of the Story

Stories may be disorganized and fragmented, flit from theme to theme, from character to character, from idea to idea with frequent hesitations and intrusions; or stories may have a rhythm, flow smoothly, be logical and coherent. Another dimension of the subject's cognitive style is the general approach taken in responding to the card. As discussed by Henry (1957), the approach on the TAT can be assessed much as it is assessed on the Rorschach. The TAT story can evolve from small details slowly built up to include larger and larger aspects until the subject has accounted for the entire card. This process can be random, shifting from detail to totality in an unorganized manner. While the degree of organization need not be directly related to the complexity of the content, a more complex story places a greater strain on an individual's capacity for ordered thinking and coherent organization.

A further way in which the stories can be revealing is through the study not only of the sequence and shift from element to element of each story but also through noting the sequence of stories. Sometimes efforts at defense occur between stories as well as in them. A gloomy, depressively toned story, short in length, limited in time span and related somberly may be followed by an optimistic, future oriented, and lengthy story; this sequence may reflect efforts to defend against strong depressive affect and concerns. Or an aggressively toned story may be followed by one in which politeness and positive regard are expressed.

Among the other rich data regarding ego processes supplied by the TAT is the manner and mode in which the stories are told (Schafer, 1958). It is crucial to consider the way the stories are told for a full personality assessment can be illustrated by the following story told by a 17-year-old girl who was hospitalized after multiple suicidal gestures, declining school performance, and increased isolation. The story was told to a black and white card derived from Picasso's painting, "Les Saltimbanques" which depicts a family of six acrobats:

There's this play written for six characters, and it's almost a ballet, and it's a very "Theatre of the Absurd" type play. These characters all received phone calls that they were wanted to try out for this play, so they all came to this small theatre and accepted to play these characters, and then they went back for rehearsal the next day, and the theatre was all boarded up and whitewashed and no sign, and they asked somebody, and they said the theatre had been boarded up for 17 years. They are all just sitting outside the theatre, and there's lots of tension between them because they argue about who's crazy and who's not, but in the end they return to their own way of life and try to forget about it, but they never can because they're always haunted by the fear they're crazy. [How did the theatre get there?] Always had been there—boarded up. Somebody just played a practical joke, and maybe—oh, I don't know—they opened the theatre just that day and bribed a man to say it had always been closed.

If, in interpreting this story, we rely on the content primarily, we could probably conclude that this patient represents people as being confused as to the boundaries between reality and fantasy, that she may feel somewhat disillusioned about reality, that people are seen as deceptive, practical jokers. We would assume that the patient is letting us know about her own experience, and we would be correct as far as we went. But when her attitude while she told the story is considered—a blend of prankish excitement and pleasure—our formulation would have to be expanded to include the observation that she takes apparent pleasure in making reality boundaries fuzzy, that she may be identifying with the practical joker in the story. Her story is also an adaptation of Pirandello's play *Six Characters in Search of an Author,* and this also serves as an intellectual buffer from the full impact of the content. A full integration of the content and her manner of presentation of the story would specify her seeming enjoyment but might conclude that in this way she is trying to defend against underlying concerns about boundaries between reality and fantasy. In this sense she reverses what she fears and converts it instead into fun and kicks.

ADMINISTRATION

Whenever possible the TAT is given in one session; it rarely requires a period longer than an hour. Our instructions for administering the test are similar to those used by Rapaport et al. (1945) and are as follows: "I am going to show you a series of pictures, and I want you to make up a story about each one. I want you to tell me what is happening in the picture, what led up to it, and what the outcome will be. I also want you to describe the thoughts and feelings of the characters."

All or part of the instructions may be repeated whenever necessary or at the subject's request. It is usually only after the subject feels he has completed his story, i.e., after each picture, that we inquire into aspects of the instructions which were not covered, e.g., the outcome of the story, the thoughts or feelings of the characters. Except for very depressed, blocked, guarded patients who might be encouraged or pressed for more information, we see what the subject produces spontaneously and feels is sufficient to meet the test requirements. It is interesting to see how often subjects persist in neglecting details during the telling of the stories, even after the examiner has called attention to previous omissions. Omissions can be of interpretive significance, e.g., when subjects routinely omit outcomes or feelings. Subjects may be asked about thoughts and feelings, outcome, events leading up to the present situation, if one or more of these areas are omitted in the story. However, the questioning is not carried out compulsively; a well detailed response to a picture excluding some aspects of the instructions would not necessarily demand further inquiry. Inquiry should also be directed at any lack of clarity, slips, neologisms, non sequiturs, or peculiar or incomprehensible comments. Striking misperceptions should also be inquired into, e.g., if the violin on Card 1 is seen as a book or is ignored. Only the most striking sexual misrecognitions should be the subject of inquiry to avoid putting the subject on guard, but a reference to a single person as "they" should be questioned, as it is usually an effort to avoid mention of the sex of the figure. In other situations where the subject avoids being specific, inquiry to that portion should also be made For instance, when a vague story is told to #15 (graveyard scene) about a man grieving for "someone who has died," it is important to find out for whom he is mourning.

Just as with all clinical interactions, whether interviews or tests, inquiry must not be leading or suggestive, but should be directed toward getting greater specificity through nonspecific questions. For instance, if in the graveyard scene the man is described as feeling sorry for what he had done, the question should *not* be "Did he kill the person?" but rather, a repetition of a segment of the subject's story: "Sorry for what he had done? What happened?" Questioning should be firm, but not inquisitorial. The general clinical skill of the tester will determine the adequacy of the inquiry.

The following 15 cards are administered in our series. (TAT designations are in parentheses.) We routinely use all these cards in a fixed sequence. This procedure appears more preferable to us than the common practice of selecting particular cards to tap possibly conflicting areas of particular patients. The fixed series, which standardly covers a variety of situations and types of interpersonal interaction, offers two advantages: it keeps any sequence effect constant, and it also minimizes the effect of a biased selection of cards on the part of the tester.

MALES AND FEMALES
   1 Boy with violin (1).
   2 Woman standing by half opened door looking into room (5).
   3 Graveyard scene (15).
   4 Silhouette of person against a bright window (14).
   5 A woodcut, showing two old men in front view, one above the other. (Not in the present TAT series but taken from the first Harvard Psychological Clinic edition of the TAT.) [1]
   6 Man's and woman's heads in close proximity (10).
   7 Picasso's "La Vie" which depicts a nude couple and a middle aged woman with baby. (Not in the present TAT series but taken from the first Harvard Psychological Clinic edition of the TAT.) [2]
   8 Man standing with arm over his eyes, woman on bed behind him (13 MF). Before cards 9, 10, and 11 are administered, either the male or female series of four cards is shown: they are described below, after card 11.

Male series
M 1 Elderly woman with back turned toward younger man (6 BM).
M 2 Faces of an elderly and a young man (7 BM).
M 3 A woman holding onto shoulders of a man (4).
M 4 A dim figure leaning against lamp post (20).
M 5 Man clinging to a rope (17 BM).

Female series
F 1 Faces of a young and old woman, the latter in the background (12 F).
F 2 Young woman with one hand against door, the other covering her face (3 GF).
F 3 Farm scene, young woman with books in foreground, man working in field and older woman standing in background (2).
F 4 A woman with hands around throat of another person on a stairway (18 GF).
F 5 Older woman sitting beside girl who is holding a doll in her lap (7 GF).

MALES AND FEMALES (follows M5 or F5)
   9 Young man lying on couch, older man leaning over him with hand over young man's face (12M).
  10 Figure on the floor beside couch, object (revolver, knife) beside him (3 BM).
  11 Blank card (16).

[1] A reproduction of this card can be found in Rapaport et al., Vol. II, 1945, p. 400.
[2] *Ibid.* p. 400.

CLINICAL EXAMPLES

In the following section, we will present a review of the major diagnostic syndromes and how they are reflected in the content and structure of TAT stories. In order to highlight the differences among various diagnostic groupings, we will use only stories told to TAT Card 10, which depicts two figures in close physical contact; generally the figure on the left is seen as male, the one on the right as female.

Depression

The severely depressed patient's record will be relatively easy to discern. He will, in telling the story, show ideational restriction, slowness in response and speech, and low mood. The stories will contain themes in which suicidal thoughts, feelings of isolation, rejection, worthlessness, and incapability on the part of the characters are emphasized. To TAT Card 10 a 29-year-old, married, severely depressed man gave the following story:

[Sigh] I don't even know—[make up a story]. I don't know what to say. [Say anything.] That's just it.—I don't—[Who are these people?] Well, one's a man and one's a woman. Somebody could have died, I suppose. Probably lost their girl or boy—in some way—[What are their thoughts and feelings?] Well, they miss him—[What will happen?] Probably will outgrow it after a long time, probably.

The following is a TAT story of a 33-year-old married, depressed woman. The story contains in its content some typical depressive features, most notably the sense of depletion of energy, the need for external support because of a feeling of being unable to cope actively with her experience which gets easily out of control. Locating some of the disturbances outside herself (the faucet, the children) reflects some efforts to externalize her own feeling of inadequacy and may be more projective than depressive, but the "tiring," fatiguing feeling and direct need to be comforted are clearly depressive:

This is the story of a woman who's leaning on the shoulder of her husband, being comforted, and after she tells him of a very tiring day where everything went wrong, he consoles her and she feels better. [Everything went wrong, anything particular you have in mind?] The sort of day when the faucet in the kitchen won't stop running and overflowing in the kitchen, where the children have fought all day, her favorite recipe didn't turn out right.

Hysteria

In hysteria a considerable amount of affective lability is noted in the stories, i.e., there may be blocking, crying, and exclamations about the fearfulness, weirdness, or prettiness of the scene. Frequently this emotional lability is coupled with story content which is quite banal and which emphasizes cliches, conventionality, and morality. Naivete is frequently present so that the stories often have a childlike quality. Pictures depicting aggressive and particularly sexual themes may elicit blocking or very brief responses which often evade the sexual or aggressive aspects of the picture. On 13 MF such subjects will often not acknowledge the nudity or comment on the sexual implication. The following story to TAT Card 10 was told by an outpatient, a 30-year-old hysterical woman who tended to experience lapses in reality testing; the story illustrates typical hysterical naivete and romanticism:

This looks like a nice man and—a sweet girl—They look like this is a happy moment—Looks like he's telling her he loves her—or something that's tender and sweet. She looks very confident and happy! It looks nice; I like it. Hm! Wait now! Maybe—well—that's right—he looks kind of older—but she looks efficient—and sweet. [Efficient?] Yes [laughs]. Doesn't look particularly efficient at the moment, but I imagine—[puts card away]. [What led up to this?] Well—I think maybe he taught school nearby, and she was a girl in the village—It strikes me as a sort of sweet, old fashioned romance. Maybe she's seen him a long time, and now it has just come to the state where he tells her that he loves her. [What will the outcome be?] I think they get married, get some children and be happy—not that they will live happily ever after, not like a fairy tale. They look like ordinary people.

Another outpatient, a 35-year-old housewife, mother of four children, with a personality organization predominantly along hysterical lines but with a conspicuous element of blandness and cynicism presented the following story:

Looks like a man and woman kissing. Or he's kissing her forehead. That's all. [What led up?] [Yawns] They could have loved each other. I don't know. Maybe they're married or getting married or something. [Thoughts and feelings?] Well, they probably love each other. [What is going to be the outcome?] Either they're married or gonna get married or something. [Which is it?] I say they're gonna get married. Their faces wouldn't look like that if they were married. [What do you mean?] Well, they wouldn't look like that after being married, that's my opinion. [How do they look?] They look like they're in love. [Covers mouth with hands.]

Obsessive Compulsive Neurosis

No attempt will be made here to distinguish among the specific defense mechanisms of regression, undoing, isolation, intellectualization, and reaction formation, since several are frequently present in the obsessive compulsive character structure. In a severe condition, a patient using these defenses may respond to the TAT with tedious, ruminative, and pedantic stories replete with reservations, doubts, and qualifications. Vacillations between alternate possibilities of actions, feelings, relationships, and strivings are often present in a context which has an intellectualized, circumstantial, rigid, third party or observer quality. Other times, detailed descriptions of objects in the picture are given, the patient refusing to make up a story or describe the outcome, since no clues are furnished in the picture. This kind of rigidity protects these patients from strong affective experience. In less severe, more intact obsessive-compulsive pictures, we see diligent, orderly, and meticulous story telling that is strongly intellectual in quality and unspontaneous. The content of the stories may contain features similar to the style of the story, e.g., hesitancy and doubting on the part of the characters, a thematic emphasis on diligence and compliance and thoroughness. The illustrative story was told by a 29-year-old male research botanist, who was admitted to the hospital with suicidal thoughts, difficulties in concentration, and some suspiciousness. Although there is a marked emphasis on feeling in the content, it is noteworthy that it is treated in a highly intellectual detailed fashion, peppered by such expressions as "what have you" and "if you will." His comment about the "sweet nothings" also belies the seemingly deep feeling:

> Could be any scene between man and wife or two lovers—assume they haven't seen each other for several weeks or months—perhaps the parting has been one of which—haven't been too many recently. Man's expression is one of both intense happiness and relief—let's say that his wife is back and they're together again. Her expression could also convey the same, although the look of happiness is not as pronounced on her features—although I can intuitively sense it's quite similar to his. At the moment he's doing the talking, she's listening. Talk is of love, sweet nothings, if you will, words suggesting how deeply he has missed her: "I don't look forward to being away from you from this time ever." She is by nod of head, by touch of hand assenting in agreement—assenting with the idea that she also feels this way. They will shortly separate from the fond embrace and with some reluctance go on about their everyday work. During the day they will make repeated contact with each other by kiss or by touch. Life will eventually return to normal—however their feelings towards each other intensified by the long parting. The expression of love passing back and forth between them will continue with renewed verve, fervor, what have you. They will perhaps in fact feel they have been—they are now better individuals for having sustained the long separation that made them realize how much they missed each other, depended on each other.—Here again, as you see quite clearly, is self-identification—me and my wife. [Why did they separate?] Chain of circumstances—in my case because of moving from the East Coast to West for a year of academic work.

Paranoid Disorders

The mechanism of projection used in this condition must be recognized as one which falls on a continuum. Projection ranges from a benign, modulated, and socially adaptive mechanism where it aids in perceiving one's own qualities in others and functions as an important ingredient in empathy, to its presence in paranoid schizophrenia at the other extreme. In extreme cases one sees gross perceptual distortions which indicate the breakdown in reality testing. In less severe paranoid conditions, one commonly sees mistrustfulness of others, questioning of motives and hyperalert watching for cues and guardedness. In the TAT, content which involves suspiciousness, distrust, sneakiness, an emphasis on malevolent outside forces or sudden changes of character woven into the fabric of the story may indicate a projective orientation. But, as with all psychological conditions, the stylistic aspects of the stories are often most revealing and are most consistently present. For example, stories may be very brief, reflecting suspicious withholding and a guarded quality, or stories may be expansive, grandiose productions revealing megalomanic tendencies. Often, stories involve legalistic, pseudological, anti-intuitive thinking in which the patient verbalizes each bit of evidence on which his story is based and justifies each conclusion about the story, often including minute details in the picture, especially facial characteristics. Misrecognitions of the sex or age of usually unambiguous characters is a clear indication of a capacity to misinterpret reality to a marked degree and in a projective manner. Questions about the tester's verbatim recording, about who will see the material or about what use will be made of it, and statements for "off the record" are not infrequently expressed by the paranoid patient.

A 21-year-old senior majoring in electrical engineering was hospitalized because of hallucinations, feelings of persecution, and confusion. The psychological examination completed two months after his admission, indicated an acute schizophrenic condition with predominantly paranoid features. His story to TAT Card 10 is as follows:

I've seen this picture before in my psychology course. I wonder what I said before. Leading up to this was probably an argument or—er—emotional rift between the two people, probably husband and wife. Now they have found a certain amount of agreement and have reconciled their differences to a certain extent. And they are showing a willingness to accept each other's differences, although the man seems to have a calculating air about his facial expression, while the woman seems more submissive—er—I would say the woman

probably has to continue to gain her way or her wants in more indirect methods. That's all I have to say about the picture. [How do
you mean the woman has to use indirect methods?] Well—er—
rather than putting her foot down and making definite demands, she
probably has to gain her way through making the man feel as though
he does have his own way. [How do you mean calculating?] His
eyebrows were cocked in a way at least, he felt he had the upper
hand in a way, or it indicated that this was more than a maneuver
from him rather than a real expression of warmth toward the woman.

Schizophrenia

A variety of TAT indications reflect schizophrenic thinking: disorganization of the structure of the story, perceptual misrecognition and peculiar verbalizations, a lack of a cohesive theme, a loss
of distance and lack of clear distinction between the patient and
the events in the picture, abrupt transformations, non sequiturs,
and temporal and affective confusion in the story. The content of
the story may be morbid or perverse. The figures may lack depth
of feelings and be isolated and withdrawn.

The following story of a hospitalized schizophrenic, an 18-year-
old male student illustrates many of these features. A preoccupation
with ego boundaries, where one leaves off and others begin is
noteworthy in the fact that the people "feel as if they are a picture"
and in the patient's efforts to set their limits as the boundary of
the picture. The story and the concrete reality of the picture seem
to get confused and are likely to reflect the patient's own confused
sense of boundaries. Other noteworthy aspects are the abrupt transi-
tions in feeling states and the miraculous way in which they alter.
The problem reflected in the story is that coming together and
intimacy seem to bring with it a fear of fusion and loss of boundaries—a typically schizophrenic fear.

Before this picture, these two people, ah, hated each other. [Takes
one of my cigarettes.] And then they were accidentally thrown together in some situation and just before this picture, a miraculous
change took place which I can't describe. In the picture they—they
feel as if they are a picture—a complete thing. And they're aware of
their limits and they accept them and after the picture, they leave

each other um—and the picture. [What are their limits?] The boundaries of the picture.

A different type of story was told by a 31-year-old hospitalized
chronic schizophrenic male teacher. What is most striking in this
story is the bland delivery and the morbid content which is over-
elaborately based on a shadow in the picture.

> Again there isn't too much in this one. These two older people are
> married, and he's dying of cancer. He had cancer of the jaw—he
> was in the hospital and had an operation, but they had to cut the
> lower part of his face away. He's going to die soon anyway, so it
> doesn't really matter. His wife is very upset to look at his mutilated
> face. He dies and that's the end of the story.

Hypomania

This condition requires the use of the very primitive mechanism
of denial which is ubiquitous in children and is often seen in adults
to a minor degree, usually in combination with repression as a more
primary defense. A. Freud (1936) discusses denial in considerable
detail citing many interesting clinical examples of the use of denial
in children both for play and reality purposes. What is involved
is the negation of pain or discomfort applied to the past, present,
and future. In fantasy, reversals can take place so that unhappiness
becomes happiness, defeat becomes victory, fear becomes courage,
and weakness is transformed into strength. In the development
from childhood into adulthood this mechanism is largely abandoned
and replaced by more complex defense strategies. Massive denial
in adults appears only when there is a psychotic loss of reality testing accompanied by hypomanic features. The question of differentiating between reaction formation and denial is frequently
raised and is difficult to answer since at times the mechanisms
seem to be the same. According to Fenichel (1945) "true" reaction formation pervades the entire character structure, so that
someone becomes a "kind" person generally whereas denial is more
geared to specific situations. But we have seen cases in which

denial also operates as an integral part of the character structure, e.g., in hypomanic characters. The context of the character structure, however, is usually informative in this regard. Thus, reaction formation is more likely to be seen in the context of an obsessive-compulsive character structure, in which other mechanisms such as isolation and intellectualization are also present; this is generally not the case with denial. A further observation which needs additional evaluation is that reaction formation is frequently a defense against overwhelming hostility, while denial tends more often to be directed against depressive feelings.

In a hypomanic record, pressure of speech, flightiness, and euphoria lead to such rapid telling of stories that the tester's intervention may be required in order to keep a verbatim record. In this kind of patient the instability of the defense is often noteworthy, so that gaiety, innocence, serenity, and good feelings may alternate with what is to be denied, i.e., depression, guilt, anger, helplessness, and despair. Attitudes of the characters in the stories and their relationships to each other are likely to arouse emotional reactions in the patient which are painful and therefore have to be denied. The following TAT story was told by a 33-year-old married woman with two children who consulted a psychiatrist because of diminution of outside activities and open aggression towards her husband and children:

[Whispers] Once upon a time—er—there was a woman Deidra, may I name her, and she's not as young, not young, in her thirties. She has met someone with whom she's fallen in love who is very tender and very warm—and that's all. [Led up?] In details, I'm not interested in details. [Outcome?] [Sigh]—Um—she has done something which has pleased him rather than saying the conventional "thank you." He's embracing her. He is feeling how fortunate he is to have found her and she is feeling how fortunate she is to have found him. [Outcome?] I was going to say they live happily ever after. She is not physically very pretty, she has a nose like a proboscis. [Laughs] But he doesn't see any of it; what is important is that he loves her. [What will happen?] No matter how awful the situation, the circumstances, of mundane living, this precious moment will go on forever.

When the patient is acutely psychotic the denial will be quite bizarre, particularly because of the peculiar juxtaposition of the denial and what is to be denied. An illustrative story was told by a 32-year-old married woman, a physician from France, who had come to the U.S. for a year's visit.

Doctor, I am so tired! How many more? [A few more.] Two people who talk together—I'm sorry I forgot to get up for the appointment. I didn't take anything. Why am I tired? I live like an animal. This is not interesting to me [referring to the TAT]. [Make up a story.] Two adults—they talk together, talk, talk, talk. [What are they talking about?] [Patient giggles] What is this, man and woman? Oui, this can be a man, but this, if this is a woman, something manqué, fail. [What is missing?] She doesn't look very girl. [Make up something] I have very poor imagination. [Try; it would be useful.] Je suis seche because I'm really—now I'm obliged to make up a story. It's not that I'm ashamed. They don't say horrible things when a man and woman begin to talk—The conversation between a man and woman doesn't really have any importance. For a man the conversation of a woman has no importance because a man is naturally selfish. What a man likes when he goes home is some rest, relax, and his wife is a piece of furniture of his house. But remember: I talk here in general, not in my personal case. I'm very serious now, and I'm sure for my husband I'm not a piece of furniture, because if I have been a piece of furniture, I'm sure my husband does not let me go away because a man need his piece of furniture each day. I'm sorry because all this story came always to my personal case. This is important for me because I've only one life and I like my life very much—I'm sorry: you ask me a funny story and I talk to you—.

The preceding cases illustrated broad and general diagnostic types. As was done with the WAIS we now return to Mrs. T.'s TAT protocol and present a response-by-response analysis of her TAT.

MRS. T.'S TAT

1. TAT 1—Boy with Violin

Reaction Time: 12″   Total Time: 52″
Uh—this child—uh—[sigh] has been studying music for a few years.

He's—he feels very deeply about music. He can hear it—hear lovely sounds in his head, but he can't get them to come out of his violin. At the time of this picture, he's sitting there very unhappy, because he can hear the sounds, but he can't create anything himself. And— uh—so he gets up and he—and very frustrated, he smashes his violin.

INTERPRETATION. One of the most striking content features of this story is the passivity and lack of action at the outset of the response. It is not until the very end that there appears an impulsive eruption of affect and aggression. As was suggested earlier in the WAIS, here too we see an initial passivity and inaction which is followed by strong action. In this instance, however, there is an indication that this activity can have a strong aggressive quality. Whether she is likely to act in an openly aggressive manner is as yet not clear. But this theme seems to be persistent. By initially identifying the figure as a child she leaves ambiguous his sexual identity which may reflect a sense of uncertain sexual identity on her part. That she is able to identify the "child" subsequently as male reflects a belated capacity for facing these identity problems. The statement, "has been studying music for a few years," is an indication of a broader time dimension and concern with the past than one commonly sees on this card, on which the boy is usually described as having gotten the violin recently. But the extended time span is accompanied by an emphasis on the lack of accomplishment: "he can't get them to come out of his violin," which has a noteworthy depressive quality. The juxtaposition of the unhappiness about hearing the sounds but not being able to get them out of his violin reflects a state of tension and a longing for an active role which is finally and only expressed through violent, volcanic activity.

Also evident is a strong investment in fantasy and a potential for it to serve as a source of gratification rather than facing frustrating and destructive aspects of the external world. In the content, nonetheless, there is an anxious but strong involvement with the necessity for external accomplishment rather than the kind of bland withdrawal one might see in a schizophrenic's story. Her emphasis on hearing sounds in one's head is reminiscent of her visualizing trends on the WAIS, and both suggest a relatively free use of primary process modes of experience rather than a rigid reliance on logical, secondary process verbal modes. The implication of passivity in the hearing of the sounds, i.e., the experience of hearing sounds which are not felt as being created by herself, suggests that a capacity for hallucinatory-like activity may be present. But inasmuch as we see no evidence for schizophrenia thus far, either in the WAIS or in this well-organized, clearly communicated initial story, we should also consider the possibility that this is a woman who may also have a marked potential for creative expression which she feels is dammed up, curtailed, and inhibited. For it is a common observation that in creative activity people experience themselves as often passively influenced by the creative process and appear able to experience entire works almost fully formed in their minds.

As regards this story, as in the WAIS, it is of interest that she shows an initial difficulty getting started in a new situation. Her vagueness and hesitation at the outset could reflect passivity but also could reflect an effort to contain her impulsive tendencies.

2. TAT 5—Women in Doorway

Reaction Time: 14"   *Total Time: 68"*
A different story each time or they—[Up to you.] Uh—this is the mother of the child with the violin. She—uh—wants—she expects her son to be a great musician. She cannot understand his feelings of frustration. And—uh—she doesn't quite understand her son. She doesn't know that he hears beautiful things. She just wants him to be famous. And she's been downstairs puttering around, and she hears the crash of the violin, and she runs upstairs and looks in the door. And—and she goes over to the son and reprimands him sharply.— That's it.

INQUIRY: [What are the thoughts and feelings of the people?] Well, the boy, as I said, is very unhappy and depressed, frustrated, because he knows he can feel something, but he can't express it to others. And the woman is just very ambitious for her son. She doesn't understand him. She just wants him to make a success of himself. She's very angry, upset, very—extremely angry with the child. [You mentioned that he can hear beautiful music.] Yeah. [Can you tell me something about that?] Well, he just—he can—uh—hear lovely things in his head—lovely sounds, you know, in his imagination, I'd guess you'd say. But he can't reproduce them on his violin.

INTERPRETATION. This story shows a representation of a mother who is punitive, who has no understanding, no warmth and no tenderness, offers no help to the child, and who has only one interest—it appears to be a narcissistic one—fame and greatness for her child. The depression and frustration discussed in the first card is very clearly repeated here vis-à-vis the very demanding mother. The very first comment that Mrs. T. makes, i.e., whether a different story is required each time, lends itself to a number of hypotheses. Most prominent are a quest for dependency; a concern with how demanding the tester is going to be and how much work she is going to have to put into the task; and the tentativeness because of a need for permission in order to go ahead and blast the maternal figure so openly. It may be, in addition, a request to be allowed to introduce continuity between cards which would serve as a way of maintaining control and keeping feelings from getting out of hand. This occurs quite frequently in paranoid patients whose observations or themes on one card may be inappropriately carried over to another because of the patient's need to relate everything together and to find hidden obscure connections between things. However, it is not an infrequent occurrence on the first two cards, which should temper the hypothesis of such paranoid trends in Mrs. T. There is further substantiation for the tendency toward fantasy and unrealistic experiences mentioned in the first card when she says that the mother doesn't know that he hears beautiful things. In this way, Mrs. T. further emphasizes the fact that this is very much an idiosyncratic experience for which there is no outside validation, and it demonstrates the gulf between the child who cannot communicate his rich fantasy life and the mother who is primarily concerned with his overt accomplishment. Although the mother is seen as "very angry, upset, very—extremely angry with the child," the mother's anger and frustration, in sharp contrast to the boy's on Card 1, never leads to a physical outburst towards the child. She is merely extremely angry, which may make her insensitive demands all the more difficult for the child to cope with. Also, this could suggest that aggression may be directed outward in an overt way only insofar as objects and not people are involved. It is interesting to note that in this relatively short story, phrases like "can't understand," "doesn't know," or "can't" occur six times. These phrases express her depression and feelings of inadequacy which are further evident in the content concerning the boy's feeling of being inhibited in his expression of his inner experience (in Card 1), and here with regard especially to what he can feel.

3. TAT 15—Graveyard Scene

Reaction Time: 3"   Total Time: 1'19"

This man—uh—very cruel person. He's never loved anyone or never outwardly would say he loved anyone. He had a wife and he was very cruel to her, very cold. And—uh—he left her and he returned home and he found that she had died. He realized how empty his life would be without her. He went out to the graveyard at night. And he's trying to tell her too late that he loved her. And he realizes after leaving the graveyard that his life has been one big farce and he kills himself. That's it.

INTERPRETATION. There is an extreme emphasis on the cold, cruel man who has never loved anybody and never shows any affection. He is at the graveside mourning for a wife whom he left and towards whom he had been very cruel.

The statement "he never loved anyone or never outwardly would say he loved anyone" is closely related to the previous stories in which a person is unable to express his inner feelings and in which, therefore, there is a marked discrepancy between what is experienced and what gets communicated. This story continues the theme of someone who suffers excessively because of this discrepancy and who inevitably is led to destructive action—in this instance of a directly suicidal nature. On one level this story may reflect an image of a paternal, older figure as cruel, demanding, cold, unloving, and ungiving, much like the maternal figure in the preceding story. These attributes may characterize for Mrs. T. the parental relationship, yet the continuity of the theme indicates that we are probably seeing as well the patient's conception of herself. It is of course significant in this story that the full recognition of the underlying love comes only after the loss, and the sequence of the story even suggests that the death follows immediately after an abandonment ("he left her"), as if it directly caused the death. Since we know that Mrs. T.'s mother committed suicide, the feeling in this story of being negligent and failing to communicate one's love adequately and perhaps being responsible for another person's death may reflect Mrs. T.'s own feelings of complicity in her mother's death. The implication that one may die from lack of love also conveys the impression that while Mrs. T. is groping for affection and warmth, she finds only coldness and cruelty.

Thus far, the stories involve frustration and depression which are resolved only through destructive and suicidal activity. We must take seriously this perceived resolution of things and try to establish with more certainty Mrs. T.'s suicidal potential.

While the stories have been relatively short, they are well organized, perceptually accurate, neither fragmented nor disjointed, and do not seem psychotic. They also lack the extreme blocking of the severely depressed patient characterized by marked ideational and psychomotor retardation. It is impressive, given the content of these stories—people blocked in their communication—that Mrs. T. is as openly communicative and frank about her inner experiences and difficulties. Despite serious suggestions of suicidal impulses, the manner in which she communicates her stories does not indicate that she has given up trying to let others in on her current depression and inner misery.

4. TAT 14—*Silhouette of a Person Against a Window*

Reaction Time: 2″   Total Time: 46″
This man is an artist and he has studied art for many years, but he can't—he's very restless, very unhappy. He can't paint like he wants to. He's standing near the window watching the sun go down. And he's very dissatisfied with the slovenly way in which he's living. And —uh—he jumps out of the window. That's it.

INTERPRETATION. The story on this card is almost a repetition of what she told to Card 1. Again we hear of somebody who has studied hard for many years, but is unable to produce in the way he wishes to. The depressive quality is striking in her description of the man as standing near the window watching the sun go down, and especially in the culmination of the story when he jumps out of the window. As in the other stories the depression quickly spreads, here from a felt lack of creative expression to a perception of external warmth and energy, the sun as fleeting and inaccessible and to dissatisfaction with one's way of living and interpersonal relationships. Thus far in these stories there has been expressed both a perception of the maternal figure as making unrealistic demands for overt demonstration of one's talent and also a perception of characters as making these very same demands on themselves. While the maternal figure may be blamed for these standards it would seem that the maternal figure's excessive expectations have been internalized. In these first four stories, there has not been a single comment about a good, warm relationship between people. Two of the four stories have had direct themes of death and suicide. Her TAT stories are becoming somewhat monothematic, which indicates the extent to which these issues preoccupy her and represent her limited ability to employ fully her current skills and creative capabilities. Thus she is being communicative but in a narrow sense; although her story telling does not show depressive retardation, the monothematic, constricted quality of the stories is, in addition to the specific content, depressive in quality, especially in view of her intellectual level.

5. *Woodcut of Two Old Men*

Reaction Time: 7″   Total Time: 49″
These are two men who've gone—they're two brothers. They've lived their lives together. And—uh—they've hated each other deeply, but neither one has expressed this hate. They grow old. And [sigh] toward the end of their lives, they both realize they're going to die— that death is very close. And—uh—they let their hate out toward each other and eventually destroy each other.

INQUIRY: [Um, what led up to their hating each other?] Just hated each other—you mean what led up to it? They were in business together. Each one thought the other was no good. They were jealous of each other when they were children. They were always in competition.

INTERPRETATION. This is another of a series of stories in which she has trouble getting started, begins to say something but checks herself, as if she has trouble orienting herself or is trying to control her thoughts. She begins the story with two men who first appear to be unrelated, but these men become brothers who hate each other deeply. Sibling rivalry is obvious here and is further emphasized in the inquiry where she first has considerable difficulty in dealing with the cause of the hatred and finally talks about them having been jealous of each other when they were children. She thus makes this into a lifelong adjustment. The hatred and morbidity is unrelieved in this presentation. Neither brother felt the other was any good, and the rivalry, the resentment, and the concomitant inability to break out of this situation is most impressive. In this story, as in several of the previous ones, there is a surprise ending. She says, "—death is very close," at which point one might have expected that they would try to make up and die peacefully. But as in previous stories, this is not to be the case, for they suddenly express their hate and eventually destroy each other. It is interesting too that one's own imminent death is here linked with the willingness to express one's angry feelings. The intense hatred, the searing, unexpressed hostility and the inevitable destruction of each other are the striking aspects of the story.

6. TAT 10—*Man's and Woman's Heads in Close Proximity*

Reaction Time: 3"   Total Time: 55"

Uh—in this story—uh—the mother and the father have just realized —received news that one of their children was killed—their only child was killed. They're heartbroken, consoling each other. And— uh—they just go through the rest of their lives with nothing, no meaning. Their child has been taken away. They suffer very deeply.

INQUIRY: [How was the child killed?] What? [How was the child killed?] In an accident—a car wreck, I guess. They were very poor people too.

INTERPRETATION. For the first time a limited possibility of warmth is expressed: parents consoling each other over the loss of their only child. The consolation, the support, and the soothing quality of their closeness is shortlived, for "they just go through the rest of their lives with nothing, no meaning." This latter statement emphasizes the emptiness of the relationship between the two, but at the same time it is an indication of the degree to which the patient is in touch with her feelings as expressed by "they suffer very deeply." The sentence change from "one of their children" to "their only child" and the emphasis on the poverty of the people reflect a gradual spread of depressive content in which things are seen as progressively worsening, pointing up the intense despair. Her response to this story is particularly noteworthy since the picture is more frequently described as affectionate caressing, or two people dancing or deeply in love, and occasionally it is seen as a reunion or a parting. With this patient, it seems that affection can only come out of great grief and suffering and is nevertheless fleeting and ephemeral, as on Card 3 where the man expresses his love toward his wife only after her death.

7. Picasso's "La Vie"

Reaction Time: 7"   Total Time: 1'22"
Uh, these are two young people that have lived together. And—uh—the mother—the woman had a child and she wanted very much to keep the child. But—uh—they couldn't afford it. Her husband was the painter and she wasn't married to him. And the mother—the son comes and takes the child away. The young girl is quite unhappy [Clears throat].

INQUIRY: [What are the feelings of the people?] Of the older woman? [Both their feelings.] Quite disapproving. She thinks that is—she dislikes the—her son's mistress or whatever it is very intensely. She's more or less taking the child just to get back at the woman. The son is dependent upon his mother for their financial well-being so there's not much he can say to prevent it. And he wants to keep on the good side of his mother. [What will be the outcome?] What? [the outcome?] What was the outcome? Uh—eventually the woman— the young girl will leave him and just continue on in a life of nothingness, because he's just too dependent upon his family. [You mentioned before that her husband was a painter. Then you mentioned that they weren't married.] No, they were living together, but not married.

INTERPRETATION. The most significant aspect of the story is the blocking around "mother," as well as the general disorganization of the story and Mrs. T.'s distractibility. She begins the second sentence with "mother" and changes it to "the woman had a child." In the fourth sentence she starts again with "mother" but shifts to the son, who, rather than the mother, takes the child away. The mother appears to loom very large in Mrs. T.'s fantasy life; she has considerable difficulty in attributing frank negative feelings and thoughts of anger and deprivation to her. The intensity of the relationship with the mother is perhaps best expressed in her defensive maneuvering to make the elderly woman the mother of the man rather than the girl's mother. One wonders whether the depiction of the passive, dependent son is not a condemnation by Mrs. T. of her own husband. Her contradictory statement that he is "her husband" but that they are "not married" also reflects an essential lack of relatedness to the man.

Once again we find a description of utter futility. The girl, after leaving the man, continues in a life of nothingness and despair, and the theme of financial poverty, as in the preceding story, may reflect inner feelings of being destitute and needy as well. Mrs. T. seems to have particular difficulty with the outcome. As in several previous stories, she seems distracted, needing repetition of the inquiry question, and she found it difficult to make up an adequate ending. This too seems to reflect her feeling of emptiness and the lack of a future for her.

It is noteworthy how Mrs. T. keeps returning to the older woman, how she only describes her feelings, and even when specifically urged to talk about the feelings of the young people, she comes back to the older woman. If we go beyond the content of the story and consider its internal structure, Mrs. T.'s emphasis on the maternal figure takes on further meaning. There is in the story a marked degree of unsureness about roles: The woman on the left is alternately referred to as a woman and as a young girl; the mistress is referred to with the impersonal pronoun "it"; and at times it appears unclear whether the young woman or the man's mother is the mother of the child. These lapses and ambiguities in communication point toward confusion in Mrs. T.'s sense of maturity (young girl or woman). They also point to possibly submerged competitive attitudes toward the mother in her child bearing role, and to some lack of differentiation of herself from her mother. Mrs. T.'s unsureness of who is doing what is also mirrored in the girl's passivity in the story.

Another consideration in interpreting this story is that the degree of cognitive disturbance is due to the nudity of the figures and sexual fantasies stimulated by it. This would support notions from the WAIS about Mrs. T.'s repressive orientation.

8. TAT 13 MF—*Man with Arm over Eyes, Woman on Bed*

Reaction Time: 3"   Total Time: 1'27"

Uh, this man is the husband of the woman. She's been very sick for many years and uh—suffering quite bad, in part, you know, terribly. And so he has just killed her—mercy killing, so to speak. And he is quite horrified by what he has done. He doesn't know if it's the right thing or the wrong thing. However, he decided that it is the right thing. And—uh—[sighs] he—no dramatic ending. He just continues to go along his merry way. He's given her an overdose of something, so as to make it look accidental—[sighs]. That's it.

INQUIRY: [When you say he just goes on his merry way—] Well, that's just a phrase. Uh—uh—he continues through his life. I mean, he doesn't jump out a window or anything. He's not sent to prison [sighs]. He just keeps on existing [sighs]. [What do you think he might do?] Might do. Well, he'll probably remarry. You mean at the moment what he might—oh, he'll probably remarry and build a—another life for himself—never, of course, forget his wife—first wife. But I think he'll feel that he did the right thing eventually.

INTERPRETATION. She goes to great lengths to try to minimize and deny the dysphoric—depressive and aggressive—implications of the story. The major expressions of her use of denial are seen in the benevolent quality of the killing, in his somewhat inappropriately "going on his merry way," and in the emphasis on what he does not do as a result of his feelings (e.g., jump out of the window), and what does *not* happen to him (e.g., go to prison). The instability of her use of denial, however, is made apparent by the breakthrough of the horrified feelings which follow his action, by the theme of futility, "He just keeps on existing," which has now appeared several times, and by the inappropriateness and incongruity of the affects in the story (he is horrified but goes on his merry way). The antecedents of her feelings of futility are specified in this story (the second in which one person is responsible for the death of another) as representing guilt and its concomitant self-blame. It seems almost superfluous to point out that in this story another death occurs, which by now is almost commonplace for her TAT. Previously, death was due to violence (auto accident, jumping out of a window, mutual destruction); in this story, however, it is caused by oral means. In questioning why this change has occurred here, serious consideration must be given to the fact that a sexual scene is often depicted in this card. One might speculate that orality and sex are closely intertwined, that is, that sexual activity is accompanied by oral fantasies (being fed and nurtured), and is generally thought of in oral terms, or consists directly of oral activity. We will have to await further data to elaborate on this speculation.

From a structural point of view of particular note is the suggestion of a mild distortion in the perception of the generation of the figures. Usually they are seen as relatively young, but the implication here is that they have been married for many years. It would seem then that she is considering them to be older than they are customarily perceived. This mild misperception is similar to her unsureness on the previous card (#7; Picasso's "La Vie") about her own maturity and about the distinctness of boundaries between generations, thereby suggesting a lack of definition between parental and child roles and a fuzzy and unclear differentiation between parent (mother) and child.

F 1. TAT 12 F—A Young Woman with an Old Woman in the Background

Reaction Time: 4"   Total Time: 1'11"
This is the picture of a woman who all of her life has been a very suspicious, conniving person. She's looking in the mirror. And she sees reflected behind her an image of what she will be as an old woman—still a suspicious, conniving sort of person. And she can't stand the thought that that's what her life will eventually lead her to. And she smashes in the mirror and runs out of the house screaming and goes out of her mind and lives in uh—a—institution for the rest of her life. That's it.

INTERPRETATION. From a perceptual point of view, looking in a mirror and seeing an image reflected behind oneself is peculiar. One would have to see the image *in* the mirror. Thus, we see a disruption in the perceptual process which is more major than the earlier misrecognitions on #7 (La Vie) and #8, but is on a continuum with them. In this case the distortion involves a spatial confusion and may hark back, therefore, to Mrs. T.'s difficulties in spatial orientation on the WAIS. The paranoid content—suspiciousness and conniving—cannot be fully appreciated in this instance unless we also consider that a frank perceptual distortion is evident and therefore that projective trends may reach psychotic proportions. Since the older woman is commonly described as a maternal figure, we can assume that the patient is communicating something about her relationship vis-à-vis this maternal figure. There is the attempt to destroy the ties to a dreaded negative maternal figure by violent means, a process which is seen as resulting in the inevitable destruction of the patient as well.

We may speculate further that she may perceive her illness and hospitalization as a direct consequence of her efforts to separate herself violently from her mother. In that her thinking becomes peculiar on this card, the depth of identification with the mother seems extreme and may reach psychotic proportions.

The feeling of being doomed to become like the maternal figure is of special significance for Mrs. T. since we know that her mother committed suicide. Her need to break the bond with the mother, therefore, becomes even more urgent, in order to free herself from being fated to repeat the mother's suicide.

Over the course of the TAT pictures we are observing increasing signs of disruptions in ego functions, also psychotic trends in Mrs. T.'s thought processes, and the more primitive defenses of projection and denial. Our earlier comments about the degree of good organization of her stories must be reconsidered in light of this shift.

F 2. TAT 3 GF—*Young Woman with One Hand Against a Door, the Other Covering Her Face*

Reaction Time: 3″   Total Time: 53″

This girl has just learned of [sighs] her—the death of her mother. She's grief stricken and happens to feel, uh—[sighs] helpless and hopeless—uh. However, she pulls herself out of th—the grief in time and and continues to make a life of her own.

INQUIRY: [What led up to this?] The—s—death of her mother? Well, she has been with her mother for many years—very close to her. And her mother was uh—uh—died from a sudden heart attack. And she's just heard the news, and it's a complete surprise to her. [And what's going to be the outcome?] Uh—nothing dramatic. She will [sighs] you know, at first shocked and sad, but will learn to live with sadness.

INTERPRETATION. In this story her thought organization improves; while a scene of grief and shock is common on this card, it is not ordinarily seen as involving the death of a mother. It reinforces our speculation about the difficulty Mrs. T. has in separating herself from her mother in order to "make a life on her own." Her belated efforts, following the stormy reaction in F 1 (Young and old woman) to distance herself from her feelings, is evident in her saying, "happens to feel helpless and hopeless—" and in her effort via denial to tone down the degree of despair and hopelessness. Denial in this instance ("nothing dramatic" will occur) neutralizes the feelings, but does not reverse them and make them gay and lively as she did on #8 (13 MF). There is a curious double meaning in the statement: "she pulls herself out of the grief in time." It could mean over a long range of time or possibly before something drastic happens. This drastic result may be either insanity or suicide, both of which have previously been associated with the mother. In line with this, there is blocking in her very first sentence before she describes the cause of her grief and again when asked what led up to it. At that point, she starts to say something other than "death," starting with "s." The likely word being blocked is "suicide."

F 3. TAT 2—*Farm Scene*

Reaction Time: 3″   Total Time: 1′28″
Well, this girl had lived [sighs] all her life in a rural community— a farm. She's quite a talented young girl. She has great possibilities, say, in the field of—oh—art. She feels her life to be restricted by her surroundings [sighs]. As this scene takes place, she has come home from studying—her school. And she is making a decision this moment to leave her home and go into the city and do what she feels she must do—study and make something of herself. She goes into the city, finds herself to be quite lost, quite unhappy, and eventu-

ally returns to her home environment to live a very mediocre life. That's all.

INQUIRY: [When you say mediocre life—] Well, just a very normal kind of role—restricted life where she has no contact with creative arts.

INTERPRETATION. Again there is the theme of an artist who fails; this time he does not attempt suicide or other destructive activity, but his life becomes empty, bland and uninteresting. This story too has a strong depressive quality with the emerging tone that change is not possible, that even when one tries to break away (as she has been trying to on the last several cards) one cannot become independent and separate (probably from mother), and one is doomed to failure. Although there are no psychotic features in this story, the question of leaving home (mother) and returning has to be seen in the light of the earlier suggestions that her thinking can become peculiar about maternal figures and that the relationship may have symbiotic elements (cf. the fluidity about generations).

In many ways this story is akin to the story on Card 1 where the boy hears the music of the violin but is incapable of reproducing it. One has the impression that in order for Mrs. T. to feel alive, to feel real, something exotic or exciting may be necessary. "Normal" for her is equated with restrictiveness, lack of excitement, and mediocrity and is the opposite of being creative and independent. One might speculate therefore that she may feel drawn to behavior that is unconventional, be it in the kinds of friends she chooses, what and how she studies, her sex life, and her relationships with people. However, the content suggests that either alternative—the free creative life or the more mediocre life—offers unpleasant possibilities. She seems consciously aware of the fact that the "artistic" life leaves her feeling lonely and depressed. In view of unconventional strivings represented here it is of interest to recall that in the WAIS she expressed considerable conflict over her unconventional morality.

The entire orientation of this story is in the direction of the past. Her first sentence is "this girl *had* lived," followed by a deep sigh which further emphasizes the involvement in things past and the generally depressive quality of this story.

F 4. TAT 18 GF—A Woman with Hands Around Throat of Another Person on a Stairway

Reaction Time: 10″   Total Time: 1′55″

Uh—these are two sisters who've lived together. They're both spinsters, each one despising the other one, getting on each other's nerves. And, uh—one day one sister goes into a complete rage, cold rage, and strangles her sister. Uh—then she locks her sister's body up in a room and continues to live in the house for many years. Then— the sisters never used to go out. They always had a maid or something that did everything for them. And finally [clears throat] the town thinks something terrible is going on in the house, and they come in and the—the sister who's remaining is completely out of her mind. She goes into the—she had been l-living with this skeleton of her other—her sister and talking with her—the dead body—er— and she's completely, you know, just insane. And they take her away and put her in a sanitarium where she eventually dies. That's it [coughs].

INTERPRETATION. This story in many ways recapitulates the story to Card 5 of the two brothers living together hating each other with the outcome of mutual destruction. There is also considerable similarity to the stories to Cards 1 and F 1 in which the violin and the mirror are smashed in an impulsive angry outburst not unlike the way the sister is killed here. The repetitive connection between death and insanity suggests that this theme represents a fundamental issue for this patient. It seems likely that the dead sister represents the dead mother and that the theme of insanity is an expression of the patient's remorse and guilt in reaction to feelings of having killed her mother. The insanity is related to the fact that the live sister continues to live with the dead sister and to talk with her. The insanity, therefore, reflects the continued presence of the dead person and the inability to separate from her. Thus, this story reiterates Mrs. T.'s difficulties in separating herself from her mother and the mother's still very real presence for her. In light of other *structural* indications of strange thinking about the dead mother, in addition to this content indication, we can infer that Mrs. T. may have experiences in which her mother seems very much with her and alive.

In terms of details of the story a few points are worthy of mention. One is the further intensification of the rage by calling it a "cold rage," which also carries the implication of premeditation or an act that has been carried out with relatively little affect and for which one presumably is more responsible. Another point is that the maid in the story is referred to as "something that did everything for them." The impersonal, mechanical, inhuman quality of this nurturant source is striking, and this is the second use of an impersonal referent for a woman (the other was on Card 7 on which the mistress was called "it"). A third point concerns a slip in the story. Towards the end of the story she mentions that the sister had been living with "this skeleton of her other—her sister—." The fact that this patient has two sets of siblings, full siblings and half siblings, seems to lend additional confusion as to who she is, to whom she is related, and how separate and distinct people can be from one another. An aspect of the story suggests, moreover, that the confused relationship between the siblings may have been heightened by and/or served as a partial displacement of Mrs. T.'s unclear differentiation from her mother. The aspect of the story to which we refer is the description of the two women as sisters and close in age whereas it is most frequent on this card for the two women to be seen as of different generations, usually one as the mother and the other as the daughter. This tendency toward misperceiving generations has already been noted in Cards 7 and 8.

F 5. TAT 7 GF—*Older Woman Sitting Beside a Girl Who Is Holding a Doll in Her Lap*

Reaction Time: 6″   Total Time: 1′35″
This is a very—uh—let's see. In this picture the mother is reading a story to her child. The child has al—[sighs]—ways—the child has always despised her mother—been very cold toward her, is a very independent sort of child. She just sits here, not listening, not caring what her mother is saying. And uh—she is—as the years go on, she gets more abusive and more cold toward her mother. And finally when her mother is a poor, a broken down old woman, she realizes the harm she has brought to her. And so the daughter then tries to make up for all her wrongdoing, but the mother dies before she can succeed in letting her know that—that her daughter really did love her—that's the story.

INQUIRY: [And how does she feel?] She—well, for the rest of her life, she feels like the chance was given her to do some good, but she waited too long, and that never again would she have the opportunity to uh—make a person feel loved when they needed it most. That's it.

INTERPRETATION. It appears that as the TAT proceeds, the stories become more and more self-evident and less effort is made to keep frankly autobiographical material out of her productions. The guilt expressed in this story is very much like the guilt of the man in the graveyard scene who all too late realized what he had done to his wife. The patient's feeling of responsibility for her mother's death comes through quite clearly here. Her comment that "she will never again have the opportunity to make a person feel loved—" is an indication of the feeling of lost opportunity that cannot be repeated and suggests that she has generalized these intense guilt feelings beyond the relationship with the mother, that she now feels incapable of making anyone feel loved. This may explain in part the feelings of inner emptiness and the marked tendency to isolate and ward off affect. This feeling also takes us back to the earlier stories in which feelings of being dammed up and unable to express thoughts and feelings were evident and the strong desire to express them was indicated. Since closeness to maternal figures is desired yet feared, her experienced difficulty in expression may reflect her ambivalence about wanting to be close and feeling guilty for not being close, on the one hand, yet also wanting to separate herself, to be independent and free.

9. TAT 12 M—*Young Man on Couch, Older Man Leaning over Him*

Reaction Time: 8"   Total Time: 1'50"

Uhm—these are two brothers. One brother has been fatally—well not fatally, but very ill [sighs]. And uh—at the moment he's asleep, his other brother comes in. His other brother loves him very much. His other brother comes in and finds his blood brother asleep and uh—is in a w—in effect, has his—hand arranged over the boy's head and is blessing him, praying to God that *his* s—his brother will be made well again. Uh—their brother does get well, goes through the peak of his sickness—saved that very night and is well or on the way to recovery. The next morning the boy who came—his—his brother

feels that he has worked a miracle and goes through life believing
that he has a personal contact with God.

INQUIRY: [How does this affect his future life—the feeling that he has
performed a miracle?] Uh—people think he's a little bit off. And he
himself believes that he is really, you know, one of the chosen people
of God. And he can't understand other people's feelings with him—
toward him when he tries to explain this miracle that he was able
to bring about. He live—he's very—lives a very bewildering life in
which he is easily hurt by other's feelings towards him. [And how
about his brother?] His brother is uh—of course uh—never says anything, but he believes his brother—his own brother to be a little bit
nutty. His brother grows up to be a very average sort of guy. And
he doesn't understand his brother. That's it.

INTERPRETATION. There is a perceptual distortion in this story in
the description of the erect figure as a young man, a brother to the
one who is asleep, as the picture leaves little doubt that this is an
elderly man. The implications of this distortion have been docu-
mented in several places already—the confused sense of generation
and the playing out between siblings of the parent-child relationship. Another lapse in efficient ego organization is evident in the
almost magical equivalence of the moment of falling asleep and
the entrance of the other brother, as if he had an ability to intuit
the precise moment of his brother's falling asleep. The perceptual
misrecognition and the magical sense of timing point toward projective modes of experience and the content—the personal contact
with God and the implied power of the mental processes—elaborates the paranoid and grandiose flavor. Some of the content can
be understood in terms of Mrs. T.'s fundamentalist religious background in which faith healing is not an uncommon practice, but
this consideration does not account for the lapses in ego organization. There is also a good deal of ambiguity about who the brothers
are and how many there are. Twice she brings in the words "other
brother" and once mentions a blood brother. One might consider
that the endless confusion about which brother is which may also
extend to whether it is a brother or sister; (note the beginning of
the word "sister" prior to "brother," indicated by italics in the
story). Certainly the relationship between these figures is quite
confused and chaotic.

The fact that this obviously older man is seen in the role of a brother, doing something as soon as the other brother is asleep, may relate to actual or fantasied incestuous sexual play between the patient and her brother leading to feelings of guilt and/or the feeling of being someone very special. The tenderness in the story "the brother blessing the one that is sick" and "the brother who loves him very much," is not sustained, and seems somewhat formal, but again, warmth is expressed only in negative circumstances, around sickness or death. In the final outcome, one brother becomes "nutty"; the other brother is an "average sort of guy," a synonym that she has used previously for feeling empty and bored.

10. TAT 3 BM—A Figure Seated on the Floor with an Object like a Gun or Knife Nearby

Reaction Time: 8″   Total Time: 41″
This is a young girl who—gone through life—had a hard life, very hard. She's worked all her life. She feels she's getting nowhere, doing nothing, till one day she comes home. She lives by herself, no husband. And she's been putting on—she's a plain girl and she was making her face up and trying to believe that she was pretty. She was used to coming home to her apartment and living a sort of a fantasy of her own where she imagined herself to be the most glamorous of women. However, this day she really sees herself in the mirror, and she just collapses in a heap weeping, bemoaning her fate. And the realization that she'd been living in a dream world in her apartment completely blasted all hopes for her, so she kills herself. That's it.

INTERPRETATION. This story speaks for itself in the directness and openness of the expression of hopelessness and depression. Here, as in the story of the two brothers on Card 5, there is a statement that leads one to think that something positive might happen: "She feels she's getting nowhere, doing nothing, till one day she comes home." But, typical of Mrs. T.'s stories, things only get worse and lead to destruction. The central theme is a confrontation with reality and facing her lack of glamor or a special quality, the message is that without make-believe, fantasy, and illusions, there is nothing left but emptiness and death. This story, therefore, is reminiscent of her story to Card 1 in which the "lovely sounds" exist only in the boy's head, and recognition of the discrepancy between them and reality results in destruction. What one sees here, then, is an open recognition of a collapse of intense efforts at denial without which there is no alternative but to kill herself. The coming home in this story and in the farm scene (F 3) and in several other stories, always represents the realization of inner emptiness and worthlessness and leads to death. This is the second story in which a woman learns important but unbearable truths about herself—first her suspiciousness and conniving (F 1) and here her lack of feminine attractiveness and desirability. The "mirror" emphasis is noteworthy and recalls her visualizing trends on the WAIS. It also recalls the story of Snow White in which a mirror serves as the oracle regarding female beauty.

11. TAT 16—Blank Card

Reaction Time: 8"　　　Total Time: 1'10"

[Laughs.] Uh—[clears throat]. This is a story about a nonentity [laughs]. He goes through life thinking that he is a person. And one day he goes into a carnival and goes to a house of mirrors. And up until this time, he'd never really looked at himself in a mirror. And so he goes into this house of mirrors and keeps looking around, but doesn't see what everybody enjoys so much. I mean, he sees nothing. And then suddenly it dawns on him that there is nothing. He is nothing, and therefore he doesn't exist any longer. And that's the end of the story [laughs]. That's it.

INTERPRETATION. Her response to this card is probably the most poignant expression of her sense of emptiness and reflects, in addition, a feeling that she exists only as a figment of her imagination. Although this seems to imply that her existence is delusional and that her ego identity has collapsed, the organization of the story is intact, she seems to enjoy telling it, and it is a rather imaginative story to this card. This observation is not meant to negate the more ominous aspects of this story which have important ties to earlier stories, namely the terror involved in taking a real look at oneself, the feelings of being nothing and essentially dead, the breakdown of denial and the permeation of depressive affect into fantasies of glamorousness, hearing beautiful sounds, having personal contact with God, and artistic aspirations. But despite indications in other stories of psychotic trends in her thinking, there is evident in this story a certain ability to play with the unrealistic experiences and shift reality around without being disturbed, although at other times she is clearly disturbed by them. And while the theme is not essentially different from other stories, she does make more of this blank card than most patients—a fact which attests to her strong investment in fantasy. It is important, therefore, that we also consider that some of her strong fantasy emphasis has creative features (regression in the service of the ego) as well as more clearly pathological regressive aspects.

Several other implications of this story also deserve comment. That there is a repeated emphasis on the dread of really confronting oneself, taking a good look at oneself without going crazy, committing suicide, or ceasing to exist, in some way undoubtedly reflects her fears of facing herself in therapy and what she will see and do. Also, there is in the story a twisting around of reality, for the house of mirrors reveals a distorted view which the patient here represents as the true, real view. (This may reflect some experience of unsureness about what *is* real.) Since the house of mirrors usually presents, in particular, a distorted—expanded or elongated—body image, this story also implicitly touches on the theme of disturbed body image. Finally, her selection of a man to represent her concerns may express tendencies toward sex role confusion.

TAT Summary

The outstanding features of this relatively monothematic TAT are her pervasive feelings of emptiness, worthlessness, and nothingness that are only flimsily defended against through the mechanisms of minimization and denial. As these defenses readily give way, depressive feelings of being dammed up in her ability to express pressing, ideational, affective, and artistic urges, of being a cruel, untrusting, unloving, and malevolent person appear, and these experiences are often transformed into violent destruction and usually self-destructive activity. This tendency to shift abruptly and violently has to be underscored, for it often follows an implication that unhappy, bland, or hateful situations may change for the better, but they never do. Invariably this extremely mild and tentative optimism is followed by a violent eruption of depressive affect which usually ends in death. At best her efforts at defense seem to *neutralize* feelings and tone them down, but leave her feeling bland, bored, and affectless. Efforts to escape a sense of emptiness take the form of a search for "heightened" experiences, e.g., artistic and possibly unconventional activity, but these too only result in depressive, lonely feelings.

Her present position as assessed by the TAT reveals considerable defensive instability. This is evident in the monothematic depressive emphasis, the absence of scenes of warmth and tenderness, except minimally and fleetingly in relationships that are absorbed in tragedy and poverty, and also evident in a variety of psychotic trends. She is strongly invested in fantasy and in idiosyncratic, unrealistic experiences, some of which have a creative quality but which take her at times to the borderline of psychosis, as we can see in the presence of some peculiar perceptual experiences (more in the structure than in the content, e.g., F 1,) and in numerous mild perceptual misrecognitions and several more major ones. These various lapses in ego organization have a projective, paranoid quality, in that she can misperceive and reorder external stimuli, and they seem to hinge largely around her most focal area of difficulty with the maternal figure. Beyond feelings of guilt concerning her mother's suicide and feelings of having been deficient as a daughter and hence responsible for the suicide, and also beyond a typical adolescent desire to establish her own separateness and uniqueness from parental figures, there are indications in the tests of a more primitive sense of being bound to the mother. She considers herself fated to repeat her life course (suicide and possibly psychosis). There is also an occasional sense of a blurring of boundaries between parent and child (mother and daughter), and this lack of differentiation from the mother dips down into the earliest genetic aspects of a symbiotic mother-child relationship. The mother is still felt to be very real and very present in her life, and a major concern is to separate from her, a process which to her seems inevitably hopeless, leading to her own destruction. At the same time her felt inability to separate from the dead mother is revealed through the continual references to emptiness, to a barren, worthless existence that in fantasy completes her identification with the mother. A similar confused sense of self-differentiation is apparent in her portrayal of sibling relationships.

There is a recurrent theme in these stories of a basic discontinuity between grandiose fantasy and reality and a belief that all illusions are shattered in the process of self-confrontation. These stories are vivid, poignant, and self-revealing. While they are markedly depressive and suggest a serious suicidal potential, they lack the extreme blocking, effortfulness, and energy depletion of many severely depressed persons and point to a strong ideational and active fantasy involvement. There is a press toward communication and a desire for self-confrontation which is viewed with terror and dread, reflecting both a likely desire for and intense fear of the psychotherapeutic process. Because of the pervasiveness of the depression and the fact that an increase in depressive feelings and concerns may push her further toward suicidal acts, therapy with her would have to proceed cautiously in removing the denial, and it would have to be directed toward an increase in her self-esteem and in her ability to differentiate herself successfully from her mother and thereby separate herself. The apparent move toward decreased levels of ego intactness over the course of the TAT cards may also represent a move toward a psychotic position. This too would point the direction of therapy toward ego building with an emphasis on diminishing the worthless and destructive feelings.

REFERENCES

BINET, A., & HENRI, V. La psychologie individuelle. *Année psychol.*, 1895, **2**, 411–465.

BRITTAIN, H. L. A study of imagination. *Ped. Sem.*, 1907, 14, 137–207.

EBBINGHAUS, H. Ueber eine methode zur prüfung geistiger fahigheiten und ihre anwendung bei schulkindern. *Ztschr. Psychol. Physiol. Sinnesorg.*, 1897, 13, 401–459.

FENICHEL, O. The psychoanalytic theory of neurosis. New York: Norton, 1945.

FREEMAN, F. S. *Theory & practice of psychological testing.* (3rd ed.) New York: Holt, Rinehart and Winston, 1962.

FREUD, ANNA *The ego and the mechanisms of defense.* New York: International Universities Press, 1936.

HENRY, W. E. *The analysis of fantasy.* New York: Wiley, 1957.

HOLT, R. R. Formal aspects of the TAT—a neglected resource. *J. proj. Tech.*, 1958, 22, 163–172.

LIBBY, W. The imagination of adolescents. *Amer. J. Psychol.*, 1908, 19, 249–252.

MASSERMAN, J. H., & BALKEN, E. R. The clinical application of fantasy studies. *J. Psychol.*, 1938, 6, 81–88.

MASSERMAN, J. H., & BALKEN, E. R. The psychoanalytic and psychiatric significance of fantasy. *Psychoanal. Rev.*, 1939, 26, 343–379; 535–549.

MORGAN, C. D., & MURRAY, H. A. A method for investigating fantasies: The Thematic Apperception Test. *Arch. neurol. Psychiat.*, 1935, 34, 289–306.

MURRAY, H. A., et al. *Explorations in personality.* New York: Oxford Univer. Press, 1938.

RAPAPORT, D., GILL, M. & SCHAFER, R. *Diagnostic psychological testing.* Chicago: Year Book Medical Publishers, 1945.

SCHAFER, R. How was this story told? *J. proj. Tech.*, 1958, 22, 181–210.

SCHWARTZ, L. A. Social situation pictures in the psychiatric interview. *Amer. J. Orthopsychiat.*, 1932, 2, 124–132.

4

Rorschach Test

In 1857, more than fifty years prior to Hermann Rorschach's experimental approach to the use of ink blots in psychodiagnosis, a book entitled *Kleksographien* was published in Germany. The author of that book, Justinius Kerner, showed that ink blots always assumed unique patterns which could not be duplicated and which often appeared to impress upon the viewer quite idiosyncratic meanings. Kerner, however, did not make the vital connection, made later by Rorschach, that different people perceive ink blots differently and that this may have important implications for personality evaluation. Thus, while Kerner's scientific contribution seems inconsequential it is probable, nonetheless, that Rorschach was acquainted with his kleksographien.

Prior to Rorschach's work, major consideration of the use of ink blots to aid in the diagnosis of personality was first advanced by Binet (1895), the originator of intelligence testing. This exploration by Binet gave impetus to a number of investigations on the use of ink blots in personality diagnosis (Dearborn, 1897; Sharp, 1899; Kirkpatrick, 1900) and in 1910 Whipple produced and published the first standardized set of ink blots. These investigators focused primarily on the content of the inkblots and used the blots as a springboard for free associations. To a lesser extent some interest was also directed to more cognitive and stylistic aspects of personality functioning by studying individual variations in preferences for synthetic or analytic modes of ideational approach. Despite its clear relevance to Rorschach's ideas, however, Ellenberger (1954) believes that it is unlikely that Rorschach was acquainted with this current of scientific interest in inkblots.

As for the direct influences on Rorschach, we know his father was an artist and that Hermann continued this interest. An interesting occurrence in Rorschach's life may also shed some light on his interest in inkblots. In the last two years of secondary school, when pupils were allowed to join student organizations similar to fraternities, Rorschach underwent the initiation rites which included giving the initiate a nickname by which he would then be known by the other student members. Significantly, Rorschach was given the nickname "Klex," the translation of which is "inkblot," and which may have already reflected some interest on Rorschach's part in inkblots and may have stimulated him further in this direction. However tempting this speculation, it is not certain that this was why Rorschach was given his nickname, for Rorschach might have been named after Kleckzel, a hero in a humorous story by one of his favorite authors. And since *klecksen* in colloquial German also means *daubing* and *Kleckzerei* and *Kleckse* refer to mediocre painting, it may be that Rorschach's nickname might merely have reflected an expectation that he would become a painter like his father. With regard to the latter possibility Ellenberger (1954) also reports that at about this time Rorschach was unsure whether to pursue a career in art or in the natural sciences.

We also know that around 1911 Hermann Rorschach engaged in a series of preliminary experiments with inkblots with a friend, and that these experiments consisted of using the inkblots like a word association test to stimulate access to the content of fantasy. These experiments, however, seem to have ceased and to have been resumed only after a long period of preoccupation with Swiss religious sects. His interest was rearoused in 1917 as a result of the dissertation of Sgymon Hens in which he described the use of an inkblot test. Rorschach's renewed exploration of inkblots culminated a little over three years later in the publication of *Psychodiagnostik*.

He tried thousands of different blots, finally selecting 15, which were reduced to 10 on the advice of his publisher. To these cards, he collected responses from 405 subjects, over 100 of whom were not patients. The following excerpt from his introduction to the English edition (Rorschach, 1942) gives a picture of the approach he took to this work:

> . . . It must be pointed out that all of the results are predominantly empirical. The questions which gave rise to the original experiments of this sort were of a different type from those which slowly developed as the work progressed. The conclusions drawn, therefore, are to be regarded more as observations than as theoretical deductions. The theoretical foundation for the experiment is, for the most part, still quite incomplete. . . .

In describing the use of the test, Rorschach emphasized the formal quality of the response process, "the pattern of perceptive process," rather than content which had been emphasized prior to his work and which in more recent times again appears to have become a major focus of Rorschach interpretation. He states in the translated version (1942, p. 16): "The interpretation of chance forms falls in the field of perception and apperception rather than imagination." In setting forth the limitations of an approach centered on the content of the material the subject produces, he pointed out (1942, p. 123): "The test cannot be considered as a means of delving into the unconscious. At best it is far inferior to the other more profound psychological methods such as dream interpretation and association experiments."

Shortly after the publication of his book, he made it clear to his colleagues that he had progressed well beyond what he had written and already considered his first work to be obsolete. It might be added that the publication of *Psychodiagnostik* had been an almost total failure. The sole Swiss psychiatric journal did not review it and the few foreign reviews that appeared either contained very brief summaries or were sharply critical. Among these was that of William Stern the German psychologist who attacked the test on the basis that no instrument could comprehend the human personality; he found fault with the methodology, the statistics, and with Rorschach's interpretations. On April 2, 1922, one year after the publication of his book, Rorschach died suddenly and unexpectedly of severe diffuse peritonitis at the age of 37.

The new test was brought to the United States by Levy, but it was not well received. Academic psychologists considered it unscientific; psychiatrists thought it too cumbersome and time consuming. Despite these objections, the use of the test grew rapidly with a multitude of modifications in procedure, scoring, and interpretation. The concern with the amount of time required for administration, scoring, and interpretation increased under the stress of World War II and the period leading up to it, and efforts were extended to harness the power of this test for large scale evaluation. It was thought that such a procedure could work effectively in selecting officers and men for particularly hazardous duty and in weeding out the unstable or unfit.

Thus, in 1941, Harrower-Erickson introduced a procedure for the Rorschach using projected slides of the cards which permitted up to 40 or 50 subjects to be tested simultaneously by their writing down responses to each card. In the same year, Munroe (1941) brought out a large-group Rorschach technique that required a minimum amount of evaluation time. This technique did not presume to have the same depth as the individually administered Rorschach; it was called an "inspection" technique and was directed primarily at spotting gross patterns of adjustment or maladjustment.

Using a different approach, Harrower-Erickson devised a multiple choice Rorschach (1943) which provided the subjects with a list of responses from which they had to choose the best one. Again, a projector was used for presenting the Rorschach slides. Later, in 1945, Eysenck proposed that this method be modified by having responses for each card ranked according to their prominence in the subject's experience.

None of these procedures, however, have proved to have a major impact in clinical work, and at present, at a time when the Rorschach test has never been more widely used for individual evaluation, reports of the group method of Rorschach testing are infrequent. There are currently simpler methods for rapid but gross personality and diagnostic screening than the Rorschach, which is an instrument par excellence, for a sensitive and detailed exposition of personality features.

In terms of its current use, one major controversy about the Rorschach Test revolves around the role of theory in the interpretation of its findings. Piotrowski (1957), for example, takes the position that no particular theoretical framework is required to interpret the Rorschach. Schafer (1954), on the other hand, states in his preface that, "No matter how helpful a clinical tool it may be, the psychological test cannot do its own thinking. What it accomplishes depends upon the thinking that guides its application." It is our position as well, that a psychological test cannot do its own thinking, and we would add that the use of the Rorschach can be taught most effectively within a theoretical framework which emphasizes the interrelationships among modes of cognition-perception and personality organization.

In order to reach such an understanding of psychological processes we have, in previous chapters, emphasized the formal aspects of test data as well as the content. Formal aspects of the Rorschach are equally important but have been increasingly overlooked. For psychological structure, as well as content of responses, affective reactions associated with the responses, and the subject's general test-taking attitude all represent important dimensions which must be considered if one is to make a comprehensive interpretation of the Rorschach. From the structural point of view, the Rorschach can be looked upon as an experimental procedure with a vast array of perceptual modalities that are available to the subject. The dimensions he uses in his response, be it the location on the blot, the color, the shading, the formal properties of the card, or the accuracy of his perception, all are hypothesized to represent generalized modes of response.

Despite the fact that the Rorschach test is the most widely used of any clinical diagnostic instrument, there is at present considerable doubt about its validity, especially about many of the structural aspects of the test. One must, however, consider in detail the types of studies which have cast most doubt on the Rorschach's validity. These studies fall into three general categories: studies in which nosological groups have served as the validating criteria; prediction studies; and studies which have employed experimental criteria.

In reviewing Rorschach research literature, the results are most disheartening in investigations in which nosological categories and clinical groups are used as validating criteria and also in those in which the Rorschach is used as an instrument of prediction of overt behavior. One may, however, seriously question whether nosological categories may be used as validating criteria since they lack clear, precise, and generally accepted definitions. There is little agreement, for instance, as to what specifically constitutes the formal diagnostic subdivisions of schizophrenia; even the general term *schizophrenia* is used in a variety of ways. Sometimes its diagnosis is primarily based on overt behavioral symptoms or on the presence of a thought disorder; sometimes it is based on a blending of the two. Rarely is it specified how the diagnosis is made. In addition, diagnostic evaluations in many clinical settings are done on admission before there has been much direct observation of the patient, and the diagnosis, in addition, is frequently made by a relatively inexperienced clinician. There is little wonder that research on the Rorschach using this type of approach turns out to be relatively fruitless (Blatt & Allison, 1967).

Another research approach used to validate the Rorschach has been through prediction studies. For example, one might, on the basis of the Rorschach, attempt to predict successful and unsuccessful discharges from state hospitals, or to differentiate the successful versus the unsuccessful parolee from jail, or to evaluate the probability of academic success for individual members of a group equated for intelligence. Such studies disregard the fact that the Rorschach can be used to gain a picture of intrapsychic balance and of internal organization, but there is no way in which one can assess via the Rorschach in what type of environment or under what social pressures a particular patient, parolee, or student will find himself. A schizophrenic may make a successful adjustment upon discharge from a state hospital if his family situation is supportive, benign, and places few excessive demands upon him. The same patient in a more pressured environmental situation may need to return to the hospital in a short time. In making any prediction, therefore, one must not only assess intrapsychic balance and organization, but one must also specify the environmental resources, strains and pressures upon the individual and how these environmental presses would interact with the particular psychological organization (Engel & Blatt, 1964). For further discussion of the importance of the differentiation between assessment *of* and assessment *for*, see Prelinger & Zimet (1964).

A third type of study which has been conducted with the Rorschach has used experimental criteria in an attempt to examine some of the underlying assumptions of Rorschach determinants. In much of this research the experimental criteria are clearly chosen and defined in terms of particular psychological processes that enter into the determinant. Interestingly, it is in this series of studies that one finds more significant results with the Rorschach. For instance, widely contradictory findings have been found in numerous research studies which have tested a hypothesized positive correlation between W responses and intelligence by simply correlating the number or percentage of all W-scores with IQ. When the quality, however, of the W responses and the processes involved were taken into consideration, a significant correlation was found between problem solving efficiency on a task involving analytic and synthetic abilities and the number and percentage of W responses of a complex and accurate nature (Blatt & Allison, 1963).

It seems that much of the research that uses nosological categories or attempts to predict behavior in complex social situations fails because the criteria are amorphous or because the demands placed upon the test are unrealistic. When the situational demands are clearly delineated and the criteria are specified and valid, there is reason to believe that the perceptual-cognitive determinants of the Rorschach will be found to be meaningful.

Another major methodological issue in research with the Rorschach seems to be the use of Rorschach dimensions as simple signs without further differentiation and refinements. Rorschach scoring categories are only gross differentiations and, as the research on the W response, for example, indicates (Blatt & Allison, 1963), the subtle yet vital differentiations made by the clinician must be included if the Rorschach is to be useful in research. As suggested by research with the Holt scoring system for the Rorschach (Holt & Havel, 1960), it may be premature to arrive at decisions regarding the validity of many aspects of the Rorschach test.

ADMINISTRATION

Since the subject will have been told initially about the testing in general, no further introduction to the Rorschach is required. The test should be started by taking out Card I and telling the subject: "I would like you to look at each card and tell me what it looks like, what it could be." Further questioning by the subject as to how he should proceed should be responded with "It's up to you," unless he is acutely anxious, at which time reassurance or further clarification may be necessary. It is preferable to put the card on the desk in front of the subject rather than to hand it to him since it will be of significance how he deals with it, i.e., whether he picks it up, turns it, etc. If he reaches for it at the time of presentation, it would, of course, be handed to him. On taking the card back, it should be placed face down where the subject cannot reach it.

Any requests by the examiner of the subject should be stated directly without leaving the subject an opening to respond negatively. For example, requests should be in terms of: "I would like you to . . ." or "I want you to . . ." rather than, "Can you . . . ?" or "Would you . . . ?"

Timing

Two time measures are taken, the first is the time that lapses between the initial exposure to the card and the subject's first scorable response. The second is taken when the subject is finished with the card. It is a good idea to leave the card several seconds longer before removing it if the subject seems hesitant. That is, unless he is highly productive, in which case an effort should be made, tactfully, to limit the number of responses to about ten per card by intervening and saying, "That's enough on this one."

We encourage subjects to look at the card longer if they want to give it up before 1½ minutes unless they have already given two responses. This is not because lots of responses are expected, but rather, in order to see the degree of flexibility and ability to shift. If the subject seems upset because he cannot give responses, he should be told that it is not important that he see more things, that we just want to be sure he has seen what he can and whether anything else occurs if he looks harder. We usually tell subjects, "Take your time, maybe something else will occur to you," if they want to give up the card quickly.

Inquiry

Although it is more common practice to conduct the inquiry after responses to all the ten cards have been gathered (e.g., Beck,

1944; Klopfer, 1942), we follow Rapaport's modification of administration by conducting the inquiry after each card and while the card is out of view. The procedure allows for a minimum of secondary elaboration by eliminating the possibility that a second view of the card will influence one's conception of the role of the various determinants, and it also circumvents the additional secondary elaboration which would result after intervening cards and responses. Since we wish to establish which determinants resulted in the formation of the particular response, we prefer to eliminate secondary elaboration as much as possible by not having the card present at the time of inquiry and not having other cards intervene before inquiry is done. An administration conducted after all the cards are given places too much emphasis on memory.

The procedure of inquiry after each card has the effect of making clear early our intentions to have subjects report what they see and to account for the derivation of their percepts. Although there is no carefully collected data as to the effects of varying procedures, this one may reduce the overall number of responses. It also may foster efforts at intact rational functioning since subjects are aware while responding that they will have to indicate the derivation and location of their responses. The importance of the immediacy of inquiry, however, overshadows these possible effects which are consistent for all subjects. It is crucial when using this method of administration to avoid biasing the subject's approach to successive responses and cards by alerting him to specific determinants. Therefore, inquiry should be kept to a minimum and leading questions avoided. The standard questions asked are, "What made it look like that?" following which, "Was there anything else that made it look like that?" If more information is sought, e.g., about the sex of figures when it is left unspecified, sex should not be inquired about directly, but rather, the subject should be asked to describe the figures or to indicate if there was anything in particular he noticed about them. If few responses are being given and are referred to in vague general terms, e.g., "animals," and if the two preceding questions elicit little information, then the subject may be asked if it looked like any particular kind of animal. Another lack of clarity that needs inquiry concerns responses in which the subject states that the color or the shape played a role in the formation of the response, e.g., sometimes color is referred to when shading is meant. If the subject says, "It looked like blood because of the shape," one might ask, "What about the shape made it look like that?" Subjects are never asked directly whether the color, shading, etc., of the cards had anything to do with the formation of their responses unless they have spontaneously referred to the determinant during the particular response.

Of particular importance is inquiry into unusual or interesting verbalizations and affect. Again, no leading questions are asked, but rather, "What did you mean by . . . ?", "I didn't quite understand what you meant when you said. . . ." The point is to indicate a lack of understanding and a desire to know more about what the subject has said. In such inquiry, as in testing and interview situations generally, it is best not to suggest alternatives about what is meant, but to indicate interest in having the subject supply the clarification. When a subject modifies a popular percept, the inquiry should be focused on the modification. For instance, to "A messed up bat," on Card I, one would ask, "What made it look 'messed up'?" and not, "What made it look like a messed up bat?" This avoids a too comprehensive inquiry and directs interest toward the unusual aspect of the response.

As for locations, these often become evident during the giving of the response or during the inquiry. If not, the card can be brought out and the subject asked to quickly point out the area, after which the card is immediately taken away.

Particularly direct questions, even after the Rorschach is completed (testing of limits), is not recommended if there is a likelihood of retesting. If few responses are given, however, one may, after all ten cards have been administered, communicate to the subject the content of the popular responses and have him locate them on the card.

THE RESPONSE PROCESS

In analyzing Rorschach test responses one makes the assumption that an individual's reaction to the blots represents a perceptual organizing process very much like the type of perceptual responses seen in everyday life. The unstructured nature of the Rorschach blots, however, makes well learned, conventional, familiar ways of reacting more difficult. In its novelty, ambiguity and relative lack of clear structure, the Rorschach brings the usually automatic and organizing perceptual processes into the forefront, thereby allowing the clinician to examine in detail the individual's adaptive modes and endeavors. Although there is no pure perceptual process independent of the organism's needs, interests, fantasies, and specific memories, one can nonetheless separate out perceptual and associative processes involved in responding to the blots (Rapaport et al., 1945). The perceptual features of the inkblots serve in a vague way as the springboard for a more elaborative associational process. The associations are then more carefully checked against the perceptual qualities of the inkblots and this in turn may lead to further articulation of the perceptual qualities, e.g., by focusing on particular areas of the cards and on particular determinants. In other words, in answering "What does this look like?" the subject must draw upon internal ideas and images in attempting to relate the Rorschach blot to particular memories of things seen, experienced or thought of in the past. The inkblot, therefore, elicits an associational process following which the associations are matched against the characteristics of the cards. With adequate responses, there is a satisfactory blending of the perceptual organizing pattern with the associative process; perception and association then are mutually dependent upon each other and interweave in a meaningful and realistic way to produce a response which matches the blot but also possesses elaborative enrichment (Rapaport et al., 1945). When either the associational or the perceptual process functions in isolation without this essential integration, however, responses are poorly conceived, badly articulated, diffuse, or distorted. Too much adherence to perceptual reality limits responses to the concrete, "inkblot" such as color naming and description; too much adherence to the associational process without depending for validation on perceptual reality will result in personalized elaborations of poor formal accuracy and in idiosyncratic verbalization. Thus, the degree of meshing of perceptual and associative processes in the responses enables one to appraise the freedom, flexibility, and reality orientation of subjects' thinking.

RORSCHACH TEST SCORES

The separate scores in a Rorschach scoring summary represent particular psychological functions of the individual. Since these functions are interrelated and are in constant interplay in the individual's adaptive endeavors, one must specify not only the particular psychological functions represented by the individual's scores, but also how these scores interrelate and balance each other. We can begin our understanding of Rorschach scores by specifying the separate scores and the functions they reflect. There are five broad categories in which most Rorschach scores fit: 1) the location of the response, 2) the level of accuracy of the percept, 3) the determinants used in forming the response, 4) the content, including the degree of conventionality of the response, and 5) qualitative features of the verbalizations and percepts. One also assesses the number of responses and the reaction time of each response, and notes the cards to which no responses are forthcoming. The first three of the above categories (location, accuracy, determinants) represent the formal characteristics of a record. They delineate the organization of the psychological functions and they represent an enduring pattern of perceptual organization and associative processes. These generally are not very susceptible to conscious censorship and distortion but represent, rather, automatic and spontaneous response processes. Although a body of research has demonstrated that the "set" of a subject, how he approaches testing and his specific preoccupations at the time of testing plus the personality of the tester may affect test scores, there is no evidence that such situational factors can significantly alter the subject's basic personality predispositions (e.g. Sarason, 1954). These situational factors may vary the intensity of the personality predispositions but are not likely to distort them in any essential way. The research on cognitive styles increasingly has pointed up the role of relatively stable ego functions which cut across various situations, lend consistency and regularity to personality functioning and free it from continual dominance by situational presses.

Number of Responses

The overall number of responses is traditionally viewed as representing the degree of quantitative ideational productivity. A high number of responses is associated with higher intellectual levels and a broader range of interests. A low number of responses can stem from a low intellectual level, depressive retardation, a meticulous striving for few but "perfect" responses, and from inhibition (Rapaport et al., 1945). The sheer number of responses, however, does not necessarily mean that the range of interests is wide or that thinking is flexible and rich. A plodding, unimaginative approach geared to the production of relatively easily seen details and banal reworkings of a few themes can produce many responses and may reflect a person who "produces" but without richness or interest. An average sized record contains about 25 responses.

Reaction Time

We assess both the time between presentation of the card and the first response and also the total time spent with each card. Reaction time is a function of factors in the subject and in the cards as well; some cards, such as IX, are more complex and harder to supply responses for. Ideational retardation (in depressives), doubt, striving for perfect responses, an influx of simultaneously experienced ideas, blocking to specific cards (e.g., the colored cards or those heavily shaded)—all tend to increase the initial reaction time (Rapaport et al., 1945). Very quick initial reaction times are obtained from unreflective, impulsive people and from people who tend to give popular responses either solely or initially before moving on to more complex responses.

The amount of time spent on each card is confounded by the fact that we encourage more than one response; therefore, the time at which the subject is willing to stop is recorded in addition to the total time actually spent with the card. This enables us to gauge the amount of effort and energy that the subject is willing to expend on the task and generally this measure will be closely related to the number of responses. It is on this measure that the striving for few but perfect responses is often apparent, for few responses will be eked out over a rather long period of time. Since some people sit with the card without trying to see anything in it, any use of this measure must also include observations of the subject's behavior.

Card Failures

The subject's failure to produce any responses to one or more cards may be due to inhibition, guardedness, or blocking. Where ideational activity is weak, as in depressives, card rejections occur, but they may also occur in guarded paranoid subjects. Often specific cards are difficult for some people, e.g., the bright colors of II, the shading and darkness of IV, VI, and sometimes VII. Card IX often produces card failures because of its greater complexity. Or specific features of the cards, e.g., the sexual implications of Card VI, can result in blocking and failure to respond on the part of repressive people.

LOCATION

The area chosen for the response indicates the degree to which the perceptual organization is geared to relatively large or small details, the extent to which complexity is emphasized, and the degree to which the perceptual impressions remain relatively global and amorphous or become well articulated. It indicates the degree to which relatively subtle and small details are used either in their own right or as the basis for fuller and more elaborated concepts. Location scores reflect an individual's willingness or reluctance to integrate the things around him. Straining for a complex integration can frequently be seen when the subject states that he cannot give a response which encompasses the whole card. He is either unable to produce a response which is a smooth, spontaneous integration of diverse elements, or he has little predilection to do so, or he strives to do so but is unsuccessful. Location scores indicate the degree to which the individual is willing to break the blots into component parts and to work with each of these separately or the extent to which he is willing to cling to the entire blot even if it means giving a relatively vague response. These formal aspects of location choice are similar to and reflect the kind of response a person might give in everyday life when confronted with a task of relatively large scope. For instance, a person may only be able to cope successfully with a situation which necessitates a clear overview. Another person may, upon surveying the situation, decide that integration is too difficult and feel confident in tackling only part of the job, or if he does not possess the ability to see the situation in larger terms, he may persist in working on the whole thing even though his efforts are poorly organized, unproductive, and relatively unsuccessful.

The major location scores are W, D, Dd, Dr, S, DW, and Do. These represent responses to the whole blot (W), to a fairly prominent part of the blot (D), or to a very small (Dd) or unusual (Dr) part of the blot, to the white space (S), to the entire blot on the basis of a single detail (DW) or to an isolated aspect of a usually more complete response (Do). Well organized and integrated Rorschach protocols show an overall balance with respect to the percentage of each of these kinds of responses within the total number of responses. D responses are most frequent and are followed by W, Dd and Dr, S, DW, and Do. In a highly organized record, the sequence of responses on any one card tends to proceed from whole to large detail to small detail. But there is a wide range of possibilities of approach and it is of value to establish for each subject his preferred mode and the situations in which he may alter it. For example, a person may shift his style of approach when highly anxious from a more general integrative one to a more limited, curtailed, narrower one. Or complex abstractions may be replaced by labored and forced integrations under strong affective arousal. The possibilities are limitless and have to be ascertained for each subject. One can in this regard, also attend to the specific area of the card to which the subject responds. Does he, for example, typically work from the top down (which may have implications of focusing initially on the higher level, more cerebral functions); does he respond to or avoid areas with specific properties such as color or sexual suggestiveness; does he respond to inner portions first and work his way outward, or does he move from the periphery to the center? Such questions often yield important insights into personality organization.

Location Score W

A variety of meanings can be attributed to this location score depending, to a large extent, on which cards the W responses are given. A W response may reflect a vague and effortless approach to the card or a highly synthesized and integrated activity. This difference is most clearly seen between Cards I or V, which readily elicit easy Ws, and Cards VIII, IX, and X, where giving a W response requires somewhat more effort (Wishner, 1948). An overabundance of W in a record reflects different psychological conditions depending on the context of the responses. For instance, in a relatively brief record it may be further indication of an uncomplicated and simpleminded view of life and the world (as in mental defectives), whereas a great many Ws in a moderately long or very long record may represent overinclusiveness, grandiosity, and a striving for unification representative of a kind of "oceanic" feeling. No Ws, or too few Ws, of course, must also be seen within the context of the rest of the record. In a short record, few Ws may simply point to a mild constriction; in a long record, the complete absence of Ws may indicate pathology of thinking since many W responses are very obvious and are frequently given in Rorschach records.

W responses typically are said to reflect integrative abilities and the capacity for abstraction and generalization. This is true, however, only when the level of complexity of the Ws is considered and not their sheer quantity. Some W responses may be simple and obvious, some diffuse and poorly conceived, and others complex and imaginative. The interpretation of Ws in a record, therefore, depends upon their qualitative features which means their level of complexity and their accuracy of form level. In an average-sized record, one would expect approximately one-third of the responses to be W responses and certainly a fair segment of this one-third to be at the higher levels of form accuracy. When this is the case, one can assume a concordance between intellectual capacity and actual functioning. A depletion in the amount of W or level of W can imply interference with intellectual efficiency as can an overabundance of Ws. Particularly when an excessive number of Ws of great complexity are evident, a tendency towards higher levels of abstract functioning is indicated and grandiosity in the thought process can be considered. In evaluating the percentage of W, it is important to take into account which location categories suffer when W is the predominant dimension of the record or which categories take the place of W when it is greatly diminished.

Location Score D

The usual expectation for the number of D responses in a record is around 50 percent and the percentage of D above that level is likely to reflect conventionality, piecemeal, undifferentiated, and unintegrated thought processes and perceptions, and, perhaps, a practical and conservative approach to life. A person of relatively low intelligence with basically unimpaired functioning, is likely to produce many Ds at the expense of both W, Dd, and Dr. In essence, a response to the D category represents a perception of and reaction to a large portion of the blot which is relatively undifferentiated and is usually, as is a simple *W*, among the more easily seen percepts in the record.

As with *W* responses, one must assess the level of complexity of *D* responses and the accuracy with which they are perceived in order to interpret their significance in terms of cognitive modes of functioning and general patterns of thought.

Location Score Dd

The *Dd* score is assigned to responses using a tiny detail of the blot, and should comprise (with *Dr*s) about ten per cent of the total number of responses. Characteristically, *Dd* does not indicate unusual or atypical small detail, but reflects the patient's attention to minute areas of the blot. Such an orientation is most frequently associated with the kind of precision, priggishness, and constriction attributed to the compulsive character.

Location Score Dr

The *Dr* score is assigned to responses when rare or unusual detail is chosen; the detail does not necessarily have to be small in size. In other words, the gross configuration of the blot itself does not suggest a particular percept, and the idiosyncratic division and the percept seem, in a way, to be arbitrarily drawn out of the blot.

Although a rare detail represents unconventional thinking, such responses can be accurately perceived and well-justified. Hence, the *Dr* response indicates a tendency to view the world in unique and unusual ways which can be either disruptive or creative, depending on the form elements of the percept. The normal record is likely to have about 10 percent of *Dr* (including *Dd*) responses. If the percentage rises above 15 to 20, strong obsessive features must be considered since the kind of intellectual squeezing-out quality that goes into the production of a large number of these responses is characteristic of obsessive personalities. If the percentage goes above 20, the possibility of paranoid thinking is also likely, i.e., a tendency to focus one's search for meaning in unusual and unexpected places.

Location Score S

White space responses are those which are based entirely or in part on background rather than on foreground blot elements, e.g., on Card I seeing the upper inner spaces as ghostlike figures merits a pure S score and seeing the same spaces as the hollowed eyes of a mask merits a primary whole response score and a secondary space score (Ws). More than one or two white space responses in a record, or more than about 5 percent, is considered evidence of an oppositional tendency and as the number of white space responses increases, the severity of the negativism and indirect resistance also increases. The rationale for this interpretation of white space responses stems from the idea that the subject is being asked to respond to the blots, and in using white space, he is responding to the nonblot portion of the card. This figure-ground reversal is rarely a conscious maneuver on the subject's part and most often indicates passive aggressive trends or other expressions of indirect hostility.

The tendency to fill in details and to use, in a sense, a blank screen as the stimulus for a perception of an object, represents, like the *Dr* response, unconventional thinking since it reveals an inverted or reverse type of thinking. Again, such thinking may be indicative of originality of thought or imaginativeness, or may suggest a negativistic orientation and, in extreme cases, may suggest delusional thinking. This is because an affinity for the white space response suggests a tendency to see something where nothing exists. When delusional thinking is present, however, signs of poor ego functioning will also emerge in other aspects of the Rorschach protocol. Attention to small white spaces has the interpretive implications of both white space and small details combined.

Location Score DW   *Confab*

The *DW* response is one that is produced by reasoning from part of the blot to a response which encompasses the whole blot, e.g., seeing the whole of Card VI as a cat only because of whiskers at the top, or calling Card II a woman because there is a vagina in the lower red area. In other words, in producing the *DW*, the subject uses a part of the blot in an expansive, vague way with little reality justification. Interpretively, the *DW* is associated with impulsivity; it is characteristic of the person who jumps to conclusions or acts impulsively. Therefore, if the final conclusion (the whole response) is purely arbitrary in quality the thinking and action it reflects are bound to be especially unrealistic (e.g., an arbitrary *DW* response involving seeing a woman on Card II as opposed to seeing the popular bat on Card I). As with other location categories, the frequency of *DW* responses, as well as their balance with other scores, is important in determining their significance. A note of caution about the *DW* responses: the record must be scored very carefully since it is easy to overscore *DW*. Often what seems like a *DW* response is simply the result of an inadequate inquiry. It is not rare for a subject to respond to a highlight or a critical detail of the blot and settle for that as the primary determinant in his response, while, in fact, he could well elaborate other details if he were simply asked if anything else about the card made it look like his percept. *DW* should only be scored when it is clear that the subject has simply embellished the rest of the response without considering its other features.

Location Score Do

Another notation with usually pathological implications is the oligophrenic response (*Do*). This response occurs to an area which is frequently seen as part of a much larger and complete percept. For example, on Card III, seeing only the head of the popular full figures is a typical *Do* response. This response indicates an inhibition, narrowing, and a constriction of thought processes; it represents a fragmentation of perception and an inability to extend one's thinking in an appropriate and meaningful way. *Do* responses are frequently seen in mental retardates and in subjects marked by constriction and by an interference with intellectual processes that produces fragmentation, e.g., depressives, organics, and some psychotics (Rapaport et al., 1945).

Ideally, a Rorschach record should be relatively free of any *DW* or *Do* tendencies.

Position Response (Po)

Although this is a most unusual type of response it needs to be listed. The *Po* response is determined primarily by the position; at times it may be exclusively by position. For instance, in Card IV in the upper right-hand quadrant the patient gives the response "heart." In the inquiry he indicates that the heart would be located in that area, but there was nothing in the blot to resemble a heart (*Dr Po At*). A line (not visible) around the center of IX is the equator, "that is where the equator would be in a map of the world" (*Dr Po Geog*). Other *Po* responses may include an additional determinant. For instance, if the patient giving the heart response had indicated that this was a devil and thus had a black heart, it would have been scored: *Dr PoC' At.*

Po responses are given almost exclusively by schizophrenics whose thought processes are circumstantial rather than based on reality, secondary process elements.

DETERMINANTS

Determinant scores indicate the extent to which form, movement, color or shading or any combination of these enter into the formation of the response. The determinant scores indicate which characteristics of the blot are responded to and the intensity of their impact. Determinants frequently serve as the subject's justification for his responses since the perceptual qualities of the inkblot tend to regulate the content or the associations which are stimulated.

Form and Form Level (F)

The use of the form determinant represents a basic but advanced aspect of ego development insofar as it demonstrates that perception is following along the lines of external reality rather than being dominated by diffuseness, physiognomic qualities, and non-logical considerations. A reliance on form by itself, solely on the outline of a percept, however, ignores any attempt to differentiate other qualities of the percept. Such an over-emphasis on form by itself reflects a factual, literal approach to one's experience, an over investment in overt and direct cues rather than in subtle differentiations and variations of internal characteristics as in an integrated use of form, shading, and color. As Rapaport et al. (1945, p. 189) states, form responses are an attempt to be "objective." They represent the processes of formal reasoning which attempt to pursue their course without anxiety or emotions interrupting or disrupting them. A high percentage of responses based on pure form, therefore, points to a banal, simple and relatively affectless way of dealing with the world and is often indicative of a "colorless" personality. The inability to move beyond the form percept, however, can also be representative of low intelligence (e.g., mental defectives) or of a depressive inability to muster up the energy to respond to complex aspects of the blots as well as an obsessive compulsive need for formal, affectless accuracy. The nuances and

F.
F emphasized responses) emphasis in
formal
intellectual
control

special sensitivities which enrich one's life experience are particularly lacking in a test record which is primarily form (F) centered.[1]

There is another class of responses which, although they may combine various determinants, are characterized predominantly by an emphasis on form. Included are those responses scored M, FM, FC, F/C, FCh, $F(C)$, and FC' which, in addition to pure F, make up the extended F responses. Both the pure $F\%$ (the percentage of the total number of responses scored pure F) and the extended $F\%$ (the percentage of all form dominant responses) serve to assess the emphasis on formal intellectual control. The extended $F\%$ may often demonstrate a strong striving for intellectual control that is not apparent in the pure $F\%$ alone (e.g., in a test record with a low or moderate pure $F\%$ but with an especially high extended $F\%$).

A pure or extended $F\%$ above 90 is high and indicates a lack of flexibility and freedom to let down one's hair and respond spontaneously and freely. However, a lesser degree of rigidity and lack of spontaneity is suggested in a record with a moderate or low pure $F\%$ and a high extended $F\%$ than in one in which both pure and extended $F\%$ are high. In such a context the extended $F\%$ points up a striving for control and containment that is not evident in the pure $F\%$.[2]

When a low $F\%$ is combined with a low extended $F\%$, an inability to modulate one's experience by intellectual controls is indicated; the two together reflect marked impulsivity, dominance by affective experience and a lack of adherence to cultural pressures for logical thinking.

Accuracy of Response ($+$, $-$)

Form level is a measure of how accurately or inaccurately, how precisely or vaguely the form of a response has been conceived.

---

[1] Of course the quality of inquiry is relevant since it is important to differentiate those responses which are truly form dominant from those which receive a form score by default. Form is scored by default if the person simply says that it is a bat because it looks like a bat; he may lack the facility with language to articulate other features and the psychologist may simply assume that form is dominant even though the statement "it looks like a bat" gives no real information about the determinants (Blatt, Engel, & Mirmow, 1961).

[2] Of course since the extended $F\%$ includes pure F responses a high pure $F\%$ is always accompanied by a high extended $F\%$.

It reveals the degree to which the characteristics of the card blend with the possibilities offered by the associative processes. Form level is determined by the frequency of occurrence of the response and by the tester's judgment and clinical experience. It is not within the scope of this book to present lists of form level scoring. The reader is referred to Beck (Vol. I, 1944), Hertz (1951), Klopfer (1942), Mayman (1960), and Rapaport et al. (1945) for the various plus and minus form responses to locations on all the cards. We follow Rapaport's recommendations to score on a four point scale ranging from $F+$, for an accurately perceived and well-articulated response, to $F-$, for a distortion of the formal attributes of the blot. The midpoints on the scale are $F\pm$ for responses which are not quite adequate $F+$ responses and have a minus element and $F\mp$ for responses which are predominantly $F-$ but not quite as poor as $F-$ responses. All pure form (F) and form dominant $(M, FC, FCh, F(C), FC')$ responses are scored in this manner and the percentage of pure F responses that are $+$ and $\pm$ $(F + \%)$ is computed as is the percentage of $+$ and $\pm$ form dominant responses (*extended F + %*).

Generally a record should consist of pure $F+$ and extended $F+$ percentages of at least 70 to 75 percent. If pure $F+\%$ or extended $F+\%$ rises above 85 or 90 percent, it should be considered high. In other words, roughly three-quarters of the pure F or form dominant responses should be made up of accurately perceived responses, leaving room for some inaccuracy. In a well-integrated person we expect to find accurate perception for the most part, but some capacity to take off from solely "hard" reality considerations. The freedom to permit oneself to respond occasionally in a less organized mode is, in fact, a defining aspect of the capacity to regress in the service of the ego (Kris, 1952; Schafer, 1958). Constrictive, rigid personality characteristics, therefore, would be most indicated by very high pure F and extended F percentages coupled with very high pure $F+$ and extended $F+$ percentages. When efforts at essentially tight, inflexible defenses are unsuccessful, however, $F\%$ is likely to be very high but accompanied by a low $F+\%$ (or a high extended $F\%$ by a low extended $F + \%$) with the low $F + \%$ indicating the failure of control. If $F\%$ is very low but $F+\%$ is high (or extended $F\%$ low and extended $F+\%$ high), the low $F\%$ would suggest that affects and/or impulses are not generally modulated sufficiently by intellectual control. The high $F+\%$ would indicate that intellectual controls, when present, tend to be rigid and inflexible. A last possible pattern in which both $F\%$ and $F+\%$ (or extended $F\%$ and extended $F+\%$) are very low would characterize a substantial collapse of intellectual and defensive controls. Thus, it is essential to consider the balance of F and extended F percentages with $F+$ and extended $F+$ percentages.

Movement Response (M)

Of all the scoring categories used in the Rorschach, there is probably more variation in the standard scoring of M than of any other single determinant, and Rorschach himself stated that, "the scoring of the M response is the thorniest problem in the entire experiment." Some clinicians score movement very broadly including any activity such as animal movement or inanimate movement (e.g., wind blowing). We adhere to Rorschach's more strict definition of M and score M only for a form perception which is imbued with kinesthetic qualities. It is only scored for humans in movement. When no clear kinesthetic activity is described, for instance, a person standing or a man smiling, M is not scored. Actual, and not implied movement, is the deciding factor. We are distinguishing here between tension and the kinesthetic quality of the response. "A person standing" may reflect some tension, but such a percept does not involve actual movement. When the figure is not a whole one, that is, when only part of the body is seen even though there might be some implied activity, as in "the head of a sleeping baby" or in a description of activity of only a portion of the body (e.g., legs kicking), M is not scored. Basically then, in order for an M response to be scored, there has to be some movement even though it may be minimal; thus, "a person standing" does not receive an M score, whereas "a person standing, turning his head" is scored M; "a person lying down" does not get an M score, but "a person lying down with arms outstretched" receives an M score. The decision to include only actual movement within the conception of M is based on the consideration that responses implying tension are often simply descriptive; a response has to go beyond simple description to merit an M score. For example, "a person standing at attention," or "a person standing very rigidly" goes beyond the descriptive statement of "a person standing" and therefore is scored for M. Since facial expressions or mood tones do not clearly imply, or are not based on, kinesthetic perceptions or perceptions of physical tension, they are not scored for M.

Human movement responses, other than the most popular ones, e.g., to Cards III and VII, are usually highly personal expressions. Of course every response on the Rorschach reflects the personality of the subject and bears the stamp of his unique cognitive processes, but the M response alone represents an identification with a human being and human activity through which feelings, aspirations, intentions, fears, and desires are expressed. It is for this reason too that we do not score animal movement in this category. It seems unlikely that animals and animal-like activity can be perceived or experienced with the same psychological significance, especially since the capacity to identify with other human beings' actions and intentions is a major psychological function related to empathy. The process of identification requires a relatively high level of psychological development; to share with or identify with another human being in action implies a fairly complex level of internal activity.

Inasmuch as movement responses derive from a complex internal ideational act they appear to reflect an individual's intellectual endowment and potential, his capacities for intellectual achievement. M is also a measure of the tendency toward introversive, rather than extratensive behavior, of an individual's tendency to emphasize the inner life of thought and fantasy. In terms of psychoanalytic ego theory, M is regarded as representative of the capacity for delay of impulse and affect expression since thinking serves the primary function of facilitating delay and planning. And M represents not only the level of intellectual endowment but also reflects the richness and vividness of thinking and the flexibility of the ideational processes. Thus, there are a variety of ideational activities, all of which are reflected by M responses, i.e., thinking may be imaginative, creative, or tend toward ruminative obsessiveness. Depending on the quality of the M response, it may also involve fearful phobic preoccupations and, in the extreme, may include delusional formations. An excessive number of Ms to the exclusion of other determinants, particularly color, indicates an overinvestment in the use of thought as a solution to life's prob-

M = Fantasy activity intellectually oriented ruminative, introspective, empathy

lems and indicates a tendency toward a lack of spontaneity in thought and action and a rigid control of impulses. As with all scores, the full interpretation of M must always proceed within the context of the quality of the particular M response, and attention should also be paid to whether the Ms depict vigorous activity or more passive movements and whether the movement tendencies are along extensor as compared to flexor dimensions. The qualitative features of M, the type of movement, as well as the formal accuracy of the perceived movement, offer further elucidation about how the thought processes operate within the psychic organization. When Ms are poorly perceived and especially when the form level is minus, one assumes that identification and empathy with others is distorted and that pathological projection may be present. People whose primary orientation is externally directed and who lack an elaborate fantasy life show markedly diminished M tendencies and responses. It is in the intellectually oriented, the ruminative, the introspective, and the fantasy dominated individuals that M responses predominate.

The notion that M reveals fantasy activity stems from an analysis of the cognitive act performed by the person in producing an M response. An M requires that the person take a static percept and imbue it with movement which is not actually present in the blot. This differs from the operation necessary for producing either form, color, or shading since these are clearly "stated" in the blot. M is the only Rorschach determinant which involves bringing something to the card which is not there in some way.

As regards the analysis of the process of forming an M response, it has been noted that people while giving M responses have reported kinesthetic experiences of the movement that is being described. Actual kinesthetic experiences, however, may occur but are not necessarily involved in movement responses. Rapaport et al. (1945, p. 212), for example, in discussing the theory that movement responses are "kinesthetic responses" because they are connected with kinesthetic experiences we have with our own bodies, conclude that there is no evidence for this view. They discount the idea that it is the same body experiences which allow us to see movement in static visual pictures that actually occur in a person who is having movement impressions on the Rorschach. Adapting Gestalt theory, they present an alternative theory, namely that it is the sensitivity to the imbalance in the perceptual field, the need for perceptual stability that allows one to experience the phenomenon of "movement." In addition, they also see the *M* response as indicating that the associative processes must have sufficient variability and wealth to have their course regulated by the perceptual imbalance and must be sufficiently flexible to offer a content for the area and resolve the imbalance. This highly integrated function is seen as requiring intellectual ability and introspection as well as empathy. A good movement response, therefore, reflects considerable ideational flexibility, versatility, wealth of associational material, and perceptual organizing ability, but may not, of necessity, involve actual kinesthetic experiences on the part of the individual. If anything, restricting a person's physical movement serves to stimulate an increase in the number of *M* responses which leads to the notion that motor activity and an emphasis on *M* (i.e., on ideation and fantasy) are inversely related.

FM (half M)

Whereas Klopfer & Kelley (1942) and Piotrowski (1957) use this category to score animals in movement, we follow Rapaport et al. (1945) in restricting *FM* either to weak, nonactive human movement, (e.g., a person standing), to large, active part human figures, or to human-like animals in clearly human activity (e.g., bears drinking a toast, monkeys kissing). This type of *FM* response is seen as a measure of constraint, of a holding back of fantasy material. Thus, a record which contains more *FM* than *M* indicates a potential for fantasy, yet, at the same time, a constriction of its expression. Like *M*, *FM* is scored for formal accuracy in the plus and minus categories, and the content has to be taken into consideration.

AFFECTIVE DIMENSIONS

Two major dimensions of the cards are utilized in interpreting the nature of a subject's affective experiences; these are the chromatic and achromatic colors. Included in the achromatic colors are not only responses to black and white, as such, but also to the variations in shading of the achromatic color. In scoring either chromatic or achromatic color, one also evaluates the degree to which the form is an essential part of the score. Thus, there are three categories within each of these scorings: (1) when form is the predominant determinant and color is used secondarily to embellish the response (*FC, FC', FCh, F(C)*); (2) when the predominant determinant is chromatic or achromatic color and form is only used secondarily (*CF, C'F, ChF, (C)F*); and (3) when color is the sole determinant of the response (*C, C', Ch*). The relative balance of the form-dominated responses, as compared to the responses in which form is relatively minor or nonexistent, gives an estimate of the degree of intellectual control and modulation of that type of affective experience. When there are no form dominant responses in a particular affective category, for example, this might indicate that these affects are intensely experienced, possibly in an overwhelming way with relatively little modulation and containment. Whereas, when categories are only responded to with form-dominated responses, this would indicate that the affects are controlled, held secondary to the intellectual processes, and are not experienced with full-bodied intensity. Ideally one should see some degree of intellectual control over emotional experiences; therefore, one expects some form-dominated responses, some color-dominated responses with form as a minor dimension as well as an occasional purely affectively determined response. When form is dominant, one must also consider the level of accuracy of the form (+ or −). For example, though form may be dominant, it may be poorly and inaccurately perceived, indicating that the efforts at intellectual control over the affective experience involve relatively poor judgment and poor reality articulation. Likewise, one has to ask whether the color is appropriate for the response. The relative degree of affective modulation and control, therefore, is determined in the different color categories by the presence of that particular type of response, the relative balance of form-dominated with color-dominated responses, and the accuracy of the form perception.

Color Responses

There is general agreement that color responses reflect an individual's characteristic handling of "affects, impulses, and actions" (Rapaport et al., 1945, p. 238). Less clear, however, is the theoretical rationale of how color responses evolve. There is no support for viewing the giving of color responses as an affective experience in itself; rather, color responses are handled "in a specific manner characteristic of [the] affective life" (Rapaport et al., 1945, p. 238). Shapiro (1960) has offered the view that color responses reflect in the perceptual sphere the degree to which "integrative, modulated, and impulsive and tension-discharge-delaying functions" are operative and their degree of successfulness. Thus, persons who are easily and primarily stimulated by vivid, diffuse colors are also likely to be hyperresponsive to their environment and to the press of internal impulses and affects. Such persons' perceptual experience and their affective and impulsive behavior are equally passive in that little active control has been exercised by the modulating and integrating ego functions. The ease of stimulation by the chromatic colors is expressed by the amount of responses which involve color and by the role played by form in the response process. The different types of color responses further illustrate this viewpoint.

FC Scores

efforts at delay of discharge capacity for interpersonal rapport

In this response form predominates over color, e.g., a red butterfly (III), caterpillars (lower center X because they are shaped like them and also the same color). The *FC* response reflects the maximal integration of the color with articulated form. Therefore, these responses reflect efforts at delay of discharge and indicate a capacity for interpersonal rapport and an ability to respond to others without egocentric or overwhelming personal expression. As Rorschach pointed out, however, it is more accurate to say that *FC*s express the "desire" to adapt, inasmuch as poor form level would reveal a lack of success in fulfilling this desire.

CF Scores

Whereas *FC* reflects a desire for emotional adaptation, *CF* indicates more "egocentric emotional responsiveness" and "affective lability" (Rorschach, 1942, p. 34). In these responses form plays a relatively minor role and these responses therefore suggest relatively little delay and little assessment of reality regarding affective reactions. Several examples are pink clouds (IX), an abstract painting (X), blood from the bears' paws (II).

C Scores

In pure *C* responses (e.g., blood seen in isolation, water colors and dyes with no formal properties) there are no efforts at delay or active perceptual organization. Pure color responses without any attempt to integrate form indicate that integrative capabilities have been overshadowed by stimulation to the point that accurate perception and logical thinking do not function. *C* responses are associated with highly impulsive actions, with unmodulated affective discharge, and also, but seemingly paradoxically, with blunted affect. If we consider that blunted affect characterizes psychological states in which "tension-discharge-delaying functions" are minimal and perceptual experience is essentially passive and unintegrated, then the apparent paradox (blunted affect indicated by pure *C*) can be resolved. Of course, states of blunted affect may be accompanied by the unmodulated expression of impulses and actions, and such uncontrolled expression would be predicted from the pure *C* responses. What is suggested is that the passive perceptual experience involved in a pure *C* response can mirror a deficiency in tension-discharge-delaying functions in either affects or impulses and actions separately or else in all three concurrently.

The significance of the three color scores is clearer in considering their possible interrelationships. Some records show no color scores of any kind and reflect shyness, rigid suppression of affects, and apathy, whereas numerous color responses are likely to reflect more emotional responsivity and impulsivity. In the normal record one expects the number of *FC*s approximately to double the number of *CF*s and no *C*s to be present. This distribution of scores would indicate marked efforts at emotional rapport and adaptiveness which are backed up by a capacity for experiencing strong affect. As *CF* and *C* begin to predominate, or the majority of *FC*s takes on poor form quality, one may expect less sensitivity in interpersonal relationships and a resultant greater impulsiveness, lability, and egocentricity. Thus, when the responses are primarily *FC*, one expects an overemphasis on rapport and sensitivity to others which often takes the form of submissive, overcompliant behavior. A record predominantly made up of *CF* responses leads one to anticipate affective outbursts and, possibly, impulsive acts. Pure *C* responses alone reflect the most extreme abandonment of ego controls; they represent either a potential for extreme impulsive discharge or a withdrawal of investment in affective response (as in blunted affect). An interesting pattern is an almost equal number of *FC* and *C* responses with no *CF* responses present. This pattern usually reflects strong efforts at rapport which are spotted by extreme affective and impulsive discharge.

In assessing the patterns of emotional reactivity, other dimensions of responses must also be considered, such as: 1) the number of *M* responses; the greater the number of *M* responses the greater is the investment in fantasy and ideation and in delay of discharge which can act as a buffer for the discharge patterns suggested by the color scores alone; 2) the content of the color responses, e.g., whether the *CF* responses involve violent aggressive content, such as blood, or more passively toned, dependent child-like content, such as cotton candy and ice cream; 3) whether the responses are given to the more vivid, stronger colors or the more subdued pastel shades; 4) the sequence of the color responses: are *FC*s given early in the record and then give way to other less integrated responses; do *FC* appear earlier or later than *CF* and *C* responses on specific color cards indicating a movement toward or away from emotional rapport; do color responses appear earlier generally and then drop out, indicating an initial arousal which is then blocked; or are color responses suppressed at first only to appear in full force later in the record? To arrive at a fuller understanding of the role of affect in psychological organization these added dimensions must be included.

Other varieties of chromatic color also exist. There is the symbolic use of color ("the red reminds me of anger"), the abstract nature of which mitigates the intensity of feeling involved via intellectualization and isolation. There are *F/C* and *C/F* scores which refer to an artificial, grafted-on use of color. In these responses color is not an integral and essential part of the response but is used to delineate areas, as in the following responses: "a map, the red represents France and the green Germany (scored *F/C*)"; another common *F/C* response is an anatomical chart with the different colors referring to different parts of the body. The perceptual artificiality involved in the formation of *F/C* and *C/F* responses mirrors efforts at adaptive rapport and affective experience that have a forced, tacked-on quality.

FC ARBITRARY. This response involves a use of color which is inconsistent with the content and for which no justification is offered (e.g., purple people and blue mice) without reference to specific memories or fairy tales. Like *F/C*, the *FC arb* response indicates an arbitrariness of perception and a failure to meaningfully integrate logical thinking with affective experience. But the *FC arb* response demonstrates a more serious loss in the critical appraisal of reality and an essentially concrete perceptual attitude since the form and color of the blot are haphazardly joined. An *FC arb* response of poor form level takes on even more pathological significance. Thus, *FC arb* responses reflect an out-of-touch quality of the affective experience.

The Experience Balance (*Erlebnistyp*)

In our discussion of movement and color separately we have already touched upon the importance of noting their relationship in an individual record. Inasmuch as movement refers to the relative emphasis on thought and delay of action, and color to the degree of affective and outerdirected expressiveness, their balance is crucial in personality assessment. Coarctated records, low in both movement and color, reflect impoverishment, inhibition, and dullness both with regard to fantasy and affects. (This is so especially if a large number of responses are given.) Dilated records, those high in movement and color, often reflect a rich, active, varied reliance on thought, feeling, and action primarily if the quality of the responses, i.e., their form level and content, do not have pathological features. Sometimes Rorschach records show an emphasis on movement or color to the almost absolute exclusion of the other. With movement present and color absent, affects and actions are likely to be inhibited and limited and ideation more prominent; perhaps even ideational symptomatology such as phobias, obsessions, or delusions may be present. With color present but movement virtually absent, the emphasis is less on delay and control and more on affective and impulsive expressiveness.

The Experience Balance is computed in the following way. Each *M* response receives one point and an *FM* one-half point; an *FC* receives one-half, a *CF* one, and a *C* one and one-half points. When color is used arbitrarily (Arb) or symbolically (Sym) it is computed in the above manner. But when color is less integrated and is of the artificial, pasted-on type (F/C or C/F), it is not directly indicated in the *EB* but is listed as an additional score. Thus a record which has two *FC*, one *C*, one *F/C*, and one *C/F* has a sum color score of 2.5 (4).

Shading Responses

Included in this category are responses which are determined in some measure by variation in lightness and darkness within the cards. These include a use of shading as surface texture, as an indicator of perspective, distance or vista, or of three-dimensionality. We follow Rapaport's classification system of scoring shading without a finer differentiation in the scores themselves as to how shading is used (e.g., vista vs. texture). Responses are scored as *FCh* (e.g., a furry bear), *ChF* (those which involve relatively vague, diffuse content such as X-rays and aerial views), and *Ch* (those which involve extremely diffuse content such as clouds and smoke).

Usually, shading responses of the *Ch* variety have been interpreted as indicators of anxiety. It is, however, also necessary to specify the ways in which the anxiety is experienced and expressed, whether the anxiety is subjectively experienced in a free-floating or specific manner, and whether it is expressed overtly in anxiety attacks or through bodily symptoms. Moreover, it is not only shading responses themselves that reflect one's experience of anxiety but also the behavior that occurs to the highly shaded cards. For example, a person who often replies with good *W* responses may avoid responding to the shading proper and instead may retreat to small, outside details of the blot; he thereby reveals a tendency to shift toward a picky, narrow, unintegrated approach when confronted with anxiety arousing stimuli. (A similar defensive maneuver but to affective arousal other than anxiety may also be seen on the chromatic cards.)

As with other test features and the psychological processes we assume they reflect, there is no direct relationship between the experience of anxiety itself and the reaction to shading. That is, anxiety may not be simultaneously experienced while giving shading responses. Shading responses may reflect anxiety, however, because of the symbolic association of darkness and mistiness with night and fearfulness. It has also been suggested (Rapaport et al.,

1945, p. 284) that anxiety serves to block the ego's efforts at organization which are crucial to enable the articulation of the more diffuse, heavily shaded inkblots into form dominant responses. Whereas unanxious people can supply the additional articulation that is needed on these cards, anxious people may be especially unable to do so.

The amount of anxiety, its intensity, and disrupting effects, increases as *ChF, Ch,* and *FCh minus* responses outnumber *FCh plus* responses. The quality of the responses and their content add further understanding of the nature of the anxiety. For example, many texture responses and some three-dimensional responses imply closeness to an object whereas vista responses imply more distance. In addition, some texture responses involve essentially sensuous and pleasurable content and others have more fearful, unpleasant connotations. Often a strong and anxious need for closeness to a comforting figure is revealed in sensuously toned close texture responses such as "a soft, fluffy fur muff like my mother's." Efforts at intellectual control over anxiety will also appear in shading responses which are distanced either spatially (e.g., threatening clouds seen in the background of the card or the kind of storm clouds one sees in Italy but not in the United States), or temporally (e.g., a heavily textured animal of an earlier era in time).

Another category of shading response is the $F(C)$ response, which includes responses in which differentiations in shading are used to define form (e.g., seeing a face in the upper central portion of IV). The $F(C)$ category also includes responses in which the shading of chromatic areas is elaborated (like the fur of the popular animals on VIII). Binder (1932) has described $F(C)$ responses as reflecting an anxious, cautious approach to interpersonal relationships as opposed to the freer rapport reflected by the *FC* response. According to Rapaport, people with many $F(C)$ responses tend to be on the watch as to how to behave in a situation, and they will try to adjust their behavior accordingly. If we consider the way in which an $F(C)$ response evolves, some further expectations can be derived about the psychological processes associated with $F(C)$ responses. Since many $F(C)$ responses involve the delineation of an unusual area within the blot, a large number of them are *Dr* responses. Hence, this type of shading response reflects a capacity for differentiating internal subleties and for more complex affective experience than is the case with the more diffuse Ch responses. The sensitivity to subleties in one's internal experience and in external reality may, like movement responses, reflect a capacity for empathy. In more pathological conditions, however, (e.g., paranoia) this sensitivity may take on a watchful, feeling-out quality. Once again, the tone of the response is important, whether depressive and anxious affect, or more pleasurable, sensuous affect is suggested.

The $F(C)$ response involving shading in colored areas is close to an FC response, but in addition reflects a certain degree of anxiety. Rapaport found that "when there is an accumulation of $F(C)$ and $(C)F$ responses to colored areas, it suggests a person given to such mingling of affect and anxiety, as is seen in complex emotions like nostalgia (sweet-sorrow)" (Rapaport et al., 1945, p. 289, footnote). Appelbaum & Holzman (1962) reported that a blending of color and shading is an indicator of suicidal potential.

Achromatic Color

These responses include those determined by black, grey, or white color. Often they refer to the presence of dysphoric, especially depressive, moods. In some way, issues around lifelessness, coldness, desolation, and loneliness are usually apparent in these responses whether to black areas which more directly connote death or to white areas with their associations to coldness and barrenness. White areas, of course, can have other implications as well, e.g., goodness, innocence, and loveliness, although imagery like "angels" seems to have an added relationship to the celestial, eternal life and hence to death indirectly. The degree to which dysphoric affect is apparent can be gauged by the extent to which C' and $C'F$ responses predominate over the FC' variety. Greater amounts of $C'F$ and C' reflect more giving up to depressive affect, most likely in a helpless, passive manner.

In an analysis of space responses, most of which make up the white color responses, Fonda (1960) suggests that space responses may indicate a drive to achieve active mastery and autonomy. It is interesting, therefore, to consider the possibility that color responses of the white variety may at times serve in defending against dysphoric affect via images of hope and purity. In a particular record, therefore, white percepts may alternate with black ones and demonstrate an attempt to defend against depression.

Blends (or Combined) Scores

Sometimes movement and chromatic and achromatic color or shading may jointly enter into a single response (e.g., Card II, black robed figures with red hats dancing, *MCC'*; Card IV, a black fuzzy bear skin rug, *FC'Ch*; or the lower third of Card IX, pink billowy clouds *C(C)F*). Blends of different determinants generally indicate a potential for more complex, richer states of affect and ideation, the nature of which can sometimes be inferred from the specific determinants present. For example, if movement (*M*) responses are often coupled with achromatic color, we would infer that fantasy activity tends to be depressively toned. If achromatic color and shading (*Ch*) are blended, anxiety and depression occur together, as in agitated, anxious depressed people. And if color and achromatic color most often occur together, interpersonal rapport and relatedness and one's affects and impulses typically involve a certain degree of dysphoria. An important aspect of blends is the degree to which they are form dominant or form takes a secondary role or is absent completely. To the degree that form is superseded by more diffuse color or shading, we are likely to see a more open, expressive or even, at the extreme, a more uncontrolled appearance of the particular affective or ideational combination. With moderate, but not excessive, dominance by form, blends often indicate a capacity for complex states that add depth and integration to one's experience.

Scoring

Each discrete response is scored separately except for alternate responses which constitute minor thematic reworkings of a basic response (e.g., on Card I the responses "moth," "butterfly," and "bat") would receive only one score. When a complex response includes segments that differ in their use of determinants, these segments are scored individually, e.g., on Card II a rocket (center space) taking off in the midst of black clouds and leaving a trail of flame from its exhaust would receive three separate scores, one for the rocket (*S F +* Rocket), one for the clouds (*D C'F* clouds), and one for the exhaust (*D CF* Flame). In addition, one should note the combining quality of the response.

When more than one determinant enters into a response, as when two figures (on Card II) in red hats and black cloaks are seen as engaged in a macabre Halloween dance, the determinants are coupled in the score (in this case, $W\ MCC'+H\ P$). Similarly, when color and shading are used separately, e.g., in a rug on Card IV, the score would be $FC'Ch+$. In tallying the responses on the summary sheet the scoring blends are listed jointly but are also separated. For example, an $MCC'+$ would be listed as such along with the other M responses, but the $FC+$ and $FC'+$ which are included within it would also be listed separately to the left of the FC and FC' notations. In computing the experience balance these blends should also be included. If a record contained one $M+$, one $MCC'+$, one $FC\mp$, one CF, and two $FC'\mp$ these would be listed in the following way:

$$M+$$
$$MCC'+$$
$$+FC\mp$$
$$CF\ 1$$
$$+FC'\mp\mp \quad \text{and the EB would be } 2/2$$

Content

The content categories form general classes of objects into which each specific response can be placed. These categories enable the examiner to make inferences about the breadth of the subject's associative processes. The main categories we use are animals and parts of animals, humans and parts of humans, objects, clothing, decorations, architecture, plants, nature scenes, geography, anatomy, sex, and food. Responses which do not fit into any of these categories are listed separately.

A variety of types of content reflects a rich array of associations, ideas, and realms of interest. It is characteristic of people with a productive, active array of interests, but it can also reflect an ideational flightiness, such as might be found in hypomanic or schizophrenic patients.

Of particular interest is the assessment of stereotypy of thought through the presence of few content areas. Rapaport lists the following factors as causing stereotypy:

a Native limitations of endowment and intelligence may seriously limit the range of conceptual realms from which the content of responses may be drawn.

b A normal adjustment which derives its stability and safety from clinging to convention and the obvious, may also restrict the range of associative material.

c The presence of strong anxiety may impair the fluidity of the subject's passing from one realm of ideas to another.

d Extreme inhibition, depressive retardation, or psychotic blocking may prevent any free passage from content to content.

e Compulsive rigidity may restrict responses to those which are most patently congruent with well circumscribed obvious details of blots.

f An all-pervading preoccupation may result in a relative stereotypy if, in its absence, the wealth and variability of ideas had been great. However, the presence of strong preoccupation in a generally unproductive picture may tend rather to increase the apparent variability. (Rapaport et al., 1945, p. 294)

Animal responses are the easiest to perceive and are most common, therefore, in certain records characterized by stereotyped thinking. While stereotypy of thinking can be apparent by elevations in any other content area, animal responses reflect its presence most strongly, especially when the animal responses exceed 40 percent of the total number of responses.

Specific preoccupations will be apparent through increases of individual or clusters of response categories. For example, a high number of Anatomy (At), Sexual, Blood, and X-ray responses is often associated with a predominant preoccupation with bodily intactness. The following factors lead to a high *At* percentage: feeling intellectually inadequate, bodily preoccupation, generalized anxiety, and extreme blocking. It is of interest, in addition, to note the balance of the number of parts of humans and animals with whole human and animal figures. A tendency to see parts primarily may show an obsessive criticalness or a fragmented, narrowed conception of oneself as incomplete and partial and a similar view of others. It may also reflect a certain degree of dehumanization and possibly of depersonalization. An extremely low *H* percentage, including whole humans and parts of humans, may reflect a lack of investment in people and may point toward schizoid, withdrawn tendencies. But an investment in people does not in itself indicate an ability to form interpersonal attachments; this must be inferred from other data such as the number and quality of FC responses, the M, and $F(C)$ responses.

One can also note on occasion particular preferences for organic or inorganic content, for what is alive and feeling, as opposed to what is mechanical and impersonal or is characterized by a formal, geometric quality. Very detached and rigid persons may at times choose more mechanical content. Plant content is of special interest, especially when well articulated and not vague, inasmuch as plants in our culture are associated with delicacy and sensitivity; such responses are likely to be shunned by males with marked masculine bravado or by women with marked masculine strivings.

Blood responses usually refer to issues around aggression, but they can also reflect preoccupation with menstruation or more general bodily concerns. Recent attempts to present Rorschach content in a more systematic and dynamic form include Schafer (1954) and Holt & Havel (1960).

Popular

Popular responses are those seen most frequently. Hence these responses reflect one's adherence to conventional ways of thinking. Stereotypy of thought leads to an increase in the number of populars, for they are easily perceived, relatively obvious and commonplace. With a low intellectual level, depressive retardation, naivete and conventionality, therefore, the P percentage is likely to be high (with 20 to 25 responses one expects a P percentage of about 20; in an average-sized record, more than this number shows stereotypy). On the other hand, a very low P percentage reflects an impoverished degree of adherence to social reality and conventional ways of thinking.

The following is the list of responses which are scored as populars (P—the most ordinary Populars; (P)—Additional near-Populars).

QUALITATIVE FEATURES

The analysis of verbalization on the Rorschach, i.e., the attempt to systematize aspects of verbalization, was initiated by Rapaport. We use most of Rapaport's qualitative scores in order to de-

Responses Scored as Populars

Card	Location	Content	Remarks
I 1.	W	P —Bat, butterfly, moth	
2.	Lower, middle, inner	P —Human form, lower ½	Also P if includes entire middle.
II 1.	W	P —2 humans	Or a common human activity.
2.	Side black	P —Bear, dog	Only if head at top of black area.
3.	Lower red	P —Butterfly, moth	
III 1.	Side black	P —Human form	Or a common human activity also as W; "leg" area must be used.
2.	Middle red	P —Ribbon, bow, bowtie	Butterfly or moth is (P).
IV 1.	W	P —Animal skin, fur rug	
2.	Lower side	(P)—Boot, shoe, foot	
3.	Lower middle	(P)—Animal head	Animal unspecified, boar, bull, cow, or dragon.
V 1.	W	P —Bat, butterfly, moth	
2.	Upper side projection	P —Leg, animal or human	Bone only is not P.
VI 1.	W	P —Animal skin, fur rug	Also lower ⅔ only.
2.	Upper D	(P)—Totem pole	
VII 1.	Upper third	P —Human head; female, child or unspecified	Also upper ⅔, or W as whole humans.
VIII 1.	Side pink	P —Animal, 4-legged	Bears, rodents, beaver, muskrat, squirrel, animal unspecified are P; cat and dog families are (P); animal with tail and 3 legs showing is P.
2.	Upper gray	P —Tree, bush	Not P if tree includes other areas (except midline as trunk).
3.	Upper middle spaces	P —Ribs, skeleton, backbone	
IX 1.	Upper orange	P —Human figure	Many variations are P, if entire orange is whole human.

Responses Scored as Populars (*Continued*)

Card	Location	Content	Remarks
	2. Outer lower pink	*P* —Human head	Embryo is (*P*).
X	1. Side blue	*P* —spider, crab, lobster	Sea animal unspecified is (*P*).
	2. Inner yellow	*P* —dog	Including special breeds.
	3. Center light green	*P* —rabbit's head	
	4. Upper green	*P* —sheep	
	5. Middle orange	(*P*)—wishbone	
	6. Upper gray	(*P*)—bug, creature	
	7. Side gray	(*P*)—bug, crab	

lineate pathology and to clarify its extent. These scores offer crucial leads to the understanding of thought processes and to the extent and type of deviant thinking. For a more recent attempt to classify verbalization and to extend Rapaport's system, the reader is referred to Holt & Havel (1960).

Combination

This score is used when contiguous areas of the blot are combined in an integrative manner. The parts remain separate and distinct and are scored separately but are interrelated (e.g., Card II, a bear with blood on his paws; Card I, two angels carrying a woman up to heaven). Combination responses reflect integrative ability and active ideational powers insofar as they involve a meaningful grouping of disparate areas. They are uncommon, therefore, in mental retardates, depressives, and in inhibited, constricted states generally. Combination responses can demonstrate successful integrations and stand in contrast to the following less successful integrations.

Fabulized Combination

This is a combination response in which contiguous areas are related in an arbitrary, idiosyncratic way. These combinations are impossible ones (e.g., Card X, worms coming out of a rabbit's eyes; Card VIII, bears climbing on cotton candy) even though each percept by itself may be of excellent form quality. The process involved in the formation of this type of response seems to involve taking spatial continuity in itself to indicate an essential relationship. Thus, such responses can occur when there is an inability to separate out perceived stimuli, when unrealistic relationships are sought among disparate events and percepts (as in ideas of reference), but these responses are not necessarily indicators of pathology. A crucial consideration in evaluating any of the verbalization scores is the attitude of the subject in giving them. When the responses are given with a feeling that the cards are really like that, or reality is actually like that, then a disturbance in the thought processes is indicated. In this case the ego has little autonomy, for it will either be bound to extremely concrete aspects of reality or else be bound to the urge of drives. When seemingly unrealistic responses are offered with a playful quality, however, one that involves the recognition by subjects that they are allowing themselves to step away from strict reality considerations temporarily, then responses like *Fab Comb's* can reflect a modulated access to more primitive modes of experiences (regression in the service of the ego). This consideration—the attitude of the subject in responding—must be included in evaluating the verbalization scores which Rapaport treated primarily as indications of pathologically deviant thought processes.

Fabulized Response

Affective elaboration of a percept merits a *Fab* score, e.g., describing a face on Card I as being either dangerous or angry. This refers to rather mild elaborations of feelings, attitudes, and qualities which can be given by introspective and sensitive people. When there is less recognition, however, that one is actively supplying the elaboration oneself, and one is convinced the cards really look that way, we are more likely to be viewing a pathological, albeit mild, intrusion.

Confabulation

This response is an extension of a fabulation and refers to the imbuing of a response with extensive and arbitrary elaboration that has little or no justification in the percept itself, e.g., to the top of Card IX, "Two evil witches who hate mankind and are out to blow up the world." Confabulation is scored on the basis of associative elaboration and not on the formal accuracy of the percept. (In the example above the response would be scored *M* plus for form.) In some cases the associative elaboration can be coupled with poor form, as to the whole of Card II, "a face screaming in agony" or to the center red of Card III, "chicken hearts bleeding, with lots of pain and weakness as when having a heart attack." When a confabulation occurs in the context of good form we can infer that basic perceptual experience is intact and that the primary disturbance is in post-perceptual, associative elaboration, much as one might see in a delusional state. More serious pathology would be indicated by the presence of confabulation and poor form. The score of confabulation tendency is used to refer to less severe confabulations and also confabulations which are accompanied by some concurrent critical appraisal or by a delayed recognition of their unrealistic nature.

Contamination

Contaminations include the fusion of two separate ideas into one (like neologisms) and the unrealistic spread of one idea into others which it comes to dominate. An example of the first kind is the response "bloody fire" to the red on Card II "because the area looks like the blood stains of wounded men and also looks like the flames of burning ships"; or on Card X, the inside yellow area frequently seen as lions and as fried eggs might be described as "a lion egg." The second type of contamination is illustrated by an example from Rapaport et al. (1945). The entirety of Card III is seen as a butterfly, because the center area looks like one. Rapaport describes this perceptual process as equivalent to seeing a man wearing a tie with a butterfly on it and thinking the man is a butterfly.

In all contaminations the defining element is the fluidity of boundaries between objects. Whereas in *Fab Comb's* the boundaries of the objects are kept distinct, in contamination an essential fusion occurs. Contamination responses are usually pathognomonic of schizophrenia, a central feature of which is a tendency not to differentiate oneself from others and to blur the boundaries of sex and generation.

Contamination tendency is scored both for partial contaminations or where critical distance is maintained. Sometimes, for instance, one sees a partial contamination when a percept is said to look like one thing but to really be another, e.g., they look like eggs, but they are really lions. In these cases the boundaries have not completely disappeared between the two ideas, but there is a quality of instability to the separateness of the boundary.

Peculiar

This includes verbalizations that are non sequiturs, cryptic, and generally illogical in terms of everyday verbal conventions, e.g., reference to the "curtains" of a vagina, or referring to an animal as "depending" from the branches of a tree instead of "hanging." For this latter example there appears to be a shortcircuiting of the usual associative process. That is, the "hanging" process seems to have touched on issues about holding on to something else and being dependent on it; these issues are compressed into the final verbalization.

Autistic Logic

Involved in autistic logic is a bizarre and highly illogical use of cause and effect relationships. Such verbalizations are given with an air of logical necessity. For example, if, on Card VIII, a wild animal is seen, then another area becomes barren and kind of wild "*because* the animal was wild"; or the popular figures on Card III are described as being in love "*because* there is a heart shaped object between them." The latter example also shows how the position of a response taken concretely can be elaborated in an unrealistic way.

Fluid

This is scored when the train of thought is not maintained, when there is loose shifting from one percept to another often in the effort to locate a particular percept. Fluid is also scored when responses or blots cannot be recalled. Insofar as the first type of fluidity involves an essentially passive experience of reality, a sense of instability of the environment and a difficulty in locating and pinpointing one's experience, it often points toward a psychotic sense of unreality. However, since memory functioning is also strongly involved in fluid verbalizations, they are frequently apparent in cases of organic brain damage or dysfunction. Often a prominent test feature in epileptics is their difficulty in keeping track of their thoughts, despite persistent efforts to do so (Glaser et al., 1963).

Symbolic

Explicit representation of an abstract idea through form or other determinants, whether employing conventional or idiosyncratic symbolism, is scored Symbolic, e.g., the center red on Card III being seen as representing a conflict between the two figures. A more extensive example from a well-functioning research subject which combines the Symbolic use of form as well as color occurred to the whole of Card IX seen upside down: "I see an imaginary essay in this. It could be a picture of the three stages of life. The origins are a little nebulous; shaped like a womb on the bottom— the place of origin. Then the green is the color of youth, aliveness, freshness, and enthusiasm which fades to red at the top, like old age. The top is flat and could be death." Although symbolic responses are not characteristic of any particular diagnostic group, they at times reflect an attempt to interpose intellectual control over more immediate affect and responsivity. A person who sees red as only symbolic of conflict distances himself from the more immediate impact of the red as blood. Symbolic responses are most likely to occur, therefore, in contexts in which there is an investment in ideational activity and in efforts to use ideation for control and delay. It will occur in the normal range but also in overideational contexts, as in paranoia and schizophrenia, and in some depressives who see portents of gloom everywhere.

Self-References

This category denotes verbalizations which indicate that the card is seen as having a specifically personal reference for the subject. Such responses indicate a loss of the test-taking attitude and the intrusion of particular preoccupations. In their extreme form, self-references indicate a disregard of the separate and impersonal reality of the cards. Percepts are viewed as actual members of the subject's family or as personally owned objects; percepts are seen as smiling at or mocking the subject. Thus, in their extreme form self-reference verbalizations reflect a concrete attitude and a loss of distance between the subject's thoughts and the cards that reaches psychotic proportions. Particularly when the percepts take on malevolent, sinister characteristics directed toward the subject, i.e., severe projections that largely ignore reality considerations, a markedly paranoid orientation is indicated. With less severe self-references, more critical distance is maintained from the card and percepts "look like" or "resemble" particular things of personal relevance but are not actually the objects, e.g., "This looks like my Scotty dog." One must keep distinct from these responses personal reminiscences and efforts by the subject to verbalize the possible psychological significance of certain responses.

SUMMARY OF THE SCORING SYSTEM

Location

W The whole or most of the blot.

D A fairly large or prominent part of the blot.

Dd A very small and clearly delineated area.

Dr An unusual or rare area, either large or small, of the blot.

S A response based on background white space rather than the foreground blot elements (S: large white areas; s: small white areas).

DW Reasoning from part of the blot to a response which encompasses the whole blot, whether or not the response matches the appearance of the blot.

Do Response to only part of a frequently seen larger, complete percept and keeping the same content for the smaller area as it has in the broader interpretation.

Po Determined primarily or exclusively by position.

Determinants

F A response based solely on the outline of the percept.

F+ An accurately perceived, well articulated response.

F± Not quite adequate F+ response with a minus element.

F− A distortion of the formal attributes of the blot.

F∓ Predominantly F− response but not as poor.

M Complete or almost complete humans in actual movement with kinesthetic qualities.

FM Weak, nonactive human movement; large active part human figures; human-like animals in clearly human activity.

FC A response based on form and color in which form predominates over color.

CF A response in which form plays a relatively minor role in comparison to color.

C A response with no attempt to integrate form.

F/C An artificial, grafted on use of color to delineate areas secondary to form (e.g., maps).

C/F An artificial, grafted on use of color to delineate areas with form secondary.

FC arb Use of a color which is inconsistent with the content and for which no justification is offered (e.g., a green bear).

FCh A response including variations in lightness and darkness within the cards in which form is dominant.

ChF Variations in shading with vague, diffuse form.

Ch Variations in shading with extremely diffuse content.

F(C) (a) Responses in which differentiations in shading are used to define form.
(b) Responses in which the shading of chromatic areas is elaborated.

(C)F Like F(C) except that shading is predominant over form.

FC' A form dominant response in which black, grey, or white color is incorporated.

C'F A response in which black, grey, or white color in primary and form secondary.

C' A response based solely on black, grey, or white color.

COMBINED SCORES. When more than one determinant enters into a response, the separate determinants are coupled together in a single overall score (e.g., Card II, black robed dancing figures with red hats which contains an M, FC', and FC is scored MCC'; Card IX pink billowy clouds would be scored C(C)F).

Content

A	complete animals
Ad	animal details
H	complete human figures
(H)	complete human-like figures
Hd	human details
(Hd)	human-like details
Obj	object
Cg	clothing
Dec	decoration

Arch   architecture
Pl   plant
Na   nature
Geog   geography
At   anatomy
Sex
Food

Qualitative

P   Popular responses given by one of every five subjects. (P) is a near-popular response.

Combination   The integration of distinct areas of the blot in a meaningful way.

Fab Comb   A combination response in which the contiguous areas are related in an arbitrary, idiosyncratic way.

Fab   Affective elaboration of a percept.

Confab   Extensive and arbitrary elaboration with little or no justification in the percept.

Contam   The fusion of two separate ideas into one; the unrealistic spread of one idea into others which it comes to dominate.

Pec   Logical non sequiturs, cryptic and illogical verbalizations in terms of everyday verbal conventions.

Autistic logic   Bizarre, illogical use of cause-effect relationships.

Fluid   Loss of the train of thought; loose shifting from percept to percept; inability to recall responses.

Symbolic   Representation of an abstract idea through form or other determinants.

Self-ref   Verbalizations which indicate that the blot has a specific personal reference for the subject.

Summation Scores

R   The total number of responses.

EB   The ratio of the sum of movement scores to the sum of the color scores. The following weights are given: 0.5 to FM and FC, 1.0 to M and CF, and 1.5 to C. F/C (0.5) and C/F (1.0) are included in the color scores as additional responses. Thus a record with 1 M,

1 FM, 1 FC, 1 C, and 1 F/C will show an EB
of 1.5—2.0 (2.5).

W%   The percent of whole responses of all the re-
          sponses.

D%   The percent of detail responses of all the re-
          sponses.

Dr%   The percent of Dr, S, and Drs responses of all
          the responses.

F%   Percentage of responses in the total record
          which are based solely on form.

Extended F%   Percentage in the total record of all form
          dominant responses, including F, M, FM, FC,
          F/C, FC', FCh, F(C).

F+%   Percentage of all pure F responses scored
          + or ±.

Extended F+%   Percentage of all form dominant responses
          scored + or ±.

A%   The percent of A and Ad responses.

H%   The percent of H and Hd responses to which
          (H) and (Hd) responses are added as addi-
          tionals.

P%   The percent of Popular responses with (P),
          i.e., near popular responses included as addi-
          tionals.

CLINICAL EXAMPLES

In the following section clinical examples of the Rorschach summary sheets of different diagnostic categories will be presented
and discussed. In addition, we will present a more fully detailed
Rorschach analysis of Mrs. T. Although it is not our typical practice to base test conclusions solely on the summary of the scores,
it is our experience that the hypotheses derived from the summary sheet usually receive ample confirmation and supplementa-
tion when other sources of Rorschach data are evaluated, e.g.,
when the attitude and affect toward the responses, the content of
the responses, the sequence of responses within individual cards
and among all 10 cards are taken into consideration. Since we
have found among psychologists that attending to scores (if a

record is scored at all) is often a neglected aspect of Rorschach analysis, we are focusing in these examples on the interpretation of the scores. Furthermore, while we also do not believe that supplying a diagnostic label is the focal task of psychological testing, it has been convenient to group these examples according to current nosology. It is possible, nevertheless, also to concentrate on the various psychological processes which are either clearly stated or implicit in the discussion of the examples.

Depression

The following is the Rorschach summary of a 34-year-old hospitalized woman with a ninth-grade education, twice married, with two children from the second marriage to a physician. Her test diagnosis was severe neurotic depression.

Summary of Scores

	$R = 5$	*EB 0/0*	
W 1	1 F + 3	1 A 3	W% 20
2ᵃ D 3	F ± 1	Ad 2	D% 80
Do 1	1 F ∓ 1		
		F% (pure) 100/100 (extended)	
		F+% (pure) 80/80 (extended)	
Fail 3, 4, 6, 7, 9, 10		A% 100	
		H% 0	
		1 P 2	
		P% 40	
Qualitative			
Fab 1			

ᵃ Scores to the left of the letters are additionals.

INTERPRETATION. The constriction and barrenness of this record immediately suggest a severe depressive, a mental defective, or a very guarded, inhibited paranoid. The patient's IQ scores (Verbal 112 and Performance 99) rule out mental deficiency, and the absence of even one peculiar, confabulation, or contamination response would tend to contraindicate a psychosis. We probably see, therefore, a depressive record par excellence—constriction of ideational activity, evident in the EB, #R, $F\%$ and $A\%$, and in numerous card rejections.

Hysteria

This Rorschach summary is of a 26-year-old married woman with two children, a high school graduate, who was seen as an outpatient. Her test report indicated an hysterical picture with strong phobic and depressive trends.

Summary of Scores

		R = 39		EB 2/5			
W	7	F+	15	A	14	W%	18
D	26	F±	7	Ad	2	D%	67
Dr	4	F∓	9	H	2	Dr%	15
S	1	M	±±	(H)	3	F%	79/90
Do	1	FC	±	Obj	8	F+%	71/74
		CF	3	Cg	2	A%	41
		C	1	Nat	1	H%	5(13)
		FCh	±	At	2	P	6
Qualitative				Food	1	P%	15
Fab	3			Number	1		
Confab tend	1			Smoke	1		
				Vista	1		
				Fireworks	1		

INTERPRETATION. Of interest in this scoring summary is the predominance of *CF* and *C* over *FC* which suggests that we may be confronted with a narcissistic or hysterical person dominated by affect and impulse. In this record, however, efforts at intellectual control are clearly evident in the relatively high extended $F\%$ (90) and indicate that hyperemotionality and affective and impulsive arousal make their appearance in spite of efforts at modulation. This would be different from a narcissistic type of person who would not strive with this much intensity to try to impose control over her thoughts and actions.

The experience balance (Color greater than Movement) points toward an hysterical picture, but the number of responses (R) and the *Dr%* are not typical in hysterical settings. These features seem to reflect the patient's productive strivings and even some superficial obsessive-compulsive features, but they are not backed up by a rich and active ideational life (since her number of *M* is somewhat low for an R of 39 and her *A%* is on the high side and suggests some stereotypy of thinking). This is probably, therefore, an intellectually striving but essentially repressive hysterical woman. The fabulations and one confabulation tendency in the qualitative column suggest trends toward fantasy elaboration which do not reach psychotic proportions but may in an hysterical person be associated with phobic formations.

Obsessive Compulsive

This Rorschach summary is of a married 31-year-old male graduate student.

Summary of Scores

			R = 37	EB 7/1(2)			
2 W	17	F+	14	A	11	W%	46
D	16	F±	3	Ad	8	D%	43
Dr	1	F∓	2	H	7	Dr%	11
De	2	M +++±∓+±		(H)	1	F%	51/100
S	1			Hd	4	F+%	89/86
3 s		FC+		Obj	1	A%	51
Qualitative		FCC′ ±		Cg	1	H%	30(32)
Fab comb	1	F/C +		Pl	1	P	7+1
Fab	1	F/CC′ ∓		Nat	2	P%	19(22)
Fab tend	2	F(C)+		Cloud	1		
Pec	2	±∓FC′++					
Fluid	1	FC′Ch ++					
		++FCh±−					

INTERPRETATION. The predominance of *M* in the EB, the vigorous avoidance of free affective experience evident in the extended *F%* of 100 suggest an obsessive-compulsive orientation. In addition, the cautious, wary, and forced interpersonal approach (indicated by the *FC*, *F(C)*, *FC′*, *FCh* emphasis) and the high *W%* which reflects some expansive features in this M dominated record point toward paranoid personality trends. One would wonder whether the several peculiar verbalizations also point in this direction. However, the good quality of the M responses and of the $F+\%$ generally argue against a severe paranoid picture, i.e., one accompanied by poor reality testing and by frankly delusional ideation. Of interest also is the relatively high $A\%$ which, along with the high extended $F\%$, indicates a rigidity and stereotypy of thought in this person whose degree of ideational productivity and investment in thought and ambitiousness is not backed up by a wide range of interests or by free, spontaneous reactivity. Lastly, the number of FC' (total of 6) as opposed to $F(C)(1)$ or $FCh(4)$ suggests depressive trends. One possible way of organizing the varied test indicators is in terms of considering that an essentially obsessive-compulsive organization is weakened to some extent and that depressive and secondarily paranoid features may be making their appearance.

Schizophrenia—Acute

This Rorschach summary is of a 21-year-old male undergraduate hospitalized after an acute schizophrenic episode with primarily paranoid features.

Summary of Scores

		$R = 27$	EB 1/4		
3 W	5	F+ 10	A 5	W%	18(30)
D	17	F— 1	Ad 3	D%	63
Dr	3	F± 5	(A) 1	Dr%	15
1 S		F∓ 2	H 1	F%	67/89
1 Do		M +	Hd 4	F+%	83/83
		FC —	(Hd) 2	A%	33
		C 2	Obj 5	H%	18(26)
		F(C) +	Pl 4	P	6 + 3
		FC' +	Nat 1	P%	22(33)
		FCh ±			
		1 Ch			

Summary of Scores (*Continued*)

Qualitative	
Fab comb	1
Fab	2
Confab	6
Contam tend	1
Pec	18
Par	1
Fluid	3
Autistic logic	4 + 1
Symbolic	4
Self-refer	1

INTERPRETATION. The qualitative scores unambiguously and immediately indicate a psychosis, in particular, schizophrenia, but in the context of a good number of popular and human responses and an adequate $F+\%$. Because of this degree of intactness, the picture is probably an acute one of recent onset. Adequate perceptions are within the patient's grasp but are subject to extensive autistic elaborations.

The juxtaposition of FC with pure C points to efforts at adaptive rapport which alternate with impulsivity and unmodulated affect discharge. The $FC-$ also highlights an impaired capacity for interpersonal relatedness. Because of the scattering of $F(C)$, FC', and FCh, it is probable that a certain degree of cautiousness and wariness is displayed in interpersonal relationships.

In the context of this much psychotic thinking, the W push (extended $W\%$ of 30) would be consistent with grandiose, expansive features. Since this is a very bright college student (Verbal IQ, 122), only one M is quite low. We know from his extended $F\%$ (89) that he is striving for rational control and the presence of a single M in contrast to the greater amount of color also attests to the ineffectiveness and brittleness of present efforts at control. Although his experience balance (EB) might suggest hysterical features, the degree to which the patient appears to be passively inundated by autistic thinking which he is little able to block in any way is also reflected in the poverty of active ideation (few M) which might serve adaptive endeavors.

Schizophrenia

This is the Rorschach summary of a 20-year-old hospitalized male college junior. His test diagnosis was early undifferentiated schizophrenia.

Summary of Scores

			$R = 19$	$EB\ 1/1$		
1 W	4	F+	6	A	3	W% 21
D	10	F—	2	Ad	3	D% 53
Dr	5	F±	2	Hd	4	Dr% 26
3 S		F∓	6	(Hd)	1	F% 84/100
		M	—	1 At	1	F+% 50/47
				Sex	7	A% 32
		FC±, arb	∓			H% 21(26)
						P 2
Qualitative						P% 10
Fab	1					
Confab tend	1					
Pec	5					
Perseveration	9					

INTERPRETATION. Immediately striking in this Rorschach summary sheet are: the extremely poor $F+$ %s which are especially prominent in view of strong efforts at control (the extended $F\%$ of 100); the one M of pure minus quality; the massing of peculiar verbalizations and perseverations, the latter largely reflecting the preoccupation with sexual content; the confabulation tendency; and lastly, the low $P\%$. These features taken together point toward a psychotic process which, because of the $M-$ and the high $Dr\%$, is likely to include ideational symptomatology such as paranoid thinking. Considering that this is the Rorschach of a college student, the low number of responses, the extended $F\%$ of 100, the few content categories and the presence of only one M reveal a tremendous struggle for containment and control and a narrowing of the focus of his interests which seems additionally unsuccessful because of this investment of energy. Noteworthy, however, is the absence of pure C or even CF and the two FC responses indicate persisting efforts at rapport, albeit of a strained ($FC\ arb$) and not well organized quality ($FC\mp$). For this reason, the psychosis does not seem to be chronic in the sense that the patient does not appear to be comfortable with it or to have lived with it over time. Rather, the attempt is toward control, as if the patient is making a last-ditch but not successful effort to hold the line against more pervasive psychotic disorganization. This latter hypothesis is strongly supported when we find that on the WAIS he obtained a total IQ of 127, a Verbal IQ of 134, and a Performance IQ of 115 and that the WAIS is relatively intact as far as signs of thought disorder are concerned.

Organic

A 20-year-old unemployed male with a sixth-grade education produced the following Rorschach summary.

Summary of Scores

				$R = 14$	$EB\ 1/1$		
W	3	F+	3	A	5	W%	21
D	10	F−	3	Ad	3	D%	71
S	1	F±	2	(H)	1	Dr%	7
1 Do		F∓	3	Hd	1	F%	78/93
		FM	±∓	Stripes	1	F+%	45/46
		CF	1	X-ray	1	A%	57
		Naming		At	2	H%	7(14)
						P	2
						P%	14

Qualitative		
Pec	4	Fail Card II
Fluid	4	
Word Finding Difficulty	2	
Perplexity	2	
Impotence	3	

INTERPRETATION. The exceedingly low $F+\%$, that is, the poor formal accuracy despite efforts at formal control (extended $F\%$ of 93), might suggest a psychotic picture but such poor reality testing in a psychotic would be expected to lead to more autistic elaboration in his thought processes, to more peculiar, confabulated, and contaminated thinking. Rather, the notations of word finding difficulties, perplexity, and impotence (the subjective sense of being unable to match one's performance to what is required and expected), along with the low form level, both in the absence of autistic modes of thought indicate an organic picture. The presence of color naming (mentioning the colors by name as a response) further corroborates the impression of organicity. The A% is somewhat high, pointing to stereotypy of thought; movement responses are curtailed to the *FM* variety, and, while these reflect some ability to buffer strong affective reactivity, the color naming and the extensive impairment in perceptual organization are likely to result in poorly organized, irrational-seeming behavior. A card failure, Card II, shows that another way available to him to help organize his reactions is through avoidance, but the fact that he does not reject Card III or Cards VIII through X suggests that his avoidance tendencies are more likely to be apparent during the initial arousal by external pressures.

MRS. T.'S RORSCHACH

In the following section we will present an analysis of Mrs. T.'s Rorschach. At the outset three summary sheets are presented: one for her entire Rorschach, the other two for the two separate sessions in which the Rorschach was administered. In the first session Cards I through IV were administered and in the second session Cards V through X. A seemingly marked difference between her functioning on these two days is the reason for presenting separate Rorschach summaries. Following an analysis of the summary sheets, we shall proceed to a card-by-card, response-by-response analysis of Mrs. T.'s Rorschach. As with the previous clinical examples, the summary sheet will be used as a general source of hypotheses regarding personality structure as one source of data. By itself the summary sheet cannot make the patient come fully alive; only a synthesis of the varied sources of test data can achieve this end.

Mrs. T.'s Rorschach Summary Sheet, Cards I–X

			$R = 54$	EB 9/7.5 (8.5)				
3	W	10^a	F+	8	A	13	W%	19
	D	35	F—	0	Ad	5	D%	65
	Dr	4	F±	8	(A)	1	Dr+S%	16

Mrs. T.'s Rorschach Summary Sheet, Cards I–X (*Continued*)

R = 54	EB 9/7.5 (8.5)		

2 S	5	F∓ 4	H	5	F% 37/89
4 s		M±,—,∓,∓	(H)	4	F+% 80/67
1 Do tend		MC′±	Hd	5	A% 33
		FM∓,±,∓,+	(Hd)	6	H% 18/37
		FMC′ —	Obj	1	P 5+4
		FM(C)±	Pl	1	P% 9(17)
		FMC∓,+symb	Na	2	
		FC(C)±	At	2	
	+	FC	1 Sex	5	
	∓,+	symb FC FCC′—	Food	1	
		F/C±	Blood	2	
		F/C(C)∓	Symb	1	
	2	CF 2	1 (Death)		
		C symb 1	1 Anal		Qualitative
	∓,±,±	F(C)	1 Homo		Fab Comb 4
		F(C)C′∓	1 Religious		Fab Comb tend 1
		(C)F 0			Fab 10
		(C)CF 2			Confab 5
	∓,—,—,±	FC′±,+,∓,±,+,±,+			Confab tend 5
		C′F 1			Contam tend 2
		C′ 0			
		FCh±,±,∓			Pec 5
		ChF 0			Par 2
		Ch 0			Pers ref 4

ᵃ Numbers and symbols to the left of scoring items refer to additional scores.

Interpretation of Mrs. T.'s Rorschach Scoring Summary

LOCATION. The location percentages are $W = 19\%$, $D = 65\%$, $Dr = 16\%$, and these reflect a distribution within the normal expected range. D and Dr are both elevated at the expense of a slightly lowered $W\%$, but the reduction in W is not large enough to be of diagnostic significance. The most outstanding feature of the location scores is the heavy emphasis on white space responses; five such responses and six additional ones indicate a great deal of unconventional thinking and may reflect marked negativism and paranoid ideation.

DETERMINANTS. The $F\%$ represents the balance between intellectual rational control and affective experience and expression.

A very low $F\%$ points to an intrusion of affects and emotions into cognitive functions, while an exceptionally high $F\%$ reflects affective constriction. Mrs. T.'s $F\%$ of 37 is distinctively low, whereas her extended $F\%$ of 89 is high, although not excessively so. This disparity between the regular and extended $F\%$'s reveals that the nonextended $F\%$ considered alone obscures this woman's intense struggle for containment of affect. That is, the slightly lower $F\%$ reflects her sensitivity and/or vulnerability to emotional stimulation, but does not reveal the degree to which she attempts to contain it, as evident in the high extended $F\%$.[3]

Though intellectual controls and defenses serve to modulate her affective responsiveness, when her responses include the affective determinants, such as color and shading, there is a marked drop in the effectiveness of her reality orientation (her extended $F+\%$ is 67 as opposed to a regular $F+\%$ of 80). It is apparent, then, that many of her resources are directed at affective containment but that the impact of affect results in some loss of capacity to successfully and accurately perceive reality.

The dilated experience balance of 9.0 to 7.5 (8.5) reveals a great investment in active ideation and fantasy as well as a highly active affective and expressive orientation. In evaluating the $M{:}C$ ratio, the quality of the Ms as well as the distribution of the color scores are important. In examining M we are interested in whether they are plus or minus and to what degree FM scores comprise the sum M.[4] With regard to the color distribution in the experience balance, we examine the relative balance of FC, CF, and C in the sum C. Here too, the plus or minus scores of FC have to be taken into account. In the case of Mrs. T., the M distribution (including pure M and blends of M with other determinants) is $2+$ or $\pm$, $3-$ or $\mp$, 4 $FM+$ or $\pm$, and 4 $FM-$ or $\mp$. Such a distribution of plus and minus scores, about as many minuses as pluses with several pure minuses, indicates ideational disturbance in this woman. The great number of M and FM in this record is especially prominent since FM is not scored for the diversity of responses that it is

[3] This illustrates the value of the extended $F\%$ for assessing the degree to which logical thought is used to modulate affective experiences. If only the regular $F\%$ were used in this case, we would be unaware of her efforts to temper emotions.

[4] It will be recalled that FM is not used for animal movement; it is only given for weak human movement or animals in clearly human-like movement.

scored for in other scoring systems. The degree of $M-$ strongly suggests that ideational pathology, possibly of a paranoid nature, is evident. That paranoid, rather than phobic or obsessive, ideational symptomatology is likely to be present is suggested by the high number of M and of $M-$ and $\mp$ in particular and also by the high number of white space responses which further supports the paranoid, negativistic, and idiosyncratic orientation of this individual's thinking.

In examining the color responses, the sum C of 7.5 (8.5) is comprised of four FC, two F/C, four CF, and one C symb. The presence of six form-dominated color responses in the sum C is another indication of the patient's attempts to modulate and control her affective reactions, although the earlier inference of the forced quality of her affective control is given strong support by the two F/C responses. It is also of interest that several of her color responses (the pure C and one FC) involve the symbolic use of color which again suggests that ideation, possibly of a paranoid nature (because of the symbolism), is used in attempts to control affects and impulses. That it is paranoid thinking which is likely to be reflected in these color scores is quite consistent with the over-ideational quality represented by the large number of M responses and the idiosyncratic quality of her thinking as indicated in the white space responses and the poor form level of many of the M responses. Although only one pure C is present, the balance of her color scores is weighted toward CF and C, since we expect a predominance of FC over CF and C. Thus, the distribution of color scores, like her extended $F+\%$, suggests that despite clear efforts at rapport and control, her modulation of affect and of impulsive behavior may be tenuous and that poorly controlled and maladaptive breakthroughs of impulse cannot be ruled out.

SHADING. There are nine shading, i.e., Ch and (C), responses in this record and in only two of them is shading dominant over form. The dominance of shading in both of these responses occurs in combination with CF. This tendency toward color-shading blends is further highlighted by the fact that six of the nine shading responses are seen in colored areas of the cards—a very unusual occurrence. It will be recalled that these types of responses (shading responses in bright colored areas) can represent "a mingling of affect and anxiety as seen in complex emotions like nostalgia (sweet sorrow)" (Rapaport et al., 1945) and also that such responses are more frequently produced by suicidal patients (Appelbaum & Holzman, 1962).

Since the shading responses are primarily form dominant, they do not indicate pervasive and free-floating anxiety, but rather, again, reflect the efforts at containment of strong affective experience. However, the fact that three of the seven form dominant responses are of $\mp$ quality shows that affective control (particularly over anxiety) is not altogether successful and that Mrs. T. is probably vulnerable to intense feelings of anxiety. Her general emphasis on form dominant (FCh, $F(C)$ as well as FC') responses is also indicative of anxious, driven, and watchful strivings toward interpersonal rapport and adaptiveness.

ACHROMATIC DETERMINANTS. Of the total of twelve responses that include C', all but one are form dominant. Thus, 22 percent of the patient's responses contain achromatic color, a very high percentage, which indicates that depression probably plays an important role in her psychological state. However, depressive affect appears to be under moderate control because only one of the black-white determinants is dominant over form and, of the remaining eleven that are secondary to form, seven are in the plus category. This drop in form level, however, indicates that depression, as well as anxiety, can disrupt her judgment.

TYPES OF CONTENT. Because of the emphasis on sexual content (five responses and one additional), we can assume that this is an area of major concern for Mrs. T. Taken together with her paranoid, negativistic, and depressive orientation, one might speculate that the problems of sexual adequacy and sexual identity are likely to be the focus of much of her thinking. The record contains a total of 20 human, human detail, or human-like percepts. In a well-integrated Rorschach one expects the number of H to outnumber the Hd responses and fewer (H) and (Hd) responses in comparison to full human content. But in Mrs. T.'s Rorschach, the H and Hd categories together have the same number of responses as the (H) and (Hd) categories, and she has the same number of Hd and of H responses. While we would infer from her high $H\%$ that she is highly invested in human beings, the equal number of H and Hd and the extensive number of (Hd) and (H) may reflect some tenuousness in her relationship with people as well as a distortion of the human image. In an overall evaluation of the content categories, we find that aside from human and human-like content, animal content, and sexual content, there is very little else that is of note. The paucity of other content categories is likely to reflect a constriction of interest.

POPULARS. The five full populars which she produces are below the expected number, especially in a record of 54 responses. This suggests trends towards alienation, unconventionality, and possibly, unrealistic thinking which are mitigated to some extent by the number of near-popular responses.

QUALITATIVE COLUMN. Although being considered last in this summary discussion, the qualitative column serves as the clearest indicator of pathology. With the exception of psychotic conditions, one rarely sees such a massing of deviant verbalizations which include five confabulations, five confabulation tendencies, two contamination tendencies, four personal references, and four fabulized combinations. In evaluating the scoring summary, one would not have to go beyond this column to make the diagnosis of a thought disorder.

SUMMARY. By combining all the information gained from the summary sheet we emerge with a number of hypotheses about the psychological functioning of this patient. (1) *Thought disorder:* There are several aspects of the summary sheet which point to this formulation, the major ones being confabulations and other deviant verbalizations and the relatively low number of full populars. (2) *Prominent projective trends:* In a record in which the sum M is 9 with almost half of the movement responses of poor form quality, one must suspect paranoid thinking. In addition, there are four personal references, a paranoid score, and several symbolic color responses, all of which lend considerable substance to this formulation. In view of the thought disorder and paranoid trends, the possibility of paranoid schizophrenia should be considered. (3) *Depression:* Comments about this aspect of her functioning have been made previously with regard to the C' scores. In reviewing the total picture there are a number of factors which do not fit in with a diagnosis of depression. The most prominent of these are the high number of responses (54) and the high sum M and sum C, especially in a record in which inquiry is given after each card. That is, the amount of productivity, energy, ideational activity, and emotional liveliness indicated by these three summary scores tends to contradict a depressive picture—one in which ideational, affective, and energy output is generally minimal and depleted. The contraindicators of depression (R, sum M, and sum C) can serve as important clues for a dynamic formulation. Rather than rejecting the possibility of marked depressive concerns which are strongly suggested in the large number of achromatic responses, we can consider that the active and colorful, the exciting and action-oriented features may serve in the avoidance or denial of an underlying depressive core. Such a constellation makes up the typical hypomanic picture. Her heightened responsivity also does not seem to arise out of the capacity for warmth and rapport, but rather, it seems to be somewhat forced and to help contain the depressive affect. (4) *Hysterical trends:* Because of the high sum C, as well as the ten fabulations and the sexual content, the possibility of hysterical features could be considered and may represent one aspect of her premorbid character structure. It is often easy to discern an essentially hysterical patient from the scoring of the Rorschach; in this case, however, there is a greater variety of characterological features than would be the case in a pure hysterical picture. That is, there is more activity, more M, and more *Dr.* (5) *Sexual adjustment:* It is quite obvious that there is a great preoccupation with sexual thoughts in view of the five to six sexual responses and the two blood responses. One might hypothesize that this is an area of considerable difficulty for her, especially when seen in a woman who is driving (number of R is 54), and negativistic (number of S is 5–11), who has difficulty in human relationships and makes efforts towards, but shows a weakened capacity for, warmth and rapport. This points towards problems in the area of sexual identity and adequate sexual functioning. One might also consider the possibility of sexual acting out because of the coupling of a high sum C with indications of illogical modes of thought. (6) *Suicidal potential:* Lastly, but perhaps of greatest importance, the possibility of suicide must be taken into consideration. The massing of chromatic shading, the impulsivity as well as the combination of depressive (introjective) and paranoid (projective) mechanisms, all in a setting of a thought disorder, may point to a suicidal potential.

In sum, the summary sheet suggests a wealth and variety of psychological trends—diagnostically, most prominent of which are those pointing toward psychotic, especially paranoid, ideation and toward efforts to deal with strong depressive concerns, possibly through denial. The summary sheet reflects an active, psychologically rich picture, perhaps somewhat constricted as regards the breadth of content references but, nevertheless, a picture in which strong thinking, feeling, and action are prominent. The richness of this picture, the relative intactness of the $F+\%$, the investment in people rather than estrangement from them, the number of form dominant responses, especially of M and FC and the absence of pure C indicate that if psychotic features are present, they are probably not chronic but more acute. This is a record suggesting inner turmoil and struggle rather than a settled, comfortable acceptance of pathology. The variety of diagnostic trends further attests to this unsettled, dynamic quality.

Mrs. T.'s Rorschach Summary Sheet, Cards I–IV

			$R = 32$		EB 7.5/7.5			
3 W	7		F+	1	A	5	W%	22
	D	19	F−		Ad	4	D%	59
	Dr	3	F±	5	H	5	Dr+S%	19
2 S	3		F∓	1	(H)	2	F%	22/81
3 s			MC'±		Hd	1	F+%	86/62
			M±−∓∓		(Hd)	4	A%	28
			FM∓±		Obj	1	H%	19(37)
			FMC'−		Pl	1	P	1 + 2
			FMC∓,+ symb		Na	2	P%	3(9)
			FC(C)±		Sex	3		
		∓,+ symb FC			Food	1	Qualitative	
			FCC'−		Blood	2	Fab comb	3
		2 CF	2		Symb	1	Fab	6
			C symb 1		1 Death		Confab	5
			F (C) C'∓		1 Anal		Confab tend	5
		± F(C)			1 Homo		Contam tend	2
			(C)F		1 Religious			
			(C)CF	2			Pec	3
		−−∓± FC'±+∓±					Par	1
			C'F	1			Pers ref	4
			C'					
			FCh±±					
			ChF					
			Ch					

Mrs. T.'s Rorschach Summary Sheet, Cards V–X

		$R = 22$	EB 1.5/0(1)				
W	3	F+	7	A	8	W%	13
D	16	F–		(A)	1	D%	73
Dr	1	F±	3	Ad	1	Dr+S%	14
S	2	F∓	3	H		F%	59/100
1 s		M		(H)	2	F+%	77/73
Do		FM(C)±		Hd	4	A%	41
1 Do tend		FM∓+		(Hd)	2	H%	18(36)
		F/C±		At	2	P	4 + 2
		F/C(C)∓		1 Sex	2	P%	18(27)
		FC					
		CF				Qualitative	
		C				Fab comb	1
	±∓	F(C)				Fab comb tend	1
		(C)F				Fab	4
		FC′+±+				Pec	2
		C′F				Par	1
		C′					
		FCh∓					
		ChF					
		Ch					

MRS. T.'S RORSCHACH COMPARISON SUMMARY

The total administration of the Rorschach took place on two separate days. On the first day Mrs. T. was given Cards I through IV; the remaining six cards were given on the second day. While such a procedure ordinarily should be avoided, the reasons for discontinuing after Card IV in this case were a very long testing session which had been preceded by an hour interview, examiner fatigue stimulated by the patient's primitive and gory ideation, and the breakdown of the air-conditioning in a windowless room.

There was a noteworthy shift in some aspects of how she dealt with the Rorschach cards on the second day. Because of this change it was thought that an analysis of Rorschach summaries considered separately for each day would be useful in giving further clues to understanding the patient.

Scoring Summary: Analysis

In comparing the two summary sheets, the most striking feature in the summary for Cards V to X is Mrs. T.'s efforts at containment. On the last six cards she gave considerably fewer responses (number of R is 22) than on the first four (number of R is 32), although the latter included three color cards to which, considering the amount of her overall color scores, she might be expected to respond excessively. The sharp decrease in responses during the second testing session, the raised D and lowered $W\%$, and the increase in the number of popular responses furnish us with the clue that Mrs. T. was making strenuous attempts at control with a concomitant result of a decrease in integrative activity and an increase in banality. It is also noteworthy that she moves from a total of eight space responses (Ss) (including the five additionals) in the first set, to three Ss, one of which is an additional, on the last set. This shift, therefore (like the increase in P), is towards more conforming behavior and less oppositionality and negativism.

The effort towards increased intellectual and cognitive control is also exemplified in the F percentages. The straight $F\%$ (the percentage of responses determined solely by form) rises from 22 on the first day to 59 on the second day, and the extended $F\%$ (percentage of form dominated responses) goes from 81 to 100. The extended $F\%$ of 81 on the first day indicates moderate efforts at intellectual control and the extended $F\%$ of 100 on the second day expresses even more rigorous efforts at strong cognitive control, rigidity, and a tendency towards blocking. Thus, she goes from lesser to greater control in the two groups of Rorschach cards, whereas she might have been expected to move toward even less control because of the presence of the last three chromatic and very stimulating cards.

Probably the sharpest differentiation between the first and second days occurs in the color and movement scores. Both, but especially the former, effect the F and extended F percentages, so differences between the two experience balances were already suggested by the differences in $F\%$. Her color sum drops from 7.5 to 0 (1.0), and her sum M goes from 7.5 to 1.5. In considering the scores that made up the sum *C* on the first four cards, it should be noted that *CF* and *C* outnumber *FC*, which indicates tendencies towards impulsive and uncontrolled behavior. On the second set of six cards, however, she has no *CF* or *C* responses, and sum *C* is entirely composed of two F/C responses that are both plus. Thus, the distribution of her color scores on the second day shows increased efforts at rapport, docility, and compliance, but in a forced, strained, and artificial way rather than with genuine mutuality and warmth.

On the first administration day, sum *M* consists of five *M* and five *FM* of which three *M* and three *FM* are in the minus category. In the second session, she produces no *M* and only three *FM*, two of which are plus, the other minus. This difference is similar to that occurring in her color responses: in the first four cards quantity is high but decreases sharply over the last six cards, and the quality of the responses also improves. The sum *M* of 7.5 on the first day reflects tremendously active fantasying and an ideational emphasis which, because of the many disturbed qualitative scores, indicates paranoid thinking. On the second day, however, she allows less free rein to her fantasy, and this clamping down of controls appears to bring with it improved reality testing. Furthermore, it may be that she is simultaneously limiting much of the originality and creativeness which her *M* emphasis suggests but which is primarily in the service of her psychosis at present.

SHADING. There is no significant change in the *Ch* responses over the two administrations, but there are very important differences in terms of the (*C*) scores. On the first set of cards she gave four (*C*) responses, two of which were form dominant and two of which were primarily (*C*) with form secondary; on the second set both (*C*) responses were form dominant scores. Thus, the interpretative trend continues in the direction already set, namely, from more sensitivity and possibly sensuousness in the early cards towards more blocking and control on the latter cards. The extent of (*C*) responses in the constricted record obtained on the second day, however, would also indicate a driven and suspicious quality to attempts at interpersonal rapport.

ACHROMATIC COLOR. Her eight form dominant *C'* responses on the first day are reduced to three and the one *C'F* response drops out on the second day. Also, on the second day all three *FC'* are in the plus category whereas the day before four of eight were in the minus category. One might conclude from this that less depressive affect appears present on the second day. But if we bear in mind that over the course of testing, especially in the second Rorschach session, she looks more constricted, less responsive, less active, and attempts fewer integrations (lower $W\%$), we might also consider that she was more depressed during the second session. Another aspect of the different picture from the first to second session, therefore, would involve a sequence from a more hypomanic to a more depressed state.

Other noteworthy differences between the two sets of cards are contained in the number of populars present; one full and two near populars in 32 responses for the first four cards is low, whereas the four full and two near populars in 22 responses on the last six cards are more within the normal range. Again, there is a very clear effort towards adaptation and towards trying to see things the way others do. This trend is also reflected in the difference between the two A percentages, which rises from 28 on the first set of cards to 41 on the second set of cards. In this case it is the 28 percent that is more within normal limits, while the 41 percent is high and reflects increased banality and stereotypy in her thinking. Moreover, in looking at the content categories, her percepts for the first set are classed under fourteen separate categories but in the second unit are classed under only seven categories. This is a further indication of constriction, and at the same time the more disturbed content, such as blood, symbolism, and death, drops out.

QUALITATIVE CATEGORIES. If one were to read the two summaries as belonging to Rorschachs of two different people, one would come to the conclusion that the first person is obviously psychotic. Such a judgment would be based on the presence of five confabulations, five confabulation tendencies, two contamination tendencies, and four personal references. On the basis of the qualitative column of the second summary sheet, one would hypothesize that the individual is relatively constricted with paranoid features (because of the EB weighted toward M with little C). The several peculiar verbalizations might suggest some trends toward unrealistic modes of thought but certainly not to a psychotic degree.

One last test feature that can be evaluated here is the reaction time and time per response for the two sets of cards. While Mrs. T.'s average response time on Cards I through IV is 8.5 seconds, which may be considered within the normal range, on Cards V through X her time per response more than quadruples to 37 seconds per card. This latter reaction time reflects increased delay and points to her efforts at control. Insofar as time per response is concerned, the average time is 36 seconds on the first set and 63 seconds on the second set. Despite the greatly reduced amount of overall verbalization during the second set of cards, her time per response almost doubles. Thus, we have one further and very clear indication of her attempts to control her impulsivity and to restrain her thinking.

The fact that we see different psychological pictures on the two days for the same individual is, of course, of great importance, for it suggests a shift of functioning from a more openly psychotic state to what might be considered to be depressed and constricted with paranoid features. While such variation may not mitigate a diagnosis of psychosis, it is indicative of Mrs. T.'s capacity to set up effective controls and to appear, at times, to be well integrated. More important, from a prognostic standpoint, the variation reveals that Mrs. T. is not settled into a chronic, hardened, psychotic position; the variation, in fact, may show a good degree of resiliency.

The fact that Mrs. T.'s Rorschach test results appear so different from one day to another raises a critical question regarding psychological organization in general and, specifically, its manifestation on the Rorschach test. For if a person can show dramatically different results on different days, one might question the reliability of the test; in other words, one might question the capacity of the test to tap more than a limited segment of personality organization at any particular time. Furthermore, one could also question the generality of test findings beyond the immediate situation and the time of testing. According to this way of thinking we might not have seen the marked shift in Mrs. T. if the entire Rorschach had been given on one day in one session. In large part these questions revolve around the consistency of personality over time and the extent of its transformation or alteration by specific situations. It is our view that while many aspects of psychological functioning may alter over time, nevertheless, there will tend to be consistency in the basic organization and patterning of defensive efforts, i.e., in the structural, stylistic aspects of personality integration. The differences in Mrs. T.'s psychological functioning appear, from the summary sheet, to be primarily in the direction of intensifying efforts at control and containment which were at least moderately present on the first day (particularly in her extended *F%* of 81). The underlying depression and the paranoid trends, however, are also present in the second testing. What is not evident in the summary of the second session is the extent of the hypomanic and psychotic potential.

But a much fuller understanding both of differences between the two days and also of consistencies and similarities can only be derived from the particular responses and her attitudes and affects during testing. We shall proceed, therefore, by turning to a card-by-card, response-by-response analysis of Mrs. T.'s Rorschach. The comparison summary discussions were presented to suggest some hypotheses about the two separate administrations and also to further indicate the value, as a guideline, of the summary sheet.

MRS. T.'S RORSCHACH

"What I'd like you to do is look at each card and tell me what it looks like, what it could be."

Card I

Reaction Time: 7"   Total Time: 1'55"
1. Just anything I see? [Yes.] Well, I see two elephants, two itty-bitty miniature elephants [D1 + D2; side figures] [1] fighting over a roach—cockroach—in the middle [D4]. You want my immediate reactions as to what I see? [D F+ A, D F± A] (W, Fab Comb.) [2] [Up to you, whatever you see.] Do you want different ideas of what I see? [Umhmm.]

INQUIRY: [What made it look like two elephants—little elephants fighting over a cockroach?] Yes. What made it look like that? [Umhmm.] Well, they were—both heads were on a slant. I saw the—ears flying out and their legs. And they were both kind of standing sideways on an elephant. They both got their—their snozzoolas—[half laughs] or their trunks or whatever you call them wrapped around the cockroach.

---

[1] These refer to Beck's (1944) location system which is used throughout the book. Location cards for responses are presented following p. 246.
[2] Designations in brackets refer to additional scores and qualitative features.

And the cockroach what have you is—the central figure. You see the two little twee—uh pincher things on the top of his head . . . [Anything else that made them look like elephants?] Uh, just the form. They just looked like elephants to me. Uh, you know, the—they were identical elephants, you know—on each side. [Anything else that made them look like elephants?] Well, other than the fact that they had the ears and the nose and the little tail-like things down at the bottom. The legs—they just looked like elephants—the whole black . . . . [Now what made it look like a cockroach?] Uh, just the basic shape. The middle figure, you know, central focus point and the—as I said, the pinchers on the top. Can't say exactly. I mean just looking at it, it looked like a bug to me—a cockroach. [Would you just point out the elephants?] [Card shown.] Here are the ears, the nose, the trunk, the legs, the tail, the same over here. [Where would the tail be?] Right there's the tail. [And the trunk?] Here. Right here. . . .

INTERPRETATION. The first noteworthy aspect of this card is Mrs. T.'s opening question, "just anything I see?" Her opening emphasis is to turn to the tester for assistance and/or relief of responsibility for what she reports. Her use of the word "anything" suggests that she is considering a free, uncontained, unthought-out approach and her need to turn to the tester, therefore, suggests that she may feel some need to have external assistance and support in containing her responses. She essentially paraphrases this concern following her first response when she says, "You want my immediate reaction as to what I see?", except that the word "immediate" adds the factor of temporal speed. It is also of interest that she puts her emphasis on what she sees, not on what comes to mind or what the card could be. This could mean that "seeing" has some special quality to her, that the perceptual sensory apparatus is highly invested; this may become clearer as we proceed.

She opens with a whole response—not the popular bat, but rather, a more complex integrative W built up from two details. This requires considerable associational and perceptual activity and energy. However, while the details are in themselves of good form quality, their interconnection seems strained, and that she is able to transform a huge elephant down to cockroach size indicates a capacity in fantasy to engage in unusual transformations and alterations of reality.

From the vantage point of the organization of defenses, this response reflects an attempt to minimize a huge attacking creature by reducing it in size and making it almost child-like and playful. Various features of the response, however, point towards considerable defensive instability, especially her inability to successfully reduce the impact of the aggressive onslaught and her somewhat disjointed comments during inquiry. From the point of view of defenses, it is also of interest that she does not avoid the aggressive impact completely beforehand or do away with it completely belatedly, but rather, she tries to convert it, and does so redundantly, into something smaller and hence less threatening. The danger is perceived but treated in a playful manner, and her affect while responding is also generally euphoric. This style of defense is strongly counterphobic in quality, i.e., what is feared is made pleasant, and is approached boldly and unhesitatingly. This type of person leaps into what she fears most.

Other aspects of this response also point toward hysterical personality features—her sensitivity to and emphasis on extensions which have phallic as well as oral aggressive connotations to her and which she has trouble describing. Her effort at description shows a blocking in memory, "whatever you call them," which indicates a repressive orientation, i.e., she naively does not know what the area is called. Her effort to label the bug as a roach also but more speculatively suggests some difficulty with the sexual implications of the word "cock."

It is unusual for the center *D* area, the usual female form, to be described as male. When areas commonly seen as of a particular sex are seen as of the opposite sex, uncertainty as to one's sexual identity is often indicated. For the patient, it could point towards a significant degree of masculine identification. The fact that she also makes this figure into a repulsive cockroach, thereby implicitly associating it with dirt, suggests a similar view of her own feminine sexuality. What she sees, in effect, in this first response is a phallic attack by a powerful animal directed at an area of the card typically seen as female. It is not too great an inferential jump to assume that this response may be describing the patient's perception of the sexual act—one in which a fearful, aggressive male attacks a repulsive, dirty, bug-like, and masculine female. Sexual identity problems, therefore, seem quite striking. This is also a first representation of an interaction and may indicate a more general conception of close contact as potentially painful and harmful.

Issues around size are prominent in this response and may reflect, in addition, different aspects of the patient's self-image—feelings of being a large and bulky figure or repulsive and bug-like. A behavioral observation tends to corroborate this interpretation: while describing where parts of the cockroach and elephants were located, she constantly pointed to herself, suggesting that she closely identified with these animals.

While this response shows a fair degree of influence of primary process content (aggression and sex) and of formal primary process features (the juxtaposition of two such discrepant creatures), it is important to note from the form level that the patient's basic perceptual processes are intact and show adequate ties with reality. Rather, it is in the associative and integrative spheres that the patient begins to move away from reality.

2. I also see some sort of demon staring at me with a beak nose—[sighs] . . . . Uh, let's see. Now that the demon's staring at me I don't see very much else. [Half laughs.] Uh gads . . . [Ws FC'± (Hd)] (Fab, Par, Pers Ref.)

INQUIRY: [And then you mentioned a demon staring at you.] Yeah, well squinting your eyes, you just saw the black form with the two— the white—you know, the two white kind of triangular things with the eyes and then down further the nose opening—very evil sort of looking thing. [What else that made it look like a demon?] It looked like it has ears and it narrowed down to a point—sharp—sharpness. [Anything else?] Uh uh. [What gave you the impression of staring at you?] I don't know. I mean the—uh, the eyes are centrally placed. They're looking straight out. They're looking at me—whoever was looking at them, they'd be looking—or visa versa.

INTERPRETATION. Responses in which patients perceive a figure staring directly at them indicate a loss of distance from the card of a paranoid nature. Inasmuch as the figure here is labeled as an evil demon, the response suggests concerns around criticism and blame and/or instinctual temptation. Imbuing external reality with these characteristics is a sign that one is attempting to project outwardly one's own impulses (temptation) or super-ego pressures (criticism). Feeling looked at directly shows an unclear separation between the card and oneself, implying that the evil intent is especially intended for the patient who is singled out for this purpose. This is equivalent clinically to a projective, paranoid attitude which finds meaning in the environment specifically directed toward oneself and usually of an evil, sinister nature. The aggressive implications of the first response—suggestive of an identification with the victim of some sort of hostile, phallic and oral aggressive attack—are further expressed in this response, which is an evil demon with prominent phallic extensions (the sharp beak, nose) and simultaneously an evil-looking opening (of the nose).

It is of interest how the patient treats this demon. She blocks momentarily and says she does not "see very much else"; then she tries to treat the demon humorously by laughing, but in so doing also indicates some recognition of her difficulty. In the inquiry, moreover, she tries to emphasize the effortfulness of seeing this response by stating that she actively had to squint her eyes which makes the demon less clear, more fuzzy-looking, and less of a direct, immediate threat. Similarly, her statement "They're [the eyes are] looking at me—whoever was looking at them . . ." also reflects some effort, albeit unstably, to shift the focus of direction away from herself toward including other people and reversing the direction to active viewing instead of being passively viewed. Thus, looking and being looked at achieve a more prominent place in this patient's psychological make-up with connotations of evilness, possibly of criticalness, and possibly of temptation.

In the inquiry Mrs. T. changes the beak-nose into a nose opening. This alternation between an extension (phallic and male) and an invagination (female) again points toward a fluid sex role identification. Her sensitivity to areas with aspects of male and female sexual anatomy also lends support to the notion that the evil demon response may contain within it guilt about being tempted by sexual thoughts or guilt about sexual actions.

3. Oh, yes I do too—see a headless angel—looks like he's conducting an . . . orchestra or something . . . That's about all, I think [W M± (Hd), (P)] (Confab. tend.).

INQUIRY: [Then you mentioned the angels conducting.] Well, there was one angel—the central figure again—the one that was the beetle —the cockroach before—is the—the form, the torso of the angel without a head, just the two little rolls on top of the neck. And uh—oh no, no, I'm sorry. The two things that they're the pincher-like things —they're the hands conducting. And of course the wings were the things that shot off at the sides . . . . [What gave you the impression of an angel?] The soaring wings, the central shape of a robe— the robe of course . . . . [You say soaring wings.] Well, they're out. They're stretched-out wings. They look you know like they are poised for flight perhaps. [Then you mentioned conducting an orchestra.] Yeah. [What gave that impression?] [Sighs.] The hands raised, as if, you know, the grand finale or something. [Anything else?] No. . . .

INTERPRETATION. The patient resists her inclination toward avoidance at the conclusion of the second response, and, instead, she produces one further response. Again, it is a response of good form quality and the third in a string of whole responses. This initial tendency toward whole responses is noteworthy in that it indicates very strong strivings for synthesis, inclusiveness, and abstraction. Soaring ambitions and expansive personality features are often reflected in records characterized by many whole responses. This last response, therefore, reflects a blending of impressions between structural aspects of the response (the number of Ws) and the content of the response (the soaring angel figure).

In its implications, this is a very rich response. For one thing, it completes a trend weakly started in the second response, that of trying to take herself out of the threatened, fearful, and passive position and placing herself instead in a more active and controlling role. What in an earlier response was a cockroach being attacked has been transformed into a figure which is directing others. Hence, the patient has been able successfully to reverse feelings of being controlled to controlling. Reversal is also evident in another way. For the demon of the second response (the projected super-ego and/or id characteristics) has been transformed into a angel; guilt and temptation are thereby converted into innocence and a denial of guilt, and what was a cockroach earlier, and dirty, unclean, and repulsive, has become pure and holy.

Indications of successful defensive efforts here include the good form of the response and the ability to work toward a more active, less fearful position. But some weaknesses of defense are also evident: the angels are headless and therefore lack a center of intellectual control, a fact that weakens the control indicated via their activity; the angels are male in the area usually seen as a female form (again pointing toward sexual identity issues and a masculine identification); the activity level of the angel is fluidly variable since its wings are alternately soaring, poised for flight, or shooting off which indicates difficulties around the expression of action tendencies; there is something incongruous about an angel with aggressive, pincher-like things also poised for flight and conducting a grand finale; the excited, climactic quality of the response, considering other suggestions of sexual preoccupations, may have a direct referent to the sexual climax. The response, in its emphasis on a grand finale (it is her last response and grand finale to the card as well), may also suggest the presence of grandiose and excited fantasies about death and life after death.

This final response, then, is an attempt at a grand denial of the preceding aggressiveness, dirtiness, fearfulness, and evil. Through a process of reversal a more pure, grandiose, and angelic self-image is arrived at. The sequence for the three responses is of interest for there is a progression toward a projective resolution before reaching the position of reversal and denial. What we see in sequence is an initial counterphobic defense which is unstable and leads toward projective ideation and finally to an expansive and more hypomanic position. Thus, as the responses proceed there is an increased reliance on more primitive defenses—projection shored up by denial. This defensive sequence, following the first more counterphobic response, suggests that some present decompensation may be underway in a basically hysterically oriented individual.

Card II

Reaction Time: 14″   Total Time: 4′30″.
1. I see two bear cubs [D1] in this balancing something on their nose, perhaps a carrot [D4]. Their paws are lifted. The—the red above [D2] looks like perhaps they've—I don't know—sort of ghastly, you know, kind of like a ghoulish sort of business—the red looks like blood and all that . . . . I'm supposed to view this as a whole—right?

[D FC'+ Ad P, D FCh± Food, D CF Bld] (W Pec., Fab.) [It's up to you.] I can pick out parts, is that it? [Uh huh.]

INQUIRY: [You mentioned at first that the bear cubs are balancing a carrot.] Yeah. [What made it look like bear cubs?] The basic black. I mean, they're—it looked like the shoulder and the head. Two bear cubs and they're nose to nose. It's just the black uh. And their noses are together and they go into kind of a cone shape. And uh they're sort of split down the middle where they've got two carrots side by side balancing on their nose. They have the ears, the basic shape of a—you know, what I would think a bear cub would look like—outline, silhouette, or what have you . . . . [What gave you the impression of a carrot?] The slender, you know, pointed object rising in—in the middle of the black silhouette. [Anything else that made it look like a carrot?] It looked like it had circular rings on it. [Anything else?] Well, it was wide at the bottom and it narrowed at the top . . . . [Anything more?] No. [Then you mentioned it looked like blood on top.] Yes, just the red. [Anything else?] Well, kind of the red above. I don't know how I got that was blood, but it looks like it was bleeding out of their chests facing each other . . . . [You say bleeding out of their chests?] Yeah, it looks like blood is kind of oozing—from the bottom part of their bodies—the chests, the shoulders of the bear cubs. I'm seeing a regular zoo today . . . [gaiety returns]. [Could you show me how you saw that—the blood?] [Card shown.] The blood—here. [Uh, huh, and you said that uh oozing from their chests.] Yeah, this is their chests, sort of, uh, you know, see . . . their paws almost . . . their shoulders. Blood's just kind of oozing out. Blood's up here. [Uh. Blood up there too?] Uh huh . . . [card withdrawn].

INTERPRETATION. Her first response, "bears," is a popular one, but, as in her first response to Card I, she takes large animals and makes them diminutive, childlike, and playful. She also takes an area often seen as a phallus and sees food instead, which points to an orally conceived image of the male organ, i.e., the phallus loses its specifically sexual meaning and is represented instead as a source of nurturance. But a potentially childlike, comic, and comfortable oral response rapidly becomes infused with more frightening fantasy. Thus, her use of the expression "basic black" has a connotation of feminine apparel and chicness which seems a strained way to deal with the depressive, dysphoric implications of the black color. Also, the balanced carrot may express feelings that oral supplies are tentative and shaky and that her present defensive position is similarly unstable. Confirmation of her defensive instability is most striking when the playful scene becomes ghastly, ghoulish, and bloody. At first she refers to the upper sides as blood, then expands this to "bleeding out of their chests," and finally she states that "blood is oozing from the bottom part of their bodies." Her thinking becomes fluid in her contradictory locations of the blood; her effort seems to be to avoid the lower, and possibly sexual, parts and to displace her emphasis upward, but her fluid thought processes at this point indicate the lack of success in this effort.

As was true of her earlier responses, the form quality remains intact. In this response it is her reaction to color that disrupts the clarity of her thinking and stimulates fearful ("ghastly"), deathly ("ghoulish"), ideation and a strong affective reaction. Since this is the first card with color, her response here suggests that her initial reaction to affective arousal is intense and generally may disrupt her thinking and lead to thoughts about body damage, mutilation, and death.

Following this response she senses her difficulty and turns to the tester for clarification and structure about whether she is supposed to give whole responses. She phrases her question in a way that suggests she expects the tester to agree that she should only give whole responses, as if there is a detail response she does not want to give possibly to the center white space since she circles it with her finger while she asks her question.

2. Well, there's one part in here that looks like oh—the vagina or something [D3]. [Runs finger up and down the blot when indicating vaginal area.] Am I—am I supposed to look at it from one angle—say this way or turn it or what? [Again, up to you.] [D FC(C)± Sex.] [Looks around room in a suspicious manner.]

INQUIRY: [Then you mentioned the vagina.] The—where the bears' paws meet or their chest—the, you know, uh things, uh—I don't know how to describe it—a narrow opening . . . red . . . . [Anything else that made it look like a vagina?] I think just the shape of it . . . . [Anything else?] Well, as I said, the red and the red. That's about it.

[Would you point out where you see the vagina?] [Card shown.] Here. [And how much of an area?] From about here to right up here to down here. [Can you outline it?] Well, this right here . . . [card withdrawn].

INTERPRETATION. The possibility that she may have seen a percept in the center space which she tried to restrain is confirmed by this response.

She seems especially flustered and tongue-tied during inquiry, and earlier, in her question about the angle at which she should look at the card, she is equally uncomfortable. For one thing, she seems to want to look elsewhere and to get away from the percept; she also asks how she is "supposed to" view the card which introduces a morally imperative quality and raises the question of whether she feels that what she sees is acceptable (i.e., right); she turns outside herself for control of ideation that is to her of questionable acceptability, and she also seems suspicious, as if she might be judged and criticized for what she sees. Her emphasis on angles of viewing and her interest in inverting the card may, on a highly speculative level, refer to concerns with sexual activity of an inverted and hence perverted nature.

The inquiry to this response failed to establish the role of the color red. It is most likely being seen as blood, since its location is the same as the blood in the first response. In all likelihood, then, she is viewing a bloody vagina which would connote menstruation and/or damage and a repulsed view of feminine sexuality and of childbearing. Once again, however, good reality testing is conveyed by the high formal level of the response.

3. ↓↑Yeah [half laughs]. Uh, I see a pretty hairy-looking bug here [laughs]. Again a—a dem—kind of a, you know, diabolical sort of bug with long, red, transparent antennae . . . [D3] [D (C)CF A] (Confab).

INQUIRY: [And then you mentioned a hairy bug.] Well, it's down where I saw the vagina. It's a red outline, looks like a—a butterfly sort of thing, but a pretty horrible looking butterfly. It has the, you know, the things sticking out like transparent antennae . . . [look of disgust]. [What gave it the impression of a hairy bug?] It had a—it's like a—hairs poking, kind of brushy. It's a brushy looking thing. [Uh huh . . . What on the card made it look hairy or brushy?] Well, I could see—well, it looked almost like a brush stroke, you know, it just looked like little hairs sticking out, you know, very—one line—that sort of thing. [Uh huh. Then you said it looked—it looked pretty horrible, pretty diabolical.] Yes. [Uh huh. What gave that impression?] What gave me that impression? [Uh huh.] I—it just looked like a grotesque sort of bug—I mean the shape of it and the—the antennae and the transparency of it. Almost like looking at it—a jellyfish like thing, you know, that you can see through . . . . Red, again the color [clears throat]. [You said again the—] Well, I mean the—the red—redness, I guess, made it look you know, bloody perhaps . . . . [Anything else about it?] No.

INTERPRETATION. This response, especially during the inquiry, is extremely fluid and presents very primitive thinking in a very direct manner. The tester at this point began to feel somewhat overwhelmed by the archaic content and by the relative openness of Mrs. T.'s sense of revulsion at herself, at femininity, and at her sexual organ which, via the bug, is represented as jellyfish-like, yet also as poking, brushy, horrible, and containing phallic-like extensions.

This response has a projective aspect; it is a diabolical bug. She almost calls it a demon, thereby relating it to her response to Card I and again suggesting major issues around guilt and/or temptation regarding sexual impulses and acts. But, unlike the Card I demon, in this response the projective, fearful ideation seems minor in comparison to the more openly depressive self-representation of herself as a transparent, flimsy, spineless, diabolical, and horrible person.

Defensive efforts are extremely shaky in this response. She clearly identifies the bug with the bloody vagina and fails in her effort at projection, juxtaposing with it prominent aspects of her self-concept (a confused combination of female and male sexual anatomy).

A major feature of this response is the lapse in ego control which accompanies sexual ideation. It should be noted that while she was giving this response she rubbed her finger around the section of the card which she had identified as the vagina. This suggests possible masturbatory activity and concerns which serve as one source of her self-repugnance.

4. Sort of reminds me of a womb [D5 + D6] might look like also
. . . looks like uh the womb giving birth or something—just as I
said, diabolical bug—sort of thing—like the birth of a, er you
know, bug . . . [mood shift from gay to upset and depressed]
[DS F(C)C'∓ Sex] (Fab Comb.)

INQUIRY: [Then you mentioned it reminded you of a womb.] Just the
—the white, you know, in the center surrounded by the dark—sort of
a seeming closedness—of being close in. And then again the—the
vagina—the opening down at the bottom. [Anything else that reminds
you of the womb?] The roundness of it, the closed-in, as I said . . .
I think that's . . . you know . . . it. [You mentioned giving birth
to something.] To the bug. Looks like the bug is coming out the
vagina—the opening . . . . [Anything else that made it look like
giving birth?] Well, just that it looks like the—I don't know—what is
it that the baby comes out of [half laughs]—uh, the vagina, is that
right? [Uh huh.] Looks like it's—the—it's having a mus-muscular
kind of spasm—the way it comes down, goes out . . . a pushing sort
of. [What gave you the impression of a muscular spasm?] The waves
—it—it—uh—the elongated vagina looks like it's contracting and er
going out—the shape of it . . . . [Could you show me how you see
it?] [Card shown.] Well, here see. This is the opening from the—this
is the womb. This is the opening and of course, here's the bug. And
it looks like this is the body of the bug—the red there, and that it
is being pushed out, being misshapen by the muscles on the side
. . . [card withdrawn].

INTERPRETATION. The culmination of one trend, the disgust of the
female sexual and childbearing roles, reaches its full expression in
this response, and Mrs. T.'s mood more clearly shifts toward increased depression.

It is of interest that, despite the graphic quality of her description of the bug earlier and of the birth process here, even including
muscular spasms, she is unsure where a baby comes out. Her
memory block here is typically repressive and in sharp contrast to
her sexual responses, the content of which appears quite close to
consciousness. In effect, she demonstrates her essential lack of
clarity regarding sexual anatomy and processes.

Her description of the "close in," "seeming closedness," "closed
in" quality of the womb introduces a note of confinement which
contrasts dramatically with her soaring, flying images. A possible

interpretation is that she sees the female reproductive role as basically constricting and confining and that it is one of the various unpleasant things she wishes to flee from.

5. ↑→↑ Also I see the form of a woman, but she doesn't have any legs . . . or she—she sort of has a leg too—a leg, but it's just one leg. She's just standing there . . . She has red hair . . . .←↓ [Ws FMC∓ Hd] (Confab tend.)

INQUIRY: [And then you mentioned the form of a woman.] Well, I— the—the white that is outlined by the black is the torso. The arms are encompassing the black. They're hanging down on the outside. [You said the white was outlined by the black?] Yes. That is the torso of the body. The arms are hanging outside of the white. They're —the black is in between the arms, you know, under the armpits and outlining the . . . and the—the head of the woman is covered by the red splotches [D2] on top of the page. You don't see it outlined— the head, but the—you can see the hair there . . . And you don't see the legs, 'cause the black comes together. It looks just like it's kind of standing on one appendature. I don't know if it's a leg or what—sort of like a stem . . . . [Anything else that made it look like the form of a woman?] Just the outline, hips and the . . . breast. [Anything else?] No. [Could you point this out?] [Card shown.] Right here—here's the hips. Here are the breast. The arms are going out here. This is the hair. This is the face in here. This is the stem . . . [card withdrawn].

INTERPRETATION. This is the most unusual response not only because of its content but in terms of its formal properties. It is the second white space response, the first being the womb, and the space, moreover, is used in a fragmented way and involves a figure-ground reversal in which the black areas are omitted and the two upper red areas serve to frame the white space between them.

In this response, further verification is evident of Mrs. T.'s disturbed experience of her body and of her femininity by the introduction of an image of women as damaged and lacking in a sufficient number of body parts (i.e., castrated). But this response is verbalized with less revulsion and disgust than the previous response and shows clear, albeit unsuccessful, efforts to reinstitute adequate defenses. Since white space responses often indicate negativistic personality traits, the figure-ground reversal here may suggest negativism, oppositionality, and perhaps rebelliousness; also, seeing a featureless woman's figure in a blank area may suggest feelings of inner emptiness and depression. Without minimizing these suggestions and the poor form level of the response, which still indicates unsuccessful adaptive efforts, it is nevertheless apparent that Mrs. T. shows some resiliency in this response; in that what was blood earlier (*CF*) is now hair (*FC*), the response reflects a move away from intense and poorly controlled affective and impulsive experience.

Another relevant aspect of this response is a theme of fragmentation, the absence of legs, and the fact that the arms are detached and distant from the body. On the first card all her responses were whole responses; here she has moved more toward details and toward unusual parts of the card. Her movement toward detail responses and the theme of fragmentation probably reflect her inability to sustain an initially strong desire to integrate and bring everything together. Her initial efforts, therefore, can be considered as a defensive effort to counteract pressing concerns about her own lack of integration, both as regards her body and her experience in general.

6. ↓ Upside down I see a—[laughs] couple more bears with their noses together [D6]. Sort of looks like they bumped noses— red [D3] symbolizing the pain they feel . . . Think that's about it . . . . That's it. [D F± Ad; D Csymb, Symb] (Fab).

INQUIRY: [Then you mentioned a couple more bears.] Well, turned upside down, it looked like older bears, more stern looking. They're more strong. They give the appearance of more strength, more bigness. Uh again they're facing each other. They look like they just bumped noses. And the red is the pain they're feeling . . . . [Anything else about those bears?] [Gesture, indicating that she sees nothing else.] [Card shown.] Here they are. Of course, the ears and the— this is the head, the thicker neck, the noses—they're just kind of splattered noses. The red is the pain they are feeling [card withdrawn].

INTERPRETATION. Her efforts at defensive reconsolidation achieve further success in this response which is essentially a return to and reworking of her first response to this card. Good form level is reestablished; distance from the earlier omnipresent blood is arrived at by means of symbolizing the red as pain, and these bears are bigger, stronger, older, and less vulnerable, damaged or deformed. Similar concerns to those indicated earlier are revealed by the fact that their noses are splattered, which suggests again that intimacy essentially produces suffering and pain, but she is able to delay calling their noses splattered until rather late in the inquiry. In view of the degree of disrupted thinking midway through this card, it is impressive that she has been this able to bounce back and institute a more adequate and reality oriented percept.

The sequence of responses over this card is of special importance. For the content starts with an attempt at childlike playfulness, proceeds through disturbed themes of feminine sexuality, childbearing, damage, and mutilation, and ends with more advanced age, seriousness, strength, and bigness. In this sequence we are witnessing a representation of a process of growth and development which, despite its regressive detours and disruptions, reaches a realistic and mature level.

Card III

Reaction Time: 3″   Total Time: 8′5″.
1. Here I definitely see two birdlike people dancing. [D1] See the two instruments behind them on each side—saxophones perhaps [D2]. They're uh—birdlike creatures are holding—they're females. They're holding something in their hand [D4]. I don't know what. They're doing sort of a spinning around motion . . . [W MC′± (H) (P); D F± Obj] (Fab).

INQUIRY: [You mentioned two birdlike people.] Yeah, [Clears throat.] They were silhouetted in black. They're facing each other. They had beaks. Am I supposed to recall how I saw it as that? [Uh huh. What made it look like that?] Well, uh, they had the shape of a woman, sort of a bustline of a woman. And it looked like they had perhaps skirts on—something coming out from their abdomen—like they had their stomach out. Their legs—they're bent sort of like they're reaching like they're in a dance—[half laughs]—some kind of frenzied sort of thing. They had the beaks that are tucked. And on the sides uh the two red splotches were shaped like saxophones . . . . [What gave you the impression of birdlike people?] Well, they were thin, angular, not thin—well, yeah—thin. They seemed to stretch. And their ne—uh they looked like their—uh their head was, you know, like a beak—like —like, you know, kind of er big. [What gave you the impression of motion?] Their stance perhaps, like they're in flight or in motion. They were just, you know, for the moment in that position. Also looked like their arms were stretched toward each other. They might have a bowl or a hat or something that they were twirling around, going around to music.

INTERPRETATION. The rapid opening verbalization of the certainty of her perception seems to indicate that Mrs. T. is aware of the fluidities in her thinking on the prior card and that she is eager to respond to more reality-based percepts now.

The figure as it is initially described is involved in lively activity, and in the inquiry a note of frenzy and flight is added. The image in its emphasis on soaring and excited activity is in ways reminiscent of the angels at the end of Card I, except here the setting is even more secular, jazzy, and sensual. In marked contrast to the activity of these figures, however, is the description of them as "silhouetted in black" which introduces a quality of formal containment and depressive immobility. A further depressive aspect of the response is the thinness, angularity, and birdlike nature of the figures, which presents them as somewhat devoid of substantial oral supplies. Once again, flight and frenzied activity seem to reflect a denial of underlying depressive affect.

Beyond the linkage of the patient's difficulty describing the stomach area with problems around oral intake her reference to "something coming out from their abdomen" (plus the big beaks) gives the female figure a phallic-like quality and suggests that being overweight, and having a protruding abdomen may be tied with fantasies of possessing a phallus.

2. ↓ Then on the other side [half laughs]—upside down, I see a— again a very strange looking face looking at me—kind of a red mouth [D3]—kind of a beak-like mouth that comes down—two teeth going

out from the roof of the mouth [Dd 28]. The mouth is opening wide on each side. [Did you say a beak-like mouth?] A beak-like mouth, yes. And then it has two teeth coming out of the roof going out [clears throat]. The two—I see two very black, cavernous eyes [D4]. It looks like—go back real deep . . . [Ws FCC'— (Hd)] (Confab tend, Pers Ref).

INQUIRY: [Then you mentioned a strange looking face looking at you.] Let's see if I can re—I don't even know if I can remember that [laughs]. I think it was the whole thing—the whole—the whole shape. Yes, yes, I do remember . . . It had two black eyes. [Right.] Yeah, uh two black eyes and they looked like they were wells—that they had quite a bit of depth—you know, that they were far back. And the red—there was a red splotch in the middle. And the mouth looked like there were fishes . . . you know, how they come down. It looked like it was spread apart on the sides and it came down in a beak-like, you know, beak of some kind at the top. And at the bottom of the—the bottom of the mouth were drawn two long slender teeth put together, you know, close together. [Card shown.] [Could you run your finger around it?] Yes. Here are the eyes. Here's the mouth. See—this is the opening. These are the teeth that are coming out. This is the upper lip. [Anything else that belongs with it?] Well, this uh—these are the jaws—I mean, you know, the—the bone. Here's the jaw line. This—the sides of the face. It comes in. This is the shoulders [clears throat]. . . .

INTERPRETATION. Her desire to establish and maintain reality ties seen in the first response has failed and has given way to more primitive ideation in this response. Her opening comment, "then on the other side," is almost a prophecy of the switch from a reality orientation to a more fantasy-autistic orientation. The personal reference, the poor form quality, and the engulfing and protruding aspects of the mouth all indicate the infusion of primitive modes of thought and archaic drive material.

By saying that she "again" sees a strange face looking at her Mrs. T. indicates that she has in mind the staring demon of Card I. The present response, like the former one, shows a reliance on projective mechanisms but it is more graphic in its description of an oral, devouring, aggressive, biting creature. Inasmuch as projection is involved, it is most likely that this fearful image—the patient's representation of what she experiences from external reality—is a projection of her own intense oral aggressive impulses. She fears being devoured by others instead of acknowledging her own neediness which is felt to be ravenous, hostile, and unacceptable. The degree of underlying, but defended against, oral aggressiveness further supports the formulation of strong and basic depressive concerns and affect. Mrs. T. also laughed several times while responding in an effort to minimize her discomfort with this image. Efforts at denial as well as projection, therefore, are evident, and, in this instance, denial weakly serves to counteract the projective danger.

The juxtaposition of prominent extensions (the teeth) with a prominent cavity (the mouth and cavernous eyes) once again is consistent with an ever-increasing number of indications of Mrs. T.'s unclear sexual identity.

3. ↓ Then again I see two—two bird heads—eagle-like heads back to back—er facing outward with two—an eye—an eye apiece . . . [D4] [D FC′∓ Ad] (Fab).

INQUIRY: [Then you mentioned you saw a bird—kind of eagle-like.] Uh they were black, uh they were facing away from each other. Their —the back of their heads were meeting. They had an eye apiece. And their—they had beaks that curved outward on each side—very mean looking. [What gave them a mean look?] They were st—well, they looked stern, strong, cruel, and I think the beak gives more of the— the cruel look. And this one eye of each—they look so uh unfeeling, you know . . . . [Anything else about them . . .] No. [Card shown.] Here—here's an eagle. Here's his beak. Here's the eye—this thing over here—beak, the head, the forehead, the two eyes. [What is this?] Well, this is the outline. Well, see they're identical—one on each side. This is the outline of the forehead and here's the beak. Uh [coughs] . . . .

INTERPRETATION. Whereas the figure in the previous response is staring directly at Mrs. T., these birds are "facing away from each other," and the power of their eyes is at least initially reduced by giving the birds only "an eye apiece." But her defensive efforts are minimally effective, and the birds and her representation of external reality become not just fearful but also unfeeling, cruel, and cold.

The fact that Mrs. T. faces these birds away from each other suggests an effort at avoidance of face-to-face and intimate contact and an attempt at separation of the figures. In part she is unsuccessfully attempting to separate herself from the immediacy of the fearful face in the second response, but it is likely that she is portraying a more general fear of intimacy and interpersonal contact.

4. ↓ Then I see two rats. I—well I see the head and part of the body and it just fades into white [Dd 22]. And they're both facing out. And it looks like they're being attacked by sort of a flying fish like effect [D5], but that they have bird beaks on their head and that the rats are bleeding on the floor [D3]. [They're being attacked by?] Uh bird fish [laughs]—flying fish with—with bird beaks. And the rats are bleeding. The rats have tails like a mushroom cloud [D4] . . . [Dr FCh± Ad, D F± A, D CF Bld] (Fab Comb, Contam tend, Confab.).

INQUIRY: [And you mentioned two rats being attacked.] Uh [clears throat] let me see—hmm. Oh yes, they are again—each one is pointing out to the side. They're identical. You can see their noses—their head. You can see the basic shape of their head. There's a white splotch in the center of each head which is the eye. They're—they look like they're in motion. They're running away and down [clears throat]. The body seems to kind of fade off. And . . . they're being attacked, I believe, I said, by a fish-like bird [laughs] flying. They're being attacked—these birdlike creatures are descending out the, the air upon their heads—descend upon—their noses. And they have little beaks and uh there's blood on the floor from the—the rats. [What made them look like rats?] The basic shape, the—they were rodent-looking shapes. (Anything else remind you? . . .) They looked— [half laughs]—looked dirty, you know. Uh they just looked like, you know, the bi—uh kind of a rat—[half laughs]—like appearance to me—ugly . . . . [And what gave you the impression of their being attacked?] They were being descended upon [clears throat] by these creatures in the air—by creatures of pointed-like they—like a lance, you know, being driven down on something [coughs]. They look like they're f-falling at that time on these rats. [What made it look like blood?] Well, it looked like a puddle of red blood. . . . [Anything else?] Well, of course, the color. [Could you show me how you see them?] [Card shown.] Here are the rats. See the basic shape on both sides. These are the eyes. This is the blood and these are the fish-like things that are coming down on—see the tail, fins. [How much of the rat do you see?] Well, see—I see the hump of the back. [Uh huh.] I see the legs here—this kind of shading here—see where the light— the grey—they're running. The body just fades off here. It's got as I said, a mushroom-like tail [clears throat] . . . [coughs] . . . [card withdrawn].

INTERPRETATION. This response probably contains the most seriously regressed form of thinking we have seen thus far in this record. Not only is the content replete with primary process thinking, but there are serious lapses in ego control evident in the regressed modes of thought. Thought disorder is apparent in the contaminatory thinking which results in a "birdfish," although Mrs. T. shows that she is not totally committed to this contamination and has some tenuous recognition of it. Thought disorder is also apparent in the fabulatory combination of the "birdfish" attacking the bleeding rat and in the confabulatory thinking and poor form evident in the extensive excursion into bizarre and highly elaborated fantasy. This response is an example of psychotic modes of thought.

The aggression suggested in the strange face and further apparent in the cruel birds, breaks through in full force in this response. It is difficult to formulate a specific, clear meaning of this response, largely because of its fluid quality and, the variety of diffuse psychosexual content. The response portrays a phallic-aggressive attack ("like a lance, you know, being driven down on something") on the noses of rats, and it is therefore probably a disguised attack on the genitals. Anal themes (dirty, ugly rats with explosive, expulsive tail areas), which are equally prominent, suggest a strongly anal conception of aggression and sexuality and a self-image as similarly being ugly, dirty, injured, and vulnerable. But the patient here may be identifying herself both with the position of being attacked and with attacking. It is of interest that here flight and motion, which at other times serve significant defensive purposes for her, become combined with an aggressive, bloody, inescapable interaction. The feeling conveyed in this response, therefore, parallels the signs of ego disorganization by indicating a sense of inevitability about the destructive interaction.

There are also several features in this response, such as the dirty quality of the rats, the fading into the white, and the mushroom cloud tails, which could have been inquired into more fully. The theme of fading off into white might be related to an effort to transform feelings of worthlessness into thoughts of purity. The comments about the body fading off also suggest the possibility of feelings of estrangement or depersonalization. Failure to conduct a full inquiry into this response was partly due to the diffuse, primitive thinking, and the difficulty of inquiry reflects the difficulty in pinning down this response.

5. ↓ I also see kind of—well, I also a very umm dominating woman standing as the central figure—very stern, very mean-looking, staring at me—looking at me—looking, you know, directly toward me. She has her hands on her hips. She looks like a character out of a Bronte novel or something, you know, of that era—uh . . . [D8 is the head; Dds 24 is the body] [S M − H] (Fab, Pers Ref).

INQUIRY: [You mentioned a domineering-looking woman.] Yes, she's very thin—looked like a spinster. She has her hands on her hips. She has a very small waist. As I said, she looked like a Victorian woman. 'Course I don't know if that's the right word, but uh [clears throat] she looks very cruel. She looks like she's looking down on you. . . . [Anything else made it look like a domineering woman?] Well [clears throat], as I said, she looks very stern, very cold, very self-possessed, with her hands on her hips . . . and cruel. [What on the card gave you that impression?] What? [What on the card made it look like that?] Well, as I said, I—you—I get the impression that I'm looking up looking up at her and she's looking down at me very—with a kind of haughty manner. I mean her stance is very erect—very cool, you know, uh—not cool, very collected, calm, very well-defined [clears throat]. [Card shown.] Here's her head. See her eyes, her nose, her mouth, her neck. This is the kind of a flounce of a collar. Here are her arms. Here's her torso here. Here are hips. She has her hands on her hips. This is her dress coming out and this is her hair up here. [Now, uh, this is her mouth right here?] Yes [clears throat]. [The eyes are—] Right there—the two. [Right in here?] Yes [coughs, card withdrawn].

INTERPRETATION. A clearly projective image is returned to, and the patient sees herself in a vulnerable position, being looked down upon and hence being criticized and being inferior. This haughty, calm, cold Victorian spinster is a striking image of harsh, super-ego pressures, a symbol of repressiveness, a vigorous opponent of libidinous thoughts and actions. She is thin and self-possessed, very collected and well-defined, not dirty and repugnant like the patient's own self-concept. Mrs. T. thereby reveals an expectation of condescending, cold, moralistic, and critical judgment by others, which, like her other projective themes, reemphasizes a perception of others as fearful, critical, condemnatory. Indirectly, it points up, as well, the underlying sense of guilt and self-abhorrence regarding any sensual impulses and her association of calmness and self-control with control over oral needs.

It is important to consider that this figure is female and that it may represent a child's perception of a stern mother. Not only are representations of warmth, compassion, and sufficient oral nurturant supplies absent, the poor form quality additionally suggests that the patient can distort her perception of reality to such an extent that she could become quite unrealistically projective and paranoid regarding her relationship to female figures, especially maternal ones.

Thus far, white space responses have been used consistently for feminine percepts—two women and a womb. At this point it is not clear how this content is consistent with negativistic or oppositional tendencies. For this patient, the white space probably has some implicit connection with concerns about purity; it may have a ghost-like connotation; it may reflect external efforts to fill a dreaded empty inner space.

6. ↑ Oh yeah, [laughs] again I see two ghoulish-looking figures facing each other [Dds 23]. They look like they're pulling apart from each other. Hair is swished back from their head. They look like Halloween figures. They're pulling apart from each other, but they're standing. [Could you slow down?] Oh yeah [clears throat]. [They're two ghoulish-looking figures looking at each other and you mentioned something about hair which I didn't get.] Well, they're pull—they're pulling back from each other—straining apart. They—they're identical. Both of them have a hook beak [adjoining the upper part of D4] and hair that kind of just flies up and away [adjoining the upper part of D5]. They're standing at the bottom of a canyon. They're—look like they might be in a boat going down a river that

goes in between the canyons [D11 are cliffs]—a very foreboding-looking thing—very gloomy. I can see the sky—silhouetted into the river [D7]. And the sun's up above [D3]. It's very hazy. It looks like it's being blurred through clouds←↑ [half laughs] [S FM∓ (Hd), Dr C'F Na, D (C)CF Na.] (Confab tend, W tend.).

INQUIRY: [Then you mentioned ghoulish-looking figures.] Well, oh you mean the two that are pulled back from each other? [Mhmmm.] Yeah, well they're in white. And they're—you just see them perhaps from the waist up. They're both swaying back from each other as they're straining from each other. And again they have beaks. They're very strange-looking, bizarre [clears throat]. They look like they're in a flat boat travelling down on a w—travelling on a river that's in a canyon. They're in the depths of this dark canyon—very cloudy and hazy. The sun is just barely seen, distorted by the clouds. [Uh huh. What made them look ghouish?] Just their—their strange shape, their straining away from each other—the whole uh atmosphere of the—the picture. It's uh you know, like two ghouls [half laughs] sitting there straining the—kind of straining—just the—the—the—uh—sort of a devilish-looking picture. [Uh huh. And what gave you the impression of uh being on a flat boat?] [Half laughs.] [The cloudiness and haze.] Well, yes, it looks like a haze uh because the sun is the red and it looks like the clouds are over the sun, distorting the—the shape of the sun. And the clouds are picking up the color and carrying it, you know, elongating it. [Could you point this out?] [Card shown.] Here are the two figures right here. See they're pulling away from each other. Here's the beak right here. It kind of descends into nowhere. This is the boat. This is the river they're travelling—see, right up there. These are the clouds. They're silhouetted in the water. This is the shape of a cliff on both sides. This is the sun in here—right here. And the clouds are picking up the color.

INTERPRETATION. This is a highly elaborate and symbolic response. Again, following a series of responses of disturbed interactions between figures on the card or between herself and a figure on the card, Mrs. T. attempts to establish separation and differentiation. The need to separate from a similar person is intense and urgent; the consequence of an inability to separate is clearly stated in the content, for the figures are on a boat in the bottom of a canyon which "descends into nowhere." Failure to extricate herself from this gloomy, devilish interaction, from a sense of being identical with a ghoulish figure, leads inevitably to oblivion and death. We know that Mrs. T.'s mother committed suicide. It is not too great a speculative leap, therefore, to assume that here Mrs. T. is indicating her struggle against an identification with her mother and against the necessity of her following in her mother's steps.

In contrast to the otherwise intensely dysphoric mood of the response, Mrs. T. appeared somewhat excited and had to be slowed down by the tester. Excitement was also expressed in the odd description of the hair as flying "up and away," which is reminiscent of the angels earlier. Other unsuccessful hypomanic features (i.e., efforts at denial) include her short-lived effort to portray these figures as Halloween figures and to include a shining sun which soon is made blurred, hazy, and yields little light or hope. Thus, as we have proceeded with our analysis of the test responses, we increasingly see that projective and hypomanic (excited, gay) orientations are unstable and give way to overwhelming and deep despair. Marked fluctuations, therefore, among depressed, elated, and projective states are likely in the clinical picture.

7. ↓ I see two girls—two young girls with bustles on their behinds bending toward each other, like they're playing some sort of game [D4]. It looks like they might be ready to kiss each other. They might be kissing—not kissing, but going to kiss each other. [Clears throat] . . . [coughs] . . . . Think that's about all I see . . . except well—do you want me to say if I see anything else? [D M∓ H.]

INQUIRY: [Then you mentioned two young girls with bustles.] Yes, they're—they look like they're bending toward each other in a kiss. They're outlined in—well, not outlined, but they're in black. They're —they're large. And they look like they're in—well, they're in a bending-over stance, leaning forward to each other with their faces, you know, just a little apart. They look like they have on an old-fashioned dress with the bustle on the bottom—and behind . . . . [What made them look like young girls?] . . . Perhaps it was the— it reminded me of a game they might be playing . . . . [Card shown.] . . . Here are their heads, see. And this is their little [half laughs] bust-line. They're bending over. This is the bustle of their skirts. Their knees kind of bent—see. They have like pony tail sort of things and their heads are facing each other . . . .

INTERPRETATION. After the last dysphoric response of gloominess and ghoulish looking figures, Mrs. T. can muster up a rather light and gay percept, though of poor form level. It is noteworthy that she has, in effect, made the ghoulish figures into little girls by inverting the card, but she still points out that they are in black. Once again the emphasis is on problems concerning intimacy and contact with others, for "they might be ready to kiss each other. They might be kissing—not kissing, but going to kiss each other." The homosexual aspect of the response is prominent and is partially defended against when, accompanied by embarrassed laughter, she notes the girls' "little bust lines" and places the girls at a very early pubescent stage of development. In another distancing maneuver she locates the figures in a past era by seeing them with old-fashioned dresses. There is a noteworthy anal reference in her description of the bustles "on the bottom—the behind" and their bent-over stance also suggests a homosexual orientation. The homosexual themes become all the more important when we consider the earlier interpretations about Mrs. T.'s difficulty as regards sexual identification and her tendency toward a phallic identity.

It is significant that she ends this response by saying that this is about all she sees, yet indicates that there is something else if the tester wants her to report it. She thus changes from an active position to a more passive one of making herself dependent upon the tester's wishes and placing responsibility for her response on the tester's shoulders. She may also be asking for help in establishing control and is perhaps seeking permission to stop responding further to the card. However, when told to go ahead, she continues.

8. Mhmmmmm. The two red things on the side look like people falling through space [D2]. They're dead people. They're falling upside down. They're dead woman—females. I don't know if they're women or girls . . . . That's it [sighs] [D FMC+ *symb* 5 H] (Death) (Confab.).

INQUIRY: [And then you mentioned two red things—that looked like

This response is scored FM for the reason that some movement is present but since the people are dead their movement is not self-propelled but rather impinges on them.

two people falling through space.] Well, the reason they looked dead is, I guess, cause they looked limp. They're falling upside down. They're being dropped. I have the impression that they've been dropped. They're falling. They look dead, cause they're just kind of all stretched out like a fluid—like something flowing. They look like they have no control of their body. They're just falling. [Anything else that made them look like dead people?] No, perhaps the color. . . . [The color?] Red—death. Uh, it's also cold-looking [said in barely audible tone]. [What do you mean?] [Laughs] I don't know. I don't know really. Uh, just kind of an impression. Maybe it's just because you think of death as being cold.

INTERPRETATION. Her earlier efforts in previous responses at flying and soaring excitedly and in control, collapse fully here and the figures return to earth, limp, cold, dead, their movement (falling) a function of an external force which has dropped them. In addition, these figures are "stretched out like a fluid" which has a thematic connotation of feelings of passivity and of being poorly put together, but also suggests that Mrs. T. has rather strange feelings and experiences about her body and an unclear definition of her body and her body boundaries.

Her description of red as "cold looking" is peculiar, and it may involve a condensation in thinking in which death has been associated with blood, but with this step in thinking omitted. She hesitates at first before indicating how the color influenced her percept, and she tries to distance herself from its impact by using the color symbolically, but she does so in a way that shows a lapse in her thought organization. Thus, in spite of relatively good accuracy of form, the content of the response, the over-elaboration of the image, the strange bodily experience suggested, and the peculiar thinking about the color red and death all highlight the sense of disturbance. It is too open an expression of death, and the fact that it occurs in the context of passivity and lack of struggle makes it especially ominous and warns us that the possibility of suicide acts must be considered. For this response seems to complete the progress toward oblivion of the people on the flatboat in the foreboding canyon.

To recapitulate, the responses to this card show a weak initial effort at denial followed by themes of oral-aggressive and phallic-aggressive attack and of a cold, unloving maternal figure, then lead to efforts at flight and self-separation to avoid inevitable death, then a last ditch attempt to defend via denial, which collapses and culminates in death. On the other preceding cards Mrs. T. showed a capacity for resiliency of defense, an ability to work eventually toward a position of strength and control. This third card, therefore, indicates that her defenses are quite unstable and brittle at present and gradually give way and result in increased subjective dysphoria and increasingly disrupted ego functioning. One consistent observation is that aggression has been seen as coming from outside herself (i.e., it is projected) or else it is directed back onto herself and connected with death. Self-initiated activity and struggle is mostly reserved for attempts at flight and separation.

The last few responses to Card III are of special interest because they also make up a series of human movement (M) responses. We see, too, that these responses are closely linked with fantasies about death and about disturbed intimacy between people, indicating that her strong fantasy investment revolves to a large extent around her present problems and may not be very free for creative intellectual activity. Moreover, the close association among her M responses, themes of death and the interpersonal relationship between women also suggests that her most central and pressing problems concern her efforts to reunite with as well as to free herself from her dead mother.

During the time that she was responding to this card it was observed that Mrs. T. was playing with a cross she was wearing, running it over her nose and crossing the chain back and forth across her nose. At other times the emphasis in the content of her responses on noses and beaks has been taken to indicate her marked involvement with genital organs, particularly with the phallus. Her preconscious motor activity seems to reflect this same involvement. It also, and perhaps more directly, points up a particular turning to a religious article, and possibly to faith, for support in the context of concerns about death and self-annihilation. However, there is also something incongruous about playing with a cross, a certain degree of irreverence toward it while relying on it. The meaning of this action is ambiguous at this point, but religious imagery has been present previously (the angels) and it has curiously combined suggestions of excitement and, here, self-stimulation with purity and holiness. This may become clearer as we proceed.

Card IV

Reaction Time: 10″   Total Time: 4′50″.
1. Well, I see a large tree [D1], as though it were a forest—sort of gloomy surroundings of a forest. Two women hiding from each other, one on each side of the tree [Dds 24: top third is the head, center third is the upper torso, and the lower third is a skirt] [D FC′± P1, S M∓ H] (Pec).

INQUIRY: [What made it look like a large tree?] The central darkness was in the shape of a trunk going out—very large and sort of branched out on top. The darkness around—the other darkness around it was like in a forest—like in—very dark uh . . . . Two women were hiding . . . . [Could you point out to me how you see them?] [Card shown.] Uh here's the tree. And here this is the foliage up here—brush-like effect. The darkness around it gives kind of like trees in the background [clears throat] . . . . [Then you mentioned two women hiding.] Oh, uh the women are the white in the black. They're on each side of the tree. And they look like women because of their shape. You can see the head in the—the top—the just the outline of the body. They're kind of bent—for—forward. Looks like they're pressing their faces against the tree hiding from each other [clears throat] . . . . Here are their heads. This is their—upper part of their body. They have on skirts. [Uh huh, and where are their heads?] They have no hands. I don't see— [Their heads.] Their heads, oh, here, these two [coughs] . . . [card withdrawn].

INTERPRETATION. The issues introduced on Card III are merely restated. The expressed need is for the women to avoid contact and to separate from each other. And the setting is depressively dark and gloomy as it was in the canyon on Card III. Once again the figures are incomplete, their bodies are damaged, and they are seen in the white space which, speculatively, may also suggest feelings of emptiness and nonexistence and may lend the women a ghost-like and death-like quality. Unlike the response of Card III, however, the form level is better here, and, although similar concerns are indicated, they are less blatant and overly symbolic. The tree the women are using as a protective screen is often seen as a phallus, so it is possible to conclude that protection is envisioned as stemming from a strong male figure and that turning toward the male organ—whether through a masculine identification or heterosexual involvement—may be seen as facilitating the necessary separation from the maternal figure and from homosexual wishes.

2. I also see a large bug, probably dead bug . . . [W F± A].

INTERPRETATION. Unfortunately, inquiry into this response was overlooked. The image of the bug previously seemed to express aspects of Mrs. T.'s negative self-image and to be linked with the birth process. Here it is a dead bug which, following upon the struggle for separation in the first response, again indicates that the separation is connected with death.

3. Uh . . . see two vultures. Well, uh they're vultures but they're also people—two men . . . . Uhh they look like they're having uh an enormous bit of pain, clutching their—their stomachs. They're back to back and their legs are bent . . . [D4 and D7 and inner space of D4] [Drs FMC'— (H)] (Confab tend, Contam tend.).

INQUIRY: [And then you mentioned two vultures.] Uh they're in white. The heads are in white, that is. They have uh pointed noses. Their bodies are in dark, in the black. The way it's shaded—the way the black, y—you know, fades into grey, it looks like they have—they're back to back and it looks like they uh—pressing arm across their stomachs. And uh also the silhouette of the black—looks like they both—well, they're identical, you know, and they have their knees drawn up as if in pain . . . . [You mentioned they looked like vultures.] Umm well, they had the head of a—they had the head of a vulture and the body of a man. . . . [What made them look like in pain?] Cause they were doubled up. They looked like they were knotting up, you know, as if they were having a stomach convulsion in extreme pain. They were drawing their legs up [clears throat]. [Is there anything else?] Just the whole stance. They looked like they were, you know, clutching in toward themselves [sighs] . . . .

INTERPRETATION. A dramatic shift toward confabulation, contaminatory trends, and poor reality articulation occurs and reconfirms

Mrs. T.'s defensive instability. This response is confabulatory because of the degree to which it is elaborated and the strangeness of vultures in this activity. The response is contaminatory in that Mrs. T. at the outset simultaneously sees vultures and people in the same area; later she can reconcile this by making the figure a hybrid one, thereby indicating that she can work herself away from the contamination. In its contaminatory aspect, therefore, this response has a borderline rather than a fully psychotic quality.

The content involves an oral aggressive, devouring creature which typically subsists on carrion, and it would seem that these creatures have a severe stomach ache. Could it be a punishment for over-indulging their ravenous appetites? Earlier test responses have already shown that Mrs. T. is attempting to ward off from recognition strong oral impulses which are conceived as destructive and hostile.

It is important to note that she displaces oral-sadistic characteristics onto men and attributes the severe pain to male figures. Since the pain and the drawn-up position of the knees of the figures could also refer to menstrual cramps or even to the birth process, Mrs. T. here could be externalizing typically female pain onto a male figure, possibly in retribution against the male. Numerous other responses also seem to point toward a disturbed conception of the female reproductive role as painful, repulsive, and linked with death: earlier concerns about the birth process in which the birth spasms are quite graphically described and in which birth is given to a repulsive, bug-like creature; the response in which the dead people are falling in a partly fluid (amniotic?) state; and the dead bug of the preceding response, which is followed here by possible birth pains.

4. Again I see a vagina [D3] . . . It uh looks like it's being penetrated. Perhaps it's a penis [D1] I don't know. It looks more—like . . . yeah, yeah [sighs]. But uh wait a minute. It looks like a penis is penetrating the—the—the anus—the anal opening [anus is in upper third of D5]. The vagina opening is further up . . . [D F∓ Sex (Anal)] (Homo, Confab).

INQUIRY: [Then you mentioned the vagina and the anus being penetrated.] That was—the thing that I said was the tree beforehand looks like the—the—looking up at a woman and you can see the vagina opening and then the—you can see the back of her—the backside of the—I don't know what you call it [half laughs]. But it looks like a penis or—or a stick, but more—more is shaped more like a penis—is pushing in from behind . . . . [What made it look like a vagina?] Well, it just looked like a diagram that one would see in a, you know, book telling about, you know, different parts of a woman . . . . [Could you show me how you see it?] [Card shown.] Here is the vagina right here. This is looking up. These are the legs, you know, going off. The—this is the, you know, and this is the opening right there. [Let's see. This is a vagina up on top.] Yes, yes, and this is the—I don't—I don't know the medical terms [half laughs]. Well, this is the—this is the behind right here . . . . This is the anus and this is the—looking up—that's the vagina opening right there . . . [clears throat] . . . [Could you also show me the vultures?] Oh, well here—here's the head, see, on both sides. And they're—well, here, I'll take this one. They're both identical. This is the—these are the shoulders drawn, you know, forward. This is the arm, the hand right there. See the lighter part, the grey there. This is a leg drawn up. This is the other one pushing down. I said they looked back to back. They weren't exactly back to back. Something was in between them. The same on this side. This is the beak like. [This would be the head then?] Yeah. [And here's the hand.] Yeah, this is the shoulder. This is the arm going and this is the hand coming over there. [Uh huh and these are the legs with the knee here.] Yes. And the other leg is bent . . . [card withdrawn].

INTERPRETATION. In this response, with its blatantly undisguised and primitive content, heterosexual and anal homosexual activities are described and are essentially equated. The theme of the penetrating stick adds a special aggressive and perverse quality to the response. Despite a mild repressive statement (her unsureness about what the backside is called) the response demonstrates a severe disruption of repressive defense. Some intellectual distance, however, is achieved belatedly by making it a textbook diagram and by using a distant rather than a present tense, but a re-establishment of defenses does not occur until after discharge of the archaic material.

The homosexual and perverse quality in this response is also emphasized by the perspective evident in Mrs. T.'s description;

she is very close to the sexual parts of the woman and seems to be looking right in. Her lack of distance from this pressing sexual material, therefore, is also reflected in her spatial closeness to the figure. She further elaborates the response by saying that she is "looking up" at the woman, thus placing herself beneath the woman. This response thus contains two views; the patient sees herself below, which, judging from previous responses, means vulnerable, threatened, and inferior; whereas the woman is being looked up at and is placed in a dominant position. Again this contradiction seems to reflect the patient's own confused notions about sexual activity, her sexual role, and about her relationships with men and with women generally. That is, prominent concerns to her are likely to revolve around who is on top, strong and dominant, and who is on the bottom, powerless, weak, and vulnerable.

5. Uhh oh yes, I also see a—a central figure—one large central figure —looking up at him. He looks like he's been impalmed on a stick. No —well, yes . . . . Well, he did at first, but he doesn't now. Well, yet he looks like he's stuck on—a stick has been driven—driven úp between his legs and he's just kind of stapled up there. He's hanging down sort of like a [clears throat] figure almost on a crucifix—on a cross—crucified. Has a very small head. Uh he's looking down. He has a beak-like looking [half laughs]. I keep saying beak—a very sharp nose—like looking down at me . . . I think that's all I see [clears throat]. [W FM± H (Rel)] (Confab, Pers Ref).

INQUIRY: [Then you mentioned there was a large central figure looking at him.] Gee, I don't remember that [half laughs]. Oh, yes, yes, the very—the final—the thing. That's the whole picture. I saw that, you know, the whole picture, the whole ink spot [clears throat]. You can see the feet—the bottom of the feet, very large, massive figure. And then stan—I'm standing at the bottom looking up, so to speak. And uh the feet, of course, are apart. And the—again, you know, what I saw as a tree is a stick that's penetrating—a stick, or you know, a plank or something. The arms are spread apart, as if, you know, hanging on a cross and the hands are flopping down . . . . And the figure has a very small head that is bent over looking down. And it has a—some sort of sharp nose or a sharp chin. I can't—it looks like ah . . . . [Uh huh, you said uh looking at him.] Yeah, it's a he. [And who is looking at him?] I am. I'm looking up at him. And he's hanging there looking down at me. [And what gave the impression of a stick being driven up into him?] Well, it [sighs] the—as I said, the legs are spread apart and then the—the black object that is pointed up—looks like he is impaled—like he—it's driven up him —just driven right up through his stomach—through his legs between his legs . . . .

INTERPRETATION. Again the patient is "at the bottom looking up," but she does not see the strong, phallic male figure often seen on this card. Rather, she reverses the direction of aggression against the male figure and tries to place herself, although below, in a more masculine, aggressive position. Her use of reversal is not complete since she also observes the massiveness of the figure and the sharp beak, as well as the fact that the figure is looking down on her. But she goes to considerable length to weaken the figure by describing it as stapled rather than nailed or hung up, as if the figure is made of paper and is not of any considerable substance. There is also a very interesting condensation in her description of this percept when she says, "He looks like he's been impalmed on a stick." This is probably a fusion of impale, embalm, and palm; hence it fuses preoccupations around injury, death, and religion.

It is of special interest that this response, which begins as a thinly veiled phallic attack on a man (giving him some of his own medicine), is shifted into a specifically religious context. We must keep in mind, too, that the previous response was rather frankly and primitively sexual and that it has been followed by a religious image and one that explicitly connotes expiation of sins and purity of heart. This card ends with indications of deep grief and guilt, with face to face contact, with a symbol of purity and suffering, as if after an excursion into sexuality, perverseness and violent aggression, she is beset with guilt and her "sins." Mrs. T.'s background was strongly religious, a fact that highlights the guilt she feels over her impulses which have burst forth in an unbridled way.

This card, in its entirety, in addition to major segments of prior cards, exhibits an almost Gargantuan excess of exposed, raw, primary process content. The powerful, primitive, and confused sexual and aggressive ideation which inundates Mrs. T.'s thinking and her guilt, self-loathing, and need for expiation, take on gigantic proportions. It is not surprising, therefore, that testing Mrs. T. was experienced by the tester as taxing and overwhelming.

Testing was temporarily discontinued at this point, since the testing session, which included an interview and the first four cards of the Rorschach, had already taken up well over two hours. The next session was scheduled for the following morning.

When the tester came on the ward for the second testing session, Mrs. T. was still asleep and had to be awakened by the nurse. She dressed rapidly and was ready within ten minutes.

Her comments prior to the beginning of the testing session were as follows:

> Oh, I'll probably see people asleep all over the place. Uh, do you have any matches? [6] [Yes, I do.] [Mrs. T. laughs.] [Do you have any thoughts about the tests so far?] Uh, I just, you know, I do—I do— the other day I just wondered—perhaps I was seeing too much, you know, looking too hard to find something—whether instead of, you know, just letting it make an impression on me. [Well, you know, different people proceed in different ways.] Yeah, yeah. Uh, other than that, nothing really.

Her opening comments reflect her conflict about passive receptive versus more active searching modes of behavior. In almost the same breath she mentions "seeing too much" and changes this to "looking too hard"; that is, she tries to give the impression that she was active and striving the day before when she often seemed overwhelmed by the stimuli and the associations they stimulated. Although she states that she is just going to let the cards make an impression on her, i.e., let herself be receptive, she also implies that she is not going to let herself see "too much."

Card V

Reaction Time: 7″   Total Time: 1′40″.

1. Well, the first thing I see is a bat-like creature. The—the whole— whole figure is involved here . . . [W F+ A P].

---

[6] Patients in the hospital in which testing was done are not permitted to have matches in their possession for security reasons. Mrs. T.'s request stems from this fact rather than from any failure on her part to supply herself with matches.

INQUIRY: [What gave you the bat-like impression?] Uh I think the shape of the thing. The wings looked like they were bent like a bat's. [Anything else that made it look bat-like?] No, I just uh— looking at it, I just got the impression that it was a bat . . . .

INTERPRETATION. She begins with a popular response without any excursion into fantasy and without any associative fluidity—a rare event in light of our previous contact with her. This indicates that she is capable of establishing reality contact and that the pervasive, primitive and archaic material elicited on the first four cards of the Rorschach, at least for the moment, is under adequate control.

2. Then I see a—a gull. [See a—?] A gull, you know, a sea gull— looks like he's sweeping off the water and is reflected in the water—I don't see much else in this . . . . Don't think I see anything else . . . [W F± A].

INQUIRY: [Then you mentioned the sea gull.] Uh yes, that was a— had a very graceful looking neck—kind of arched—arched neck with a long curved beak. Uh wings are spread over its back . . . . [Anything else that made it look like it?] Well, it—it just looked like it was—you know, its belly had just hit the water or something. It was gliding or something. [What made it look like as if the belly had just hit the water?] Well, there's a dark line running through the central part of the picture which would—looks like a water line. And you can see the reflection of the bird in the water . . . . [Could you run your finger around it?] [Card shown.] This is the beak—the head of the gull. This is the wings uh right here. This is the tail—water around the reflection right here . . . [card withdrawn].

INTERPRETATION. The theme is flight, except that the bat is transformed into a more graceful seagull, an image portraying more feminine attributes than any previous response. Nevertheless, the seagull is seen as male, and in the inquiry the "sweeping off" position changes to "just hit the water." The content of the response (the fusion of male and female characteristics, the unsuccessful attempt at flight and soaring, the hurt to the stomach area) have all appeared earlier and have been commented upon. There is little further elaboration or clarification of their meaning. It is important, however, in terms of the earlier question we raised regarding the reliability of the two Rorschach sessions, to note that the same basic themes and issues thus far seem to be apparent in the second session although in a more muted form. As such, this fact would indicate a consistency in Mrs. T. from the first to second day.

This is an "easy" card to respond to because of its press toward the popular bat and its general outline. But these two responses do reflect increased control in reality testing on Mrs. T.'s part.

Card VI

Reaction Time: 47"   Total Time: 3'20"
1. ↓↑→ [Smiles.] Uhmmm. . . . [half laughs] ↑ Uh the only thing I see in this uh—well, the—first this looks like a penis here [center of D3] [D F+ Sex].

INQUIRY: [You mentioned that first it looked like a penis.] Yes. [What made it look like one?] It was just shaped like—li—uhh. [Draws on table.] Then I said also it looked like two—[Well, before you go on to something else, uh is there anything else that made it look like a penis?] No, shape uh.

INTERPRETATION. Her reaction time of 47 seconds is the longest we have seen thus far and this, in addition to much card turning, indicates considerable conflict and hesitation. With a great deal of reluctance, she finally indicates that she sees a penis. There are two important aspects in this response; on the one hand, we get the impression that the penis predominates and attracts her very strongly when she refers to it as "the only thing" and "the first thing." One sees her attempts to suppress the response by delaying it, by the way she tries to change the subject during the inquiry. On the other hand, her embarrassment and discomfort with the percept seem more appropriate than was her ease and openness earlier. And there is also an impressive lack of bizarre elaboration and confabulation which were also so evident earlier, especially on sex responses. She responds with good form level again and seems to be maintaining the more controlled and integrated style she showed in her two responses to Card V.

2. Or else it looks like two little monsters uh belly to belly [D3]
↓ [D F∓ (A)] (Fab Comb tend).

INQUIRY: [Then you mentioned uh two little monsters.] Well, uh
they were—there's a line, you know, a dark line dividing the—the
elongated [sighs] thing, and on each side I could see a—I don't
know how to ex—it looked like uh two worms with wings lying—I
mean facing each other—not facing, but you know, identical to each
other . . . . And that's—[Hmm, what made them look like monsters?] Uh well, they were strange-looking. Umm uh they were ugly.
You know, think that's it. [Then you said before that uh they were
belly to belly.] Yeah, well they're—most of the things that I've seen,
you know, that are identical—they're facing in opposite directions.
Well, these were facing toward each other. [Anything else that made
them look like little monsters?] No. [Where do you see them?] [Card
shown.] Here—see here's one—right here, there's a wing-like thing,
little eye—kind of a rodent shaped head, one on each side [card
withdrawn].

INTERPRETATION. The penis of the first response, to which she was
greatly attracted, is divided in half and reinterpreted as little
monsters, worms with wings, strange, ugly looking creatures. Mrs.
T. indicates in this manner the degree to which she is both fasci-
nated by, repelled by, and depreciative of the phallus. Its potential
danger, suggested by the term "monster," is minimized by describing the monster as little and then is even further reduced as a
threat when the monsters abruptly are seen instead as worms with
wings, i.e., as small, relatively harmless yet repulsive animals. The
phallic objects previously seen were large and penetrating and now
they have a diminutive, unthreatening quality, and Mrs. T. even
acts somewhat coquettish in her inability to repeat the word,
"penis." This response also illustrates how fragmentation of a
percept and a lapse in synthetic functioning, turning the monster
into a worm with wings, can serve in efforts at gaining a sense of
control and mastery. In much the same way we saw on the first
day on Card I a similar defensive effort to reduce potentially
threatening images in size in order to limit their fearfulness, and
we also saw an early shift from an expansive approach to a more
fragmented one (from Card I to II). Again, therefore, despite
apparent differences from the first to second day, there is con-

sistency in Mrs. T.'s repertoire of styles, of defense, and of adaptation.

Conflicts over intimacy also receive further expression in this response in the effort to pinpoint whether the worms are facing each other and are identical to each other. The worms are seen in "belly to belly" contact, which puts them in close contact and possibly in a very sexually suggestive position. Often, previously, face to face contact involved criticism, condescension, fearfulness, guilt, and temptation, and the patient felt it necessary to try to portray figures facing away from or trying to separate from each other. That Mrs. T. is aware of the constancy of the theme of "identical" figures suggests some awareness of her fears about being too similar to and too intimate with others.

3. ↓ And the top of the picture—in the other direction I see the pinchers of some kind of bug, but I don't see the rest of the bug [Dd 21]. Uh it's like a—well, cockroach sort of thing [Dr F+ Ad] (Do tend).

INQUIRY: [Then you mentioned pinchers of a bug.] That's at the other end of the picture, you know, turning it upside down. And uh just saw two curved little black objects that looked like the pinchers of a cockroach or any other type of bug. . . . [Anything else that made it look like pinchers of a cockroach?] No.

INTERPRETATION. This tiny detail response is in sharp contrast to her earlier more grandiose and vivid percepts. As with the "worm with wings," it reflects an attempt at fragmentation to limit and contain her responses in order to regain control, although there is a minor breakthrough in her statement, "It is a cockroach sort of thing." In the inquiry she is quite reluctant to elaborate on the response, and she restricts it to the two small details at the bottom of the card. Aggressive implications in the pinchers are thus vastly diminished because of the size and the fact that they belong to a bug.

4. ↓ Oh then I see the [sighs] two heads with the very elongated noses, little bitty eyes, very sharp chin, and they—the heads are identical of course backed up against each other—very long skinny

neck [D1]. . . . ←↓↑ Think that's all I see in this. That's it. ↓ [D FC′+ Hd.]

INQUIRY: [And then you mentioned the two heads.] Uh they were about—they—they involved most of the black and uh they were identical. And they were silhouetted in black—you know, they were in black. And uh the white—white dot on each side of their eyes. And they just had the shape of you know, an ex—uh exaggerated features of a head. [Anything else?] No. [Could you point out the faces?] [Card shown.] The faces—here is the nose and the chin, the neck. There's the eye, both sides, uh [card withdrawn].

INTERPRETATION. This is a very well perceived, form dominant response, and it shows a complete re-integration following the minor disruption of her perception of the pinchers of a cockroach. While she describes the two heads as having sharp chins and elongated noses, they do not have beaks as was the case on the first four cards. However, they are once again backed up against each other which, along with the emphasis on the silhouette, again indicates her intimacy concerns. The silhouette also is an expression of her sensitivity to the somber tones of the card and, as before, suggests depressive features as well as formal containment via an artistic, aesthetic mode. The "little bitty eyes" are particularly noteworthy for, as part of the content of the response, they mirror the cognitive, perceptual mode that Mrs. T. has shifted towards, i.e., that of narrowing and limiting her field of perception, seeing less, and seeing details and small details to the exclusion of more expansive, ambitious whole responses. It is impressive that through this means she is thus far able to stay within the bounds of realistic thought.

Card VII
Reaction Time: 45″   Total Time: 3′40″

1. ↓↑→↓↑ Having trouble seeing anything in this. Uh I see two —two heads of [sighs] girls facing each other with pony tails floating out into the air [D1]. And they look like they're uh—these two heads are on top of two more heads that are turned away from each other [D3] [D F+ Hd P] (Pec).

INQUIRY: [First were the heads of two girls.] Yes, they were the— they—black. They were the top. They were identical on each side facing toward each other. S—they had the shape of a young face, you know, the chin—it was small. They had pony tails. [Anything else that made it look like the face of a young girl?] Think just the face and the shape. [Then you mentioned pony tails floating in the air.] Yes, that was the—the dark—you know, the sort of thing that goes floating in the air [half laughs] back behind the head. [How do you mean goes floating in the air?] Well, i-it—it—hmm—how do I mean floating? [Uh huh.] It just is uh—well, instead of a pony tail usually goes down, this one's going up. It just looks like it's kind of— well, I don't know—suspended in mid-air.

INTERPRETATION. There is considerable blocking on this card and her anxiety and apprehension are evident in the delayed response and card turning. Further, she acknowledges her difficulty by saying that she is having trouble seeing anything. Once more there is a turn toward containment and an effort to hold her ideation in check. The form quality of this response is quite good, and the only peculiar feature is the statement about "floating" pony tails. The comparison of floating here and the gliding response on Card V, with the more driven and violent action of hair swirling on Card III, suggests a relaxation and a reduction of the frenzy of her fantasy life. In the inquiry she becomes aware of the inappropriateness of her description of the pony tails floating, and rather than attempting to justify the response by an illogical explanation, she blocks on it. The control here, as on Cards V and VI, demonstrates an impressive degree of resiliency.

Although there is significant change toward increased control, we still see the theme of identical objects on either side, an emphasis on a sharp intrusive aspect of the percept, in this case, the chin, which is deemphasized and made smaller. Depressive features are still suggested by the emphasis on the blackness of the percept. It is interesting that in many ways we are seeing in these responses the same themes and emphases which, instead of being elaborated on in an expansive or exaggerated way as before, are now treated in a diminutive form. This tendency was evident at the outset of the Rorschach when she stressed "itty-bitty" qualities. Thus, again what we seem to see on the second day is an intensification of defensive efforts that were initially present on the first day. This point bears emphasis because it supports the assumption that there is, despite shifts in intensity from time to time, a certain degree of consistency and regularity to personality style and organization that cuts across various situations. From the point of view of research using the Rorschach, therefore, this would suggest that it is essential to attend to basic styles and the organization of psychological processes as well as to test scores.

2. These look like heads of very angry uh misshapen men in a way [D3] [D FCh∓ Hd] (Fab Comb., Confab).

INQUIRY: [Then you mentioned these two heads on top of two others.] Yes, uh their necks were connected to the top of—I said two heads that were turned away from each other. And uh were—heads were weird looking, you know, distorted. They're not—they weren't really shaped like heads, but they were. And uh I think I said that they looked angry—uh sort of expression over the eyes or something. I got the impression of anger. [Uh huh, anything else that made them look like angry heads?] Well, uh, as I said, uh they were shaded light grey over the eyes which made it look like they were frowning—I guess that was it. The mouth was—the chin or, you know, hard-set. [Uh huh, anything else?] No. [Uh huh, could you point out to me how you see them?] [Card shown.] The heads at the bottom? [Well, both heads.] Well, here's the two girl heads—facing each other and the pony tails going up. And here are the two heads underneath. And see the way the shadow there looks like they're frowning—and nose and chin. [Could you run your finger around the head—the lower heads.] The lower heads—right there. I guess this is kind of a top-notch [laughs]—forgot about that. [And how are the heads connected? How do you see them?] Well, it looks like the neck of the top head t—growing out of the—the heads of this [half laughs] bottom head [card withdrawn].

INTERPRETATION. She does not see the lower part of the blot as being the torsos of the girls but rather as two additional heads of misshapen and angry men. At first the heads are described as "connected"—a forced and arbitrary relationship—which restates Mrs. T.'s problems around intimacy, her expressed sense of being attached to and stuck to others (e.g., to her mother) and her need to separate herself and break these too close ties. Later in inquiry, however, her thinking becomes more frankly arbitrary and unrealistic when the top (female) heads are said to be "growing out" of the lower (male) heads. In that each of the two areas becomes less specific and one area becomes an extension of the other and becomes integral and merges with it, this response reflects a deeper concern with ego boundaries than is suggested by the word "connected." We begin to notice, therefore, that the adaptive controls in the more recent responses are beginning to lessen in effectiveness. However, it is significant that the concern with ego boundaries was not expressed spontaneously but came out during the inquiry in response to the tester's questions. This delay in expression shows greater control than would an initial expression of the same thought. Once again we note a striking consistency with her functioning on the first day on Cards I through IV. For now, as then, her initial efforts at control and her resiliency seem to give way gradually to more poorly organized modes of thinking. We would, therefore, come to a similar conclusion about this characteristic of her psychological functioning from either the cards administered on the first or second day, although the intensity of her disruptions is markedly muted on the second day.

From the point of view of its content, this response portrays female heads emerging from misshapen male heads and suggests a sexual metamorphosis and the identity confusion we have seen all along. The content indicates that under a girl is a misshapen, angry man, and we infer this to be the patient's basic view of herself.

The comment "kind of top-notch" is ambiguous but may represent an attempt to use humor to deal with some loss of control.

3. See a butterfly with square wings [D4]. . . . Uh that's about all I can see in this . . . [D FC′± A].

INQUIRY: [Uh huh. And you mentioned a butterfly with square wings.] This is—was the umm the lobe—the group of heads I saw. The body was [sighs] a black line and the wings were the dark splotches, you know, over on each side—square. [Anything else that made it look like a butterfly?] No.

INTERPRETATION. The butterfly is accurate in form and of almost popular content. At the same time, however, her comments about the black line and the wings as dark splotches are depressive. An insect which is usually characterized as having gay and feminine qualities is, instead, characterized by somber, cumbersome, and unpleasant features.

4. ↓ Uh I see also the silhouette of a—a woman turned—uh I just see her silhouette [Ds7]. I can't tell if she's turned backwards or forwards or what. . . . That's all I see in this one [S FC′+ Hd].

INQUIRY: [Then you mentioned a silhouette of a woman.] Yes, uh she was in white, silhouetted by the dark, you know, looked like she was standing perhaps in the—with the—the light on her or something. And uh I couldn't see any features. She was either facing directly toward me or directly, you know, or with her back toward me. And you could see the outline of her hair and her—their collar and their shoulders. . . . [Anything else that made it look like—] No. [Can you run your finger around it?] [Card shown.] Yeah. Here's the whole shape right here. And this is her hair, her head—there—the roll of her collar and her shoulders. . . .

INTERPRETATION. This response is one more in a long series of feminine percepts seen in white space areas and therefore repeats a class of responses seen from the first to second days. The anonymity of the female figure is stressed further by the emphasis on the silhouette and the light blurring out her features. The issue of establishing contact or achieving separation is again expressed in her concerns about whether the figure is facing her or turning away and in her peculiar uncertainty at one point in inquiry as to whether she is describing a single figure or several figures.

The frequency of this type of response, a female figure in a white space area, indicates a marked investment in white, ghost-like females. The fact that here this investment is coupled with issues over intimacy and separation suggests a link of these themes with Mrs. T.'s thoughts about her deceased mother.

Card VIII
Reaction Time: 23″   Total Time: 4′5″

1. Um goody. ←↑→ Um . . . I see two—two rats [D1]. They're raised upon their legs walking. [I'm sorry I didn't hear you. They're raised up?] They're raised up on their legs—yeah. They're sort of

arching up. They don't have any tails. . . . Uh ↑ uhm ↓↑ [D F+ A P].

INTERPRETATION. Upon being presented with the first chromatic card after four achromatic cards, Mrs. T. opens with a statement of childlike pleasure, "Oh, goody," but proceeds to describe two rats in a state of tension, possibly ready to spring, and tail-less. This is one instance where the content of her response, which tends to be dysphoric, is discrepant with her affect. We can conclude from the discrepancy that her affect is probably somewhat forced. Nevertheless, as has been the case ever since Card IV this first response is a popular one and shows no bizarre elaboration.

In terms of its content, this response brings to mind the rats whose tails were cut off by the farmer's wife. If our inference is correct, this response would reflect again an attempt on the patient's part to minimize the potential danger from male figures and their genital powers. As such, this response could reflect the patient's effort to counteract a basically phobic, fearful orientation.

2. Think this also reminds me of—of diagrams of illustrations I've seen of the human body in color [D2+ Ds3] [clears throat]. I see sort of a pelvic region [D2] and a rib cage [Ds3] [clears throat]— sort of a grotesque figure here. → Uh . . . ↓ again [Ds F/C(C)∓ At (P), (Sex)] (Fab).

INQUIRY: [You said it reminded you of a—of a diagram illustrating the human body.] [Coughs.] Yes, uh the—the pelvic bones sort of, you know, the arch in red which fade into an orange. You see the—the rib cage—very tiny rib cage. It was in white, I think, surrounded by blue. Then uh there're blue streaks in the white that look like— there's shading that goes under the ribs. . . . Um I said—I believe I said it was grotesque because uh the rib cage was so out of proportion with the size of the pelvic area. . . . [Anything else that made it look like an illustration?] Just the—just the impression of looking at it. The different colors, you know. [What specifically made it look like a pelvis?] Uh it looked like the—the bone structure of a pelvis. [Card shown.] [Point it out to me.] Uh here's the pelvic bone right here. Here's the rib cage up here—the ribs [card withdrawn].

Location Cards for Original Testing

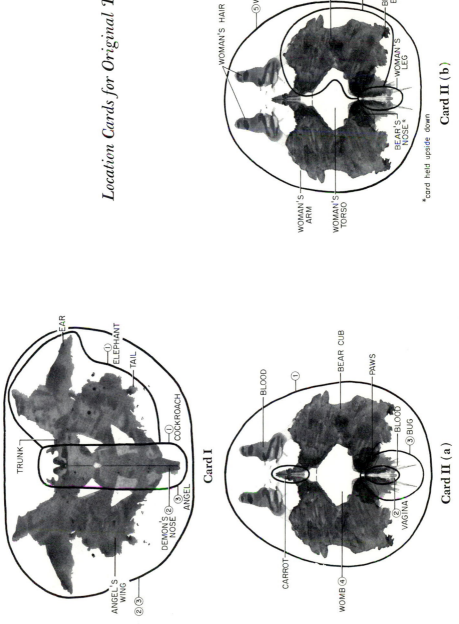

Card I

EAR
① ELEPHANT
TAIL
① COCKROACH
ANGEL
TRUNK
DEMON'S NOSE ②
③
ANGEL'S WING
② ③

Card II (a)

BLOOD
①
BEAR CUB
PAWS
CARROT
WOMB ④
BLOOD
③ BUG
② VAGINA

Card II (b)

WOMAN'S HAIR
⑤ WOMAN
BEAR'S NECK*
⑥ BEAR*
BEAR'S EAR*
WOMAN'S LEG
BEAR'S NOSE*
WOMAN'S ARM
WOMAN'S TORSO

*card held upside down

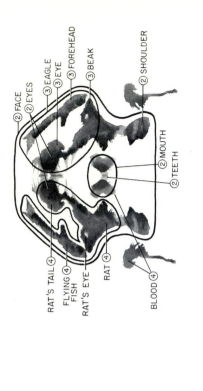

Card III (a)

SAXOPHONE 1
PEOPLE FALLING 8
PEOPLE 1
BOWL or HAT 1
RIVER
SUN and CLOUDS 6
CLIFF 6
HAIR
BEAK
6

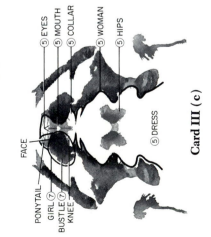

Card III (b)

FACE 2
EYES 2
EAGLE 3
EYE 3
FOREHEAD 3
BEAK 3
SHOULDER 2
MOUTH 2
TEETH 2
RAT'S TAIL 4
FLYING FISH 4
RAT'S EYE
RAT 4
BLOOD 4

Card III (c)

EYES 5
MOUTH 5
COLLAR 5
WOMAN 5
HIPS 5
FACE
PONYTAIL
GIRL 7
BUSTLE 7
KNEE
DRESS 5

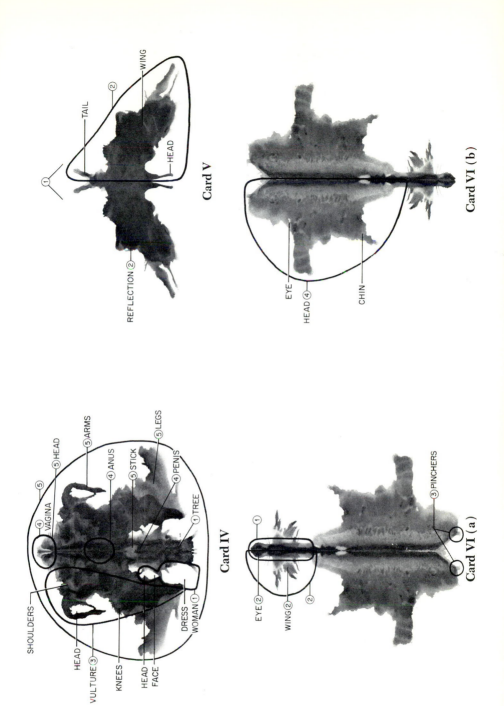

Card IV

SHOULDERS
⑤ HEAD
⑤ ARMS
VAGINA
④ ANUS
⑤ STICK
⑤ LEGS
⑤
④ PENIS
① TREE
HEAD
VULTURE ③
KNEES
HEAD
FACE
DRESS
WOMAN ①

Card V

WING
TAIL
②
HEAD
①
REFLECTION ②

Card VI (a)

EYE ②
WING ②
②
①
③ PINCHERS

Card VI (b)

EYE
HEAD ④
CHIN

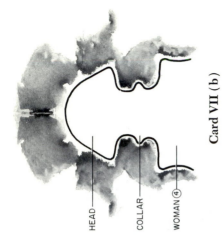

Card VII (a)

TOPNOTCH
EYE
①
②
③

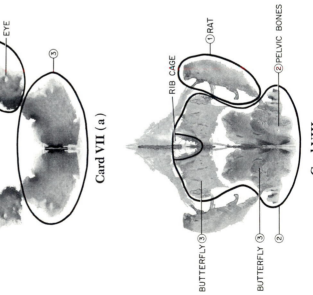

Card VII (b)

HEAD
COLLAR
WOMAN ④

Card VIII

RIB CAGE
①RAT
②PELVIC BONES
BUTTERFLY③
BUTTERFLY③
②

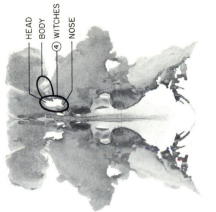

Card IX (b)

HEAD
BODY
④ WITCHES
NOSE

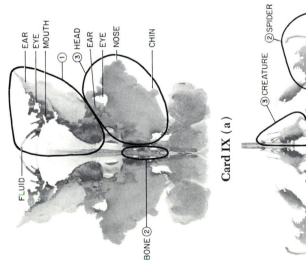

EAR
EYE
MOUTH
①
③ HEAD
EAR
EYE
NOSE
CHIN
FLUID
BONE ②

Card IX (a)

② SPIDER
③ CREATURE
④ FALLOPIAN TUBE

Card X

Location Cards for Retest

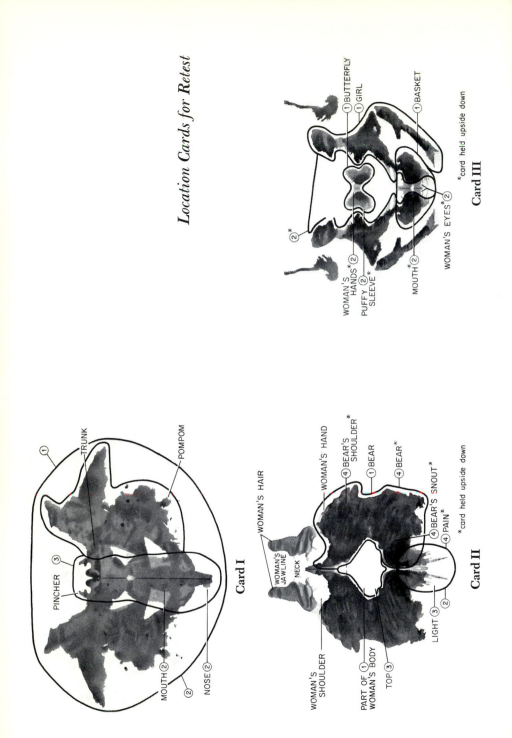

Card I

TRUNK
POMPOM
PINCHER ③
MOUTH ②
NOSE ②
②
①

Card II

WOMAN'S HAIR
WOMAN'S HAND
④ BEAR'S SHOULDER*
① BEAR
④ BEAR*
④ BEAR'S SNOUT*
④ PAIN*
*card held upside down
WOMAN'S JAWLINE
NECK
WOMAN'S SHOULDER
PART OF ① WOMAN'S BODY
TOP ③
LIGHT ③
②

Card III

① BUTTERFLY
① GIRL
① BASKET
*card held upside down
②*
WOMAN'S HANDS* ②
PUFFY SLEEVE* ②
MOUTH ②
WOMAN'S EYES* ②

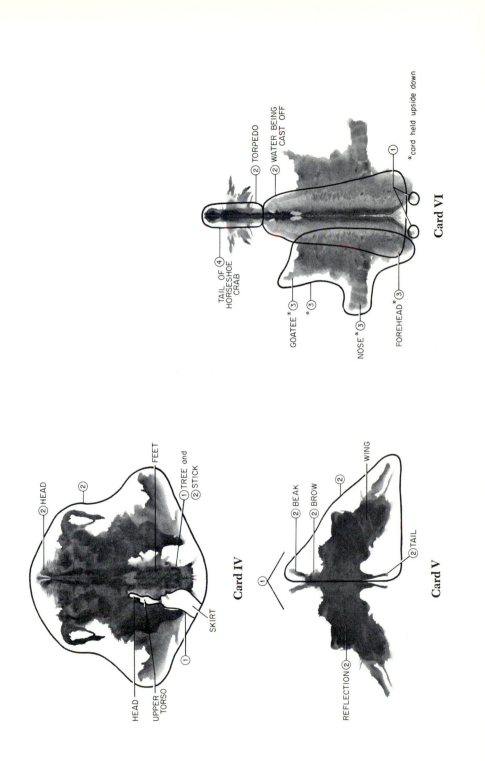

Card IV

② HEAD
②
FEET
① TREE and
② STICK
HEAD
UPPER TORSO
SKIRT
①

Card V

② BEAK
② BROW
WING
②
② TAIL
①
REFLECTION ②

Card VI

② TORPEDO
② WATER BEING CAST OFF
①
TAIL OF HORSESHOE CRAB ④
GOATEE * ③
* ③
NOSE * ③
FOREHEAD * ③
*card held upside down

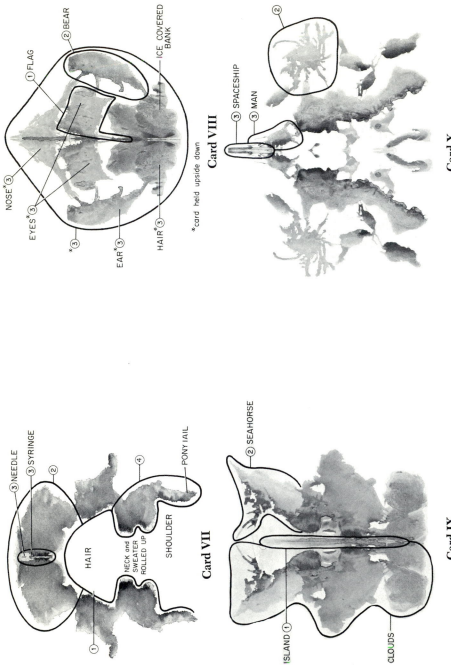

Card VII

③ NEEDLE
③ SYRINGE
②
④
①
HAIR
NECK and
SWEATER
ROLLED UP
SHOULDER
PONY TAIL

Card VIII

① FLAG
② BEAR
NOSE* ③
EYES* ③
* ③
EAR* ③
HAIR* ③
ICE COVERED
BANK
*card held upside down

Card IX

② SEAHORSE
ISLAND ①
CLOUDS

Card X

②
③ SPACESHIP
③ MAN

INTERPRETATION. Although she seemed to respond with pleasure to the introduction of the colored card, it is noteworthy that her first response did not involve color and that the content of her response belied her forced affect. In this second response she makes an attempt to use color, but once more, it has a forced and pasted-on quality. Her inability to utilize the colors in an integrated way suggests that her affective expression has become quite stilted. The affective reaction at the beginning of the card along with the subsequent stilted use of color, suggests a lack of depth and genuiness in her emotional reactions. It is important to consider that her responses to the earlier colored cards (II and III) suggested very poor control over her affects and impulses. In this later card she appears to be introducing increasing control but in a forced, somewhat put-on manner.

The comments about the disproportionately large pelvic area demonstrate the degree to which sexual areas stand out and compel her attention. She even spoils the form level of her response by integrating the pelvic area with the commonly seen rib cage. The sexual connotations of this response are further supported by the fact that after the response was given, Mrs. T. shifted her position and placed her skirt so that she would be sitting in a less revealing manner.

3. Think I see—butterfly. In fact, I see two butterflies. Uh one of them in blue [D5]. The other one is in red [D2]. And it looks like the blue one is connected to the bottom one. . . . And that's about all I see in this. . . . That's it [D F+ A; D F± A].

INQUIRY: [Then you mentioned uh butterflies.] Uh the bottom butterfly was the red—the red and orange. And [sighs] uh it's connected to the—the butterfly bl—above which is in blue. And it looked like the blue butterfly is in some manner connected—connecting it to [half laughs]—can't say legs, but it's connected to the—the red butterfly. [What made it look like a butterfly?] The shape. The—the red one, of course, it looked more like a butterfly really as far as the shape of the wings, go. The—sort of the reason they both look like butterflies is they both have a main body with wing-like formations on both sides. . . . [Anything else that made them look like butterflies?] No.

INTERPRETATION. In these final responses, we see adequate form level, but they are accompanied by a repetition of her readiness to join things together. Here the butterflies become linked physically and again point up Mrs. T.'s perception of herself as tied to and linked to others and probably to her mother in particular. However, in comparison with other cards, it is important to note that she does not elaborate the connection in a bizarre way.

These responses are difficult to score for color; she claims when questioned that only the shape influenced her perception, but several times she refers to the red and blue butterflies. It seems, therefore, that she was probably mentioning the color only in order to indicate the location of each butterfly and did not use the color as an integral part of her percept. Thus, she here seems to approach *FC* responses but to stop short of a full and adaptive use of color. On this card, therefore, her several responses include color only in a forced manner (*F/C*) or else seem specifically to omit mention of color even though it could readily be included in the response. What we may conclude is that her efforts at increased control in the second half of the test thus far involve a superficial, forced display of affect coupled with a rigorous avoidance of more full-bodied affective experience.

At the end of this card, Mrs. T. said "That's it," but appeared dissatisfied with her responses and her inability to see anything else. At this point she had her left hand over her left eye while her right hand was rubbing her other eye as if she were literally trying to avoid seeing the card (see, in this regard, Card III, response 3, the birds with one eye apiece). In this behavioral way, she demonstrates her efforts at avoidance, at blocking her perception and narrowing her field of vision—probably in order to defend herself against other more disturbing thoughts or percepts.

Card IX

Reaction Time: 1'25"   Total Time: 6'25".
The colors distract me from seeing anything [long pause]. All I see are shapes just . . . . Okay I see something.
1. ↑ Uh, two figures facing each other and they're very uh hideous-looking things [D3]. They're creatures. I don't know what they are. They have long beaks [D7] with the little horn-like growing off of the nose or the, you know, the ear that's on top of their head that goes off in a point. They look like they're leaning back laughing at

each other. It also looks like they're—ejecting some kind of fluid or something out of their cones over their nose . . . . [Dd25] . . . [long pause] [D FM(C)± (H)] (Fab, Pec).

INQUIRY: [You mentioned two figures facing each other.] They were —the uh figures were orange and uh they had the basic shape of a head, but they uh were uhh sort of demons. They were laughing at each other, so they uh—you know—not a merry laugh at all. Uh and they had the, as I said, the long noses with a lot of little horny things growing off of them . . . . And the ear uh pointed up—the pointed ear on the back of the head . . . . [You mentioned ejection of some kind of fluid.] Yes, out of the umm—out of their no—their—not out of their noses, but out of the things that are growing off of their noses . . . sort of the—looked like a fluid—a transparent fluid—or— that they—shooting off toward each other. [What made it look like that?] Well, it was a very light, light orange compared to the rest of the orange. It was in a line coming out of one of the protrusions off the nose . . . . [Uh huh . . . And then the creatures that are facing each other ejecting the fluid.] [Card shown.] Oh well here [clears throat]—here's the head of one. And this is the nose. This is the fluid coming out the the, you know. And their mou—their mouth is there—their eye, their ear. [Uh huh, and how—how much of that do you see?] Um I see it all the way down to here. [Uh huh.] This is just their body, their, you know neck . . . [card withdrawn].

INTERPRETATION. Her opening comment that color distracts her from seeing anything supports the interpretation made on Card VIII that her strained reactions to color demonstrated an attempt to deny the disruptive effect that color has on her perceptual associative processes. Her comment, "All I see are shapes," further emphasizes this point and indicates that she attempts to block out or avoid the disruptive color rather than try to cope with it and integrate it. In an effort to combat the too strong impact of color, she takes one minute and 25 seconds to respond, by far the longest reaction time of any card. This interpretation must be tempered slightly, however, by the fact that this is probably the most difficult card in the series.

Mrs. T.'s delay in responding is partially effective, for her first response is a weak human movement response of good form quality. But as she begins to elaborate the response, she returns to the mode of functioning previously seen on the first four cards, namely, extensive fabulation which reaches almost confabulatory proportions. Because of her marked efforts at control on Cards V through X, the appearance of this mode of functioning is especially striking and firmly establishes consistency between Cards I through IV and V through X. Although she tries to avoid involvement, as indicated by her hesitation in giving the response, she cannot resist emphasizing and elaborating the phallic intrusive features of horns, little horny things, and pointed ears, or the ejaculatory-seeming fluid being ejected from the "cones over their noses." This response involves two interacting figures, face to face, and the interaction is perceived as phallic, aggressive, and mocking. The thinly veiled reference to ejaculation further reflects the breakdown of repressive defenses (such content is too little disguised), and it also reflects Mrs. T.'s perception of male figures and their sexual activity as basically angry, mocking, and hideous. Inasmuch as Mrs. T. seems to be striving towards a masculine identification, it is likely to be an identification with a phallic, intrusive, ejaculating male. Her statement that the fluid is not coming directly out of the nose but from something grafted onto the nose, could suggest a wish to alter her physical anatomy to fit her desire to achieve masculinity.

2. [Watching examiner very closely.] I see just one little bitty thing in here that uh looks like a bone—a human bone [lower ⅓ of D5]. As I said, the colors distract me from seeing anything in this . . . [long pause] [D F∓ At].

INQUIRY: [You mentioned it looked like a bone.] Oh, it was outlined in ink. You know, it looked like a pen drawing with color—just— [half laughs] well, to me it just looked like a bone. [What gave it the quality of a human bone?] I don't know [half laughs]. Just—I just thought of a human bone when I saw it. [Was there anything at all that gave you that impression?] No, I can't think of anything. I just looked at it and just thought that there was a human bone. [Could you run your finger around it?] [Card shown.] [Examiner clears throat.] Here. [Card withdrawn.] [Do you have an impression now?] Do I have an impression now? [Uh huh.] It just looks like a bone [laughs].

INTERPRETATION. The sequence from the phallic aggressive emphasis of the first response to the "little bitty" bone repeats a defensive pattern from Card I and indicates that in this response Mrs. T. is attempting to minimize the power and repulsiveness she equates with males and with their penises in particular. A counterphobic quality is also evident in her giggling and in her placing the card on her lap for the first time and freely and casually moving the card around. However, she again notes the distracting colors and covers her eyes while giving the response, both of which emphasize her need to shield herself from the fuller, more aggressive, and fearful implications of her percept.

In terms of defensive processes, this response is of interest in that the content of the response ("itty bitty") and the structure of the response (showing a shift to a relatively small detail from her previous response) reflect parallel processes. When we also consider her behavior and attitude toward the response (shielding her eyes, giggling, and placing the card in her lap near her genitals) we can round out and complete our interpretation: her counterphobic and hypomanic maneuvers are unstable and do not hide her underlying repressive orientation.

3. Well, I see two—two heads in blue, facing away from each other . . . . [D11] They uh—they're ugly and they're certainly unusual looking [half laugh] . . . . A sad old man . . . and uh let's see— sort of look like they have an animal's ear on their—back of their head . . . ↓ [D F∓ (Hd)] (Fab).

INQUIRY: [Then you mentioned two heads facing away.] Uh they were in blue and uh they looked like fat, you know, the heads of fat men. And they had uh the great big little bump of a chin and you know everything's fat. Their neck's very fat and fat noses [sighs]. And on back the hair—the head they had a uh—looked like a bear's ear or something on their head . . . . [Anything else that made them look like fat heads?] Uh just the size. [And what made them look ugly?] Uh the sh—the shape of their heads. They were just ugly—ugly-looking—a big bulbous sort of nose . . . . [Dd24] [Run your finger around it.] [Card shown.] Uh here's the mouth and the—the little chin and the fat neck on both sides. [Did you say this is the nose here?] Yes. [And this is the chin.] Yeah. [Can you point to any other parts of the head?] Well, the eyes [Dds29], the forehead, the ears back here, then the . . . [card withdrawn].

INTERPRETATION. She continues the defensive efforts she began in the last response and further derogates the male figures by making them fat and ugly and further weakens their virility by seeing them as sad old men. Some aspects of defensive instability reenter, however, in that the grafted-on extension and the bulbous nose are equally emphasized. Her reference to the "great big little lump of a chin" vividly illustrates her need to minimize the length and strength of extensions and reflects the only partial effectiveness of her defenses. Weak defensive efforts are also apparent in the phobically-toned description of the ugliness of the figures.

She sees this response in the green areas but calls it blue. It is not clear why she did this—the inquiry omitted any questions about it and also about what made the men look sad. A possible reason for her misidentification of color is that the perception of the color was influenced by the content of the response. That is, the attitude of sadness influenced her to see a blue (sad) color.

4. ↓ See two witches—hmm with long hook noses. Just—I see their head and their bodies kind of just fade off. They're facing toward each other, kind of hovering [small spaces adjoining the top center of D6] . . . . I believe that's all I can see—I can see in it . . . [S FM∓ (Hd)].

INQUIRY: [Clears throat.] [And you saw two witches.] Yeah, they were in white, uh very small figures . . . . They had—only thing I could really see were their heads and their bodies just kind of curled around —faded away. [I'm sorry, did you say that the only thing you could see were their heads and the—] And well, I could see the general form of the body, but it had no distinctive uh features [yawns]. Oh, excuse me. [Uh huh, what made them look like witches?] The shape of their heads. They had the long narrow curved nose and the sharp chin—sort of hair that kind of was pulled off of their face, you know, in—in the air behind them. They were curved uh—bodies were curved up and they were humped over looking down [yawns]. Gee . . . . [Anything else?] [Card shown.] No. [Could you run your finger around it?] Here are the face, there's the nose. This is—the white is the shape of their head. [Uh huh.] And that's the hair, here's the nose, the chin. And the body's curling around—see.

INTERPRETATION. After seeing only male figures or symbolic representations of the phallus, a marked shift occurs toward two female figures. Again, as on Card III and IV, the females are seen in the white space and are now fading off and hence even more ghost-like. We have already speculated on the relationship between these ghost-like female figures and Mrs. T.'s dead mother, but the perception of these figures as witches also suggests a perception of the maternal figure in phallic, hostile, and evil terms. It is of interest that the threat of these figures is minimized by making them "very small," but their hovering quality and their elevated position reveal their fearfulness, and their prominent noses reveal their phallic quality.

During this card Mrs. T. often watched the tester very closely, looking directly into his face while he was writing. When he looked up, she would smile coquettishly while talking sweetly and biting her nails occasionally. This was most predominant during the inquiry and after discussing the noses of the first response. She may, in part, have been looking for the tester's reactions to her percepts, and, like the content of her response, the interaction with the tester had a suspended, watchful quality. She may also have been showing that she is identifying with the hovering female by hovering over the tester, and in this way, she would also be reversing her basic fearfulness of male figures.

Card X

Reaction Time: 15"   Total Time: 3'50".
1. [Grimaces.] I see quite a lot of bugs umm, not bugs, but just creatures. You know, you'd look through a microscope and see them crawling around. They're all over the place . . . . Um . . . you want me to describe the bugs to you? They all—some form of creature. Uh would you like me to describe them uh? [Up to you.] [W F/C± A.]

INQUIRY: [What gave you the impression of looking through a microscope and seeing these things?] Uh they were, well, of course they were large—And they looked like the sort of [half laughs] things one, you know, would see through a microscope, uh having, you know, seen some weird-looking little creatures through a microscope myself, they just make me think of that. And they're not the sort of things one sees everyday. [How's that?] Uh well, you know, they're not—they don't look like the bugs and little things that one would see, you know, just normally . . . . [Uh huh, but what on the card gave you the impression?] What? [Of looking through a microscope.] Well, I just uh—nothing really on the card. I just thought like I—it was a picture of—well, I don't know. I just felt like I was seeing these things through a microscope, not that there was actually anything that looked like a microscope or—

INTERPRETATION. She greets this card with a grimace and a frown and seems rather disturbed by it. An almost hysterical, phobic-like quality is evident in her expression of disgust about the bugs who are "all over the place." In attempting to contain these strong feelings she achieves some distance by viewing the scene through a microscope, making it more removed, small, and under scientific, intellectual control. In a further attempt to maintain distance she says that they are not the kind of things one would see every day. The score for color (the F/C) is based on comments during the inquiry to the third response of this card, during which reference is made to the overall ugliness of the picture and to the discrepancy of the bright colors with the misshapen figures which makes the figures look masquerading. Thus, it appears that as Mrs. T. proceeds with this response, her defensive controls become considerably weaker, and the struggle to maintain at least a superficial affective display becomes more marked.

One of the means used to achieve distance in this response, the microscope, also has just the opposite effect, that of enlarging things and making the creatures appear even more overwhelming and threatening. And her various emphases on facing, looking, being seen, squinting, or covering her eyes continues on this card and points up her strong investment in visual, and possibly voyeuristic modes, in visual curiosity more generally, and sexual curiosity specifically. This response, like others earlier, also demonstrates how modes used for gratification, in this case looking can also simultaneously serve defensive purposes.

2. The ones that I see most, you know, come out most—and they are the—they're in blue. They're spiders [D1] [clears throat] . . . [D F+ A P].

INTERPRETATION. Because of the popularity of the response and the absence of spontaneous verbalizations which might lend this response a unique cast, it was not inquired into. Two aspects of the response are noteworthy however: her emphasis on the fact that it is the popular animals which stand out and her alternation between a position of active viewing ("I see") and one of passive viewing ("came out most"), between an active position and one of feeling subject to outside forces.

3. And I see [sighs] two little creatures in grey that look like they're standing face to face and arguing with each other [D8] . . . uh . . . um. . . .→ [sigh] It's a very ugly picture, I think . . . ↓ [D FM+ (H) (P)] (Fab, Par).

INQUIRY: [Uh huh . . . You mentioned two little creatures in grey.] Yeah, they [half laughs]—they uh looked like something one would see in a cartoon by Al Capp—humorous looking things. They were standing face to face arguing with each other. [What made them look like they were arguing?] Uh they had—looked like they had what one would—might call an arm raised toward each other. And they— their mouths were open [clears throat]. They looked like they were frowning perhaps . . . . [Uh huh, and what gave you the impression of this being uh an ugly picture?] [Patient coughs.] The fact that it— tha—that—I don't know. The—the, the creatures that I could see were very ugly looking, misshapen . . . . Uh you know, they all had grotesque sort of like appearance [clears throat]. [Uh huh, anything else that made them look—] Uh the colors. I mean it was a very colorful picture, as far as that went, but they—the colors just didn't go with what I saw, which made it even uglier to me, like they were masquerading perhaps . . . [coughs].

INTERPRETATION. This is the third in a series of responses of plus form and the second popular response. Nevertheless, it demonstrates a marked degree of defensive instability, for the content at first is aggressive and ugly (and face to face); then, in inquiry, a major effort at defense via humor (denial) appears, only to be followed by a reiteration of the themes of ugliness, misshapenness, orality, and aggressiveness (likely reflections of her own self-image).

4. ↓ And I see something in green that looks like uh [clears throat] a uh female reproductive organs—uh Fallopian tubes, and the—the womb, and then the uterus [D10] . . . uhh . . . ↑↓ Uh the main impression I get out of this uh is the looking through a microscope . . . . I really don't see anything else but this . . . [coughs] [D F± Sex].

INQUIRY: [And then you mentioned female reproductive organs.] Yes, they were in green and they—they were uh—they were—looked like, you know, a diagram of them—uh the inside. A curved Fallopian tube leading down into the—the womb with the opening at the bottom going—going into the uh uterus . . . . [Point out where you saw this.] [Card shown.] Here, and then there's the womb. And here's the opening [clears throat] [card withdrawn].

INTERPRETATION. This is the fourth consecutive response of good form level, and of particular importance is the fact that the form level is maintained on a response with sexual content. Her emphasis now is on internal organs rather than on external genitalia, and her stammering and hesitation suggest embarrassment about this response. She seems to be able to talk freely about Fallopian tubes, but has some trouble with the word "uterus" and also "vagina" which she refers to as "an opening." Her embarrassment toward sexuality, and her need to distance herself is again seen in her reference to the microscope. But in comparison with her sexual content on earlier cards, autistic elaboration is notably absent. In general, the responses to this card are fairly well articulated and show relatively little pathological thinking or archaic content. As such, these responses attest to Mrs. T.'s ability to reestablish more adequate reality testing and control. There are, however, numerous indications of disturbance on this card, which have been already discussed, plus an avoidance of the direct use of color except as it is pasted on, having a masquerading, ungenuine quality. A positive sign is the recognition, to some degree, of her own masquerading tendencies—her reliance on denial which gives little comfort for her intense depressive and fearful projective experiences.

RORSCHACH SUMMARY—MRS. T.

This is an altogether unique Rorschach, both in terms of the content of the verbalizations and the change that occurred in the quality of responses from the first four cards to the last six. In order to review what appeared as almost two distinct types of responding, a comparison of the two summary sheets was presented earlier. In the response by response analysis, however, we began to see how a certain degree of consistency of personality organization was also evident from the first to second day. At this point we shall view the test in its entirety.

One of the outstanding features of Mrs. T. is her striking shifts in ego-functioning and ego control. There is little question about the presence of psychotic features which are variable in nature and at times have a paranoid and depressive quality, and at other times a hypomanic, grandiose quality. However, there are few disruptions of boundaries between separate Rorschach images and little suggestion therefore of severe issues about ego boundaries; there are few trends toward contamination, no autistic logic, and no signs of withdrawal from interpersonal relationships. The absence of these test signs lessens the probability of a full psychosis or schizophrenia. Her psychotic trends here are best described as borderline.

Counterphobic defense is also evident, but it too, like the projection and denial, is unstable, unsuccessful in its attempt to ward off fearfulness and depressive self-loathing. In terms of the arrangement of defenses, it is probable that an initially hysterical, repressive organization has broken down, that counterphobic efforts have not maintained any equilibrium and have yielded to the more archaic defenses of projection and denial.

It appears that the depression is quite deep and severe, and that her attempts to overcome it through efforts at projection and denial result in breaking reality ties. The extreme fluidity of Mrs. T.'s sexual identity is apparent throughout the record in her repeated depreciation of femininity coupled with her identification with a phallic approach that at times takes on intrusive and sadistic qualities. Her attitude toward men is compounded with envy and a desire to minimize, and depreciate their strength and take this strength onto herself.

We see that she is counterphobically attracted to what she fears most, that her thinking is preoccupied with sexual themes, with heterosexual and homosexual and with perverse sexual and possibly auto-erotic activity. These are little disguised and are associated with essentially disgusting, anal, or fearful fantasies, contrary to religious, moralistic, Victorian scruples from which she is unable to free herself. Thus, she seems full of self-loathing, unable to achieve a desired image of herself as being in control, active, soaring, innocent, guiltless, clean, thin, and self-possessed. Instead, we see repeated indications that Mrs. T. feels dirty, damaged, guilty, vulnerable, voracious, fat, sensual, passive, and uncontrolled.

The triad of paranoid, depressive, and hypomanic features, plus her impulsivity strongly point to the possibility of suicide that might occur under circumstances of despair, possibly combined with delusional-like thinking (for instance, the dead mother is calling), or it could occur impulsively during a hypomanic period, possibly the result of an "accident" or due to a continued search for new and further limits of experiencing herself as vital and lively. To some extent, sexual themes may appear uppermost at times in her thinking, but a more prominent issue is her felt attachment to the maternal figure—and a suggestion at one point in the test that the sense of attachment may even approach feelings of being fused and blending with her. Mrs. T.'s suicidal ideation bears directly on the relationship with her mother; she often reveals her need to separate from the dead mother or else be carried along with her into oblivion or death. The struggle to free herself is intense, and, because of the instability of her defenses at present and her difficulty in extricating herself, the danger of suicidal activity needs to be seriously considered.

As for Mrs. T.'s adaptive resources, her capacity to reinstitute defenses after the discharge of archaic material indicates resiliency in her functioning. With effort she seems capable of establishing control in the face of external stimulation which earlier disrupted her thinking and suggested she could be impulsive and have stormy affective outbursts. Her resiliency appears based on her ability to shift to a more curtailed, narrow, fragmented mode of perception and experience with stilted affective control. Psychotherapeutic strategy must take this into account. That is, pressing Mrs. T. toward a free associative, analytic approach might only push her towards increased outpouring and bizarreness; whereas a more structured approach, at least initially, with control and clear limit setting, would probably be more effective.

REFERENCES

APPELBAUM, S. A., & HOLZMAN, P. S. The color-shading response and suicide. *J. proj. Tech.*, 1962, **26**, 155–161.

BECK, S. J. *Rorschach's Test*. Vol. I. *Basic processes*. New York: Grune & Stratton, 1944.

BINDER, H. Die helldunkeldeutungen im psychodiagnostischen experiment von Rorschach. Schweiz. *Arch. Neurol. Psychiat.*, 1932–1933, **30**, 1–67, 233–286.

BINDER, H. The "light-dark" interpretations in Rorschach's experiment. *Rorschach Res. Exch.*, 1937, **2**, 37–42.

BINET, A., & HENRI, V. La psychologie individuelle. *Anée psychol.* 1895, **2**, 411–465.

BLATT, S. J., & ALLISON, J. Methodological considerations in Rorschach research: The W response as an expression of abstractive and integrative strivings. *J. proj. Tech.*, 1963, **27**, 269–279.

BLATT, S. J., & ALLISON, J. The intelligence test in personality assessment. In A. I. Rabin (Ed.), *Projective techniques in personality assessment*. New York: Springer, 1967.

BLATT, S. J., ENGEL, M., & MIRMOW, E. L. When inquiry fails. *J. proj. Tech.*, 1961, **25**, 32–37.

DEARBORN, G. Blots of ink in experimental psychology. *Psychol. Rev.*, 1897, **4**, 390–391.

ELLENBERGER, H. The life and work of Hermann Rorschach. *Bull. Menninger Clinic*, 1954, **18**, 173–219.

EYSENCK, H. J. A comparative study of four screening tests for neurotics. *Psychol. Bull.*, 1945, **42**, 659–662.

FONDA, C. P. The white-space response. In M. Rickers-Ovsiankina (Ed.), *Rorschach psychology*. New York: Wiley, 1960, Pp. 80–109.

GLASER, G. H., NEWMAN, R. J., & SCHAFER, R. Interictal psychosis in psychomotor temporal lobe epilepsy: an EEG psychological study. In G. H. Glaser (Ed.), *EEG & behavior*. New York: Basic Books, 1963.

HARROWER-ERICKSON, M. R. Directions for administration of the Group Test. *Rorschach Res. Exch.*, 1941, **5**, 145–153.

HARROWER-ERICKSON, M. R. A Multiple Choice Test for screening purposes. *Psychosom. Med.*, 1943, **5**, 331–341.

HERTZ, M. R. Frequency tables to be used in scoring the Rorschach Inkblot Test. (3rd ed.), Cleveland, Ohio: Psychology Department, Western Reserve Medical School, 1951.

HOLT, R. R., & HAVEL, J. A method for assessing primary and secondary process
259

in the Rorschach. In M. Rickers-Ovsiankina (Ed.), *Rorschach psychology*, New York: Wiley, 1960, Pp. 263–319.

KERNER, J. "Klexographien," Part VI. In Pissin, R. (Ed.), *Keiners Werke*. Berlin: Bong & Co., 1857.

KIRKPATRICK, E. Individual tests of school children. *Psychol. Rev.*, 1900, 7, 274–280.

KLOPFER, B., & KELLEY, D. M. *The Rorschach technique*. Tarrytown-on-Hudson, New York: World, 1942.

KRIS, E. *Psychoanalytic explorations in art*. New York: International Univer. Press, 1952.

MAYMAN, M. *Rorschach form level manual*. (Unpublished Manuscript), 1960.

MUNROE, R. L. The inspection technique. A modification of the Rorschach method of personality diagnosis for large scale application. *Rorschach Res. Exch.*, 1941, 5, 166–190.

PIOTROWSKI, Z. A. *Perceptanalysis*. New York: Macmillan, 1957.

PRELINGER, E., & ZIMET, C. N. *An ego-psychological approach to character assessment*. New York: Free Press, 1964.

RAPAPORT, D., GILL, M., & SCHAFER, R. *Diagnostic psychological testing*. Chicago: Year Book Medical Publishers, 1945.

RORSCHACH, H. Psychodiagnostik: *Methodik und ergebnisse eines wahrnemungsdiagnostischen experiments. Deutenlassen von zufallsformen.* Bern: Ernst Bircher, 1921. In English, *Psychodiagnostics*. (Trans.) Lemkau P., & Dronenberg, B. Bern: Huber, 1942. New York: Grune & Stratton, 1942.

SARASON, S. B. The clinical interaction. New York: Harper & Row, 1954.

SCHAFER, R. *Psychoanalytic interpretation in Rorschach testing*. New York: Grune & Stratton, 1954.

SCHAFER, R. Regression in the service of the ego: Relevance of a psychoanalytic concept for personality assessment. In Gardner Lindzey (Ed.), *Assessment of human motives*. New York: Holt, Rinehart & Winston, 1958.

SHAPIRO, D. A perceptual understanding of color response. In M. Rickers-Ovsiankina (Ed.), *Rorschach psychology*. New York: Wiley, 1960, Pp. 154–202.

SHARP, S. E. Individual psychology: a study in psychological method. *Amer. J. Psychol.*, 1899, 10, 329–391.

WHIPPLE, G. M. *Manual of mental and physical tests*. Baltimore: Warwick & York, 1910.

WISHNER, J. Rorschach intellectual indicators in neurotics. *Amer. J. Orthopsychiat.*, 1948, 18, Pp. 265–271.

5

In this chapter we shall try to bring together the findings from the WAIS, TAT, and Rorschach, and then present the final test report on Mrs. T.

In reviewing the various test indications, we are immediately struck both by apparent differences and marked regularities and it becomes imperative to try to organize these findings. For example, we note from the WAIS a basically repressive, passive, helpless orientation which is defended against in an unstable way via an active, phallic-aggressive mode of functioning. On the TAT, by contrast, there is more open giving in to depression and the desire to be active is present but more curtailed, held back, and dammed up. Moreover, more primitive defenses appear as well as psychotic thought processes particularly as regards the relationship with the maternal figure—the inability to separate from the still real but dead and negative mother. With the Rorschach, psychotic trends in thinking are also evident, as in the TAT, as well as a similar fluctuation among depressive (introjective) and projective states but unlike the TAT we also see more of the efforts at denial, more of the push toward excitement, frenzy and activity, and more extensive preoccupation

Summary of Mrs. T.'s Tests

261

with sexual issues. Nevertheless, as on the TAT, the more basic issues revolve around feelings of being attached to and even, on occasion, feeling fused with the maternal figure.

As regards the question of psychosis, since the WAIS is quite intact and free of indications of psychosis, whereas the TAT and Rorschach both show some psychotic indications, the patient at most could be considered to be in a borderline psychotic condition. For the orderly WAIS demonstrates a high level of ego functioning in structured situations and suggests that even in an interview situation her thought organization would be free of peculiarities of thought or fragmentation of ideas. Neither an acute nor a chronic schizophrenic would show this degree of ego intactness. When we take a further look we also find that much of Mrs. T.'s thinking on the TAT and Rorschach is also unaffected by psychotic thought processes—that her perceptual experience is undisrupted for the most part, that the formal organization of her thinking is not severely or pervasively impaired. Rather, *at times* she ideationally overelaborates her experience, gets fluid in her thinking, expresses a peculiar thought or shows relatively mild perceptual misrecognitions. Moreover, she also shows that she can often reconstitute from these lapses in ego organization, and that she is not bland or withdrawn interpersonally. Her ego resources are impressive and rule out a full psychotic state and suggest at most borderline psychotic trends.

On all the tests we see an easy accessibility to more primitive primary process modes of functioning; in her visualizing trends on the WAIS; in the content of the TAT in which "lovely sounds" and other unrealistic experiences and illusions are frequent; in the structural aspects and perceptual organization of the TAT as well; and in the extensive drive elaboration on the Rorschach. Although they are accompanied by feelings of being dammed up or can reach psychotic levels or are relatively monothematic, they also can have a certain richness and imaginativeness at times that bespeaks actual creative potential.

On the WAIS Mrs. T. looks more repressive and hysterical but with the TAT and Rorschach the more primitive defenses of denial and projection become prominent. We can conclude therefore that in her most intact integrated functioning she looks hysterical and in addition is probably inclined toward counterphobic behavior. All the tests show a struggle against passivity and fearfulness but interspersed throughout are representations of the passive, vulnerable, and female role that she desires to defend against. Included in these representations is an underlying perception of sexuality as an aggressive activity, an attack on a female by a powerful, dominant, and damaging male. In a typically hysterical fashion male strength and power is feared but envied and both elements of a masculine identification and counterphobic attempts to minimize phallic power and make it playful and harmless are present. There are suggestions that what she fears she may instead seek out to try to demonstrate her fearlessness. Thus, although she appears terrified by sexual activity, she simultaneously shows a hypersexual emphasis in her thinking and possibly in her actions as well.

It is of interest that we see a moralistic, conventional, hypersocial emphasis on the WAIS scatter, but such frank sexual imagery on the Rorschach. It is important to consider, however, the degree to which her ego organization is lessened in effectiveness and shows fluidity with this imagery and also the degree of religious moral concern that accompanies it and points to the relentless guilt and self-loathing that Mrs. T. feels about her sexual impulses and behavior. Thus we would conclude again that the basic orientation is moralistic, conventional, and repressive (cf., the memory trouble with sexual words), that her repressive defenses have lessened in effectiveness and that she has moved away from this position—counterphobically, but has been unable to go against her basically straight-laced, moralistic conscience. In this regard minor suggestions of concerns about being confined in some way on the WAIS are repeated, more boldly, on the TAT and Rorschach, and on the Rorschach, especially, are juxtaposed against images of flying and soaring. The images of confinement are likely to reflect her conception of the "mediocre," unartistic, dull life she wishes to reject but is unable to because of the depression and guilt that ensues. Her "soaring" images are repeatedly masculine in nature, active and hence show that a masculine identification may serve in efforts at evading a tied down, small town, confined, and feminine position. It is significant, too, that her feelings, especially on the TAT, are so markedly dominated by a sense of being dammed-up and unable to express inner thoughts, affects, and creative impulses and that her concern is with how to get these inner urges out in the open. One alternative is clearly via a move toward an excited, soaring, expansive, and hypomanic orientation (cf., the content of her Rorschach responses and her color scores). But such efforts appear to be experienced by her as illusory, masquerade-like, and ungenuine, and the stronger and deeper feelings remain dammed up and their expression feared. (A variety of test signs converge in this direction: the content of carnivals and make-up; the quality of some of the color scores [F/C] which show a push toward forced, superficial affective expression; her detached, undisturbed attitude toward many of her more disturbed images, particularly on the Rorschach; and her overall productivity on the first part of the Rorschach.)

Impulse expression is more basically feared by Mrs. T., and not just sexual and sensual impulses, but also aggressive impulses (which are sometimes minimized and temporarily made playful but are more consistently projected outward or are introjected and take the form of self-blame), and strong, oral impulses which are felt to be ravenous and unacceptable and displaced onto men. On the surface, the stern, thin, repressive, moralistic, calm, and controlled Victorian maternal figure represents the repudiation of the instincts that Mrs. T. tries to reject but which probably serves as the dominant female model for her. In this regard, it is of interest that one means of control for Mrs. T. is to fragment her perception, to narrow her field of perception, make things diminutive (on the second part of the Rorschach); that is, by perceptually creating the very constricted, contained, narrow, small-town view she tries to reject but is forced to rely on for adequate protection. This reflects her ambivalence about breaking away from her narrow constraints and seeking out a free, spontaneous independent Bohemian existence. (In this regard, see her initial helplessness, difficulty in orienting herself without external strength and support in the WAIS.)

On a deeper level, her ambivalence in this regard reflects her conflicted attachment to a maternal figure who is seen as cruel and punitive, who is dead yet is felt to be still alive and exerting very real pressures. In fact, her marked sexual preoccupation probably serves to obscure more basic concerns about separating and differentiating herself from the attachment to this mother who destroyed herself (see Rorschach Cards III [responses 8–10], IV [response 1] and VII; TAT #F1). The sense of attachment may even take on a quality of being fused with and undifferentiated from this mother in a very primitive, symbiotic sense. More often it is a feeling of being connected to the mother and unable to separate from her and circumvent fate and the inevitable doom from following in her footsteps towards insanity and suicide. Simultaneously (TAT #3, #F5) she seems to feel directly responsible for the mother's death, seeing herself as deficient in her ability to have loved the mother sufficiently to keep her from suicide. A large segment of her guilt and her self-loathing seems based on this feeling of implication in the mother's death, that is, for what she feels is an essential badness on her part.

This is a basically severely depressed woman who feels dirty, voracious, fat, sensual, damaged, guilty, and vulnerable, and who depreciates her feminine attributes. She can also be impulsive (see her Rorschach color scores, her monothematically depressed and impulsively toned TAT, and some problems around impulsivity even on the WAIS). Inasmuch as she feels inextricably bound to her dead mother and feels she may be carried along into oblivion with her and is impulsive at the same time and somewhat projective, the danger of suicidal acts has to be seriously considered.

One last consideration is the likelihood of organic components. Neither the TAT nor the Rorschach show any particularly organic signs, e.g., word finding difficulty, lapses in the train of thought, forgetting what she has said or is trying to say, perseveration, or other disruption in the formal attributes of thinking unaccompanied by drive intrusion. Thus, on the basis of the WAIS, we can conclude that some mild organic features, probably toxic, may be present but do not seem to interfere with her overall psychological functioning.

MRS. T.'s TEST REPORT

Analysis of Test Results

Because of a multitude of trends it is difficult to focus on a single major psychopathological feature in the test record of this woman. Projection, repression, and denial are prominent in a setting of borderline psychosis. A basically repressive orientation appears to have broken down, as have attempts at counterphobic behavior and have led to the appearance of more primitive mechanisms of defense—projection and denial—and toward psychotic trends. The tests reflect, therefore, a decompensation of a hysterical character structure.

What perhaps is most glaring is the patient's feelings of worthlessness, inconsequentiality, of a void, and an almost echoing inner hollowness. In a variety of forms the themes of being nobody and nothing, of having nobody, of expecting nothing in the future but lifelong hospitalization or sudden peaceful death are reflected. It is then her intense feelings of depression often under the cover of Pollyannish denial, which at times give way to a hypomanic denial, that have the major impact on her at this time. This must be viewed in conjunction with thought processes that can be as bizarre, confabulated and flamboyant as those of an acute schizophrenic as exemplified in this response on Card II of the Rorschach: "A pretty hairy looking bug, diabolical sort of bug with long, red transparent antennae. Sort of reminds me what a womb might look like also (pause) looks like a womb giving birth to something—just as I said, a diabolical bug sort of thing, like the birth of a bug." What is most noteworthy about this and other responses like it is the being in touch with very primitive and archaic fantasies without intense experiences of anxiety, blocking or other of the psychological or physiological manifestations that frequently accompany the expression of primary process thought in an individual. This must be considered all the more impressive since she is able to respond to relatively impersonal tests like the WAIS without severe disruptions, or the intrusion of highly charged material. Her intellectual functioning is only mildly impaired; in other words, she is capable of a level of performance in the Very Superior range, approximately 10 IQ points above her present level. At this time she receives a Full IQ of 121, a Verbal of 123, both in the Superior category, and a Performance IQ of 116, falling in the Bright Normal classification. It is quite clear then, that she has capacities for ego control which, however, tend rapidly to disintegrate in the face of increased affective stimulation.

Some of the major aspects of her present psychological status are sexual identity and hostile fantasies; sense of self and body images; Oedipal issues; the dead mother and remarried father; and suicide potential and adaptive strengths.

The feelings of worthlessness and the deep depression which this patient experiences are expressed in a multiude of ways, but none more descriptive than her shameful and disgusted thoughts about her body, its size, its structurelessness and missing phallus, its ugliness and lack of control over it. She views herself both as a huge ungainly animal as well as a little dirty, hairy, crawling bug. She makes it clear that at times she becomes the most glamorous of women in a fantasy that rapidly shatters, giving way to thoughts of death and suicide. The phallic emphasis for both male and female objects, the frequent slips of tongue relating to male-female confusion as well as her sadistic fantasies about males (e.g., on IV of the Rorschach: ". . . he looks like he's stuck on—a stick has been driven up between his legs, just kind of stapled up there—the black objects that is pointed up . . . looks like he is *impalmed*, it's driven up right through his stomach.") bespeak of her wish to be a man, to have a penis. These fantasies appear very close to consciousness, they are little defended and it seems likely that she is preoccupied with thoughts in this area. This male-female ambivalence is very graphically expressed around issues of body size. Being male is equated with largeness, massiveness, and an elephantine quality (the trunk not being the least important consideration in the latter). The female is likened to a bug, a cockroach, a hairy ugly little thing. Her own body image fluctuates between these two positions, with occasional hybridization. Her overweight, her somewhat unkempt appearance as well as her lack of make-up must be considered in the light of the above formulations.

There is little in the record that reveals an investment in things feminine, or a personal quality that contains nurturant, tender, warm feelings. There are representations of desperate longings for contact, for warmth, and closeness, but these are not on a level of mutuality; they are the need expressions of someone in the psychological position of a child capable of taking in, but not able to give. Her preoccupation with male and female sexual organs, the pronounced orality and some of the somewhat perverse contacts as represented on the Rorschach (e.g., a penis entering the anus), would suggest that her sexual activity has taken a variety of forms, at times probably quite bizarre. One might speculate that sexual activity itself, in view of the absence of warm, tender, and loving feelings, may be a way of achieving the closeness that she so desperately looks for or it may be an avenue for achieving a heightened level of excitement which helps to make her more aware of being alive and dispels to some extent the inner emptiness. Under conditions of heightened external stimulation, her denial mechanisms are most operative and it is at such times that she will appear hypomanic. The normal life, the average situation, all mean emptiness for her, somehow the world is never as rich and as full as her fantasy.

She is continually confronted by this reality situation where she is not a genius, where she feels herself to be a total failure as an artist, an identity which she has striven for, and where her desires to be a man or a glamourous, exciting woman cannot be fulfilled. Faced with such a situation she sees only two possible outcomes to her life which appear repetitively in the tests: death or a lifetime in a mental hospital. Death has a positive value for her, she sees death as releasing and peaceful, as somehow making up to her mother, thus assuaging her guilt for the hostile acts, fantasied or actual, toward the mother, and also as continuing her intense attachment to the mother who she feels unable to separate herself from. Oedipal issues are also quite pronounced, possibly being in part responsible for her guilty feelings. While in some ways the father's remarriage may have aided her in dealing with her more open sexual feelings, it also made her intensely angry toward her father, experiencing violent competitive attitudes and harboring death wishes towards her new half-siblings. At the same time she feels homeless and alone.

Expressions of grandiose paranoid thoughts are present in juxta-position to introjective features and feelings of worthlessness. Her feelings of nothingness have been commented on previously but the following pathetic story given to the blank card of the TAT can express her position most directly:

Card 16, Patient: [laughs] Uh [clears throat], this is a story about a nonentity [laughs]. He goes through life thinking that he is a person. And one day he goes into a carnival and goes to a house of mirrors. And up until this time, he'd never really looked at himself in a mirror. And so he goes into this house of mirrors and keeps looking around, but doesn't see what everybody enjoys so much. I mean, he sees nothing. And then suddenly it dawns on him that there is nothing. He is nothing and therefore he doesn't exist any longer. And that's the end of the story [laughs]. That's it.

In view of her very tenuous psychological position, her powerful death wishes and her openness to an acute psychotic decompensation when self realization and self or other confrontation of fantasy occurs, therapy at this time might be best formulated around helping her to integrate, to close over. She is not without ego strengths so that there is something on which to capitalize. Around highly personal material her thinking becomes confabulated and her pathology becomes strikingly emphasized so that at times she appears on the tests as if in an acute psychotic state in which reality testing mechanisms have been completely overwhelmed. That she has the capacity to rebound is a considerable asset, and she also seems sufficiently anxious and uncomfortable and therefore eager to seek a therapeutic alliance, but whether she is capable of withstanding the continuous impact of a probing type therapy is highly questionable.

In summary, the tests reveal a borderline psychotic position with wide fluctuations between good reality testing and excursions into strikingly primitive, archaic, and often bizarre thoughts. Severely depressive as well as grandiose paranoid expressions highlight her record. The suicide potential of this woman is very great since it is not likely to be an impulsive act, but a carefully planned procedure to put an end to her present suffering and escape into the "peaceful" state of death.

6

Retesting
Mrs. T.

Two and one-half years after the first testing of Mrs. T. she was retested. In this chapter we shall present these later tests in order to demonstrate the process of a retest analysis. Again we shall proceed test by test, presenting her summary sheets or responses and then commenting on them insofar as they reflect a change from her earlier psychological functioning.

Retesting was done several months before Mrs. T.'s discharge from the hospital. During the two and one-half year interval she was seen clinically as having improved slowly and having made sufficient gains to be ready for discharge and continued outside therapy. Testing was requested as a further aid to assessing her readiness for discharge. One important piece of information regarding Mrs. T.'s life at this time was the fact of her father's progressive deterioration from a chronic disease which had been diagnosed one year after the first testing and one and one-half years prior to the second testing.

One of the most outstanding changes in the WAIS is an increase in Performance IQ by 19 points which indicates a marked change in Mrs. T.'s functioning. This increase is due to improvement primarily on Blocks

270

Mrs. T.'s WAIS (Original Testing)

Verbal Subtest Scaled Scores		Performance Subtest Scaled Scores	
Comprehension	17/15	Picture Arrangement	17
Information	12	Picture Completion	11
Digit Span	12	Block Design	13
Arithmetic	11	Object Assembly	10/13
Similarities	12	Digit Symbol	12
Vocabulary	16		

Story Recall:　　*Immediate* 19　(−1 *tendency*)　　*Delayed* 18
Verbal IQ 120/118　　*Performance IQ* 116/120
Full Scale IQ 120

and Object Assembly and, to a lesser extent, on Digit Symbol; it suggests not only improved visual-motor coordination but the likelihood of less striking depressive features. Since a major aspect of the Object Assembly subtest is that it demands insight, once one knows the nature of the object to be assembled the scores can be greatly enhanced particularly through time credits. Some of Mrs. T.'s improvement on Object Assembly, therefore, may be due to practice effect from the previous testing on which she eventually had insight into all the objects. It is impressive, nonetheless, that she is now extremely fast and efficient. As for the other Performance subtests, it is not our experience that they are facilitated to any noteworthy degree by practice, especially with an intervening period of two and one-half years. Their increases most likely reflect an alteration in psychological functioning.

Mrs. T.'s WAIS (Retest)

Verbal Subtest Scaled Scores		Performance Subtest Scaled Scores	
Comprehension	15/16	Picture Arrangement	18
Information	16/15	Picture Completion	12/13
Digit Span	11	Block Design	16
Arithmetic	10/13	Object Assembly	16
Similarities	15	Digit Symbol	14
Vocabulary	14		

Story Recall 22/18
Verbal IQ 120/124　　　　　*Performance IQ* 135/136
Full Scale IQ 128/131

Her Verbal IQ is essentially the same as before but noteworthy improvements in Information and Similarities are evident. These changes show a firmer grasp of her basic fund of information, less blocking in memory, and improved abstract thinking. We can, with this testing, confidently rule out the possibility of any current organic brain dysfunction, mostly because of her present Similarities and Block Design scores.

Differences of one or two scaled score points are not usually considered to be significant unless there is some overall pattern to them, e.g., a two-point drop only in Similarities and Block Design which together would suggest some disturbance in abstract thinking. But a change in several points can be viewed as a trend. The drop in Comprehension, therefore, especially since it reflected an especially high investment in conventionality before, can be seen in conjunction with the improved Information score as a lessening in the underlying but strongly repressive, moralistic strivings. The drop in Vocabulary is unusual and hard to account for but is only two scaled score points lower and not of major import. Digit Span and Arithmetic are approximately the same as before. The additional score for Arithmetic this time, however, suggests that temporary inefficiencies accounted more for the low score; since Mrs. T.'s additional score stems from improvement based on the tester's questioning her incorrect responses, her delayed improvement also suggests that she may do better with support and encouragement than she did before. Thus, her improvement would be seen as partial.

It is of interest that some Verbal subtest scores are higher and some lower than before, whereas all Performance scores are higher. Furthermore, the fact that the Performance IQ is 15 points higher than the Verbal IQ more clearly than before indicates a person with a strong orientation toward action, activity and possibly acting out behavior. Often such a discrepancy between Verbal and Performance IQ's reflects a person who is action oriented at the expense of introspection, intellectuality, and internal reflection. Such a pattern therefore is common in hysterics, narcissistic character disorders, and psychopaths. However, Mrs. T.'s Information score in this testing, if anything, suggests considerably less repressive organization since Information has increased by 4 scale score points and is now roughly equal to Comprehension. While the scatter of the Verbal subtests at the first testing revealed a repressive organization, the Performance scales in the current testing suggest some action tendencies but not to the exclusion of thought and planning (see also the continued elevation of the Picture Arrangement). There also appears to be some reduction of her depression indicated by the increased ideational and motoric efficiency. Thus, Mrs. T.'s depression seems to be diminished with the consequence of an increase in ideational efficiency and a possibly more realistic internalization of her difficulties. She seems to be around mid-point in her therapeutic progress with a diminution of depression and a decrease in her utilization of repression, introjection, and projection but with an insufficient stabilization of internalization to contain fully her acting out.

Information   *Scaled Score 16/15*

Score	Item	Response
1	1. Flag	
1	2. Ball	
1	3. Months	
1	4. Thermometer	
1	5. Rubber.	Tree, a plant. Wait a minute, I don't know. I was pretty dumb last time on this too. A plant, yeah.
1	6. Presidents.	Uh, Eisenhower, Truman, Roosevelt, uh, FDR, and Kennedy.
1	7. Longfellow.	Poet.
1	8. Weeks.	52.
1	9. Panama.	S.
1	10. Brazil.	South America.
1	11. Height.	Five feet, six inches.
1	12. Italy.	I don't know. [Guess.] Rome.
1	13. Clothes.	They absorb the heat.
1	14. Washington.	February 22.
1	15. Hamlet.	Shakespeare.
1	16. Vatican.	It's the holy city of the Catholic faith, or it's a place where the Pope lives, the Pope's house.
1	17. Paris.	3,000 [shrugs].
1/0	18. Egypt.	It's in Africa, it's, uh, wait a minute, borders on the Mediterranean on the Southeast part of Africa.
1	19. Yeast.	Ferment?
1	20. Population.	160 million.
1	21. Senators.	100.

Information (Continued)   *Scaled Score 16/15*

Score	Item	Response
1	22. Genesis.	The creation of the earth and mankind.
1	23. Temperature.	100 degrees centigrade.
1	24. Iliad.	Homer.
0	25. Blood Vessels.	Capillaries, the great big ones, the aorta or whatever you want to call 'em, and the veins.
1	26. Koran.	Oh, it's to the Moslem religion something similar to what our Bible is to Christians.
1	27. Faust.	Goethe. That's one I found out, checked up on [laughs].
0	28. Ethnology.	The study of culture?
0	29. Apocrypha.	I don't know. [Any idea?] No.

INFORMATION. She still shows a mild difficulty getting started involving unsureness rather than mishearing and she comments on her earlier intellectual inadequacy. In response to 12 (Italy), she says she does not know and avoids the circuitous personalized route by which she reached it before. She is able to guess the answer but she is less willing spontaneously to extend herself. Since her previous answer had involved an intrusion of possible preoccupations about moral and immoral behavior, it is of interest that the intrusion is now absent by means of an initial avoidance but that when asked to face the question she is able to. This suggests that efforts to block out disruptive issues by means of avoidance and repressive maneuvers may now be more successful, though still partial.

Reference to the "Pope's house" is idiosyncratic although ambiguous at this point. But as we proceed it is impressive that the various items involving numbers which she missed previously are now responded to accurately and relatively smoothly (Paris, Population, Senators, Temperature). Also while she does not obviously resort to visualizing Egypt's location, she does place it incorrectly in the "southeast part of Africa." Her concerns about bodily organization are still evident; her miss on "blood vessels" is new; it also reveals a preoccupation with bodily functioning, and her reference to the "big" vessels is consistent with the earlier tests' indications of particular concerns about body size. On "Faust" she states that she had obtained the answer after the first testing. Although this suggests that her general improvement in Information may be due to her having made a special effort to learn the correct answers, it is important to take into account the long interval between testings and the fact that people characterized by a reliance on repression who look up answers after testing most often by the time of the second testing forget them completely or remember looking them up and have them on the tip of their tongues but find them inaccessible. The fact that she could obtain the answers and retain them this successfully is no small achievement. Another change in Information is the absence of the sense of being overwhelmed and needing to call on God.

We would conclude therefore that her functioning seems smoother and less personalized. Some of the same issues are still apparent but in a more muted way.

Comprehension   *Scaled Score 15/16*

Score	Item	Response
2	1. Clothes.	
2	2. Engine.	
2	3. Envelope.	I'd mail it.
2	4. Bad company.	They might pick up bad habits.
2	5. Movies.	What should you do? Alert the manager quietly.
2	6. Taxes.	To support the government.
1	7. Iron.	Oh, while you're feeling ambitious, pursue your interest while you have the incentive.
1	8. Child labor.	To protect children from being exploited by people who know how to manipulate a little better than they do.
2	9. Forest.	In the daytime? Well, I might climb a tree and figure out what direction the sun was, where the sun was in the sky and follow that general direction if I wanted to go west or east. But I'd probably stay right where I was and wait till people found me.
2	10. Deaf.	Because they have nothing to relate, if they can't hear, they have nothing to relate what a word or sound might be, nothing to imitate, put it that way.
1/2	11. City land.	Business, profit, less room, concentrated business opportunity, or housing, lack of housing space, profiteering [laughs].

Comprehension (*Continued*)   *Scaled Score 15/16*

Score	Item	Response
1	12. Marriage.	Well, uh, one thing is I think to protect them from, wait a minute, I think it's a health precaution in terms of having children. [More?] Blood type, if it will be a danger to have children or to the child, they find out. I guess it's a protection also to both partners in case they have VD, and I'm sure some sort of morality enters into it, social morality, but I don't know.
2	13. Brooks.	I think it means that people who know a little about everything and not much about anything tend to run off at the mouth, sort of a superficial way of relating to people.
1	14. Swallow.	One experience doesn't determine the whole way you might see something.

COMPREHENSION. Again some similar personal concerns are evident in this testing: the shift from an active, responsible position to a helpless, passive one (in the "forest" item); the feeling that one can lose one's ambition and incentive easily; and the concern with space and confinement (in the "city land" item). And one concern seems even more prominent than before: the emphasis on people manipulating others, on profiteering, on needed protection ("marriage" item) which reflects angry feelings of being at the mercy of others who can take advantage of her.

But in some respects Comprehension also shows fewer intrusions by depressive concerns (see the "envelope" item and the dropping out of the oral issue in the "swallow" item), and by impulsive trends (now there is more restraint and the manager is told "quietly" although a struggle for delay is apparent at present). The focus instead is on an untrustworthy external environment, although some oral emphasis is still evident in the strong comment "running off at the mouth" (in "brooks"). In her response to the "forest" item previously, she stated that she "actually would sit" until somebody found her, whereas now she would "probably stay" where she was until people found her. The difference in verbalization is of interest. Although both answers point up a passive, helpless trend, what was definite and actual before is now only

probable and therefore not absolute, and now there is no reference
made to sitting. Thus, in a subtle way there is a suggestion of less
passivity.

Arithmetic   *Scaled Score 10/13*

Score	Item	Time	Solution
1	1. 15″ (3 + 4 blocks)		
1	2. 15″ (3 − 1 books)		
1	3. 15″ ($4 + $5)	1″	$9.00
1	4. 15″ (10¢ − 6¢)	1″	4¢
1	5. 15″ (25¢ from 6)	1″	$1.50
1	6. 30″ (inches: 2½ ft.)	4″	Wait a minute, 30.
1	7. 30″ (6¢/orange: 36¢)	1″	6
1	8. 30″ (24 miles at 3/hr.)	3″	8
1	9. 30″ (7 2¢ stamps)	1″	36¢
0/1	10. 30″ ($18 − $7.50)	2″	Uh, $11.50. [How get?] Oh, I got it wrong, should be $10.50 [laughs]. I subtracted $7.50 from 18.
0/1	11. 60″ (+1 10″) (2/31¢: dozen)	9″	Oh, 1.81 [How get?] I multiplied, you said a dozen cans, I took 2 into that is 6 and take 6 times 31, 1.86, I think.
2	12. 60″ (+1 10″) ($400 = 2/3)	3″	Uh, 600.
0	13. 60″ (+1 15″) ($60 less 15%)	10″	Oh, God [laughs] 45? [How get?] I guessed. [?] I really did. I don't know anything about math. [How might you go about it?] I think you divide 15 into 60 and subtract that from 60. I think that's how, I'm not sure.

Arithmetic (Continued)   **Scaled Score 10/13**

Score	Item	Time	Solution
0/1	14. 120″ (+1 20″) (8 men — 6 days)	30″	Wait a minute—oh God—uh, 108? [How get?] Let's see, 6 men, 8 days, I multiplied 6 times 8, 8 times 6, that is, I got 54, but it's 48. I doubled 54, but I should have doubled 48. I don't know why, but I did. [Answer?] Uh, wait a minute, 48 and 48, 96.

ARITHMETIC. Arithmetic is faster and her misses to 10 and 11 seem due to impulsivity and hastiness. Overall, she shows some temporary inefficiency now but less of the necessity to repeat questions and the effortfulness in keeping her thinking focused on the problem. On the more difficult questions she resorts more to the behavior we observed on the first test—the call for external help, anxiety, and self-depreciation. Her functioning now, as we saw from the scatter, shows both impulsivity and some improved concentration and ideational clarity.

Similarities   **Scaled Score 15**

Score	Item	Response
2	1. Orange.	Both fruit.
2	2. Coat.	Both clothing.
1	3. Axe.	Both used to cut.
2	4. Dog.	They're both animals, of course so am I [laughing] Yeah, OK.
2	5. North.	Directions.
2	6. Eye.	Sensory.
2	7. Air.	Essential to life.
2	8. Table.	Uh, both are furniture.
2	9. Egg.	Beginning of life.
2	10. Poem.	Forms of art.
0	11. Wood.	One, also is derived from wood.
1	12. Praise.	Uh, both are forms of judging behavior.
2	13. Fly.	Both are living.

SIMILARITIES. She is generally smoother and more accurate now except for her added comment in which she points up her "animal" nature—a facetious remark about her devalued conception of herself and of her impulses. But this comment does not spoil the level of her response as her concerns did before (on 8, "table", and 9, "egg").

Story Recall I (Score 22)

Dec. 6 / Last week / a river / overflowed / in a small town / 10 miles / from Albany./ Water covered the streets / and entered the houses./ Fourteen persons / were drowned / and 600 persons / caught cold / because of the dampness / and cold weather./ In saving / a boy / who was caught / under a bridge / a man / cut his hands./
Response: Dec. 6. Last week a river overflowed in a small town 10 miles from Albany. Fourteen people were drowned and 600 people were missing. Wait a minute, the dampness and coldness seeped through the town. A small boy, oh, no, a man, in the process of rescuing a small boy who was caught under a bridge, cut his hand.

Story Recall II [1] (Score 18)

Dec. 6./ Last week / a river / overflowed / in a small town / 10 miles / from Albany./ Water covered the streets / and entered the houses./ Fourteen persons / were drowned / and 600 persons / caught cold / because of the dampness / and cold weather./ In saving / a small boy / who was caught / under a bridge / a man / cut his hands./
Response: [makes face] Last week a river overflowed into a small town 10 miles outside of Albany. Fourteen people were drowned and because of the coldness, cold water and dampness 600 people caught cold. In the process of rescuing a small boy caught under a bridge a man cut his hand.

STORY RECALL. Her score on Story Recall I is a little higher now, but she still exaggerates the disruption of the flood, this time spe-

[1] Was given after Digit Span, Digit Symbol and Picture Completion were administered.

cifically emphasizing a loss (600 people "missing") and shows some uncertainty about whether the boy or the man is in the saving role, thereby implying a reversal of roles (the latter a major theme of her first TAT). But this time, even though she does not improve her score on Story Recall II, she recuperates more from her earlier errors than she did on the first testing. Nevertheless, personal pre-occupations are clearly evident now as before.

Digit Span	*Scaled Score 11*
Number of Digits Forward (6)	**Number of Digits Backward (6)**
(3) (correct)	(2)
(3)	(2)
(4) (correct)	(3) (correct)
(4)	(3)
(5) (correct)	3 2 7 9 : 9 7 3 6
(5)	(4) (correct)
(6) (correct)	1 5 2 8 6 : 6 8 9 5 1
(6)	(5) (correct)
5 9 1 7 4 2 8 : 5 1 9 7 4 2 8	(5) (correct)
4 1 7 9 3 8 6 : 4 1 9 7 3 2 6	(6)
(8)	8 1 2 9 3 6 5 : 5 6 9 3 2 1 8
(8)	4 7 3 9 1 2 8 : 8 2 1 9 3 4
(9)	(8)
(9)	(8)

DIGIT SPAN. Although one point lower on Digits Forward, the difference in testing is negligible.

DIGIT SYMBOL   69

DIGIT SYMBOL. She now completes 70 symbols as compared to 65 on the first testing. Her symbols—her Us—are more like the sample now but give the appearance of being quickly done. In fact, there is one uncorrected error (below the 36th number, a five, she put the symbol for a two) and for the 66th number—a nine—she put the symbol for an eight but spontaneously corrected herself. As on Arithmetic, her errors here reflect some hastiness and impulsivity which accompanies her generally improved functioning. This finding again supports the hypotheses drawn from her subtest scatter about her partial improvement, that is her increased ideational control but also her current action orientation.

Picture Completion   *Scaled Score 12/13*

Score	Item	Time	Response
1	1. Door.	1″	Doorknob.
1	2. Pig.	1″	Tail.
1	3. Girl.	1″	Nose, bridge of nose, and ear. [Intended?] Well, both were intended. [?] The nose.
1	4. Car.	2″	Door handles.
0	5. Card.	4″	The nines on the other corner.
1	6. Pitcher.	1″	The water being poured into the glass.
1	7. Glasses.	2″	The connector between the eye glasses.
1	8. Violin.	3″	The fifth string. 19″ God oh mighty, I think it's a fret that's missing instead of the string [points].
1	9. Boat.	1″	Oarlock.
0	10. Bulb.	6″	Something to plug the light into.
0/1	11. Flag.	3″	The rest of the flagpole and not enough stars either. [Intended?] Flagpole is the most obvious.
1	12. Man, dog.	2″	Dog tracks of the dog.
1	13. Map.	2″	Florida.
1	14. Ship.	2″	Smokestack [smiles].
1	15. Crab.	3″	Crab's leg.
1	16. Vanity.	3″	Reflection of the arm.
1	17. Man.	4″	Finger.
1	18. Sun.	2″	Man's shadow.
1	19. Horse.	2″	Stirrups.
0	20. Woodpile.	15″	I don't see that anything is missing.
1	21. Girl.	2″	Eyebrow.

PICTURE COMPLETION. Her Picture Completion score is not improved, but on item 6 (pitcher) there is less emphasis on external support; on 8 and 14 there is less blocking in memory; and no anal or phallic referent on the crab item. Some new disturbance which is unclear in its meaning occurs on the violin item to which she reacts strongly.

Block Design   Scale Score 16

Score	Item	Time	Solution
4	a.	5″	*4 3 2 1*
	b.		
4	1.	8″	Makes error at first, makes face and corrects. *3 2 1 4*
	2.		
4	3.	7″	*4 3 1 2*
4	4.	6″	*4 3 2 1*
4	5.	7″	*3 2 1 4*
4	6.	13″	*2 4 3 1*
6	7. (2′)	25″	*5 7 4 1 2 3 6 9 8*
6	8.	36″	*7 4 8 5*W *1 9* 6R *2 3* Corrects *5* after *1*; corrects *6* right after placing it.
5	9.	1′11″	At first has 4 blocks in bottom row, two in center and two in top row. *7 4 8* 9W *9* (as 4th block in row). *6 3 2.* Oh [Removes most blocks leaving *9 6 3*] *8 5 2 4 1 7.*
6	10.	37″	*9 8 6 7 4 5 2 3 1*

Bonus Scores
(Basic Score 4)

Item	5	6
7	31″–40″	1″–30″
8	46″–70″	1″–45″
9	61″–80″	1″–60″
10	61″–80″	1″–60″

BLOCK DESIGN. She is more efficient now, getting full bonus credit on 7 and 8 and she is more efficient on 6. Her style of responding is more variable now on 7, 8, and 9.

Picture Arrangement   *Scaled Score 18*

Score	Item	Time	Seq	Solution
4	1. (1')	a. 2″ b.	WXY	
4	2.	a. 2″ b.	PAT	[Scoops cards up. Apologizes when she is asked to leave them in order.]
4	3.	4″	ABCD	
4	4.	6″	ATOMIC	
4	5.	13″	OPENS	
4	6.	8″	JANET	
6	7. (2')	16″	EFGHIJ	He's got someone planted down there who's feeding his line fish.
6	8.	13″	SAMUEL	He has a manikin with him and he's sitting there and he looks back and he is aware that it looks like he's making out with a live person and he gets embarrassed, pushes the manikin aside.

PICTURE ARRANGEMENT. She is faster on 8 and therefore gets full credit on this subtest now. She introduces an indirect oral theme on 7 in the diver who is "feeding" the line with fish and her expression "a live person" on 8 is strange. This latter expression implies that the manikin may be conceived of as a dead person and may have its roots in depressive feelings and concerns of Mrs. T.'s about her sexual responsivity and about herself more generally. One positive change in the eighth story is the shift from an external emphasis on people actually watching to an internal recognition of how it might appear to others. The shift is from externalization to increased introspectiveness and internal ideational elaboration. This is important to note because comprehension suggested she might look more projective now, more ready to see the source of difficulties as outside herself. Again we see Mrs. T. at a midstage of improvement, showing increased introspection and capacity for internalization.

Object Assembly   *Scaled Score 16*

Score	Item	Time	Solution
7	1. (2′)	12″	LLAAH Done sloppily.
13	2. (2′)	23″	Ear, ear, eye, nose, lip, neck.
10	3. (3′)	37″	Thumb, forefinger, index, wrist, fingers.
12	4. (3′)	16″	Rump to back legs, back, head, front legs, trunk.

BS	Item 1(5)	2(9)	3(7)	4(8)
6	16″–20″			
7	11″–15″			
8	1″–10″			
9			41″–50″	
10			31″–40″	31″–50″
11		36″–45″	1″–30″	21″–30″
12		26″–35″		1″–20″
13		1″–25″		

OBJECT ASSEMBLY. The difference between tests is due to her rapid insight into the "hand" item, possibly the result of her earlier delayed insight and possibly another suggestion that personal concerns are less intrusive into impersonal tasks.

Vocabulary   *Scaled Score 14*

Score	Response
2	Where you sleep.
2	Seagoing vessel.
2	A hard form of coinage, coinage.
1	A season of the year.
2	Uh, make something workable.
2	The first morning of the, first meal of the day.

Vocabulary (Continued) Scaled Score 14

Score	Response
1	Material.
1	Cut.
1	Construct.
2	Hide.
2	Extremely large.
2	To go about something quickly.
2	Uh, a group of words which form a complete thought.
2	Control.
2	Begin.
2	Think about.
2	Cave.
2	Point out.
2	Home-like.
2	Devour.
2	End.
2	Hinder.
2	Guilt.
0	Uh, resting place.
2	Uh, uh, incomparable.
2	Hesitant.
1	Tragedy.
2	Bravery.
2	Quiet.
0	Uh, monument.
2	Sympathy.
2	Touchable.
1	Outside.
1	Uh, strikingly apparent. [Explain?] Well, wait a minute, maybe I'm getting this wrong. Well, somebody has the audacity to do something, affrontery is a better word.
2	Threatening.
1	Lecture.
2	Burden.
0	Cheat.
1	Stab.
1	Comedy.

VOCABULARY. An analysis of her responses to individual words may enable us to account for the difference in scores between testings. With "bed" she is less flustered and does not elaborate her answer as much. She is less elaborative on "ship" and also on "winter" where her lack of elaboration diminishes her score. Her definition of "repair" now shows less emphasis on damage but is followed by a disruption in communication in response to "breakfast" in which she at first substitutes the word "morning" for "meal". The fact that food is initially absent suggests concerns about being unnourished and unfed, but may at the same time, like the several responses preceding it, point to efforts to block out from consciousness earlier depressive feelings of coldness, isolation, damage, and neediness.

On the next word—"fabric"—she was not asked to tell more about its meaning following her spontaneous definition so we do not know whether she would have introduced her earlier notion of covering something. She changes her definition of "assemble" from "congregate" (which has more of an interpersonal quality) to "construct" (which is impersonal and more active in a masculine sense) which may reflect some lessened involvement with people in preference for activities. The next item of interest is 19, "domestic" which is undisrupted now. Her response to "consume" is more accurate, stronger and has a specifically oral-aggressive quality. It may reflect increased acceptance of full bodied orality but it may also reflect some of the concerns about her animal nature that she alluded to during Similarities; it is consistent with her difficulty in defining "breakfast." Four items later (24) "sanctuary," she spoils her original definition by describing a sanctuary as a "resting place," introducting a note of passivity and/or death which generally has been less evident in this WAIS than in the former one. A continued though diminished concern around death may be also suggested by the response of "monument" to the word "edifice." She has more difficulty defining "audacious" than before which may reflect her still present problems in the area of active self-assertion. Most of her other slightly poorer responses on this testing are not especially revealing—except that her definition to "travesty" now may reflect some increased reliance on denial and desire to see things as pleasant.

WAIS Summary

All in all, then, the second WAIS shows that her functioning is generally smoother, clearer, and more precise. She shows an increased emphasis on internal ideation and more control over her thought processes, less difficulty with numbers and memory; she is faster, more efficient and shows fewer personal intrusions. Although the problems revealed in the first testing are still clearly evident around passivity and activity, around depression, oral needs, her "animal" instincts, her role vis-à-vis adults and her projective trends —these problems are less intrusive and do not interfere with her cognitive functioning as much as they did on the first WAIS.

MRS. T.'S TAT (RETEST)[2]

1. TAT 1

Reaction Time: 5″   Total Time: 1′20″
Here's a little boy who would rather be outside playing, and he has to study the violin, and at the time of the picture he's sort of morosely looking at the violin, debating whether or not he's going to practice as he's supposed to or go out and play with the kids. So he decides to go out and play with the children because he himself is not interested in the, it's not his wish to study the violin.

INTERPRETATION. There is a dramatic shift in the two stories toward the more popular and commonly told story. It suggests a move toward more conventional ways of looking at things and a quieting down of her intense fantasying. Moreover, in the content, impulsive, destructive action is omitted as is the feeling of frustration and the emphasis on passive fantasy. Rather it is now a story in which activity and interpersonal contact are sought out, somewhat with a defiant emphasis on the boy's prerogative to take self-instigated action and not do what he is supposed to do. Although the content is rebellious, the story in its overall quality is more conventional, less expressive than before, but also less disturbed.

2. TAT 5

Reaction Time: 3″   Total Time: 1′35″
Here's a woman who was asleep. She heard noises downstairs and they frightened her so she decided to come down and check out the

[2] The same TAT series was used in the retesting except that F5 (TAT 7GF), 10 (TAT 3BM), and 11 (TAT 16) were omitted.

noises, which is what she's doing, by peering around the corner with sort of a little bit frightened, but determined look on her face, to find out what the noise is. It's the radiator, so she goes back upstairs and goes to bed.

INTERPRETATION. As in 1, she tells the more usual story now of a frightened woman but adds that there was really nothing for her to be frightened about. In comparison with the negative portrayal of the maternal figure on this card in the first testing and the degree of rich personal communication then, this story is relatively banal. The need to minimize the fright at the end contrasts markedly with her opening TAT stories before in which objects ended smashed (Story 1) or people ended angry (Story 2). Her minimization this time suggests that her defenses are now geared toward toning down dysphoric concerns, anger, and fear. The conventionality of the story is reflected in the minimization of the fright and it presents a relatively undisturbed view of experience with more focus on external happenings than on internal processes. One interesting aspect of the story now, however, is the portrayal of the incident as interrupting the woman's sleep to which she returns afterward. The choice is for a more passive position, which like Mrs. T.'s selection of theme may reflect present efforts to avoid the recognition of problems, difficulties, and fears.

3. TAT 15

Reaction Time: 3"   Total Time: 1'30"
Here's a man whose wife has been dead for years and years, but he still can't get over the tragedy of it, and he hasn't found anything else in his life, so he continuously comes back to the graveyard and mourns her because he's found nothing to replace, or to fill, his loneliness. So he spends the rest of his life yearning for something he can never have and dies a lonely old soured-up man.

INQUIRY: [How did his wife die?] Oh, she was killed. [How?] Train-wreck [smiles]. That's the first thing I think of. [Soured-up?] Well, he just, he didn't have, he was so resentful of her having died that he never allowed himself to look for something else, could never get beyond resenting and hurting over her death enough to try and replace it with something, try to replace her absence with something fulfilling. [Toward whom resentful?] Life itself, he just bore a grudge, felt everything was against him and did nothing to correct it.

INTERPRETATION. The man's cruelty, his implication in his wife's death, the sense of lost opportunity, the lack of expression of love and the suicide are now absent in the story to this card. What we see instead is a man who is unable to bear a loss and who yearns for what he cannot have. Mrs. T.'s use of the expression "soured-up" adds an oral cast to the story, as if oral supplies have gone bad. Inasmuch as this story seemed on the first testing to reflect feelings about Mrs. T.'s dead mother, the feeling she represents here, an unsuccessful struggle to relinquish one's involvement with a dead person, may reflect Mrs. T.'s felt inability to give up her nurturant needs or to find adequate substitutes for them. Like Story 2, the source of disturbance is sought in the outside world but here is accompanied by a recognition of doing this.

4. TAT 14

Reaction Time: 8″   Total Time: 2′25″

I remember my old story about this and it's one that comes to mind again. It's a story of an artist who hasn't been able to find anything satisfactory to paint in a long time. He's felt dissatisfied and inhibited in his way of expressing himself. So he stops painting for a while and sort of gets outside of himself and sees the world, not in terms of traveling, but sort of looking at the sky, which he's doing here, and a period of time relating himself again to nature and to people, and eventually goes back to painting with a freer and more satisfying form of expression. I don't think that's the same story after all. I'm not sure. Can't remember now. Remember the picture though.

INQUIRY: [Relating himself to nature and people?] I think what I was thinking of is that he, or, he had withdrawn so much into his own self in trying to find a way to express himself through an art form that he had forgotten that he needed things and people outside of himself to help him find a way of expressing himself and in relating to other people, it is like in a way, meeting himself again too. [?] Well, beginning to realize and acknowledge his caring for something other than his own subjective thoughts, feelings for others besides himself, opened a new, freed him, just freed him.

INTERPRETATION. Even though she claims to remember her former story, and thinks she is retelling it, her story is markedly different. We no longer see the accelerated spread of depression, or the depressive view of nature (the setting sun), or suicide. The story, like Story 2, starts out with a disturbance which is resolved by the end of the story. This is in sharp contrast to many of her stories on the first testing in which there was a faint suggestion of something positive happening which deteriorated rapidly toward destruction and death. The story now is more positive; people and nature are sought out and have happy consequences. The push is to get "outside" oneself and the content of the stories up to this point reflects an emphasis on external happenings as opposed to the pent-up, dammed-up, self-absorbed characters in her previous testing. It is of particular importance that Mrs. T. is unsure whether this is the same story she told before. Such verbalizations have a decidedly repressive quality as if her earlier severely depressive, suicidal thoughts are now unavailable to her and blotted out. Thus, her movement appears to be toward a more repressive position—her stories are more conventional and positively toned— almost naively so. One would hope she could integrate her past experience with current reality but she seems to be sealing it off from recognition and, like the character in this story (and in Stories 1 and 2), may be seeking out external activity to facilitate this process. This latter possibility was also suggested on the WAIS in the increased proclivity toward action indicated by the elevation of the Performance over Verbal IQ. The combination of increased effectiveness of repression with increased acting out potential similarly reflects the fact that Mrs. T. seems in midstream in regard to working through and consolidating her therapeutic gains.

5. Woodcut of Two Old Men

Reaction Time: 16"   Total Time: 2'15"
This is a nightmare that a man is having. He's been having problems in deciding what he wants to do as opposed to what his father wants him to do. In this dream, he becomes vividly aware of feeling oppressed by his parents' demands, wishes for him, and that he feels unable to separate what he wants to do from what they want him to do even if it were the same thing. The next day when he wakes up, he's quite aware of the problem he has and spends a period of time trying to separate what he feels he can do, and what he feels his parents want him to do, at the end of which time he finds himself able to live more in terms of his own desires.

INQUIRY: [What to do?] Well, he's in college and his parents want him to go into an engineering course and he doesn't know if he wants to go into engineering or some other field and for all he knows, he might really want to be an engineer, but he becomes confused as to whom he's doing it for, himself or his parents. I'm not sure if he becomes an engineer or not, but the important thing is he gets himself to a position where he can realize what has, where his wishes are, his interests are, and where his parents are and to proceed from there.

INTERPRETATION. The violence and smoldering hate of her first story is muted here by making the scene a dream, not an actual occurrence but a symbolic expression of a conflict between parents and child over the child's choice of career. Although the tester neglected to establish what was happening in the picture beyond the fact that the paternal figure is probably doing something to the son which reflects the demands he is making, the general tone of the story sharply reduces the aggressive impact and murderous outcome of the first story. Mrs. T. is able to distance herself from the intense aggression and indicates the importance of issues around individuation and separation from parental figures. This theme was prominent in the first tests but here it is treated as a typically adolescent conflict about his ties to his parents. This is another TAT story in which aggressive interaction and destruction are not inevitable as they were before. It is the fourth story in this series in which a positive, satisfactory solution to a problem is arrived at.

6. TAT 10

Reaction Time: 5"   Total Time: 1'55"
Here's an old couple that have had to work very hard all their lives and have had quite a full life in terms of caring, in terms of sharing good times and bad times. At the time of this picture, they're just sort of loving each other, no particular crisis or anything involved in it. They just want to be close to each other. There's no real end to this, they just continue in the kind of life they've led, having to work for what they get and deserving it, and eventually dying having lived a really rich life.

INTERPRETATION. The strong depressive elements of the earlier story are now completely absent and instead fullness of life, love, and closeness are emphasized. Although there are references to "bad times" and "hard work" included in the story, some effort to deny any severe difficulties is reflected in Mrs. T.'s comment that there is "no particular crisis or anything involved in it." By specifically drawing attention to what is absent she emphasizes it and thereby demonstrates the process, more strained here, that has been apparent throughout the present TAT, namely, her use of denial in order to present an optimistic picture of reality. We must bear in mind that she has not gone to excessive lengths to do this, e.g., by stressing only happiness, gaiety, and joy, but instead has indicated a recognition of difficulties which she tries to view optimistically. In this story the denial is more forced and suggests she is trying especially hard to see things positively and to ward off the stark, pervasive dysphoria we saw in the first tests.

7. Picasso's "La Vie"

Reaction Time: 9″   Total Time: 3′10″
This is a couple who have lived together, very much in love with each other, and they've had an illegitimate child. The girl's mother who's quite provincial finds them and takes their child away from them, condemning them for the life they've led, saying they obviously couldn't raise a child with any sort of—intelligence, put it that way, and so she stalks away from them with the child, threatening to expose their affairs to the world if they try to get the child back and the couple decide to hell with it, they would rather have the child and they go eventually to the mother and take the baby back, and the mother doesn't say anything because it would reflect too much on her, and she doesn't want to quite ruin her name. So there's no great scandal evolving from the situation.

INQUIRY: [Feel when mother takes the baby?] They're very frightened. At first they are concerned with the threat of being exposed so to speak, but then they realize that exposure, so to speak, is not going to alter their own love or the love they have for their child, though it would probably make things more difficult.

INTERPRETATION. Again, a well organized story, with a happy ending in which a "great scandal" is avoided, replaces the cognitive disturbance and futility in the first story. And like other stories in this present series, what initially looks like a dire situation is overcome actively and resourcefully and leads to interpersonal closeness rather than "a life of nothingness." The mother here is more openly opposed, although the difficulty of going against her is still quite apparent. Mrs. T. is also able to represent the woman as the girl's mother and interestingly it is the girl's impetus to action that retrieves the baby. Although the basic attachment to the maternal figure still seems very strong, at least in fantasy Mrs. T. can represent an effort to move away from her. The absence here of suggestions of a lack of differentiation of herself from her mother also attests to a beginning ability to separate herself from her mother.

8. TAT 13 MF

Reaction Time: 8″   Total Time: 2′40″

This is a man's wife. She's been ill for a long, long time, she's a lovely woman, and they've been very much in love, very close to each other in their relationship. But he had seen her suffer so much and she had begged him to kill her, and at this moment he's debating, he's in anguish whether he should give in to her wish or not because of her acute pain. He doesn't know if he can live with the feeling of having killed her. Can I end the story saying I don't know what happens? [Try to make something up] Very conveniently she's going to die, so he doesn't have to make the choice. I boxed myself in on that one [smile].

INQUIRY: [Wrong with her?] She had cancer. [Feel?] He feels a relief because she had been in pain so much and it also took the decision or burden off him, or to take away her life and her pain.

INTERPRETATION. Somewhat conveniently the woman dies and relieves the man of his decision. Mrs. T. acknowledges how she "boxed" herself in and how she is willing to use any technique to avoid the full impact of the guilt and depression that would follow from the killing. It is that sole feeling—relief at the avoidance of guilt—that dominates the man's feelings to the exclusion of any grief about the woman's death. Mrs. T., therefore, seems aware of how she tries to ward off depressive affect suggesting that her present optimistic position is not secure and solid but involves considerable conscious effort on her part. This story is closer to her original one than any other thus far and Mrs. T. is even willing to leave the outcome in doubt showing that she has more trouble in recuperating from the theme here than she has had as yet during the retesting. In some respects, however, the story now shows a less inappropriate use of denial than did the first one.

F1. TAT 12F

Reaction Time: 15"   Total Time: 2'45"

Here's a, this is a woman who, oh, lives with her mother and her grandmother, and uh, they can't get away from each other, they're just sort of bound together. They get to a point where they can't really tolerate each other, yet they can't get away from each other. So the youngest finally one day reaches a point where she feels like her grandmother is just feeding off her, and not letting her have a life of her own. They can't even look at each other anymore. So she finally decides that rather than stay in this sort of confined life it would be better for her, even if she doesn't know what lies ahead of her or anything, to leave her home, which she does.

INQUIRY: [Why can't they get away from each other?] They've just lived together all their lives and they're all too frightened of the unknown and would rather tolerate the hell of living with each other than to take a chance. [Who in the picture?] Grandmother. First it was the mother, but on second thought, she looked too old, but my first thought was the mother. [Outcome?] I think the woman'll have enough of whatever it takes to find a life for herself outside her former existence.

INTERPRETATION. The theme now, as before, involves a desire to separate from an intense attachment to a maternal figure but now the ending is more hopeful, the thought processes in the story telling are considerably less disrupted, and there is a more rational representation of the problem and a more adaptive solution. Some fluidity is indicated in the lack of clarity as to whether three women or two women are involved but this is relatively mild compared to the former peculiar perceptual experience. The need clearly is to get away but the feeling is still basically one of being inextricably tied to a negative, orally destructive mother. And the earlier emphasis in the first tests on soaring and fleeing to escape a sense of confinement and lack of freedom is here explicitly related to the desire to separate from the mother but the difficulty is in accomplishing this. There is a further suggestion that it is the maternal figure's needs to hold on to her, her oral incorporative tendencies which Mrs. T. must flee. In part, this may be a projection of her own intense neediness and inability to give up the mother

but with the optimistic note that, though potentially painful, this
must be accomplished.

F2. TAT 3GF

Reaction Time: 3″   Total Time: 1′35″
This is a young girl that has just heard of tragedy in the family. She's
terribly unhappy, crying, feeling the pain of her parent's death. But
she realizes that she still has her own life and she finds a way to live
with the feeling of missing her parent and proceeds to have a life of
her own, even become a parent herself. [Places on pile.]

INQUIRY: [Both parents die?] No, the father. [How die?] Heart attack.

INTERPRETATION. The story is similar to the first one but is more
positive in its outcome and shifts from the loss of the mother to the
vague loss of a parent who on questioning is specified as the father.
Much like trying in F1 to see the older figure as a grandmother,
this seems to reflect some desire to distance herself from the cen-
trality of her mother to her. Again the desire is for independence
but the major preoccupation is with the intolerable loss.

F3. TAT 2

Reaction Time: 4″   Total Time: 2′40″
This is a girl who has lived in the hills of Arkansas all her life. She
is quite dissatisfied because through her schooling and education she's
gotten an itch to see other worlds than Arkansas, and she's faced with
what is sort of an emotional dilemma for her, whether to stay with
her brother and mother in Arkansas and share the farm life, help her
mother who is pregnant and can't do much work or should she go find
out about the things she's just discovering through her education.
She's sort of torn between family obligations and love and her own
wish to go beyond her present life. . . . She suffers with this for a
while and makes her choice. I think she leaves Arkansas [smiles].

INQUIRY: [Who on farm?] Her father's dead, just died recently I
guess, and it's just her mother and her brother and they're poor
people, and she's needed there. But she feels other needs.

INTERPRETATION. Her new story reiterates the difficulty separating,
leaving home (from a rural to an urban setting), and maturing

except now there is more recognition of the difficulty in pulling herself away, more recognition of her ties to home. Nevertheless, she also sees the situation to a large extent as helping her mother and her being needed rather than primarily in terms of her own needs to remain. But the story now no longer includes the expansive ambitiousness and the inevitable depression or sense of emptiness. This is the second story in this series in which a father has died—a move away from the emphasis on the mother's death in the first TAT and possibly a direct representation of her concerns about her father's own imminent death.

F4. TAT 18GF

Reaction Time: 6″   Total Time: 1′30″
These are two sisters that have lived together for a long, long time, they're old maids. They've always been very sweet to each other, but underneath they really despised each other, and one day it just got to be too much for one of the sisters, and she killed her sister. But she didn't get away with it. She was caught and spent the rest of her life in jail.

INQUIRY: [Led up to killing?] She didn't like the way she, just something very trivial, like the way she dusted the bannister or stairway. Just frustration after frustration built up. [Frustration about?] Oh, I think she was frustrated because of her own life first of all, the fact that the only person she did have was her sister, that there was no one else in her life. They had lived too closely for too long until every resentment grew out of proportion and it just blew up on her. [Feel after?] She felt badly, guilty, but also like maybe it was the first definite thing she had done in her life.

INTERPRETATION. She continues mildly to distort the usual perception of these two figures as of different generations and also includes the sudden eruption of a longstanding rage which leads to the murder of the sister. What is different is the absence of the theme of insanity and the strange behavior toward the dead sister. Now it is more a direct issue of crime and punishment and there is more emphasis on the superficial sweetness of the two sisters as well as the recognition of the intensity of the love and involvement with her. This is another indication of the difficulty and conflicted feelings about separating herself except through violent means.

The story represents Mrs. T.'s problems around generations and her confused relationship with her siblings.

9. TAT 12M

Reaction Time: 5″   Total Time: 2′15″
This is a faith healer at a revival who promises the people that he can cure everything, cure them completely and a young boy who has been crippled all his life is brought to the evangelist and there's a big meeting and he's supposed to be cured magically. At this point the evangelist is going to cure him, has his hand over his head and the result is that the boy doesn't get cured, he's always been hopeless as far as his crippledness goes, and the man's exposed as a fraud, and run out of town.

INQUIRY: [Boy feel?] I think the boy realized even before that there wasn't any chance of being cured but he sort of went along with his family because they don't want to face the fact and he thought that this disappointment that would come to his parents might make them more aware of the truthfulness of his condition.

INTERPRETATION. The perceptual misrecognition of the age difference between these two figures is now absent, as well as the magical timing of the entrance of the brother, the stress on the "personal
contact with God," the confusion of the siblings, the sense of
estrangement between the people and the theme of insanity. Thus,
both in its formal organization—perceptual accuracy and structural organization of the story elements—and in its content, the
present story demonstrates improved efficiency in ego functioning.
Interestingly, the boy in this story is crippled and remains crippled
but is certainly without illusions. The emphasis in the story is now
on passive compliance, going along with the act without conviction,
and since the card represents a healer and a patient, this story may
be taken to indicate angry feelings about the fear and/or the wish
for the therapist to fail in his healing role. The story also involves
a debunking of mystical aspects of religion more clearly and un-
ambivalently than the earlier story; it may reflect a more pronounced
move away from her religious background which may be another
aspect of her struggle for separation and individuation.

TAT Summary

Like the WAIS, the current TAT demonstrates improved efficiency
of ego organization. More usual, conventional ways of looking at

reality are evident. The monothematic depressive quality, the sense of being dammed-up in her expressiveness, the major emphasis on fantasy, and the violent destructive and suicidal activity are either absent or considerably muted. There is only one perceptual fluidity (related to the number of women in F1) and two mild perceptual misrecognitions but these do not reach the psychotic levels of thought organization present in the previous TAT. Rather the psychological picture now shows a more clearly repressive orientation with strong efforts to minimize feelings of distress, emptiness, misery and futility and instead to see things more optimistically and hopefully (see TAT Story 4 specifically). Characters now are less self-absorbed and preoccupied with fantasy, and strive more to engage themselves with other people and outside activities—to some extent in an effort to facilitate the process of warding off from consciousness the intense dysphoric concerns apparent on the first TAT. At the same time, however, there is an increased recognition of the ties to the maternal figure. While Mrs. T. feels impinged upon by outside forces and externalizes the reason for the ties to the maternal figure often as stemming from the maternal figure's desire to hold on to her, there is nonetheless a more open acknowledgment of her own needs for this attachment. Separation, individuation and maturity are still sought after but her thinking about them is not as disrupted, confused, depressed and angry as before, which also suggests a clearer, more realistic view of her development.

Her present defenses are not altogether stable. Her efforts at minimization and denial are sometimes forced and self-conscious, but she seems in a transition stage trying to shut out dysphoria and to be optimistic, trying to more actively involve herself in things "outside" and to recognize more the extent of her own need to hold on to her mother and to her constricted, "confining" rural background. With this increasing recognition of the symbiotic ties to her mother comes the potential for mature separation and individuation through positive identification.

Some prominent changes are immediately apparent in the summary of Mrs. T.'s Rorschach retest. Her overall productivity ($\#R$) is lower; her qualitative column is noticeably freer of pathology scores; her production of Movement responses is lower, but her production of Color responses is slightly elevated; her $F+\%$s (regular and extended) are improved; and there is no direct sexual content. The reduction of qualitative scores and the lowering of M

Mrs. T.'s Rorschach Retest Summary Sheet

			R = 37	EB 5.5/8.5				
5 W	10	F+	11	A	11	W%	27
D	20	F—	0	Ad	3	D%	54
Dr	4	F±	6	H	5	Dr%	19
1 S	2	F∓	0	(H)	1	F%	46/81
2 s	1	M+∓∓+		Hd	3	F+%	100/84
1 Do	0	MC'+		(Hd)	1	A%	40
		FMC∓		Obj	5	H%	22(27)
	∓	FC++∓		Pl	1	P	7
		CF	4	Sunset	1	P%	19
		C(C)F 1		Na	1		
		C symb 1		Light	1	Fab	5
		F(C)+∓±		Pain	1	Confab tend 1
	1	(C)F		Water	1	Fab comb	1
	+	FC'+		Fireworks	1		
		ChF 1		Underwater	1		

taken together indicate less autistic elaboration, less fantasy investment, and probably less reliance on projection and psychotic modes of thought. The improved $F+$% further indicates increased reality testing and ego control. Since her sexual responses previously seemed the result of weakened repressive defenses and were often accompanied by much disrupted thinking, their absence now also suggests increased control—possibly via repressive modes which are now blocking them out. The reduction in the total number of responses, like her M responses, reflects a curtailment of her ideational productivity. It is of interest that her fantasy is more limited and that her affective experience at the same time appears unchanged. In fact, if we consider that she gives 30 percent fewer responses to the second Rorschach, then the slight increase in the sum of her color scores is even more impressive. Her experience balance thus is still dilated as regards sum M and sum C but is more clearly repressive now.

The change in the picture of her summary sheets therefore suggests more organized and efficient psychological functioning which may be accompanied by a more noteworthy reliance on repressive defenses.

In order to evaluate Mrs. T.'s change further, we shall proceed to a card by card analysis of the present Rorschach with our emphasis placed on the differences between the two Rorschachs.

Card 1

Reaction Time: 1'   Total Time: 3'
1. Here we are with the elephant again. I see two elephants touching trunks and their hooves are together, one on each side, with their ears flying off in the breeze, pompons on their tails [D1 + D2] [D F+ A].*

INQUIRY: [Elephants?] They had the shape of elephants.

2. I see a total, the whole thing together as a mask, very devilish thing, with ears and sort of horn-like things, eyes and mouth that's grinning with the nose coming down [Ws FC'+ (Hd)] (Fab).

INQUIRY: [Devilish?] It was leering, sort of smiling, grinning. I think the way the white was shining through for the eyes, sort of luminosity, and the horns, sort of fitted a caricature of a devil's face you might see.

3. ↑↓↑ Well, sort of a cockroach in the center of the thing, sort of goes off into the grey blob on the sides, very indistinct. Only thing that really resembles a roach is the very top where you see the sort of pinchers coming out [D4] [D F± A].

INTERPRETATION. She again starts out with elephants, also fighting and still minimized in their strength by the presence of pompons on their tails, but much less effort is invested in minimizing them and making them childlike and playful. Secondly, the elephants are not integrated in an incongruous way with the cockroach as before.

The demon is now seen as a mask, still with fearful, sinister, and lascivious intent, but more intellectual distance is achieved from it from the fact that it is a "mask" rather than an actual demon and because it is not seen as staring directly at her. That is, she acknowledges its fearfulness to her more easily and smoothly and shows more control over it than before.

She now ends the card with the cockroach and omits the confabulated angel response of the first test.

This card in general shows less push toward W responses and

* Location cards for retest responses are presented following p. 246.

hence toward expansive and grandiose integration. The fabulized combination and the confabulation tendency are dropped out, her communication is clearer, less fluid, and her defensive efforts are less strained and struggling. The same problems are unmistakably present—the need to minimize the fearful phallic male image (the pompon on the tail), the projective trend, the perception of the female form as bug-like. But there is, nonetheless, little indication of the earlier sexual role confusion, less personalized elaboration, less sense of direct threat from the images on the cards, less need to retreat to expansive denial, manic frenzy, and fluidly sexualized and moralistic themes. In a subtle way, only, in the image of the elephants' ears "flying *off* in the breeze" do we see a much less intense representation of these latter tendencies. This card, in sum, demonstrates a lessened reliance on projection and denial as well as a diminution of defensive instability and of primitivization of thought processes.

Card II

Reaction Time: 5"   Total Time: 2'25"

1. Well, I see a red-headed female standing behind two bears that are rubbing noses [D1] and she has her hands on the forehead of each bear. [Her hair is D2; her head is in the space between D2; and her hands are the red portion of the blot on top of the heads of the D1 animals.] Her figure is obscured by the bears, which are in the foreground [Drs FMC∓ H, D F+ A P] (W, Fab Comb).

INQUIRY: [Female?] Well, mainly the hair, well the red was the hair and it surrounded an area which took an animal shape; sort of a silhouette of the head, neck, shoulders, and then you couldn't see the rest of her figure other than a small portion because because the bears that were facing each other obscured it. And then you could see her hands, they were red, so I don't know if they could be hands, but gave the impression to me of a woman resting her hands on the bears' heads.

2. Then I see a butterfly. That's the red in the bottom of the picture [D3] [D FC+ A P].

INQUIRY: [Butterfly?] Well, it was the color, the red had a shape of a butterfly, the way the wings got very slender at the end, tapering.

3. And I see a top, the child's toy top, that's spinning very fast [Ds 5] and shedding a red light as it goes around [D3] [S F+ Obj, D CF Light].

INQUIRY: [Top spinning?] It was the form of a top. The white area in the middle of the inkblot had the distinct form of a top and the reason it looked like it was spinning was that the color that was formerly the butterfly looked like a reflection that was being cast off by something spinning in a light and sort of casting off a light.

4. ↓ I see two grumpy old bears that have just hit their noses together [D6] and it hurt because the red, where I see the butterfly, signifies pain [D3]. They're in profile, the bears [D F±Ad, D C*symb*. Pain] (W, Fab, Agg.).

INQUIRY: [Grumpy?] Well, this is turning the picture upside down. Well, they look like strong bears, had much bigger shoulders and heads than the other bears and they looked like they were pulling back from each other the way the bodies were postured. Looked like they had just hit each other and were pulling back.

INTERPRETATION. To this card she gives several fewer responses without any of the peculiar verbalizations and confabulations evident earlier. The "ghastly," "ghoulish" bloody bear cubs, the "diabolical" bug, the severely disrupted sexual and reproductive imagery are no longer evident. This time she starts with the red haired woman who is integrated somewhat forcedly with the bears but the previous spread of aggression and damage is no longer present and the woman is described as more physically intact and less poorly put together. Whereas last time she tried at the outset to defend through childlike and oral imagery which quickly broke down and led to increasingly disturbed imagery from which she was eventually able to extricate herself, her responses this time are more orderly, more smoothly verbalized and better defended. It is impressive, for example, how the vagina is now a butterfly, how the womb giving birth to a diabolical bug is now a child's top "shedding a red light as it goes around," and how the prior percept of bloody bears or a damaged woman are pleasantly brought together in a friendly and affectionate interaction (with the woman resting her hands on the bears who are rubbing noses). Only at the end of the card does an aggressive theme appear, but again it is subdued by the symbolic nature of the pain and the bears' noses are no longer spattered. Only the positioning of the bears gives away Mrs. T.'s still present concern with separating herself from too painful aggressive interactions. Thus, this card shows major signs of improved psychological functioning, largely achieved through the absence of former confabulatory elaboration and the substitution of pleasant, unaggressive, childlike imagery. Her ineffective efforts in the first Rorschach to present such an undisturbed childlike view of reality is here more solidly realized; it demonstrates the current effectiveness of repressive defenses and Pollyannaish denial.

Card III

Reaction Time: 7″   Total Time: 2′20″
1. Two girls doing some sort of dance [D1], facing each other with baskets [D4] in their hands and a butterfly in the middle [D3] [W M+ H P, D F(C)+ A P].

INQUIRY: [Butterfly?] Sort of had the, well, it looked like what a two year old would draw as a butterfly, had the shape for the wings and center darkness for the body. Very little. [Anything else?] Just the overall shape.

2. Oh, [laughs] there's the old lady again. I remember the one, a woman, sort of a very Victorian, prudish sort of woman, sitting right boom in the middle of somethings, sitting with her hands clasped in her lap with a very frowning countenance, has a very disapproving look on her face as though she doesn't approve of anything that was going on around her [D8 is the head; Dds 24 is the body; Dd 29 are puffy sleeves and Dd 28 are her hands] [DrS M∓ H] (Confab tend).

INQUIRY: [Prudish?] I think first of all, was the clothes she was dressed in, looked like straight out of Jane Eyre, also was sitting sort of straight and prim, very restrained. And she had a frown on her face, disdainful sort of expression. [Disdainful?] Well, one thing, she sort of looked, gave you the impression she's sitting there alone, nothing around her seemed to relate to the central figure. She looks like she's drawn herself away from things. [When *E* asks her to point out, she says she thinks *E* will have to look hard to see it. *E* questions. She says, "You'd ask about the girls, this must be less obvious. And I think I had trouble showing it to Dr. _____ the last time.]

INTERPRETATION. The number of responses drops from thirteen to three; poorly perceived minus responses, confabulation and contamination tendencies are now successfully held in check, and the overelaborated content—the strange concerns with death, external attack, and frenzy—are conspicuously absent. Two of her three responses are carry-overs from the first Rorschach and she can more clearly locate the Victorian woman and is not directly threatened by her and does not lose distance from the card. The woman is now seen as sitting, she is not "staring" or "looking down," and her hands are in her lap rather than on her hips. Although there is something odd about how Mrs. T. relates the woman's position on the card to her psychological stance ("drawn . . . away from things"), it is noteworthy how this previously very threatening woman is now seen only as frowning and disdainful, relatively passive and somewhat withdrawn.

As regards Mrs. T.'s shift to a more effective repressive position, this card is also of interest. The frenzied dancers are now more mildly dancing with baskets in their hands, and the butterfly which ends the card has a childlike quality. Mrs. T.'s disturbed thinking is muted now; and the content of her responses shows a parallel muting. It is calmer, more benign, and subdued, and again reflects the increased effectiveness of repressive defenses.

Card IV

Reaction Time: 8″   Total Time: 3′25″

1. Here again, I remember what I've seen. Two women playing hide-and-go-seek. Old fashioned women. [Dds 24: top third is the head, center third is the upper torso and the lower third is the skirt). It's an old fashioned scene, looks like it takes place in a garden party. They're wearing old fashioned gowns and are sort of teasing each other by hiding behind a tree trunk you see going up in the sky [D1] [s M∓ H, D F± Pl] (Fab).

INQUIRY: [Hide-and-go-seek?] Well, they look like they were, well, they were hiding from each other. Well, they were out of sight of each other, looking around a tree, and just reminded me of things I've read when the women played games. I don't know, something like that. [Old fashioned?] I think the clothes, the hoopskirts, or the long skirts. [Garden party?] I think I just associated it with stories I read, plus the fact they were hiding behind a tree, you don't find that in a living room.

2. Oh, uh, I don't know if I saw this before or not. I see a figure, the whole thing is a figure you see from a foreshortened view, you're looking up at it. The feet are enormous and the rest sort of tapers up

to a small head and the hands are sort of dangling down, arms held out to the side. And it's either being held up by a stick or is leaning against a stick [W M+ H] (Fab).

INQUIRY: [Kind of figure?] Sort of looks like a distorted clown, sort of a macabre sort of thing. [Distorted?] I think first of all, the angle at which you see it sort of throws everything out of proportion, the hands flopping off at the side, the smallness of the head as it goes away from you.

INTERPRETATION. Again, the responses are decreased in number and interestingly, Mrs. T. for the second time gives a response which she regards as equivalent to a former one but which is altered considerably. It is as if she is not consciously aware of the degree of primitive thinking she displayed previously, for the women hiding from each other in a dark, gloomy forest are now old-fashioned benign ladies playing a game at a garden party. This shift is an impressive accomplishment of repression and denial. Moreover, the confabulated and confused sexual imagery is left out and the mixed up religious, sexual, and aggressive image of the male figure is transformed into a clown which although "distorted" and "macabre" is more passively supported by the previously destructive murderous impaling stick. This reflects a disparagement of male figures but without the intense sadistic fantasies seen previously. This card, like others in this Rorschach series, follows similar trends toward perceiving reality as childlike, pleasant, playful, and asexual.

Card V

Reaction Time: 2″   Total Time: 1′10″

1. A bat. The whole thing is a bat [W F+ A P].

2. ↑↓← A sea gull that's just hitting the water, landing on the water and the reflection is being picked up. ↓ It's a bat from both directions [laughs] [W F± A].

INTERPRETATION. Little change is evident on this card except that the sea gulls are now landing instead of "sweeping off" the water. She quickly rephrases "hitting the water" to "landing on the water," thereby reducing the aggressive impact. "Landing" also connotes a position of settled rest more than "sweeping off" and this shift in the content may reflect Mrs. T.'s more settled, less soaring position at present.

Card VI

Reaction Time: 18"   Total Time: 3'25"

1. ↓ In the very top of the picture I see again sort of the pinchers of a rodent, not a rodent, a bug, but it doesn't have a body actually, just sort of the very top [Dr F+ Ad] (Do tend).

INQUIRY: [Pinchers?] They had the distinct shape of sort of symmetrical pinchers shape coming out.

2. ↑↓ I got the impression of something going through water, you're looking down from above and you see something that looks like a torpedo [center of D3], something hurtling through the water and casting off a weight [D1] [D F+ Obj, ChF Water] (Comb, W).

INQUIRY: [Something going through the water?] There was a distinct line that looked like it was cutting through water because it casted off a lighter grey area that looked like foam and then it went back into the dark area.

3. ↓ I see two large heads with necks but nothing, no real, no body, sort of goes into nothing, back to back, back of the heads pressed together, big nose, goatee [D1] [D F± Hd].

INQUIRY: [Heads?] Let's see if I can remember. Oh, just the shape, again sort of a distorted shape, tremendous nose, goatee. The dark line again was the separation of the two.

4. Also, the whole thing together's sort of a horseshoe crab with the shell being the darker area and the thin darkness being the, I guess you'd call it the beak, I don't now, the tail [laugh] [W F(C)∓ A].

INTERPRETATION. Now she reverses the card immediately, probably to get away from the sexual image she began with last time. Two of her responses remain the same (the pinchers and the heads) and there is less fragmenting of her perception now. She is still sensitive to the area of the card often seen as a phallus and which she saw as such before, but now makes it into a torpedo. In this way she conveys an impression of the male organ as aggressive and potentially damaging. But it is a more disguised percept than before, reflecting more the sensitivity to phallic-like extensions and the symbolic elaboration of sexual themes that one sees in hysterical settings.

She ends the card with a horseshoe crab now, but there is some fluidity of thinking around whether the extension of the horseshoe crab is called "the beak" or "the tail" showing an oral-anal equivalence. Her repeated emphasis on the absence of bodies (of the rodents and the heads), the quality of "sort of going back into nothing" is reminiscent of several of her responses on the first Rorschach in which things fade away, are unsubstantial and ghost-like. The horseshoe crab has the very opposite characteristic of a well-defined and hard-shelled body and it is of interest that Mrs. T. ends with the firmer, stronger image which may reflect her increased sense of having more substantial, tougher boundaries between herself and others and of being less vulnerable psychologically than she was earlier.

Card VII

Reaction Time: 10″   Total Time: 2′35″

1. ↓ I see the silhouette of a young girl with a sort of Dutch boy haircut that was squared off, and a turtleneck, you can see the roll of the material around the neck and you see the shoulders, in silhouette [Ds 7] [S F+ Hd].

INQUIRY: [Young girl?] The pony tail probably, and they had chubby looking cheeks. Oh, wait a minute, you're talking about the girl with the Dutch boy haircut, just the haircut, I guess, it's a young kid's haircut.

2. ↓ And a butterfly at the top with big square wings (D4) [D F+ A].

3. And a syringe with a needle [Dd 26] [Dr F(C)± Obj].

INQUIRY: [Syringe?] The shape, and yeah, the shape of the syringe then you could see the very thin strip of white that made it look like a needle.

4. ↑ Oh, and two girls looking at each other with pony tails, they're sort of being whipped up into the air behind them and the rest of their bodies are so indistinct, can't see them ↑↓↑ [D1] [D F+ Hd P].

INTERPRETATION. The odd fabulized combination with the near blending and fusing quality drops out as does the theme of anger and body damage. Sexual role confusion is still indicated by the girls with boys' haircuts and by the phallically toned percept of a syringe with a needle in an area frequently seen as a vagina. But the severity of the sexual role problems does not reach the proportions of peculiar synthetic thinking as it did before, and is therefore less disruptive to the efficiency of her ego functioning. The syringe response, like the torpedo of Card VI, shows a symbolic treatment of a sexual area and, although it indicates unclear sexual role differentiation, it again shows a typically repressive defense.

It is noteworthy in addition that the young girl (with the boy's haircut) is wearing a "turtleneck" sweater; that is, she is little exposed but rather well protected and sealed in, much in the manner of the horseshoe crab of Card VI.

Card VIII

Reaction Time: 10"   Total Time: 2'20"

1. I see two blue flags sticking out of a central orange pole and the flags are each one flopping off to the side [D5] [D FC+ Obj].

2. I see a bear [D1] standing on an ice-covered bank that's picking up color of the sun and the bank is next to water and the whole scene is reflected back [D F+ A P, D CF Nat] (W, C/F tend).

INQUIRY: [Ice-covered?] Mainly because of the varied colors, only way these colors could be there is if it were ice-covered and picking up the reflection of the sunset perhaps.

3. ↓ Oh, I see the head of a dog with blue eyes [D5], pink ears on each side [D1], sort of a grey snout [D4] and a big flounce of pinkish hair on top [D2] [W FC∓ Ad] (FC$_{arb}$ tend).

INQUIRY: [Dog's head?] The shape with, well, you see the _____, sort of the shape of the snout, the nose, like the shape of a dog's snout. (Anything else?) Ears, that's right, just the overall shape.

INTERPRETATION. She now opens with a good *FC* response and does not introduce the theme of connectedness again. Nor is she drawn to the prepotent rib cage. In all, she now uses color in three of her four responses, two of which are *FC*. But one *FC* has an arbitrary quality (the dog with *pink hair*) and her *CF* tends toward *C/F* since the color is not integral but is reflected onto the scene. Thus, her use of color now is both adaptively oriented and also mildly forced and arbitrary whereas before on this card it was primarily superficial and forced. This means that her use of color in an adaptive way is partially successful, a fact which also attests to her increased but still tentative adaptive affective experience.

Card IX

Reaction Time: 20"   Total Time: 2'50"

1. ← Well, I see the sunset. You can see an island [D5] way off in the distance—the whole sunset, well, the ocean is around it and picking up all the clouds and reflecting them back, a lot of colors in the clouds, big puffy clouds [W C(C)F Sunset].

INQUIRY: [Sunset?] Well, the shape, looks like the shapes of big puffy clouds, you could see it was reflected, the colors, the pinks, the blues, the sort of violet, looks like a painting of the sunset to me. [Reflection?] 'Cause it was duplicated and there was a distinct line in the middle that sort of looked like an island, wasn't as puffy or gauzy looking, had more of a solid look. [Puffy and gauzy?] I think the shapes of the colors were sort of balloon shaped, especially the pink, you could see colors sort of coming through colors.

2. I see sort of two, well, they look like the beginnings of what might be a seahorse [D3], but they sort of go into nothing, well, anyway, they have the shape of a seahorse, the chest and stance, the head of a seahorse and it goes into a beak-like affair that departs from what I think a seahorse ought to look like [D F+ A] (F/C tend).

INQUIRY: [Seahorse?] Well, as I said before, I think it was the swell of the chest, the head thrown back, and the head didn't fit the picture, I think just the first impression of the form. [Anything else?] No, also the distinction of the color from the other colors, and it separates itself from the other colors. [How did that influence it?] It just helped to separate it from the rest of the shapes.

INTERPRETATION. Less disturbed thinking is apparent; she is less distracted by and more able to use the color; the sexual themes are omitted as well as the strange phallic aggressive interchange and the "hovering" witches. Her use of color though is similar to Card VIII in that she uses it more in a reflected than an integral way and dilutes it intellectually even more by seeing the scene as a painting. It is significant too that two of her three CF responses thus far (the ice of VIII and the response here) involve sunsets, ice, islands, and seem, therefore, to have implicitly depressive undertones. Note also her contrast of the puffy look of the clouds and the transparency of the colors to the solid look of the island—again reflecting her concerns about her as yet not securely attained sense of solidity and stability.

Card X

Reaction Time: 5″   Total Time: 2′50″
Is this the last one? [Big smile]
1. Oh, here we are at the World's Fair. I see a lot of fireworks bursting all over. All the colors are very gay. A lot of different colors exploding in the sky [W CF Fireworks].

INQUIRY: [Bursting?] You saw the colors, they were sending out colored lights, flares.

2. And also, it's like looking into an aquarium and you see all sorts of strange sea creatures, crab-like things and seaweed, like a Walt Disney underwater shot, sort of all the little separate things that might exist in the water [W CF Underwater].

INQUIRY: [Sea creatures?] Well, they don't have any definite shapes, they sort of did remind me of movies I've seen of beasts that live under the sea. Weren't familiar to me as any particular thing, just vaguely like fish, sea creatures, and I think the vivid colors, like I have seen in pictures of water creatures.

3. See two men, two creatures, sort of comical characters, arguing with each other. They have all sorts of antenna sticking out from their heads [D8]. And sort of a space ship sitting behind them [D 14]. They look like they just landed and they're kind of arguing with each other about what it all means. Mostly, I just see the sort of crab-like shapes and fish-like shapes that look like they might be in an aquarium [D MC′+ (H), D F± Obj] (Fab, W).

INQUIRY: [Comical characters?] Well, they sort of [laughs] they struck me as humorous, I don't know why, squatting little grey creatures with exaggerated antenna that look like, well, they just impressed me as being comical. [Arguing?] The expression on their faces. They looked bewildered by it all. [Space ship?] There was a grey cylinder-like form behind them and being as they looked like creatures from another planet, that in turn reminded me of what a space ship might look like.

INTERPRETATION. The microscope is no longer present but the theme of looking and seeing into (an aquarium) persists. Superficial affective display gives way to stronger, less masquerading affective expression; fearful, misshapen figures disappear; her sexual response is no longer alluded to. A certain amount of emphasis on soaring and its link to phallic excitement (e.g., the space ship, the torpedo on Card VI, and the fireworks here) is still evident but more controlled than in her responses generally on the first Rorschach. In her response to this card the emphasis is on gaiety, excitement, and humor, and it is a relatively successful emphasis. The essentially arguing, bewildered space men are converted into humorous, unthreatening, playful creatures and Mrs. T. carries off this conversion with relative ease in comparison to her first Rorschach.

Rorschach Summary

The current Rorschach reveals an increased reliance on repressive defenses and on denial both of which are relatively successful in keeping in check the former intense dysphoric, aggressive, and disrupted sexual imagery. Mrs. T.'s thinking shows few remnants of the clearly psychotic trends she showed earlier, less confabulatory elaboration, fewer peculiar verbalizations, and less grandiose fantasy. The problem areas specified in the analysis of the first tests are still evident in this Rorschach but more subtly and indirectly. Her color balance still suggests strong affective display which now is often depressively toned but her present defenses seem rigorously directed toward warding off from awareness direct recognition of anger and unhappiness. Nonetheless, she does seem relatively able to maintain a benign, pleasant, childlike, and playful view of things.

Analysis of Test-Retest Results

The tests indicate striking improvement in many ways from her position at the testing of two and one-half years ago. By and large the same issues still concern her, but their impact seems much less intense and her capacity to deal with them considerably greater. At the time of the first testing her functioning often resembled that of a borderline psychotic individual. Almost all of the evidence of thought disorder has disappeared and presently she is not psychotic. Although personal concerns, particularly involving her attitude toward maternal figures, do intrude into her functioning, she generally maintains sufficient defensive solidarity to sustain adequate reality testing and prevent overwhelming dysphoric affect. The organization and control of her thinking has improved considerably without being accompanied by marked constriction; repressive defenses are now more marked and more successful. Her present functioning is much less uneven than previously and considerable potential for creativity is suggested. Nonetheless her position is still somewhat precarious, and her present defensive efforts—repression and denial—often seem too vigorously directed toward maintaining a primarily benign, pleasant, childlike, playful view of reality. Thus, although she appears to be moving toward greater growth, difficulties still remain to be faced and coped with.

At the time of the first testing, her self-image was of a shameful, ugly, dirty, ungainly, disgusting creature. Her feelings of worthlessness and underlying depression were very intense. These feelings and attitudes are evident in the present record as well, but their intensity is much diminished and depression is coped with fairly successfully. She can permit herself to experience some dysphoric affect and the denial now is less unstable and extreme, and the marked grandiosity shown two and one-half years ago is no longer evident. Though her underlying self image still seems to include something like a "cockroach" or "bug," these feelings do not as readily break through and overwhelm her as they did earlier. In general, the affects now are less intense and better modulated. Disturbing fantasies about her body are still evident, but are not as intense or bizarre as previously. She demonstrates far less explicit preoccupation with anatomy and sexual organs now, but seems instead to have feelings of uncertainty regarding the shape and nature of her body, to be unsure of its boundaries and its attractiveness and unable to experience her body in a consistent, comfortable, familiar way. She sees many percepts on the current Rorschach, for example, which have no bodies or indistinct bodies.

Closely related to these feelings about her body is confusion in sexual identity. Previously, femininity seemed to be consistently regarded in an intense negative manner and there was little evidence of any strong wish to be feminine. Women were ugly castrated creatures with "horrible," "misshapen" genitals. Presently she seems to be striving to achieve an identity as a women and to regard femininity in a more positive manner. She sees many more feminine percepts, and the intensity of feelings of revulsion and disgust toward women and female genitalia have diminished considerably. However, strong negative attitudes regarding female sexuality are still evident and it is necessary for her to deny them. Heterosexual relations are still frightening and she tends to retreat to a more childlike position to escape heterosexual involvement.

She views women, especially mother figures, as stern, cruel, strict, and punitive. It is around issues of mothers and women in general, that her serious lapses in reality testing occur. Her intense involvement with a forbidding mother figure is reflected in a Rorschach percept seen in an unusual area and of poor form level, of "a very Victorian, prudish sort of woman . . . sitting with her hands clasped in her lap, with a very frowning countenance, has a very disapproving look on her face as though she doesn't approve of anything that was going on around her." It seems likely that her conflictful attitudes toward femininity are related to her identification with this negatively perceived maternal figure.

There are many indications in the present record that separating herself from her mother, breaking these ties and establishing a separate identity, is a major issue. Several times on the Rorschach she sees reflections or emphasizes the line between two figures suggesting concerns about duplication and individuation. The TAT has many stories about separating one's own desires from one's parents, breaking away from the ties which bind one to home and parents. This is seen as a terribly frightening but necessary course. Thus, in one TAT story a girl feels that her grandmother, with whom she lives is "just feeding off her and not letting her have a life of her own . . . So she finally decides that rather than stay in this sort of confined life, it would be better for her, even if she doesn't know what lies ahead of her or anything, to leave home, which she does. . . . I think the woman will have enough of whatever it takes to find a life for herself outside her former existence." These efforts at separation represent strivings toward growth, not evident in the earlier record. She seems to be reaching out for contact with others, toward "relating [herself] again to nature and to people" and is much more aware than previously of the dangers of having "drawn herself away from things" and "withdrawn so much into [her] own-self." She is conflictful about such reaching out and still somewhat mistrustful but seems to be moving toward greater contact with others.

She appears to deal with her fear and jealousy of men by mockery and disparagement which seems to have replaced the intense sadistic fantasies evident at the first testing. She sees men as distorted, macabre, clown-like figures who are ineffectual and need support, but also appears to have strong wishes to be a man and have a penis. These wishes seem less intense and more indirectly expressed than previously, but the phallic concern is still evident. Thus, where she saw a penis on the first Rorschach, she now sees a torpedo. Homosexual problems also seem less intense than previously.

The strength of paranoid trends is somewhat less than on the first records. Earlier there were expressions of considerable grandiosity as well as a large number of self-referents, such as percepts seen as "staring at me." Projection is still, along with denial, her predominant mode of dealing with aggression. She still shows a strong investment in fantasy, and some of her percepts are elaborately described as devilish, grinning, leering, etc. But she has much greater control over these fantasies and the boundary between fantasy and reality seems more clear.

Her intellectual functioning is now smoother and more consistent. The improvement in her IQ score (now: Verbal IQ 120, Performance 135, Total 128; previously: Verbal IQ 120, Performance 116, Total 120) is mainly on the performance tests, where the 19-point rise probably reflects the decrease in depression as well as better organization and greater efficiency. Some of the improvement may be a function of practice. She is attempting to cope with significant depressive feelings of guilt, worthlessness, and ugliness and to achieve some sense of separation from an extremely overbearing mother image and seems to be moving in the direction of growth.

7

Postscript

In this concluding chapter our main purpose is to round out the clinical picture of Mrs. T. First we will present a diary she kept for several days some months after being admitted to the hospital and shortly after a change of therapists. The diary was kept without any awareness on Mrs. T.'s part at the time that she would eventually be discussed in a book. Following this, an interview with Mrs. T.'s therapist conducted seven months after testing and dealing both with the usefulness to him of the test findings and with his impressions of Mrs. T.'s hospital course will be included. Finally, we will note briefly some aspects of Mrs. T.'s life following discharge from the hospital.

MRS. T.'S DIARY [1]

July 5

A day that I wish would end forever—Crap, I feel badly. Tonight I helped restrain Betty for what seemed to me hours. She's mute and possibly becoming catatonic. She fought and I had to force her to still—never a sound from her—just tears and tense fighting muscles. What did it make me feel like? Can I be honest? Part of me enjoyed being strong and able to hold some sort of crazy pleasure—I was like a hulking Negro aide who gets some kind of hideous thrill out of such things. The other part of me felt sick

[1] This material was not available at the time of the interpretation of her tests. All names in the diary have been changed.

and terribly, terribly sad. Sad for Betty—sad for me. SAD. Sick because of the other part of me—the part I hate; the part I love. A bad day.

Dr. Singer leaves for the next two weeks. I don't know how much of the way I have felt most of the day has to do with that. I spoke to Jean—her birthday. I wonder if I will ever see her alive again. She and Aunt Miriam are spending the evening with Dad, Bob and Mary. My stomach is in my throat when I think how much I wish I were there and the time was years ago—then I could crawl up to Mommy or into an "Oz" book and forget that Arlene is sick, Mommy's dead, Joe's gone, Daddy's helpless in his hurt, and that Dr. Adams is gone. Will I ever learn how to live with my feelings for Adams. All night I've been hurt—feelings that somehow I've been left, that people reject me—so I have to reject them first like getting angry with Fred—maybe part of my pleasure in being with Betty is that I was treating her like I want people to treat me—people held her, Dr. Singer held her—she was a hurt frightened puppy. I am too on the inside—on the outside. I am a big strong fe-*male*—I want to cry Dr. Adams out too—and the others. He left me. She left me. He left me. Three people—three words—three hurts.

July 5 (Continued)

I stopped writing for awhile, but why should I. Maybe I'm afraid that I'll write myself completely out—It's like there's so little there. Today I read what was written last night as a sort of warm up for therapy but I don't want to turn this into that because then I'm not writing for myself but for therapy. I can't even be true to myself for 24 hrs. Big exposée all the time. Like I think I'm unique for having sadness. Horse shit! Fuck, fuck, fuck, FUCK YOU BUDDY. See what this place had done for me. No inhibitions—Never was able to even whisper the word before without cringing with all sorts of half modesty. It's as easy as saying God—God, fuck, God, fuck. Oh fuck myself for being such a phooney. And not even a real phoney at that—a real phoney feels all the way phoney—like Norma. No, wrong. Like maybe God. Which is best? To be phoney —but real and not exist or my kind of phoney—unreal yet existing.

Fuck me—it's like the rose bit—a phoney is a phoney is a phoney.
Confusing but I know that after death I'm going to go to hell—
which doesn't even exist. Except in the mind and that's what scares
me—what if my mind doesn't die—keeps on going. That thought
really hangs me up—my stupid mind being sad and *knowing* it
for eternity. Oh, an unreal fuck to an unreal mind that death
might make real. Am I trying to shock me or an unknown reader
that I am very dishonestly writting for. I felt I gotta write something down that would make me die of shame if someone ever
read—that way I'd damn sure be writing just to me! Rightto, old
fucking girl—purge your black soul. I masterbate—and I think
of the sex act when I do it and it makes me ashamed and every-
time I say "never again" and I'll probably do it for the rest of my
life. I bite my toe nails, pick my nose—(Dr. Singer just came in to
see how I was—I said O.K. and acted casual. I'm a liar—I wish I
could say terrible, terrible, terrible. Like Fuck, Fuck, Fuck—3 little
words, 3 times, 3 hurts.)

July 5 (continued)

I got repetitive for dramatic effect. What am I ashamed of? The
most truthful answer I can give is probably—me. More specific
if you please, you fuckin' fake. I had a homosexual affair with
Erica when I was 11 or 12 or 13. Great—I'm getting better—worser.
Certainly shittier. I killed my mother—not really but it sounds very
psychiatric and my doctor would just looove to hear me say it
because that would mean I had exposed therapeutically some deep
unconscious motivation for my horrible guilt feelings—thereby
having found the maglignancy, we could chop it out and presto
—cured. But, try tho' you may to convince me otherwise dear doctor, I did not kill my mother. She, unfortunately, killed herself. But
I do think that that's when something BIG started dying in me too.
I'm sort of the walking, talking rotting death type. Wind me up
and I eat, I sleep, I dream. I also write a lot of horseshit. Just read
this over. It's fun. I wish I could share it with someone. Like who?
You, I guess. See, now I'm writing to the reader. Look, whoever
is reading this now—if you're doing so with my consent—then you
can be damn sure that, even if I haven't said it, I must really trust
you and your reaction. I call this stuff horseshit but if someone

else did—! I probably must love you too—but not necessarily because for me love and trust don't go hand and hand like some goddamn ass said they did. I've been able to love several but haven't half way trusted them. Actually the only person I've been able to love and trust at the same time was probably Dr. Adams—Arlene almost—but not quite. Certainly not myself. And, in case, you are someone reading this without my invitation—then you're a sneak and a cowardly cheat like me and you better start getting frightened because you too will have a hell.

Maybe "lonely" is the word that should be where all the "SAD'S" are.

July 6 EARLY AFT.

This is turning into a sort of life-line for me. Makes me feel like I'm doing something—what, I don't know. A big release. I don't want to start feeling for this like Benton felt about the stuff he wrote. It was a real obsession for him. But maybe it would be good for me to be at least obsessed about something. My mind is gummy today—no motion, just sticky discomfort inside of me. Truthfully, I don't feel like anybody likes me today. —or I don't care for them. I get so damn uncomfortable when people talk to me. I don't know what to say. Hypocrite. Like I smile and say "great" and inside the thought is "drop dead, leave me alone, go screw, and, oh god, please hold me in your arms and rock me." I wish I was all the way the split personality type—maybe me #I & me #II might be friends and be content just to be together alone.

Night

This whole ward is boardering on mass insanity. In the almost 9 months since I've been here I've *never* seen it as crazy as now. It's like everyone is hanging on cliff just ready to drop all the way. Like tonight—First to set the scene—7:30. A Treasure Hunt activity that was definitely the most insane thing going—created of course by way-out Shirley. Clue's written in Hebrew, clues with algebraic formulas with no solution possible, impossible clues, sick,

sick, sick—no winner of course. Then a large group of us with loud rock'n'roll music, banging of pool balls, and TV clatter in the background. Jack with a group in one corner talking about the joys of heroin; Fred in another group talking about past-thievery, Frank turning his belly button on and off. Betty running around making absolutely no sense—She is really psychotic—Shirley running up and down the emotional scale every 5 minutes, and so on—really nuts—me included. Oh, the hell with it! No one will *ever* read this! I think its cramping my style or my honesty. I feel like flipping out but it would have to be an act and that couldn't happen. Relax. Let me wander, wonder, thunder, scumder. The squirrel died and is rotting outside. Dean would be upset if he knew this. I heard the boys calling him the SPCA today. He has a thing about animals. I think I do too. Like for Joe. That choking feeling again. Where's Karen? I want to talk to her about how I feel but she's never got time now with Betty, Nancy and the banging head bit. I resent their monopoly on people I like talking with. I also resent Sandra's monopoly of Fred even tho' I really do care for her. Fred and I have been sort of on each other's back for the last two days. Maybe we let ourselves be too close and honest the other night. I've been a real bitch with him while all the time I want to grab him up in my arms. It's a screwed up relationship—something like this couldn't exist on the outside. Maybe I let myself feel too much for him—it's like he's a substitute for Joe. I was extremely jealous of Joe. Shit—I'm jealous of anyone I really care about. It's like my hold on them is so weak that anyone could displace me therefore I've got to keep others away from them

sleep now. sleep all day tomorow—Like sleep forever—
[Sketch, "RELAX"]

where do the eyes go when I go asleep—roll up into my forehead? Someday someone will put pennies on my eyes. Then I'll really be dead to the world.

"I could not stop for death
So death he stopped for me . . ."

Yeah, Ruth, he sure did and now you're either crawling around in a worm's belly or being dusted off the furniture by Mr. Clean. You poor dead woman. I really used to think there was such a thing as the Littlest Angel. When did that dream die? I'm really trying to think this one through [sketch of star]. Maybe when I found out that stars don't have 5 points. But they do! they do! [Sketch of star with 5 numbered points.]

Crazy July 8

The weekend was indescribable—mad, mad people. Hilarious in many ways but as Gage said "Every laugh is part pathos." Betty I would like to rock like a little baby—Nancy I would enjoy knocking the hell out of. POW! . . . Right in the kisser. —Talked to Arlene—still has psychiatrist—Dr. Saunders—I also have a Dr. Saunders while Singer's gone. Wish he would hurry back. Oh Joe. Dry mouth and Joe worries back. I know something's happened to him. Shit—I can't write for the past 2 days. What's happened that I'm so occupied with all this surface crap. I've missed Fred but now I feel he's part with me again. All this tough bitter stuff, he *has* to go thru. I can't stand being around him when he's as consistently vulgar as he's been lately. "Eat me this, fuck you that" are only his more mild forms of expression. But I feel no hurry—I think that he and I will sort of care for each other permanently— Don't know about Tony tho! Shirley yes. I'm learning how to love and hate and how to feel sad and lonely. It's a painful lesson.

July 9

And it's bullshit—ref. to July 8. Couldn't express myself then, don't know if I can now. Good old negative approach. Talking to Jim tonight about things that shake him. Many times when I hear some of the mental stuff some of these kids go thru' it's hard for me to understand cuz' I never feel tho' I've gone thru' any thing that deep in feeling—I feel uncomfortable—like I'm here as some sort of pretender and it bugs. Either I can't or won't allow myself to remember or it just didn't happened. But something Jim said tonight in regard to his "hitting the panic button" for a minute or so on a walk last night reminded me of a similar experience—It's something I've never spoken of to anyone—not even Dr. Adams— because it happened during what I think is the most horrible thing I've ever done. It was during the summer of when I went up to

Bridgetown about buying a horse and ended up shacking with John
Jos. Foster or whatever . . . who ever he was. I don't remember
much about it—some goddamn horrible night. more that seemed
terribly unreal the whole time—Jesus Christ, I'm a real whore. No
wonder I don't want to remember—it's the only real thing I kept
from Adams—that & sleeping with Britt before I took the pills.
What am I? Too chicken to reveal the true slut in me. But what
Jim reminded me of was the time I was in the restaurant with Mrs.
Mayee and she introduced me to some older friends. I turned around
and said, "Hello, hello, hello, hello . . . excuse me" and took out
of the restroom. The feeling I had when I turned to them—like
complete panic, feeling that my eyes were rolling back into my
head and that my face was one big nervous twitch! Jesus it was
horrible—the clammy sweats and everything. Palmer came in and
asked what was wrong—I was so mortified—I lied and said that
it was some sort of nervous thing that I was seeing a doctor for."
And thats about all I can remember. I just a feeling of terrible
shame about the whole week . . . Anyhow I think occasionally
about what happened in the restaurant but shut it out quickly. I've
never tried to figure out why it—or anything else for that matter—
happened. Like I did it and there's no excuse for it and I'm too
ashamed to talk about it. Just thinking about John Joseph and all
that makes me sick with myself. It was like I was going from
minute to minute shamelessly with no touch with reality. Like New
Years with Art and Bart and the other guys. About this panic it's
happened since and before to a lesser degree—To some extent it's
why I'm so uncomfortable shopping and being in situations with
new people—I feel so uncomfortable with myself—an anxious feelings,—like I might jump out of my skin. There's other things that
go into this that I feel but I just don't express. Not to myself—
not to anybody! Sometimes I feel like I'm being driven wild by this
stuff that's just underneath that I can't pull out—take now. I feel
like beating my head and screaming—what are these feelings!
What are they? For Christ's sake, help me!! That's why I think
of Pentathol—Anything that would take away this wall—if only
just a moment—and let some of the craziness out. Then maybe I
could work from there. And I really know that, despite all my outside shit of feeling well, underneath I am really sick. Maybe as
sick as anyone in here—God knows. And it scares me to face this

the few times that I do. It's like the more I become aware of the fact that I'm pretty sick inside the more I become aware that somehow I can't reach it—I want, at times, to run away from it before the frustration kills me in a sense. It's hell—I feel the times I come the closest to touching what's in me is when I dream—And my dreams are mostly crazy scrambled nightmares but at least they come close to what is real in me. I can't understand or express them, but I can *feel* them. [later]

What dreams have bothered me the most likely? Several but one I haven't mentioned in therapy probably is the most important. Unfortunately like most of my dreams, I can only remember pieces —anyhow this one was sometime around the doctor change. I had a penis and kept trying to hide it from others—in the dream, I knew I shouldn't have the damn thing or maybe it was that I shouldn't have breasts. Either way, it was a horrible thing—like I had done something really bad. These people somehow found out and kept pointing at me like I was some kind of monster. Then I had to have intercourse with my father to prove that I wasn't a man. I dreamed the actual intercourse in which I sat on my father's lap facing him but I didn't know what he looked. As I remember, although there was a lot of feeling of repulsion, I also felt some sexual pleasure and while I was having intercourse I looked and the penis was gone. People kept looking at me saying now somehow that this was the right thing to do. I didn't have any climax and the dream moved to something else, I don't remember what. One thing I do remember vaguely is that my father kept being referred to as George. Another dream around that time was one I just remember exactly a very short piece of—Dr. Adams and I were running in the rain. He was holding my hand and pulling me out of the storm toward a shelter. As far as I can remember I believe it was the most secure, wonderful feeling I've ever had during a dream. When I woke up I felt like crying when I realized it was not real. I feel pretty misty when I think about it even now. God, I really lost something when he left. It's almost identical to the feeling I had when I first went off to camp and felt so damn homesick for weeks. It's also how I felt when Rusty died the second day I was in boarding school. I wish I could cry—I feel like it.

July 12 or 13

I want to be a Joppolo—ref. to Hersey's *A Bell for Adano*. "He is our future in the world . . . . . no plan, no hope, no treaty . . . . . could ever guarantee anything. Only men can guarantee, only the behavior of man under pressure, only our Joppolos." I really would want to be like this man. Mommy was—in her unique way—to G'town like the Major was to Adano. Not so dramatic maybe but—just as penetrating and lasting. Also this is probably a part of what killed her. Wonder why so many of the really good people end up dying early or something. Maybe it's like the poem, "To an Athelete Dying Young" like maybe people who die at the height of their giving of themselves are remembered more for their goodness *or infamy* then those who sort of outlive their quality and are actually seen as old, creaking, helpless people. It dissalusion— but it shouldn't. God, how it must feel to know that you've outlived your capacities—so you maybe don't realize it—only those around you do—ick. But why do I want to make others around me happy —maybe just because I want them to like me so I can be happy? Jesus, maybe I shouldn't even question myself as long as there's a good end product—but is it true that the end result justifies the means. Nuts—I don't know. At times I think I'm awfully shallow but on the other hand I am interested and I do want them to be as happy as possible, yet so often I've done just the opposite and made some people very unhappy including myself. Like I sort of have to do penance. "Repent all yee sinners!" Wonder if there is anyone who has never sinned. By sinning I don't mean the Bible type—that's a lot of hooey. To sin is to hurt yourself or someone else without a justifiable reason. Shit—I don't mean just that—I'm not *this* surface but hell I don't want to get all hung up in the abstract just now. Besides why write it down. It's like trying to paint a garden—you think you've got a realistic picture of what is like, then you've just got a picture that isn't true anymore—new flowers, dead ones, new weeds, etc. Like everything moves—expands —maybe contracts—maybe disappears. Man, I can't write tonight. There's some little bumbs on my bosooms and I keep picking at them. Damn my chest is ugly. I'm like a kid who can't say the word, breasts. I feel like it's a bad word or something—Anyhow I *hate* my "breasts"—ugh—they don't even deserves to be called that. "Udders" is a better word in my case. Too bad Mickey Spilaine couldn't have designed me—I'd be some babe instead of some bag. Nuts! I know I could be pretty damn good looking if I'd lose weight and god—I like too. Yet when anyone tells me I'm pretty, part of me wants to kiss him—part wants to *slug* him. Why? Why de-doo, why-de-day? And why do $7 + 7 = 14$? Why not 15? Hey—just found a blue vein in my breast. God forbid that I should have any of the characteristics of the normal woman's breast. Wow I'm getting to be an oldtimer with that word—breast, breasts, breasts, breastii-like fuck—an empty word. Odd how a mouthed sound can stir so many different feelings. Wonder how much would be changed in this world if there had never been such a thing as "voice". No singing, no laughing, no crying—like the greatest would be no, "sorriee, yew have de/ailed the wronga numb-ber . . . puleze check yewr . . . . ." God, all I'm doing now is putting dark lines on a piece of paper. And now, ladies and gentlemen, time for your predawn nightmares.

July 16

There's a goddamn cricket right outside of my window that is annoying the hell out of me: Brr Brrr Brrr—and I loved them at Lakeland—guess night sounds of the country have become strange to me—and I hate the idea of that happening. The past few days I've been thinking an awful lot about the country—small towns, dirt roads, walking thru' fresh fertilizer, cows lying down when there's the feeling of rain coming, being able to see a storm off in the distance instead of crappy buildings—the whole bit. Hell, the only time, or *maybe* times, I've seen a sunset since I've been in here has been when I was in Adams's office late in the aft—I get angry when I look out and know by the clouds that the sun really must be beautiful—and I can't see it!! Shit!! Anyhow I'm homesick for it *all*. And once I get out of here—no more cities for me. They scare hell out of me anyhow. Jack's grandfather used to tease me that I was really the corn-fed country girl. I hope to God I am. City life is shitty—shitty life is city. So I'll go to Vet school and end up takin' care of pigs and mules—and man would I ever be happy! Lately I've even been able to have wonderful phantasies about this and what's so great about them is that for once I feel that something I dream about might really be in my realm of possibility. For such a long, long time I've not been to even believe the tiniest bit in my daydreams—they were like completely *unreal*. Maybe it's not so much that I couldn't believe in them but more the case of choosing such impossible subjects. Like being thin. I might not stay as fat as now but never will I be anywhere near the skinny state no matter how much I lie to myself and others about once being thin. Pipe dreams, kid! And my other wierd phantasies—Oz and all that. But I'll never stop hoping that Oz exists. In my opinion—even if a sort of wistful desire for a childhood dream to be true is labeled as immature and a bit crazy, I don't give a fat damn. I just wish more people could have the dream. Another sort of place that has always stuck in the back of my mind is a fictional glade in a forest that I read years ago in *Rusty and the Rockfall*—not sure if that's the right title. Wonder if that has any connection with me naming the dog I loved so much "Rusty". It's odd but I never think of Rusty without thinking of Mommy and viceversa. It's even that way in my dreams. Wonder if a little bit of that is due to the fact that they both died while I was away in boarding school? I think I loved them both about the same amount—and sadly enough it was easier to show Rusty my love than it was for mother. And now, it's Joe that so much of my love goes for. I keep getting this fear that somethings happened to him and it honestly tears me up. I guess actually I do have an obsession and it's Joe. It's not as apparent as other people's obsessions—but it's always with me: Joe—And when I went east with Mrs. Loper I almost didn't go because I had to leave Joe & then I worried the whole time I was gone. And the hardest thing to leave when I came here was Joe. And if I had had *any* idea of how long it would be—I would have *never* left—Mainly because of Joe. It makes me feel sort of like child desertion.

INTERVIEW WITH MRS. T.'S THERAPIST [1]

EXAMINER: Going back to her coming in and the testing, did the test findings in any way contribute to treatment positively or negatively?

[1] Transcription of interview 7 months after initial testing.

THERAPIST: Yeah, I think in general positively. I believe . . . yes, I recall . . . . She was uh quite anxious about them at the time, but that was very brief—and I don't think it interfered with treatment in any way. I think it helped a lot of these feelings of emptiness, and being alone—well this really terrible feeling she gets about losing contact with people. I think probably we got into that more rapidly than we might have otherwise. The direct reaction was certainly much bringing out of all kinds of these feelings about how inadequate she was, how poorly she had done, how stupid she was.

EXAMINER: Uh huh. How about more specifically how you were concerned in reaction to the test report and general findings?

THERAPIST: Well, you scared me for a little while as I told you.

EXAMINER: You mean you proceeded more cautiously?

THERAPIST: For a little while, yeah. But I think it made me, you know, more cautious than I would ordinarily be. I think I really spent some time thinking about, you know, really trying to apply what you said to what I do in therapy. And you said you would —did not think she could tolerate—you made some statement that you did not believe she could tolerate uncovering therapy. I don't think I am aware of that consciously bearing on what I do in therapy. It kind of comes from what the patient is doing and the material that comes up. But what was coming up, you know, I think could only be classified as kind of uncovering therapy. So I was kind of concerned about it—whether I should be doing something different—whether I ought to be slowing her down, trying to steer her away from some of the things that were happening. So I thought about this quite a bit. And I talked to the Assistant Director of the hospital about it. And I went back to doing what I do. So I suppose for a little time you could say it—it certainly made me think about that. And I was kind of concerned about it—you know, how fragile she was. I don't think she's as fragile as one would get the picture from your report.

EXAMINER: Uh huh.

THERAPIST: The things she's been able to tolerate. She had medication only once since she's been here which was the night she met her new therapist. She got some thorazine that night from Dr. J. and he doesn't do this readily, so she was really very upset that night. And again it goes back to the stuff you picked up. I think for the first time seeing her new therapist she accepted the fact that I was really leaving. She got these terrifying feelings of emptiness and had to ask to go into seclusion. She felt in a way, you know, that I was taking everything with me, that she was going to be left in a kind of a void. I think some feelings of real derealization. The world was kind of just going to be black and be void. And this feeling that, that only if you're dead should you be so lonely, so that somehow being dead would make it all right, but otherwise really afraid she couldn't stand it. But since then she's seemed to work it through fairly well. I don't know. She may get very upset when I go. But I have a feeling she's not been yet as upset as she got at that time. Oh I think the fact that she's never really required medication other than occasional Benadryl uh to sleep ever since she's been here. Uh I've never seen, you know, anything really—oh real evidence of thought disorder, and real confusion in thinking at all. She handles things very well. She's a fascinating patient to work with.

EXAMINER: Was there anything else about the test report in general that was helpful or not helpful in any way?

THERAPIST: I think an awful lot of it was very helpful in the sense that I certainly—the stuff certainly came out—the suicidal preoccupations were pretty plainly indicated there. I think the sexual confusion has come out even more strongly clinically than on your written report—really a fantastic amount of stuff around this. Very conscious of this as a child—how hard she tried to be a boy. She said that when she heard that you'd turn into a boy if you could kiss your elbow, she damned near threw her shoulder out of joint. Even now she's terribly uncomfortable if the situation comes up where she has to dress like a girl. She will avoid mirrors. If she sees herself in the mirror, well, one day she went back, took off her clothes, and put on her blue jeans and sloppy shirt again, going over to a part time job where she had to dress up where she felt like she was playing at being a woman. This made her terribly uncomfortable. I think these things were indicated in your report, but are even more striking somehow clinically.

EXAMINER: Uh huh.

THERAPIST: I think that the report indicated before I was seeing it so much this sense of emptiness and probably more strongly her earlier suicidal preoccupations, although this was pretty evident, I think, when she came in.

EXAMINER: How were these items that preceded the clinical material and the therapy material helpful in terms of your treating her?

THERAPIST: I think that's an awful hard question to answer. I think uh—I think anything is helpful—any kind of knowledge you have about a patient. And when things start to come, you—you know, you've—I think your mind kind of automatically puts things together and kind of adds them up and I think it's helpful too. I haven't looked at the report real recently. I can still remember very vividly for instance, that story she told to the blank card which, you know, helps to give you a sense of what she's going through, what she's feeling, you know, not saying you can put your finger on real definitely. But I think that story, for example, was very helpful. I think you remember the one that she answered to the white card.

EXAMINER: Oh yes.

THERAPIST: The house of mirrors.

EXAMINER: Uh huh. In line with this, I wonder would it have been useful to you, do you think, if for instance, you had the possibility to actually go over her other clinical material, test material per se?

THERAPIST: It might have been. We did discuss it I think more than you do sometimes because you had done this. You remember I came up and we spent an hour talking about it. Uh I think that was helpful.

EXAMINER: Uh huh, uh huh, you—

THERAPIST: Little things. Knowing how bright this girl is. She was constantly oh talking about her failures in school, talking about how dumb she was . . . Uh you know, I was aware that she had a very good vocabulary from the way she talked. But I don't think you know, I—I would have been as immediately aware of what a big discrepancy there was, cause she's really a terribly bright girl.

EXAMINER: You're aware of this now in—in treatment?

THERAPIST: Yeah, I think so. But I don't think I would have been so quickly.

EXAMINER: Uh huh.

THERAPIST: It's hard to tell though cause I know the test results too. She's a bright girl.

EXAMINER: Is there any other information that you might have thought of that would have been useful if it would have been included in the test report?

THERAPIST: I don't know. What kind of thing do you have in mind?

EXAMINER: I—I don't really know. Uh this uh—

THERAPIST: I don't know what else you could have gotten—

EXAMINER: Putting the uh—sort of putting the burden on you. Is there anything else that you might think of that could have been included or might have been or should have been that—

THERAPIST: No. That—that's like saying what else could have come out in the test results that didn't. Again I'd have to look at them. I have a feeling that her tremendous fears around homosexuality have come through much more strongly in treatment than they did on the test results, although the confusion was there. I think this has been more evident clinically now. She was not aware of . . . she was pushing it down pretty drastically before. It came out first in fears about herself and these were of course very much intensified. Now she's getting into the point of talking more and more now about this really crazy mother of hers. It became quite evident in that she became conscious of really feeling that her mother was probably latently homosexual. I don't remember that this was as prominent in the test results as it has been clinically. I just don't know what kind of thing you might have gotten at that wasn't in the test results.

EXAMINER: Uh huh. What have been some of the other major themes that were prominent with her during the past year?

THERAPIST: Oh, it's been about eight months now. There's been a tremendous amount of material particularly recently around the mother's suicide, again this feeling of really being empty, following this kind of intolerable empty feeling, you know, that she will never make contact with anybody again. Certainly the separation brought this out very strongly. Behind this very clearly a feeling that she is responsible for the mother's suicide. As a child she had once gotten angry at her grandfather and screamed at him she wished he were dead. And he died several days later. I think we've set up a relative view of this feeling. Then there's been a great deal of incestuous material. Her brother apparently quite a sadistic man—he began to force her into sexual play at an early age. I don't think she's ever been able to talk to anybody about this. It lasted about four years at which time she went into a rage and chased him with a knife and really intended to kill him. As I said, she's never really been able to get angry since consciously. Then a lot of material on why she really couldn't tell anybody, uh her position in the family as being—having come along much later—her brother is older and her sister is older. And then there's a gap and then her. The mother was getting more and more sick—treated her very confusingly in a way. She would be screaming and hollering at her and then would suddenly reverse herself and beg forgiveness from her even as a child about what a horrible mother she was, how awful she treated her. She would be thrown in a position of comforting the mother and saying, "That's all right. You're really not that way." lying about it. When trouble would happen the older children would often blame it on her. Several times the parents would take the older children's word for it and she began to feel that nobody really listened to her, that she was just guilty per se. This she feels is the reason why she couldn't tell anybody about what her brother was doing, because nobody would have believed her. That clearly fitted in with some kind of fantasy things, because she felt that it was her fault anyway. And yet she got a lot of gratification out of it. It was—at least her brother was showing interest in her. Then there kind of developed a whole— well really we got back into this through looking at the whole repetition of her relationships which have been just repetitive of this situation with the brother. She can only relate to a man who treats her in a very sadistic way, walks all over her and pushes her around. And more recently around feelings when it was discussed whether I would keep on with her. After it was decided that I wouldn't see her after I left the hospital staff there was a lot of material which indicated that in some way she had had to sabotage this. In some way she had sent out signals, done things which would make the staff so uncomfortable that they would feel that she was not ready to go to therapy outside the hospital for fear they would lose hold on what was going on with her. And then behind this it became very clear that any

relationship that she really wanted or a man that she really
looked up to, would have liked to have gone with, she had to
sabotage it in one way. One man that she particularly was in
love with and I think still is, she very clearly destroyed any
chance they had of going together. So this has kind of been a
theme, why she always gets herself in a spot where she's the one
to get hurt, and then break up, this kind of withdrawal, eating
fantastic amounts of food to try to fill up this feeling of emptiness,
going to bed with her old Oz books and a stack of peanut butter
sandwiches. Really just pulling away from everything. Oh a lot
of material I think around really very early deprivation. She
sucked her thumb until she was thirteen and still does in her
sleep sometimes. Has this wiggler toe—did she ever talk to you
about that? Started out as a silk blanket when she was a little
kid. Apparently kind of a transition object at that time. And when
the blanket wore out, she found she could get the same sensation
with a silk tie. And only recently she realized it always had to
be her father's tie and she steals ties from him. And even now she
keeps at the bottom of her bed one of her father's silk ties and
she loops it through her toes at night and then wiggles her toes
and gets the sensation of kind of warmth, of comfort; it certainly
has a masturbatory quality about it. Again very overdetermined—
used to drive her mother crazy. She used to walk around the
house with it between her toes and really provoked her mother
into blowing up about this. Gets really panicky if she loses it.
One of the maids once threw it out changing the linen. Well
she raised the roof at the maid.

EXAMINER: What's the prognosis would you say?

THERAPIST: I think—I think if she can stay in treatment long enough,
it's very good. I really think she has the capacity to work with
these things, to experience them, to take at least enough distance
to see what she's doing. She was talking the other day about you
know in the eight months what has really happened. She said
the only thing—the real thing she thinks—is that now she knows
she has a choice. And she never knew this before. She said, "I
can go back to doing what I was doing." She was drinking more
and more, going from party to party just seeking stimulation.
She was taking quite large amounts of Dexedrine, starting to become promiscuous, merely just seeking out any kind of contact

to try hanging on. But she said, you know, "My feeling was uh you know, this was just what I had to do. I mean everything I've done has been kind of this way." And she said, "Now I've got a choice. I know that I can do something different. I can go to school and make something of my life. I—I really didn't have any feeling like this before." And she said, "I may go back and do exactly the same thing, but now I know that I don't have to, that there's another way." This was said in a very real way and I think that's pretty significant—can really see that. There's a tremendous temptation now to get her father to take her out. And when I go—she can—she'll be able to do this. "Is it worth it getting involved with another therapist when you're going to have to leave him again? I don't know if I can go through all this suffering"—quite aware that she can talk her father into getting her out of here any time she wants to. She was very tempted to do this, just like she was tempted kind of to get Daddy to buy me. But again you know the awareness she has. She said, "I knew"—she said, "my father was even disturbed at how young you are. Then S. comes in [her new therapist]. He's much younger than you." She found herself when she last talked to her father complaining that her next doctor was so young, knowing that this bothered her father. And she—and her father's very wealthy. He's always bought her way out of trouble, really bought her anything she's wanted. And she could talk about uh getting Daddy to put pressure so that she could continue seeing me. Then she said, "You know, if uh my Daddy did this, uh your chances of being any help to me would be gone."

This week, we got into how the termination was particularly difficult and partly my fault, 'cause this decision about my continuing to see her or not kept being put off and put off. Everybody else in the hospital knew whether they were going to change therapists several weeks before she did. And she got terribly disturbed about this. [And the more she was disturbed?] I don't think I was aware at the time because of this feeling that you know, that she was so guilty about it, that she had to sabotage it in some way, which made it really enormously difficult for her. And all kinds of feelings that she had never been able to talk to anybody like this before. She had to keep me in some way and all this stuff. Practically went through a fantasy pregnancy. She hadn't menstruated since she came in. Just at the time this decision was to be made, she suddenly became terribly concerned about the fact that she hadn't menstruated in all this time. She began to feel that she was pregnant. She put her fingers in her vagina and felt that her cervix was way down and softer than it had been before. Following the examination and finding out that she was not pregnant, she began to menstruate the next day for the first time in eight months. And she said, "You know, losing a doctor, it'd be nice to have a baby to take his place." [1] But anyway this—there were all kinds of fantasies about me, about being in love with me, sexual feelings about me. But with this business last Wednesday and working it through and yesterday it was kind of like I was a real person again. She said, "You know. I'm going to be sad to see you go." She talked about the other day seeing me go home and she said, "For the first time I thought, now he's going to his home, to his wife and kids. He must be kind of excited about his new job. I'm sure he's kind of sad to leave here, but you know, he's probably pretty happy to be starting something new. I'll be sad to see you go. And I—I think I'll be able to work with the new doctor." This was the first time I've heard that she's talked that way. So I think that the temptation to get Daddy to pull her out, uh you know, unless something goes wrong in the next couple of weeks, I think she'll probably stay.

EXAMINER: Now in going back to what we were talking about before about retesting. Uh do you have any thoughts about uh well on the one hand what advantage there would be at this point of retesting her and what kind of information would come from it?

THERAPIST: I don't think there would be any advantage right now until she settles in again. But I would like to see you know what kind of changes there are uh in terms of a lot of the things she's seen about herself.

EXAMINER: Uh huh. Would you expect the tests to be quite different?

THERAPIST: I don't know how much different, but I think I would think I would expect them to be different. I think after she'd really started with somebody, it might be, because she has a real

[1] Significantly, it was this fantasy that Mrs. T. eventually tried to act out two years later at the time of her discharge from the hospital.

sense of—of the relationship filling up this emptiness. And she talks about my going away. And it's a fragmentation, you know, that everything—that her feelings fragment somehow when somebody leaves. And then she can't pull them back together again. You know, it's only around a relationship like she's had in therapy that somehow she begins to pull these things together and begins to see herself at all as—as an individual. I would think, you know, if she has the same kind of relationship with her new therapist that this might make quite a bit of difference. The terror around this emptiness, uh you know, which I think is indicated in the Rorschach, I didn't—you—I don't think I really saw that clinically although there were, there were evidences of it in the way she described her mother's death and the kind of things she felt, but I don't think I was really aware of it until what happened last week when she really accepted the fact that I was going. Had this real terror of being alone, that this was going to go on, you know, this was the way she pictured death. Same time, you know, she's felt—many times she talked about death not in terms of "I'm going to kill myself" maybe in the future, but you know that someday this is inevitable. Uh you know something involved in the identification with the mother. Somehow it's just going to happen. And the trouble is you know somehow it's out of her control. And some of this feeling certainly has come back at this time. I don't feel that she's immediately suicidal. I don't feel that as much as you know "K" [The hospital director] is concerned about it and some of the others, although you know it's possible at this termination, but I just don't feel that now. But in terms of ultimately if she should walk out or discontinue treatment I think there'd be a very strong likelihood she'd kill herself. But she sees this emptiness and death as the same thing. At the same time she feels this inevitability of death. She's kind of terrified by this picture she has of the void which is cold and empty. "You feel things but you're all alone. You know, it comes both ways. I'm terrified of this. I'm terr— therefore I'm terrified of death. On the other hand it would give me a reason for feeling so alone. You know, I can't stand it now because there isn't any reason. At least then I wouldn't have to wonder why it is that I feel this way."

EXAMINER: In general as regards psychological tests and test reports here or anywhere else for that matter have they been useful, in what way they could have been more useful, what has your experience generally been?

THERAPIST: I think in general they've been particularly helpful here. I don't know whether I could use—should use her as an example because I've talked with you more than I ordinarily do. But I think there is much more—at least on some of the tests I've had there's more attempt here to indicate how patients may relate to another person which I think has been helpful. I remember Jack L. specifically that there was a statement uh about a prediction about how he would deal with a relationship which I think was very helpful. It was accurate. It worked out that way. And I think it was very helpful for me to have had this suggestion which was in my mind when he began to deal with me in this way. I think that kind of descriptive material has certainly been especially helpful. I think it's always helpful to be able to talk with the psychologist about what went on.

EXAMINER: Uh huh.

THERAPIST: And in general I try to do this. I've talked to _____ [one of the authors] several times. And it's always helpful when you have specific questions. Uh Mark P. for example who turned out very differently than my initial impression. You know how he got here. Course he came under unusual circumstances. He was tricked into coming. He had all kinds of reasons for being very disturbed. He looked so flat and facetious and superficial and when he just was crossed in any way, became very paranoid and suspicious. There were indications in this history and in the early material that this had been going on for a long time. And I had a lot of questions on whether there was deterioration you know, whether this was a slow chronic downhill course. And this was the question I asked and the test results indicated that there wasn't deterioration. And this has turned out I think to be very accurate. He's one of the best patients I've had all year and you know, has changed more in a brief time than any other patient I've had. Just finally getting to someone that he could really begin to talk to he experienced tremendous relief. And I don't see any evidence now that this is kind of a chronic progressive thing. That was very helpful just as an example that comes to mind.

EXAMINER: Uh you're going into private practice now. Do you think that you might use psychological testing in private practice?

THERAPIST: Yeah, I think uh there might be times when I very definitely.

EXAMINER: Are there any particular kinds of patients that you would think about testing more so than others, or particular situations?

THERAPIST: Well, one I've just indicated. It was something I had a lot of concern about at the time . . .

EXAMINER: Uh huh, uh huh.

THERAPIST: Because of the way he was acting. I think it was very helpful in the way I began to deal with him. You know, to have this feeling that that it wasn't a chronic slow deterioration. And I'm sure that it helped in how well things are going with Mark because it reassured me in a lot of ways. I think that would be a time when I would certainly. I think in suspicions of borderline patients it's very helpful.

EXAMINER: Is there anything you feel is unique about psychological testing different from a consultation say with another therapist?

THERAPIST: Yeah, I think there are a lot of things different. Well just with Mrs. T., of course, she's in some way unique, but the kind of stuff around the TAT, say, which I don't think you get from another—you know, talking to somebody else who had just interviewed her, cause I don't think she would talk that way. But as you said, you know, that's one of the most striking TAT reports I've ever seen cause she's got a vivid imagination. And but these themes were very relevant to her. And I don't think you'd get that from an interview. You know, I'm not saying that somebody who'd seen her a year couldn't give you a lot of this same stuff, but you'd never get it better out of her cause I don't think she could talk about it in terms of herself. A lot of the oral-aggressive stuff which you picked up early—I think you could probably—all this business around the su—the thumb sucking and this business, you could probably see it. But I didn't really begin to get it until she talked about some dreams in which—which were really just as striking as the Rorschach. Uh one I remember very vividly. She had a dream of a bunch of friends who were crossing a body of water by this swinging bridge. And sharks were leaping up out of the water and just biting off chunks of flesh. And she could see the bones and this sort of thing. But I think that was indicated in the—in the Rorschach before I began to hear that kind of material.

EXAMINER: Well, thank you very much.

FOLLOW-UP OF MRS. T.

Soon after retesting, Mrs. T. was discharged from the hospital. However in short time, because of a variety of abrupt, unexpected losses of several close relatives and of a boy friend, and repeated efforts to try to become illegitimately pregnant, she became more depressed and seclusive, ate ravenously, and had to reenter the hospital. During this second hospital stay she attended several college classes outside the hospital, finished her final exams and did well on them. Her intention at this point was to continue outpatient therapy with her first hospital therapist [an interview with him appeared earlier]. However, she soon confided that once again she had a substitute relationship to turn to in order to circumvent the loneliness she anticipated and dreaded upon leaving the hospital. This time she revealed that she planned on marrying someone she was going out with—a secret she had kept from the hospital staff for fear they might have objected to her discharge because of it. Her therapist confronted with this secret and with details of the instability of Mrs. T.'s intended spouse raised serious questions regarding the desirability of a marriage which might only repeat her former marriage and the sadistic relationship with her brother and which had as its primary purpose avoiding being alone. Inasmuch as the therapist opposed the marriage Mrs. T. felt it would be impossible to be in therapy with him and at the same time try to make a go of her marriage. Therapy was terminated. Six months later Mrs. T. became pregnant although her marriage appeared to be getting worse. She now tried to contact her therapist, was unable to reach him by phone and instead took a slight overdose of barbiturates. The next day she was able to reach the therapist and resumed therapy with him until the birth of her baby. The delivery went well; Mrs. T. felt happy and decided once again to stop therapy and try to make a go of her marriage. Her efforts in this regard were unsuccessful; repeated arguments and angry departures by the husband led to a separation, followed by frantic but futile efforts by Mrs. T. at reconciliation. At this point Mrs. T. decided once again to reenter therapy which brings us up to the present. Interestingly, she has been able to hold herself together relatively well. She had lost a considerable amount of weight while in the hospital and was somewhat magically transformed into a rather attractive well-groomed young woman. She has been relatively successful in maintaining this new appearance except for sporadic weight gains during bad periods in her marriage. Moreover, she has been able to maintain many social contacts and has resumed several creative activities. In large part a point of stability is her strong feelings toward her baby which may help motivate her exploration of her problems yet may also obscure her terrors of loneliness and emptiness.

Index